Neural Network PC Tools

Neural Network PC Tools
A Practical Guide

with a Foreword by Bernard Widrow

Edited by

Russell C. Eberhart and Roy W. Dobbins

The Johns Hopkins University Applied Physics Laboratory,
Laurel, Maryland

Academic Press, Inc.
Harcourt Brace Jovanovich, Publishers
San Diego   New York   Boston   London   Sydney   Tokyo   Toronto

This book is printed on acid-free paper. ∞

Copyright © 1990 by Academic Press, Inc.
All Rights Reserved.
No part of this publication may be reproduced or transmitted in any form or by any means, electronic or mechanical, including photocopy, recording, or any information storage and retrieval system, without permission in writing from the publisher.

Academic Press, Inc.
San Diego, California 92101

United Kingdom Edition published by
Academic Press Limited
24–28 Oval Road, London NW1 7DX

Library of Congress Cataloging-in-Publication Data

Neural network PC tools : a practical guide / [edited by] Russell C.
    Eberhart and Roy W. Dobbins.
        p. cm.
    ISBN 0-12-228640-5 (alk. paper)
    1. Neural computers. 2. Neural circuitry. 3. Microcomputers.
I. Eberhart, Russell C. II. Dobbins, Roy W.
QA76.5.N42827   1990
006.3--dc20   90-727
                                                                 CIP

Printed in the United States of America
90 91 92 93   9 8 7 6 5 4 3 2 1

To Francie, Mark, and Sean;
to Leonie, Lorien, and Audrey;
and in Renée's memory.

CONTENTS

CONTRIBUTORS

Numbers in parentheses indicate the pages on which the authors' contributions begin.

Maureen Caudhill (189),   11450 Grassy Trail Drive, San Diego, California 92127

Roy W. Dobbins (9, 35, 59, 81, 111, 161, 215, 295, 393),   The Johns Hopkins University Applied Physics Laboratory, Laurel, Maryland 20723

Russell C. Eberhart (9, 35, 59, 81, 111, 161, 177, 215, 295, 393),   The Johns Hopkins University Applied Physics Laboratory, Laurel, Maryland 20723

Gary Entsminger (285),   Rocky Mountain Biological Laboratory, Crested Butte, Colorado 81224

Larrie V. Hutton (161, 235),   The Johns Hopkins University Applied Physics Laboratory, Laurel, Maryland 20723

D. Gilbert Lee, Jr. (137),   The Johns Hopkins University Applied Physics Laboratory, Laurel, Maryland 20723

Vincent G. Sigillito (177, 235),   The Johns Hopkins University Applied Physics Laboratory, Laurel, Maryland 20723

Thomas Zaremba (251),   The Johns Hopkins University Applied Physics Laboratory, Laurel, Maryland 20723

FOREWORD

I am pleased to have been asked by Russ Eberhart and Roy Dobbins to write the foreword to this book. It has been three decades since my frequently referenced article with Hoff, on adaptive switching circuits, that discussed the Least Mean Squares algorithm [13]. My first hardware version of Adaline, shown in the accompanying photograph, is also approaching its 30th birthday. How time flies!

After my original work in the neural network field, I did some developmental work in the adaptive filter area. I still believe that if an electrical engineer had developed the back-propagation algorithm, we'd be working with "massively parallel adaptive filters" instead of neural networks. Oh, well.

A few years ago, about the time of Rumelhart and McClelland's three-volume tome on parallel distributed processing [2,4,5], I said to myself, "What the heck, adaptive filters are in pretty good shape. I think I'll work on neural networks again."

In the past few years, there has been an absolute explosion in the amount of work being done in the neural network field. It seems somewhat analogous to the far-reaching social and political changes sweeping the world as this book goes to press in 1990.

Just as I have to watch the morning news to keep abreast of changes in governments in Eastern Europe, I have to read my morning mail (which now includes e-mail) to keep abreast of developments in neural networks. With all the fine neural network applications both working and under development, I feel that neural networks are here to stay! And I'm sure that the most exciting applications are yet to come.

As president of the International Neural Network Society (INNS) and fellow of the Institute of Electrical and Electronics Engineers, with a special interest in its Neural Networks Council, I'm in a position to see most major publications in the field. In fact, I am asked to review a significant percentage of the new books.

It is thus from a position of some experience that I say that an exposition on the practical applications of neural networks has been greatly needed. I believe that this book fulfills that need in an extremely fine fashion.

Many books have been written that emphasize the theoretical aspects of neural networks. Some have gone as far as presenting equations for various network topologies. One or two have even included demonstration software illustrating different network topologies.

Equations and demonstrations, however, are only a starting point for engineers and computer scientists. What we need, for our real-world practical applications, is a carefully thought-out methodology that takes the systems approach. By that I mean an approach is required that starts with a systems analysis and goes all the way to the computer code necessary to implement the design developed from the analysis.

This book does that. It is a practical and thorough approach to applying neural network tools to everyday problems. And, as the case studies illustrate, these applications aren't limited to the scientific and engineering fields. In this book, you can even learn how to use neural network tools to compose music and analyze the commodities futures market.

Another issue dealt with, at least implicitly, in this book is that of terminology. The glossary near the end of the book contains proposed definitions for a number of terms we use in our everyday neural network efforts. While I personally may not agree with each and every definition, I wholeheartedly endorse moving toward a commonly accepted terminology. It's pretty hard for a person new to the field to sort through literature that refers to processing elements, processing units, units, neurons, nodes, neurodes, etc., all of which refer to exactly the same thing.

Through their participation in the Ad Hoc Standards Committee of the IEEE Neural Networks Council, chaired by Evangelia Tzanakou of Rutgers University, Russ Eberhart and Roy Dobbins, with their colleagues from academia, industry, and government, will be grappling with the issue of definitions. I'm sure that their committee is in for some interesting discussions over the next few years.

Also helpful to folks new to neural nets is the appendix on additional resources. Of course, as president of the INNS, I feel bound to ask that you pay special attention to the information on our society!

As Russ and Roy say in the introductory chapter, you really don't need a supercomputer, a million dollars, and an interdisciplinary team of experts to put neural networks to work. All you need is a personal computer and this book. I'm sure you'll enjoy it!

Bernard Widrow
Electrical Engineering Department
Stanford University

Introduction

Russell C. Eberhart
Roy W. Dobbins

In the past few years, neural networks have received a great deal of attention and are being touted as one of the greatest computational tools ever developed. Much of the excitement is due to the apparent ability of neural networks to imitate the brain's ability to make decisions and draw conclusions when presented with complex, noisy, irrelevant, and/ or partial information. Furthermore, at some primitive level, neural networks appear able to imitate the brain's "creative" processes to generate new data or patterns.

It is hard, especially for a person unfamiliar with the subject, to separate the substance from the hype. Many of the applications being discussed for neural networks are complex and relatively hard to understand, and many of the available hardware and software tools are either too simplistic to be useful or too complicated and expensive to be affordable and understandable for the average engineer or computer scientist.

The hardware and software tools we describe in this book, with few exceptions, are available to most technical people, and we have written the book to help the typical engineer, computer scientist, or other technically oriented person who is interested in solving practical problems with neural networks. You'll need some background in algebra to understand some of the equations for network training and operation, but the algebra required isn't any more involved than most folks have had by the time they graduate from high school. The most complicated mathematics we'll use involves summing a series of subscripted variables.

It is true that a deep understanding of biologically derived neural networks requires knowledge in a variety of fields, including biology,

Neural Network PC Tools
Copyright © 1990 by Academic Press, Inc. All rights of reproduction in any form reserved.

mathematics, and artificial intelligence. But none of this knowledge is needed to understand the neural network tools presented in this book. Probably the best background for getting the maximum benefit from this book is liking to "muck about" with computers. If you're comfortable running a variety of software and occasionally (possibly with some trepidation) fiddling with programming simple stuff in a language such as BASIC or C, you'll feel right at home here.

It's a myth that the only way to achieve results with neural networks is with a million dollars, a supercomputer, and an interdisciplinary team of Nobel laureates, though some commercial vendors out there would like you to believe it.

You don't need a supercomputer or a parallel processing machine to do something useful with neural networks. It's not even necessary to have a MicroVAX or a Sun workstation. A personal computer such as an IBM PC/AT or workalike is a perfectly adequate hardware base. A plain vanilla PC, XT, or workalike is even sufficient; it's just that the slower clock speed is going to make things take longer. With simple hardware and software tools, it is possible to solve problems that are otherwise impossible or impractical. Neural networks really do offer solutions to some problems that can't be solved in any other way known to the authors. That's no hype!

What *is* hype is that neural networks can solve all of your difficult engineering or computer problems faster and cheaper than anything you have ever tried. It is a myth that neural networks can leap tall buildings in a single bound and that they can solve problems single-handedly. They are particularly inappropriate for problems requiring precise calculations: You'll probably never successfully balance your checkbook with a neural network. (But then, how many people have actually used a personal computer for this task?)

Another statement that qualifies as *mostly* myth is that you don't need to do any programming at all to use neural network tools. This is at best misleading. It's true that a neural network trains (learns) and runs on input data and according to a set of rules that update the weights that connect the processing elements, or nodes, and that the learning of the network is not, strictly speaking, programmed. It's also true that computer-aided software engineering (CASE) tools will become more available in the next few years and that little or no programming expertise will be required to use these tools to generate executable neural network code. But it's also true that in the real world of neural network applications, some programming is required to get from where you start to a solution.

Furthermore, although it is accurate to say that neural networks can play a key role in the solution of several classes of problems that are difficult, if not impossible, to solve any other way currently known, it is almost always true that the neural network portion of the solution is only a relatively small part of the overall system. In terms of the total amount of computer code, the network often accounts for only about 10 percent of the total solution. It is an absolutely indispensable 10 percent, and success would not be possible without it, but it is important to keep it in perspective. Preprocessing and further manipulation of the data to form pattern files for presentation to the network typically involve much of the code. Interpreting and displaying the results often account for another large portion.

Another myth about neural networks is that you need to know something about neural biology to understand them. Nothing could be further from the truth. In fact, for most engineers and computer scientists, neural network tools can be considered just another (powerful) set of resources in the analysis toolkit. Furthermore, a good case can be made for the argument that neural network tools are technical descendents of analog computing just as much as they are descended from biology or neurology.

In Chapter 1 (Background and History), the development of neural networks and neural network tools is reviewed, and other ways to describe neural networks, such as connectionist models and parallel distributed processing, are discussed. A brief background of the biological derivation of the technology is presented, and some of the main differences between biological structures and neural network tools are reviewed. Neural network development history is presented by defining and reviewing the accomplishments in four "Ages" of neural networks: the Age of Camelot, the Dark Age, the Renaissance, and the Neoconnectionist Age. This chapter should go a long way toward dispelling any mystery the reader might feel surrounding the subject.

Chapter 2 examines in detail the implementation of two neural network architectures currently used on personal computers. Although there are about 12–15 neural network architectures in fairly general use as this book is being written, most of them are variations of one or more of five or six main architectures. And of these five or six, most readers can probably get started with only two or three.

The personal computer implementations include examples of the back-propagation and self-organization (Kohonen) network architectures. The back-propagation network is the most commonly used network structure for solving practical problems on personal computers. After the back-propagation notation and topology are introduced, the forward calculations and method of back-propagating errors are presented. Training and testing the back-propagation network are briefly discussed.

The self-organizing network model often associated with Dr. Teuvo Kohonen of Finland is then presented, with its topology and notation first, followed by network initialization and input procedures, training calculations, and tips on how to run the network.

Source code written in C for implementing each of the networks is listed in Appendix A, and a diskette with source and executable code is available from the authors for a nominal fee.

Chapter 3 (Systems Considerations) discusses some of the systems aspects related to incorporating neural network tools into analysis procedures, including the data preprocessing that is almost always required prior to building pattern files for analysis by the network tools. Included is a discussion how to classify problems and how to decide whether or not they can be efficiently and successfully solved using neural network tools. We also look at some of the roles that networks can play.

No matter what kind of system is being designed, whether it uses neural networks or not, one of the very first steps is to develop a system specification. We review some of the issues related to this development and describe a few of the tools available, from very informal ones to more formal structured analysis tools.

Also included is a comparison of neural network tools with expert systems. It will be seen that though examples of "expert" results must be used to train the network, there is no need for extensive "knowledge engineering" activity to define meticulously each and every rule and situation the system may ever encounter. Rather, examples of "correct" behavior can be presented to the network for training; this training can be implemented by an engineer or programmer with little or no knowledge of the subject matter.

The following chapters review the software and hardware tools available to implement the various network architectures. The software tools are particularly important to understand, because it is here that most people begin their explorations of neural networks. In fact, much can be done with just a PC/AT or workalike and the appropriate software.

Chapter 4 (Software Tools) details the software aspects of implementing and running neural network tools on a personal computer. Some of the software tools available commercially are briefly discussed. Following these discussions, Chapter 5 (Development Environments) presents a computer-assisted software engineering (CASE) tool for code development, named CaseNet.

Despite the best efforts of the software developer, certain applications may require speed assistance from custom hardware. More and more of this hardware is becoming available at reasonable prices. Particularly attractive for some applications are transputers, dedicated hardware parallel coprocessing boards that can be plugged into a PC/AT. The hardware implementation of neural network tools is discussed in Chapter 6.

The next two chapters discuss measuring the performance of neural network systems (Chapter 7) and analyzing networks (Chapter 8). Training and testing of networks are reviewed. In training, guidelines for quantifying such things as the number of training iterations and values for learning and momentum factors in back-propagation networks are discussed. Relative to testing, the subject of testing network tools is reviewed, including figuring out how to select a set of training and testing patterns and knowing when an application of a network tool has been successful.

In Chapter 9 (Expert Networks) a new type of AI tool is introduced: the expert network tool. These tools involve expert systems linked with neural networks to form hybrid systems that can do things neither neural networks nor expert systems can do alone. It is believed that variations of these hybrids may form a powerful new basis for AI development.

For many readers, the most important part of the book may be Chapters 10–14, which present case studies. Each case study tells the story of the process required to solve a real-world problem with neural networks. These case studies are presented in detail, including the reasoning that went into the choices for network architecture and training, and the preprocessing steps that were required before data could be presented to a network tool. Here the reader will gain an appreciation of why the neural network itself may be only 10 percent of the overall code of a given system.

Although the problems that the reader wants to solve with neural network tools may seem significantly different from those presented as case studies, we believe that the approaches, methods, and reasoning discussed are generally transferable to many other situations. By studying the case studies and thinking about them, readers can develop their own methodologies for applying neural network tools to problem solving.

The first case study discusses a system designed to analyze electroencephalogram (EEG) waveforms to detect epileptiform spikes. Spikes are abnormal EEG waveforms that can indicate neurological problems. The importance of preprocessing is emphasized by the two approaches used to form pattern files: one using raw EEG data to build the files and the other using calculated spike-related parameters. Both approaches represent significant preprocessing. Also emphasized is the iterative nature of developing neural network tools, particularly when an inter-disciplinary team is involved.

The second case study deals with how to determine whether a certain kind of radar signal return is valid. The third presents a down-to-earth neural net approach for analyzing commodities markets. The fourth investigates the possibilities of using neural networks in a system for optical character recognition. The fifth is an example of using neural nets to compose music. In addition, Chapter 6 on hardware presents a mini case study on the categorization of ship patterns.

The book is designed to be read in sequence, up to the case studies. The case studies themselves, however, can be read in any order.

Appendix E is a resource guide to further information. First, organizations and societies devoted to neural network theory and applications are briefly described, with contacts for each. Next, the major conferences, workshops, and symposia that are being held regularly are listed. Then, additional publications such as journals and magazines that are devoted to neural networks are listed, with a brief description of each. Finally, computer bulletin boards with activity related to neural network development are listed to provide readers with additional resources.

A glossary of neural network terms has been assembled with the help of many people working in the neural network field. If more than one commonly used definition of a term exists, more than one may be given. As illustrated in the glossary, there are a significant number of terms in the neural network field for which universal definitions, agreed to by all in the field, do not exist. Even terms as basic as *architecture* and *layer* as applied to neural networks are used in different ways by different authors.

Throughout the book, a few things will become evident, probably a little bit at a time.

1. When you are considering neural network tools and systems, the traditional distinctions between hardware and software get a bit fuzzy; distinctions between data and program are often almost nonexistent.
2. In this book, we are primarily interested in problem solving and applications rather than physiological plausibility. We really don't care too much whether what we do reflects what actually goes on in the brain or any other part of the nervous system.
3. We are not concerned with searching for artificial intelligence (whatever that is), or even for a neural network tool from which intelligent behavior will emerge. Again, the focus is solving problems.
4. Your activities as a neural network tool developer and user are some-

what different from what you may be used to in other technical work. Working with neural networks requires you to play two roles. The first is the hands-on active design, develop, test, and debug role you're probably used to. But the second, just as important as the first, is the more passive observation and analytical thinking role. You'll often not get what you expect from a neural network. Most of the time, if you take the time to observe and think, rather than "bash to fit and paint to match," you can learn something very useful.

There are four application areas for which neural networks are generally considered to be best suited. The first three are related, and the first and third do one kind or another of classification.

The first area is classification as reflected in decision theory; that is, which of several predefined classes best reflects an input pattern. The number of classes is typically small compared with the number of inputs. One example from the case studies is a decision whether or not a given segment of EEG data represents an epileptiform spike waveform or not. Another type of analysis that can be considered as classification is the ability of neural networks to construct nonlinear mappings between high-dimensional spaces. Some types of video image processing by neural networks are examples of this area.

The second area is often referred to as content addressable memory, or as associative memory. A typical example is obtaining the complete version of a pattern at the output of the network by providing a partial version at the input. (The input and output nodes of the network may sometimes be the same nodes.) This process is sometimes described as obtaining an exemplar pattern from a noisy and/or incomplete one.

The third area is referred to either as clustering or compression. This area can also be considered a form of encoding, rather than classification. An example is significantly reducing the dimensionality of an input, as in the case of speech recognition. Another example is reducing the number of bits that must be stored or transmitted to represent, within some allowed error margin, a block of data. In other words, the original block of data can be reconstructed within the allowed error with fewer bits than were in the original data.

The fourth area is somewhat different from the first three in that no classification is involved. It involves the generation of structured sequences or patterns from a network trained to examples. For instance, if a network is trained to reproduce a certain style of musical sequence, then it is possible for the network to compose "original" versions of that type of music. As another example, a neural network may be trained to model, or simulate, something. Because of inherent randomness in the process being simulated, there may be no "right" answers, but the system can perhaps be described statistically. The network simulation may then be designed to reproduce these statistical qualities. This area can be extended to many areas of application and represents the ability of a neural network system to be "creative."

The number of specific neural network tool applications for personal computers that reflect the four areas grows, it seems, daily. The following is a list of application areas the authors have gleaned from a variety of sources including books, technical papers presented at conferences, articles in journals and magazines, and advertisements for neural network hardware or software. This list, despite its length, is not meant to be complete. Furthermore, the authors do not guarantee the authenticity of each of the applications; some of them have the faint aroma of snake oil.

analysis of medical tests
circuit board problem diagnosis
EEG waveform classification
picking winners at horse races
predicting performance of students
analysis of loan applications
stock market prediction
military target tracking and recognition
process control
oil exploration
psychiatric evaluations
optimizing scheduled maintenance of machines
composing music
spectral analysis
optimizing raw material orders
selection of employees
detection of explosives in airline luggage
speech recognition
text-to-speech conversion
selection of criminal investigation targets
analysis of polygraph examination results
optimization of antenna array patterns
optical character recognition
modeling the operation of the brain

Perhaps one or more of these applications will catch your imagination or trigger your thinking of yet another area you would like to explore. The remainder of this book is designed to assist you in your explorations.

CHAPTER 1

Background and History

Russell C. Eberhart
Roy W. Dobbins

Introduction

The subject of neural networks is broad as well as deep, covering disciplines ranging from medicine to microelectronics. It is not the purpose of this book to address neural networks generally, neither is it the authors' intent to explore subjects related to biological or neurological neural networks. Instead this book focuses on neural network based tools, for personal computers, that can solve practical problems. For the most part, computers with 80286, 80386, or 68000 microprocessors are used as the hardware platforms on which the neural network based analysis systems discussed in this book are implemented. Common examples of these personal computers are the IBM AT, the Compaq DeskPro 386, and the Apple Macintosh, although workalike machines are just as useful. Each of the editors of this book uses a name brand machine at work and a workalike or clone at home.

Because neural network tools are derived from the massively parallel biological structures found in brains, we briefly review this derivation in this chapter, prior to the detailed introduction of neural network tools.

First, however, we present the definition of a neural network tool, or NNT as it is referred to in the remainder of the book. An NNT is an analysis tool that is modeled after the massively parallel structure of the brain: It simulates a highly interconnected, parallel computational structure with many relatively simple individual processing elements, or *neurodes*.

Neural Network PC Tools

Individual neurodes are gathered together into groups called *slabs*. Slabs can receive input (input slabs), provide output (output slabs), or be inaccessible to both input and output, with connections only to other slabs (internal slabs). Although the concept of slabs is not essential to understanding neural networks, it will be used throughout this book. It is the author's belief that slabs provide a useful and concise mechanism for representing and discussing networks.

Neural network tools are characterized in three ways. First is the architecture of the NNT, which is the particular way the slabs are interconnected and receive input and output. Second is the transfer function of the slabs, that is, the function that describes the output of a neurode given its input. Third is the learning paradigm used for training the network. These three characteristics can be thought of as the top level attributes of an NNT. As will be seen later in this chapter, the three attributes cannot always be varied independently. For example, certain architectures preclude certain learning paradigms.

The *T* of NNT suggests the final element of this introductory definition of NNTs. The tools are hardware/software systems that can be implemented on personal computers, such as 80286, 80386, and 68000 microprocessor-based machines.

Much of the rest of this chapter is devoted to expanding these central ideas about NNTs. However, now that a basic definition of an NNT has been stated, it is useful to review the development of neural network theory and technology.

Biological Basis for Neural Network Tools

Introduction

Every day of our lives, each of us carries out thousands of tasks that require us to keep track of many things at once and to process and act upon these things. Relatively simple actions, such as picking up a glass of water or dialing a telephone number, involve many individual pieces of memory, learning, and physical coordination. The complexity of such "simple" tasks, which most of us do all the time without "thinking" about them, is underscored by the difficulty involved in teaching robots to perform them. Performance of these tasks is made possible by our complex biological structure.

Neurons

Studies over the past few decades have shed some light on the construction and operation of our brains and nervous systems. The basic build-

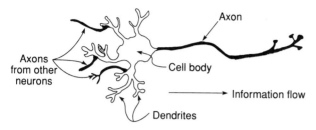

Figure 1-1 Biological neuron.

ing block of the nervous system is the neuron. The major components of a neuron include a central cell body, dendrites, and an axon.

Figure 1-1, a conceptual diagram of a neuron, is a sketch of only one representation of a neuron. There are many kinds of neurons, and to get more detailed information on their configuration and functioning, you should refer to a book on neuroanatomy or neurology, such as House and Pansky [1]. The neuron represented in Fig. 1-1 probably resembles a motor neuron more than most other types, such as sensory neurons, but it is meant only to convey the basic configuration and terminology. Note that the signal flow goes from left to right, from the dendrites, through the cell body, and out through the axon. The signal from one neuron is passed on to another by means of a connection between the axon of the first and a dendrite of the second. This connection is called a *synapse*. Axons often synapse onto the trunk of a dendrite, but they can also synapse directly onto the cell body.

The human brain has a large number of neurons, or processing elements (PE). Typical estimates are on the order of 10–500 billion [2]. According to one estimate by Stubbs [3], neurons are arranged into about 1000 main modules, each with about 500 neural networks. Each network has on the order of 100,000 neurons. The axon of each neuron connects to about 100 (but sometimes several thousand) other neurons, and this value varies greatly from neuron to neuron and neuron type to neuron type. According to a rule called Eccles law, each neuron either excites or inhibits all neurons to which it is connected.

Differences between Biological Structures and NNTs

There are significant differences between a neural biological structure (as we currently understand it) and the implementation or representation of this structure in NNTs. Before we summarize a few of these differences, note that the neurode, or processing element, in an NNT is generally considered to be roughly analogous to a biological neuron.

(We say "generally" because some researchers use an entire NNT to model a single biological neuron.)

1. In a typical implementation of an NNT, connections among neurodes can have either positive or negative weights. These weights correspond to excitatory and inhibitory neural connections, so Eccles law is not usually implemented in NNTs.
2. Information about the state of activation, or excitation, of a neurode is passed to other neurodes to which it is connected as a value that roughly corresponds to a direct current (dc) level. In biological neural nets (BNNs), a train of pulses across a synapse carries the information, and higher absolute values of activation result in higher pulse rates, so that alternating current (ac) frequency, or pulse repetition rate, generally corresponds to activation level. There are exceptions to the pulse rate carrying information in biological nets, but they are relatively unimportant for our discussion.
3. There are many kinds of neurons in biological systems. An NNT is typically implemented with only one type of neurode. Occasionally, two or three types of neurodes are used, and as the technology of NNTs develops, more sophisticated tools may make use of several neurode types in each implementation. On the other hand, some studies indicate that any required implementation can be carried out with as few as two types of neurodes [2].
4. Neurons in BNNs typically operate on an individual cycle time of about 10–100 milliseconds (msec). The basic clock frequency in an 80286 or 80386 based microcomputer is generally 10–30 megahertz (mHz), which results in a basic cycle time for the computer of 0.03–0.10 microseconds (μsec). Even if we take into account the number of multiply–accumulate operations needed to calculate and propagate a new value for a PE (typically 10–100 μsec), the basic cycle time for an individual PE is still only about 1–10 μsec. Note, however, that in some ways speed is deceiving. Despite its slower cycle time, the brain is still able to perform some tasks orders of magnitude faster than today's fastest digital computer. This is because of the brain's massively parallel architecture.
5. There is a significant difference between the number of neurodes in the typical NNT and the number of biological neurons involved in any task in a BNN. Typical NNTs are implemented with anywhere from a few dozen to several hundred neurodes.

Each of the 1000 main modules in the human brain described by Stubbs [3] contains about 500 million neurons, and it is almost certain that several (perhaps many) of these main modules are involved in any simple task. Of course, for any practical application, most of us wouldn't have the foggiest notion of how to utilize effectively an NNT with 500 million neurodes! There are many other differences, of course, but those described should give you a rough picture.

Where Did Neural Networks Get Their Name?

If NNTs are so different from BNNs, why are they even called *neural network* tools? Why not something else? The answer is that the background and training of the people who first implemented useful NNTs were generally in the biological, physiological, and psychological areas rather than in engineering or computer science.

One of the most important publications that opened up neural network analysis by presenting it in a useful and clear way was a three-volume set of books entitled *Parallel Distributed Processing* [2,4,5]. The chapters in the first two volumes were authored by members of the interdisciplinary Parallel Distributed Processing (PDP) research group, who were from a variety of educational institutions. Several members of the PDP research group are cognitive scientists. Others are psychologists. Computer scientists are definitely in the minority; and judging from the professional titles and affiliations of the PDP authors, none is an engineer.

Had the concept of massively parallel processing initially been developed and made practical by electrical or computer engineers, we could be using "massively parallel adaptive filter" tools instead of neural network tools, or they might be called something else that has no reference to the word *neural*. Neural networks do have technical roots in the fields of analog computing and signal processing (back in the days of vacuum tubes, no less) that rival in importance their roots in biology and cognitive science. We review this engineering heritage in the next section of this chapter.

Much of the neural network effort in biology, cognitive science, and related fields came about as a result of efforts to explain experimental results and observations in behavior and in brain construction. Why should we engineers and computer scientists care about experimental results in brain research and cognitive science? For one thing, as Anderson [6] points out, if we can find out what kind of "wetware" runs well in our brains, we may gain insight into what kind of software to write for neural network applications. In other words, cognitive scientists and psychologists may provide us with some important information for reverse-engineering NNT software.

Neural Network Development History

Introduction

We have divided the history of neural network development into four segments, which we call *ages*. The first age begins at the time of William James, about a century ago. We call this the Age of Camelot. It ends in 1969 with the publication of Minsky and Papert's book on *perceptrons*. Next is the Dark Age (or Depression Age) beginning in 1969 and ending in 1982 with Hopfield's landmark paper on neural networks and physical systems. The third age, the Renaissance, begins with Hopfield's paper and ends with the publication of *Parallel Distributed Processing*, Volumes 1 and 2, by Rumelhart and McClelland in 1986. The fourth age, called the Age of Neoconnectionism after Cowan and Sharp's review article on neural nets and artificial intelligence [10], runs from 1987 until the present.

This history is traced somewhat differently here than in other books on neural networks in that we focus on people, rather than just on theory or technology. We review the contributions of a number of individuals and relate them to how NNTs are being implemented today. The selection of individuals is somewhat arbitrary because our intent is to provide a broad sample of the people who contributed to current NNT technology rather than an exhaustive list. Some well-known neural networkers are mentioned only briefly, and others are omitted. We discuss the selected people and their contributions roughly in chronological order.

The Age of Camelot

We begin our look at neural network history in the Age of Camelot with a person considered by many to be the greatest American psychologist who ever lived, William James. James also taught, and thoroughly understood, physiology. It has been almost exactly a century since James published his *Principles of Psychology* and its condensed version *Psychology (Briefer Course)* [7].

James was the first to publish a number of facts related to brain structure and function. He first stated, for example, some of the basic principles of correlational learning and associative memory. In stating what he called his Elementary Principle, James wrote,

> Let us then assume as the basis of all our subsequent reasoning this law: When two elementary brain processes have been active together or in immediate succession, one of them, on re-occurring, tends to propagate its excitement into the other.

This is closely related to the concepts of associative memory and correlational learning.

He seemed to foretell the notion of a neuron's activity being a function of the sum of its inputs, with past correlation history contributing to the weight of interconnections:

> The amount of activity at any given point in the brain-cortex is the sum of the tendencies of all other points to discharge into it, such tendencies being proportionate (1) to the number of times the excitement of each other point may have accompanied that of the point in question; (2) to the intensity of such excitements; and (3) to the absence of any rival point functionally disconnected with the first point, into which the discharges might be diverted.

Over half a century later, McCulloch and Pitts [8] published one of the most famous neural network papers, in which they derived theorems related to models of neuronal systems based on what was known about biological structures in the early 1940s. In coming to their conclusions, they stated five physical assumptions:

> 1. The activity of the neuron is an "all-or-none" process. 2. A certain fixed number of synapses must be excited within the period of latent addition in order to excite a neuron at any time, and this number is independent of previous activity and position on the neuron. 3. The only significant delay within the nervous system is synaptic delay. 4. The activity of any inhibitory synapse absolutely prevents excitation of the neuron at that time. 5. The structure of the net does not change with time.

The period of *latent addition* is the time during which the neuron is able to detect the values present on its inputs, the synapses. This time was described by McCulloch and Pitts as typically less than 0.25 msec. The *synaptic delay* is the time delay between sensing inputs and acting on them by transmitting an outgoing pulse, stated by McCulloch and Pitts to be on the order of half a millisecond.

The neuron described by these five assumptions is known as the McCulloch–Pitts neuron. The theories they developed were important for a number of reasons, including the fact that any finite logical expression can be realized by networks of their neurons. They also appear to be the first authors since William James to describe a massively parallel neural model.

Although the paper was very important, it is very difficult to read. In particular, the theorem proofs presented by McCulloch and Pitts have stopped more than one engineer in their tracks. Furthermore, not all of the concepts presented in the paper are being implemented in today's NNTs. In this book, comparisons are not made between the theories and conclusions of McCulloch and Pitts (or anyone else) and the current theories of neural biology. The focus here is strictly on the implementation (or nonimplementation) of their ideas in NNTs for personal computers.

One concept that is not generally being implemented is their all-or-none neuron. A binary, on or off, neuron is used as the neurode in neural networks such as the Boltzmann machine [2], but it is not generally used in most NNTs today. Much more common is a neurode whose output value can vary continuously over some range, such as from 0 to 1, or -1 to 1.

Another example of an unused concept involves the signal required to "excite" a neurode. First, because the output of a neurode generally varies continuously with the input, there is no "threshold" at which an output appears. The neurodes used in some NNTs activate at some threshold, but not in most of the tools we'll be discussing in this book. For neurodes with either continuous outputs or thresholds, no "fixed number of connections" (synapses) must be excited. The net input to a neurode is generally a function of the outputs of the neurodes connected to it upstream (presynaptically) and of the connection strengths to those presynaptic neurodes.

A third example is that there is generally no delay associated with the connection (synapse) in an NNT. Typically, the output states (activation levels) of the neurodes are updated synchronously, one slab (or layer) at a time. Sometimes, as in Boltzmann machines, they are updated asynchronously, with the update order determined stochastically. There is almost never, however, a delay built into a connection from one neurode to another.

A fourth example is that the activation of a single inhibitory connection does not usually disable or deactivate the neuron to which it is connected. Any inhibitory connection (a connection with a negative weight) has the same absolute magnitude effect, albeit subtractive, as the additive effect of a positive connection with the same absolute weight.

With regard to the fifth assumption of McCulloch and Pitts, it is true that the structure of an NNT usually does not change with time, with a couple of caveats. First, it is usual to "train" NNTs, such as back-propagation and self-organizing networks, prior to their use. During the training process, the structure doesn't usually change, but the interconnecting weights do. In addition, it is not uncommon, once training is complete, for neurodes that aren't contributing significantly to be removed. This certainly can be considered a change to the structure of the network.

But wait a minute! What are we left with of McCulloch and Pitts' five assumptions? If truth be told, when referring to NNTs we are in most cases left with perhaps one assumption: the fifth.

Then why do we make such a big deal about their 1943 paper? First, they proved that networks of their neurons could represent any finite logical expression; second, they used a massively parallel architecture; and third, they provided the stepping stones for the development of the network models and learning paradigms that followed.

Just because NNTs don't always reflect McCulloch and Pitts' work doesn't imply in any way that their work was bad. Our NNTs don't always reflect what we currently understand about BNNs either. For instance, it appears that a neuron acts somewhat like a voltage-controlled oscillator (VCO), with the output frequency a function of the input level (input voltage): The higher the input, the more pulses per second the neuron puts out. NNTs usually work with basically steady-state values of the neurode from one update to the next.

The next personality along our journey through the Age of Camelot is Donald O. Hebb, whose 1949 book *The Organization of Behavior* [11] was the first to define the method of updating synaptic weights that we now refer to as *Hebbian*. He is also among the first to use the term *connectionism*. Hebb presented his method as a "neurophysiological postulate" in his chapter entitled "The First Stage of Perception: Growth of the Assembly," as follows:

> When an axon of cell A is near enough to excite a cell B and repeatedly or persistently takes part in firing it, some growth process or metabolic change takes place in one or both cells such that A's efficiency as one of the cells firing B, is increased.

Hebb made four primary contributions to neural network theory.

First, he stated that in a neural network, information is stored in the weight of the synapses (connections).

Second, he postulated a connection weight learning rate that is proportional to the product of the activation values of the neurons. Note that his postulate assumed that the activation values are positive. Because he didn't provide a means for the weights to be decreased, they could theoretically go infinitely high. Learning that involves neurons with negative activation values has also been labeled as Hebbian. This is not included in Hebb's original formulation, but is a logical extension of it.

Third, he assumed that weights are symmetric. That is, the weight of a connection from neuron A to neuron B is the same as that from B to A. Although this may or may not be true in BNNs, it is often applied to implementations in neural network tools.

Fourth, he postulated a cell assembly theory, which states that as learning occurs, strengths and patterns of synapse connections (weights) change, and assemblies of cells are created by these changes. Stated another way, if simultaneous activation of a group of weakly connected cells occurs repeatedly, these cells tend to coalesce into a more strongly connected assembly.

All four of Hebb's contributions are generally implemented in today's NNTs, at least to some degree. We often refer to learning schemes implemented in some networks as Hebbian.

In 1958, a landmark paper by Frank Rosenblatt [12] defined a neural network structure called the *perceptron*. The perceptron was probably the first honest-to-goodness NNT because it was simulated in detail on an IBM 704 computer at the Cornell Aeronautical Laboratory. This computer-oriented paper caught the imagination of engineers and physicists, despite the fact that its mathematical proofs, analyses, and descriptions contained tortuous twists and turns. If you can wade through the variety of systems and modes of organization in the paper, you'll see that the perceptron is capable of learning to classify certain pattern sets as similar or distinct by modifying its connections. It can therefore be described as a "learning machine."

Rosenblatt used biological vision as his network model. Input node groups consisted of random sets of cells in a region of the retina, each group being connected to a single association unit (AU) in the next higher layer. AUs were connected bidirectionally to response units (RUs) in the third (highest) layer. The perceptron's objective was to activate the correct RU for each particular input pattern class. Each RU typically had a large number of connections to AUs.

He devised two ways to implement the feedback from RUs to AUs. In the first, activation of an RU would tend to excite the AUs that sent the RU excitation (positive feedback). In the second, inhibitory connections existed between the RU and the *complement* of the set of AUs that excited it (negative feedback), therefore inhibiting activity in AUs which did not transmit to it. Rosenblatt used the second option for most of his systems. In addition, for both options, he assumed that all RUs were interconnected with inhibitory connections.

Rosenblatt used his perceptron model to address two questions. First, in what form is information stored, or remembered? Second, how does stored information influence recognition and behavior? His answers were as follows [12]:

... *the information is contained in connections or associations rather than topographic representations. ... since the stored information takes the form of new connections, or transmission channels in the nervous system (or the creation of conditions which are functionally equivalent to new connections), it follows that the new stimuli will make use of these new path-*

ways which have been created, automatically activating the appropriate response without requiring any separate process for their recognition or identification.

The primary perceptron learning mechanism is "self-organizing" or "self-associative" in that the response that happens to become dominant is initially random. However, Rosenblatt also described systems in which training or "forced responses" occurred.

This paper laid the groundwork for both supervised and unsupervised training algorithms as they are seen today in back-propagation and Kohonen networks, respectively. The basic structures set forth by Rosenblatt are therefore alive and well, despite the critique by Minsky and Papert, which we discuss later.

Our last stop in the Age of Camelot is with Bernard Widrow and Marcian Hoff. In 1960, they published a paper entitled "Adaptive Switching Circuits" that, particularly from an engineering standpoint, has become one of the most important papers on neural network technology [13]. Widrow and Hoff are the first engineers we've talked about in our history section. Not only did they design NNTs that they simulated on computers, they implemented their designs in hardware. And at least one of the lunchbox-sized machines they built "way back then" is still in working order!

Widrow and Hoff introduced a device called an *adaline* (for *adaptive linear*) [13]. Adaline (Fig. 1-2) consists of a single neurode with an arbitrary number of input elements that can take on values of plus or minus one and a bias element that is always plus one. Before being summed by the neurode summer, each input, including the bias, is

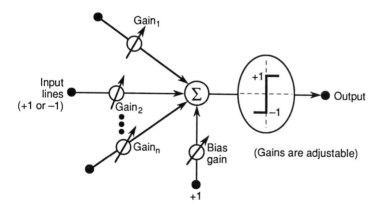

Figure 1-2   Adaline, an adjustable neuron.

modified by a unique weight that Widrow and Hoff call a "gain." (This name reflects their engineering background because the term *gain* refers to the amplification factor that an electronic signal undergoes when processed by an amplifier; it may be more descriptive of the function performed than the more common term *weight*.) On the output of the summer is a quantizer that has an output of plus one if the summer output, including the bias, is greater than zero, and an output of minus one for summer outputs less than or equal to zero.

What is particularly ingenious about the adaline is the learning algorithm. One of the main problems with perceptrons was the length of time it took them to learn to classify patterns. The Widrow–Hoff algorithm yields learning that is faster and more accurate. The algorithm is a form of *supervised* learning that adjusts the weights (gains) according to the size of the error on the output of the summer. Widrow and Hoff showed that the way they adjust the weights minimizes the sum-squared error over all patterns in the training set. For that reason, the Widrow–Hoff method is also known as the least mean squares (LMS) algorithm. The error is the difference between what the output of the adaline should be and the output of the summer. The sum-squared error is obtained by measuring the error for each pattern presented to the adaline, squaring each value, and then summing all of the squared values.

Minimizing the sum-squared error involves an error reduction method called *gradient descent*, or *steepest descent*. Mathematically, it involves the partial derivatives of the error with respect to the weights. Don't worry about this mathematical jargon if you haven't studied calculus because Widrow and Hoff showed that you don't have to take the derivatives. They are proportional to the error (and its sign) and to the sign of the input.

They further showed that, for n inputs, reducing the measured error of the summer by $1/n$ for each input does a good job of implementing gradient descent. You adjust each weight until the error is reduced by $1/n$ of the total error you started with. For example, if you have 12 input nodes, you adjust each weight to remove $\frac{1}{12}$ of the total error. This method provides for weight adjustment (learning) even when the output of the classifier is correct. For example, if the output of the summer is 0.5, the classifier output is 1.0. If the correct output is 1.0, there is still an error signal of 0.5 that is used to train the weights further. This is a significant improvement over the perceptron, which adjusts weights only when the classifier output is incorrect. This is one reason the learning of an adaline is faster and more accurate.

Widrow and Hoff's paper was prophetic, too. They suggested several practical implementations of their adaline:

If a computer were built of adaptive neurons, details of structure could be imparted by the designer by training (showing it examples of what he would like to do) rather than by direct designing.

An extension of the Widrow–Hoff learning algorithm is used today in back-propagation networks, and their work in hardware implementation of NNTs heralded today's cutting-edge work in very large-scale integration (VLSI) by people including Carver Mead and his colleagues at the California Institute of Technology [41]. Dr. Widrow is the earliest significant contributor to neural network hardware system development who is still working in the area of neural networks.

As the 1960s drew to a close, optimism was the order of the day. Many people were working in artificial intelligence (AI), both in the area exemplified by expert systems and in neural networks. Although many areas were still unexplored and many problems were unsolved, the general feeling was that the sky was the limit. Little did most folks know that, for neural networks, the sky was about to fall.

The Dark Age

In 1969, Marvin Minsky and Seymour Papert dropped a bombshell on the neural network community in the form of a book called *Perceptrons* [16]. While it could be argued that neural network development in the late 1960s had suffered from an overdose of hype and a paucity of performance, nearly all funding for neural networks dried up after the book was published. This was the beginning of the Dark Age.

Most of Minsky and Papert's book is about simple perceptrons, with only an input layer and an output layer (no hidden layer). Furthermore, neurons are threshold logic units, so only two states are allowed, on or off. The authors' analysis of simple perceptrons was generally correct, but even this part of their book had a disturbing undertone, because of the authors' style of writing and because of what was not said. Their writing style is illustrated by statements such as "Most of this writing [about perceptrons] is without scientific value" and "It is therefore vacuous to cite a 'perceptron convergence theorem' as assurance that a learning process will eventually find a correct setting of its parameters (if one exists)" [16]. Words and phrases such as "vacuous" and "without scientific value" project a sort of holier-than-thou attitude not likely to make friends and influence people. The book didn't say much about perceptrons' good points; it isn't so much about what perceptrons *can* do as what they *can't* do.

The coup de grace came in the last chapter, where Minsky and Papert wrote, "our intuitive judgement [is] that the extension [to multilayer perceptrons with hidden layers] is sterile." This statement has proven to be a serious mistake and, in the opinions of some workers, a conscious "hatchet job" on a research area whose proponents were competing with Minsky, Papert, and their colleagues for funding. Perhaps the most serious effect of the book is that it drove a wedge between the "traditional" AI folks (those who work with expert systems) and the neural network people. This is particularly disturbing because it is becoming increasingly apparent that, at least in many areas, major breakthroughs in AI are going to require a combination of approaches.

The approach of expert systems is going to be combined with NNTs to form hybrid systems. Call them *expert network tools*, or ENTs. These ENTs will likely play an important role in complex systems such as those used for medical diagnosis. They are discussed later in the book. Suffice it to say that these two areas of AI need to cooperate closely, not merely coexist.

It has now been more than two decades since *Perceptrons* was published. Have the authors seen the error of their ways? Not if you believe what Papert said in a recent article [17]. He admits that "there was *some* hostility in the energy behind the research reported in *Perceptrons*, and there is *some* degree of annoyance at the way the new movement [in neural networks] has developed. . . ." From the tone of the rest of the article, one concludes that this is an understatement. Papert is playing his same old tune in stating that "the story of new, powerful network mechanisms is seriously exaggerated," and he is still exhibiting the same holier-than-thou attitude in references to *Parallel Distributed Processing* [2,4,5] as "the current bible of connectionism" [17]. He displays a lack of familiarity, both with computer technology available in 1970 and with the current power of NNTs:

> The influential recent demonstrations of new networks all run on small computers and could have been done in 1970 with ease. . . . the examples discussed in the literature are still very small. Indeed, Minsky and I, in a more technical discussion of this history (added as a new chapter to a reissue of Perceptrons), suggest that the entire structure of recent connectionist theories might be built on quicksand: it is all based on toy-sized problems with no theoretical analysis to show that performance will be maintained when the models are scaled up to realistic size.

It isn't clear what computer Papert had available in 1970, but authors of this book were working with state-of-the-art Data General Nova computers, with 4 Kbytes of memory, that had to be bootstrapped by *hand-setting* front panel switches each time the machine was turned on. Mass storage was paper tape that was read, or punched, by an ASR-33 teletype at 10 characters per second. Although there was also limited access to a Nova computer with a disk drive, the bulk of our work was done with paper tape. The programming languages available were Assembler and BASIC. Period. And the machine ran at about one megahertz.

"Mainframes" at universities were typically PDP-11s with 8 Kbytes of memory, operated in "batch mode" by computer high priests who required you to drop off your punched cards one day and get your results (often limited to error messages) the next. It would have been close to impossible to code, train, and test any significant network on these machines. Networks now typically have more weights than these machines had memory locations.

The computers we used to write this book have clock speeds of 10–25 mHz, memories of 1–16 Mbytes, and hard disks of 20–110 megabytes; and they are cheap machines, costing less than one-third of the Nova *in constant, uninflated 1970 dollars.*

The "recent demonstrations of new networks," mentioned by Papert, have depended heavily on the new, inexpensive, powerful microcomputer technology. Far from being toy problems, recent applications ranging from biology to military are significant and sizable. Some of these applications are reviewed in this book, so you can judge for yourself. As for being "built on quicksand," let the record speak for itself: Successfully implementing significant applications is more important to many of us than pontificating theory. It is hoped that you will heed the call to reunite the two areas of AI so that problems will be solved that can't be approached by either discipline alone. A merging of the two areas should result in an AI field with significantly expanded capabilities.

In the decade following the publication of Minsky and Papert's book, the number of researchers toiling in the neural network vineyards dropped significantly. For those who remained, progress continued, but in smaller steps. Now we will look at the work of the Dark Age developers who have a continuing impact on the field, particularly those whose contributions led to currently used techniques in NNTs.

In 1972, two researchers on different continents published similar neural network development results. One, Dr. Teuvo Kohonen of the Helsinki University of Technology in Finland, is an electrical engineer; the other, Dr. James Anderson, is a neurophysiologist and professor of psychology at Brown University in the United States. Although Kohonen called his neural network structure "associative memory" [19] and Anderson named his "interactive memory" [20], their techniques in network architectures, learning algorithms, and transfer functions were almost identical. Despite the similarity of their results, these men do not contain a single item in common! This is illustrated by their lists of references.

We focus here on Kohonen, partly because of the current implementations of Kohonen's work in NNTs (we review and apply Kohonen's networks extensively in the next chapter) and partly because of his interest in applications such as pattern recognition and speech recognition. This is not to diminish in any way the work done by Anderson, which was and continues to be important and relevant. In fact, a book recently edited by Anderson and Rosenfeld [6] is arguably the best compilation of the significant work in the neural network field. Each paper in the volume is prefaced by excellent introductory material that places the paper in context. Anderson has been interested more in physiological plausibility and models for his network structures and learning algorithms.

One of the most notable things about Kohonen's 1972 paper is the neurode, or processing unit, that he uses. It is linear and continuous valued, rather than the all-or-none binary model McCulloch–Pitts and Widrow–Hoff. Not only is the output continuous valued, but so are the connection weights and input values. Remember that Widrow–Hoff used continuous values to calculate the error values, but the output of the neurode was binary.

Also notable is Kohonen's use of networks with many simultaneously active input and output neurodes, which are necessary if we're considering visual images or spectral speech information. Rather than having the output of the network represented by the activation of a single "winning" neurode or the activation level of a single multivalued neurode, Kohonen uses activation patterns on a relatively large number of output neurodes to represent the input classifications. This makes the network better able to generalize and less sensitive to noise.

Most notably, the paper lays the groundwork for a type of NNT very different from that evolved from the perceptron. The current version of the multilayer perceptron most commonly used is the back-propagation network, which is trained by giving it examples of correct classifications, an example of supervised learning. Current versions of Kohonen's networks, sometimes referred to as *self-organizing* networks, learn to classify without being taught. This is called *unsupervised learning* and can frequently be used to categorize information when we don't know what categories exist. It is also possible, as we'll discuss in the next chapter, to combine Kohonen unsupervised architectures with architectures such as back-propagation to do interesting and useful things.

Dr. Stephen Grossberg of the Center for Adaptive Systems at Boston University, the second Dark Age researcher discussed here, appeared on the neural network scene about the same time as Minsky and Papert published their book. He continues to be one of the most productive, visible, and controversial personalities in the field. His work is often abstract, theoretical, and mathematically dense. It is extremely difficult to wade through his papers, because many of them refer to work described in several previous papers. He seems to be more concerned with the physiological plausibility of network structures than with providing tools for practical problem solving.

In his early work, Grossberg introduced several concepts that are used in a number of current neural network architectures. In the past few years, he and Dr. Gail Carpenter, his spouse, have introduced and developed a network architecture known as adaptive resonance theory (ART). His early concepts include the "on-center off-surround" gain control system for a group of neurons. This basically says that if a neurode in a population of neurodes is strongly excited, the surrounding neurodes will receive inhibition signals. This lateral inhibition idea is also used in Kohonen's self-organizing structures. Grossberg also contributed much to the theories of network memories, that is, how patterns can stay active after inputs to the network have stopped. He wrote of short-term memory (STM) and long-term memory (LTM) mechanisms, how the former are related to neurode activation values and the latter to connection weights. Both activation values and weights decay with time, a feature called *forgetting*. Activation values decay relatively quickly (short-term memory) whereas weights, having long-term memory, decay much more slowly.

Note that there is a basic difference between the Grossberg networks and the network structures we've been discussing so far. In the latter, the interconnecting weights are trained and then frozen whereas Grossberg's patterns are presented to the networks to classify without supervised training. Activation values of the neurodes have no memory. The only thing determining the activation values is the pattern currently being presented to the network.

Grossberg gives neurodes (or groups of them, called *cell populations*) short-term memory (STM), so that the current activation value depends on the previous one as well as on the average excitation of other connected populations. In accordance with on-center off-surround, Grossberg's earlier papers [24] describe an inhibitory effect of activation values of connected populations.

He also wrote about a different kind of neurode response function (output versus input) that had been discussed earlier: a *sigmoid* function. A typical sigmoid response function, described in 1973 [24], is illustrated in Fig. 1–3. In this paper, he shows that signal enhancement and decreased sensitivity to noise can occur if the signals transmitted be-

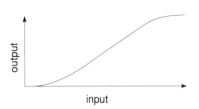

Figure 1-3 Sigmoid function.

tween cell populations are sigmoid functions of the populations' average activity levels. This sigmoid function differs in several respects from the one we use with our back-propagation networks in the next chapter. For one thing, it only plays an inhibitory role, even when it is used as part of the shunting self-excitation term for a neurode population. For another, it is always nonnegative in Grossberg's implementation [24].

Another concept incorporated into Grossberg's network models that differs from those discussed previously is the learning algorithm. In models such as Widrow–Hoff and the back-propagation network, the learning signal is proportional to the error in the output, that is, the difference between the desired and actual values. In Grossberg's model, learning is computed from the *sum* of the desired and actual values, represented in some of his models by input and learned feedback signals.

Over the past several years, Grossberg and Carpenter have been developing their adaptive resonance theory (ART) models, which incorporate most of the features described. There are three versions of the ART system, ART 1, ART 2, and, very recently, ART 3. The ART network paradigm has been described as "one of the most complex neural networks ever invented" [25].

ART 1 networks can process only binary input patterns. Because almost all NNT applications require continuous-valued patterns, we won't consider ART 1 in this book. ART 2 networks are even more complicated than those of ART 1, and can process discrete-valued input data. They cannot, however, process continuous-valued data. In addition to their complexity and limitations, to the best of the authors' knowledge and to the best of the knowledge of others cognizant of ART 2 [26], insufficient information has been published to implement ART 2 networks on personal computers. Neither ART 1 nor ART 2, then, appears to be a candidate for practical applications on personal computers. In fact, Caudill [25] reports that

> When these [ART 1 models] are implemented in a software-only simulation
> (such as that provided by at least one of the available commercial simula-

tors), computational overhead is so great that the network is unacceptably slow on anything short of a Cray.

In the authors' opinion, it is best to view the ART models as powerful research models rather than as available NNTs. If you want to learn more about them, the most effective way is to look at the books that are a collection of papers by Grossberg and Carpenter [21,23]. Drs. Carpenter and Grossberg have also published a relatively readable article that is primarily focused on ART 2 [27]. For more easily understood explanations of ART, see Caudill [25].

The third researcher we'll discuss in our tour of the Dark Age is Dr. Kunihiko Fukushima of the NHK Broadcasting Science Research Laboratories in Tokyo, Japan. Dr. Fukushima has developed a number of neural network architectures and algorithms but is best known for the *neocognitron*. The neocognitron was briefly described first in English in a 1979 report, but the first thorough English language description appeared in 1980 [28]. Subsequent articles have reported developments and refinements [29,30,31].

The neocognitron is a model for a visual pattern recognition mechanism and is therefore very concerned with biological plausibility. As stated by Fukushima, the goal of the work was "to synthesize a neural network model in order to endow it [with] an ability to [perform] pattern recognition like a human being." The network originally described is self-organized and thus able to learn without supervision.

Later versions of the model utilize supervised learning. Fukushima et al. in the 1983 article admit that the supervised learning situation more nearly reflects "a standpoint of an engineering application to a design of a pattern recognizer rather than that of pure biological modeling" [30]. Because the network emulates the visual nervous system, starting with retinal images, each layer is two-dimensional. An input layer is followed by a number of modules connected in series. Each module consists of two layers, the first representing S-cells (the more simple visual cortex cells) and the second representing C-cells (the more complex visual cortex cells). Cells are nonnegative and continuous valued.

Weights from C-cells in one layer to S-cells in the next layer are modifiable, as are those from the input to the first S-cells. Weights within a layer, from S-cells to C-cells, are fixed. There are a number of "planes" within each layer. Each cell receives input from a fixed, relatively small region of the layer preceding it. By the time the output layer is reached, each output cell "sees" the entire input as a result of this telescoping effect of decreasing the number of cells in each plane with the depth into the network.

It is beyond the scope of this summary to describe the neocognitron fully, but it exhibits a number of interesting features. For example, the network response is not significantly affected by the position of the pattern in the input field. It also recognizes input correctly despite small changes in shape or size of the input pattern. Recent versions cope even better with deformation and positional shift than early versions, and, when presented with a complex pattern consisting of several characters, are able to pay selective attention to the characters one at a time, recognizing each in turn [31].

The neocognitron itself has not been implemented to any significant degree on personal computers (although several of the concepts have appeared in current NNTs), probably because of the model's complexity. For example, in the network of the 1980 paper [28], an input layer of 256 cells (16 × 16) was followed by three modules of 8544, 2400, and 120 cells, respectively. In addition to the complexity introduced by over 11,000 neurodes, the neocognitron has multiple feedforward paths and feedback loops, resulting in a computing complexity that is daunting.

One important thing that Fukushima figured out, however, was how to deal with learning of inner "hidden" cells (neurodes) that are neither input nor output cells. He assumes not only that you know what your desired response is but also that you know what computational process needs to be followed, stage by stage through the network, to get that response. Knowing the computational process is only possible in certain well defined cases, such as the one described by Fukushima, in which the 10 digits, 0–9, were being recognized in handwritten form. Nevertheless, it was quite an accomplishment.

It may be interesting to note in passing that Fukushima calls his output cells (those that perform the recognition) *gnostic cells*. We assume he is using the word in the context of the suffix -*gnosis*, which means knowledge or recognition, rather than in connection with the Gnostic religous cults of late pre-Christian and early Christian centuries.

The Renaissance

Several publications appeared in the period from 1982 until 1986 that significantly furthered the state of neural network research. Several individuals were involved, one who published his first two landmark neural network papers by himself, and others who, in addition to their individual efforts, published as a group. We call these folks the Renaissance Men.

The individual who published by himself is Dr. John J. Hopfield of the California Insititute of Technology. In 1982, Hopfield published a paper that, according to many neural network researchers, played a more important role than any other single paper in reviving the field [32]. A number of factors were responsible for the impact of Hopfield's 1982 paper and follow-on paper published in 1984 [33]. In addition to what he said, how he said it and who he is are quite important. We'll briefly describe what he said below, but first let's take a quick look at who he is and how he presented his findings.

Much of the significant work in neural networks during the Dark Age was done by biologists, psychologists, and other researchers we could label "carbon based." Hopfield is a well-respected physicist. One might say that he is a "silicon-based" researcher. In presenting his findings, he brought a number of areas into a coherent whole. He identified network structures and algorithms that could be generalized and that had a high degree of robustness. Significantly, he pointed out throughout his papers that his ideas could be implemented in integrated circuitry, which is why we call him silicon based. He presented his networks in a manner that was easy for engineers and computer scientists to understand, showing the similarities between his work and that of others. In short, he got the attention of the technical world.

He didn't introduce too many new ideas; he just put them together in new, creative, and brilliant ways. One new idea was his definition of the energy of a network: For a given state of the network, the energy is proportional to the overall sum of the products of each pair of node activation values (V_i, V_j) and the connection weight associated with them (T_{ij}), that is,

$$E = -0.5 \sum T_{ij} V_i V_j \qquad (T_{ii} = 0) \qquad (1\text{-}1)$$

He showed that the algorithm for changing V_i, described below, makes E decrease and that eventually a minimum E is obtained. In other words, he proved that the network has stable states.

Many of his ideas are incorporated in the networks that we look at in the next chapter, but we don't present the Hopfield net in detail. Instead, we review the version of his network that uses binary neurodes, as presented in his 1982 paper [32].

The network Hopfield described in 1984 [33] is similar except that it contains continuous-valued neurodes with a sigmoidal nonlinearity. The same general mathematical method is used for computing network values in each case. Despite the continuous sigmoidal nonlinearity, inputs to the network must be expressed in binary form. This arises from the network equations (to be shown) and presents significant problems in using this version of the Hopfield net in many applications.

A very simple example of a Hopfield network (the original 1982 version) is illustrated in Fig. 1-4. Each neurode is binary; that is, it can take on only one of two values. Hopfield used values of 1 and 0 but

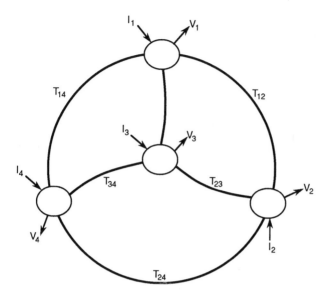

Figure 1-4 Simplified four-neuron Hopfield network.

subsequently showed that values of 1 and −1 result in simplified mathematics. We use 1 and −1. The value that the neurode assumes is governed by a *hard-limiting* function. By this we mean that if the net input to a neurode is greater than or equal to some threshold value (usually taken to be 0), then the activation value is 1; otherwise it is −1.

Before we go through the operation of the network, two limitations of Hopfield networks should be mentioned. The first is that Hopfield networks can reliably store and recall only about 15 percent as many states as the network has neurodes. For example, a network with 60 neurodes can store about 9 states. A second limitation is that the patterns stored must be chosen so that the Hamming distance is about 50 percent of the number of neurodes. The Hamming distance between two binary patterns is the number of bits in which the values are different. For example, the patterns 1 1 1 1 1 and 1 −1 1 −1 1 have a Hamming distance of 2.

From the first limitation, you can see that we're stretching things to say we can store almost anything in a four-neuron network. We'll pick the patterns 1 1 1 1 and −1 −1 −1 −1 as the two we'll store. We *store* the patterns by initializing the interconnecting weights according to Eq. 1-2. The equation says that a weight is equal to the sum over all stored patterns of the product of the activation values of the neurodes on each end of the connection:

$$T_{ij} = \sum_p V_i V_j \qquad (T_{ii} = 0) \tag{1-2}$$

In our simple example, the sum over the two patterns of V_iV_j for each pattern is always $1 + 1 = 2$, so each of our weights is 2. Now let's see how the network updates the activation values of the neurodes, recovering complete patterns from partial ones.

The activation values of the neurodes are updated asynchronously and, in Hopfield's original configuration, stochastically. To be updated *asynchronously* means that they are updated one at a time, rather than all at once as is the case with the back-propagation networks, which we'll look at in the next chapter. Updating *stochastically* means that a probability is involved in which a neurode is updated at a given opportunity. For example, if it's the turn of neurode number three to be updated, a random number between 0 and 1 is generated. If the number generated is greater than, say, 0.5, the neurode is updated. Otherwise, it isn't updated.

Keeping in mind the hard-limiting function described earlier, we find that Eq. 1-3 describes the process for calculating the net input to a neurode, where I_i is the external input to a neurode.

$$\text{Net input to neurode } i = \sum_{i \neq j} T_{ij}V_j + I_i \qquad (1\text{-}3)$$

The activation value of the neurode will be 1, if the net input is greater than or equal to zero and -1. Let's look at how this network, trained to "remember" the two states of 1 1 1 1 and -1 -1 -1 -1 deals with an imperfect input pattern.

Let's input a pattern of 1 1 1 -1, which has a Hamming distance of 1 from one of the two remembered states and assume that the four neurodes now have these values. One way to think about this is to consider the weights T_{ij} set to 0 during the external input process. Then the activation state of each neurode assumes whatever we input to it.

Now we asynchronously and stochastically update the activation states of all four neurodes. If one of the neurodes with a value of 1 is selected first, we calculate its new activation function. (We are no longer applying external inputs, so I_i is 0 for all neurodes now.) Using Eq. (1-3), you can see that each of the three neurodes with a value of 1 has the same net input whichever one is selected: $2(1) + 2(1) + 2(-1) = 2$. Because $2 > 0$, its activation value doesn't change.

When the neurode with the activation value of -1 is selected and updated, its activation value is changed to 1 because the net input to it is $2(1) + 2(1) + 2(1) = 6$. As soon as this happens, the pattern is stable, no matter how long you continue, because the net input of any neurode selected is now greater than 0. We have thus successfully recovered one of the remembered states.

Similarly, you can see that the other remembered state is recovered if you start with any pattern with a Hamming distance of 1 from

$-1\ -1\ -1\ -1$, such as $1\ -1\ -1\ -1$. If you start with a pattern with a Hamming distance of 2 from each of the remembered states, the state recovered depends on which neurode has its activation value updated first. That seems only fair because the test pattern was halfway between the two remembered states.

Although this was a simplified example, the same principles apply to a large Hopfield network. You should be able to work out more useful examples for yourself with the information given.

Hopfield's work was noticed almost immediately by the semiconductor industry. Within three years of his 1984 paper, AT&T Bell Laboratories announced the first hardware neural networks on silicon chips, utilizing Hopfield's theories. Cal Tech cohort Carver Mead has continued the innovations, fabricating hardware versions of the cochlea and retina.

Just prior to AT&T's announcement of the chips in 1986, the other Renaissance men, the Parallel Distributed Processing (PDP) Research Group, published the first two volumes of their *Parallel Distributed Processing* [2,4]. The third volume followed in 1988 [5]. Although it is difficult to pinpoint when work on these volumes began, a meeting organized by Hinton and Anderson in 1979 seems to be the first meeting that involved a significant number of the PDP group. The Renaissance, kindled by Hopfield, burst into flames with the release of their books. A total of 16 researchers comprised the PDP Research Group, and anywhere from one to four of them wrote each chapter in the first two PDP volumes. Drs. James L. McClelland and David E. Rumelhart edited the first two volumes and contributed to the third.

It is hard to overstate the effect these books had on neural network research and development. By late 1987, when the authors of this book bought their copies of volume 1, it was in its sixth printing. The software that was included with volume 3 sold more copies in 1988 than all other neural network software combined. What accounted for the unparalleled success of *Parallel Distributed Processing*? In one sentence: The books presented everything practical there was to know about neural networks in 1986 in an understandable, usable and interesting way; in fact, 1986 seemed to mark the point at which a "critical mass" of neural network information became available.

Recall that neural network models have three primary attributes: the architecture, the neurode transfer functions and attributes, and the learning algorithms. The PDP books presented various manifestations of these three items, building several network types as examples. The most read and quoted are probably chapters 1–4 and chapter 8 in volume 1. Be prepared to read chapter 8 at least twice. It is entitled "Learning Internal Representations by Error Propagation" and contains the nuts and bolts derivation of the back-propagation algorithm for multi-level perceptrons; It may be the most quoted reference in neural network literature as of early 1990. Other chapters also represent landmarks in neural network development, such as chapter 7 on Boltzmann machines, written by Drs. Geoffrey Hinton of Carnegie-Mellon and Terry Sejnowski, then of Johns Hopkins University, now at the Salk Institute in San Diego. Hinton started out, with McClelland and Rumelhart, to be one of the editors of the books but decided to devote more of his time to the Boltzmann machine work.

Certainly one of the most significant contribution of the PDP volumes has been the derivation and subsequent popularization of the back-propagation learning algorithm for multilayer perceptrons, published in a landmark article in *Nature* [34]. At about the same time that Rumelhart, Hinton, and Williams developed the back-propagation learning scheme, it was developed by Paul Werbos and Dave Parker [52].

We devote a significant portion of the next chapter to implementations of the back-propagation model in NNTs for personal computers. A number of other models and mechanisms are not covered in any significant way, including interactive activation and competition, constraint satisfaction (including the Boltzmann machine), the pattern associator, and autoassociators and competitive learning.

The Age of Neoconnectionism

Since 1987 we have been experiencing the Age of Neoconnectionism, named by Cowan and Sharp [10]. The field of neural networks and the development of neural network tools for personal computers have expanded almost unbelievably in the past several years. It is no longer feasible to assemble "all there is to know" about the current state of neural networks in one volume, or one set of volumes, as the PDP Research Group attempted to do in 1986–1988.

The list of applications has expanded from biological and psychological uses to include uses as diverse as biomedical waveform classification, music composition, and prediction of the commodity futures market. Currently, another shift is occurring that is even more important: the shift to personal computers for NNT implementation. Not that this is the only important trend in neural network research and development today. Significant work is occurring in areas ranging from the prediction of protein folding using supercomputers to the formulation of new network learning algorithms and neurode transfer functions.

It seems that this is a time to regroup and take a snapshot of those tools that are being developed solely for personal computers. Personal computers have changed drastically since the introduction of the first

Altairs and Apples. The increased capabilities (speed, memory, mass storage, communications, and graphics) and reduced cost of personal computers make the implementation of very useful and inexpensive NNTs universally attractive. The rest of this book looks at NNTs for PCs in the Neoconnectionist Age.

CHAPTER 2

Implementations

Russell C. Eberhart
Roy W. Dobbins

Introduction

This chapter illustrates how to implement a few examples of neural network tools (NNTs) on personal computers. We'll do these implementations step by step, with explanations along the way. Each NNT architecture (topology, model) has been selected because of its successful track record in solving practical problems on PC-based systems. We have selected our implementations to provide a spectrum of examples in various areas, including supervised and unsupervised (self-organizing) training, and feedforward and recurrent algorithms.

There is no such thing as a standard definition of any of these implementations. For example, there is no universally accepted example of a back-propagation implementation. Different people implement it in somewhat different ways. Sometimes it's even hard to find consistency within one person's implementation of a network model. For example, the computer code listed in Appendix 3 of Dr. Tuevo Kohonen's notes for his tutorial on self-organizing feature maps does not in all cases reflect the network equations presented in his text [37].

Such inconsistencies, even in one researcher's publications, are understandable. Neural network models evolve over time, and researchers implement their models differently as research and development proceeds and as application requirements change. Thus, the PC implementations presented in this chapter are not meant to represent generic versions of any model. They are merely representative samples of a few NNTs that the authors believe are potentially useful to a wide range of users.

The source code for each of the NNTs and the peripheral programs are listed in Appendices A and B. The C language was chosen for implementation of the examples in this book. Other languages, such as Pascal, were also tried in some cases, but the speed of the compiled programs was faster using C. Even more speed could have been obtained by using assembly language, but heavily annotated C source code is much easier to understand for most people who do programming.

A diskette with the source code described in this chapter is available from the authors. It is particularly handy if you want to make changes to the code for your applications. The diskette is also handy if you don't program, don't have a C compiler available, or don't want to key in the source code yourself, because it also contains compiled, ready-to-run, versions of the NNTs.[1]

The Back-Propagation Model

Introduction

To describe the back-propagation model, we first look at each of its elements and how they combine to form the back-propagation topology.

The notation and terminology for the back-propagation NNT are introduced.

The ways input is presented to a back-propagation NNT are described, and normalization techniques and options are introduced.

We present the equations that describe the network training and operation. These equations are divided into two categories: feedforward calculations and error back-propagation calculations. The feedforward calculations are used both in training mode and in the operation of the trained NNT; back-propagation calculations are applied only during training.

Finally, we discuss a version of computer source code that implements theequations into an NNT. Pattern, run, and weight file structures, that are needed as part of the back-propagation NNT, are also discussed.

We describe the back-propagation model in terms of the architecture of the NNT that implements it. The term *architecture*, as applied to neural networks, has been used in different ways by different authors. Often its meaning has been taken to be basically equivalent to *topology*, that is, the pattern of nodes and interconnections, together with such

[1] Send $20 in U.S. dollars to Roy Dobbins, 5833 Humblebee Road, Columbia, MD 21045, if you live in the United States or Canada. If you live in another country, please send $26 U.S. to help defray the air mail cost.

other items as directions of data flow and node activation functions. In this volume, architecture means the specifications sufficient for a neural network developer to build, train, test, and operate the network. Therefore the architecture is not related to the details of the NNT implementation, instead; it provides the complete specifications needed by someone for implementation.

Topology and Notation

A simple, three-layer back-propagation model is illustrated in detail in Fig. 2-1. Each neurode is represented by a circle and each interconnection, with its associated weight, by an arrow. The neurodes labeled *b* are bias neurodes. Of the many ways to implement back-propagation, the configuration of Fig. 2-1 is the most common.

In Fig. 2-1, we introduce the NNT notation that is used throughout the book for back-propagation networks. Just as there is no standard for back-propagation network implementation, there is no standard for notation. In fact, the different notations used by various authors often make it difficult to understand what they are describing. We use a notation that is substantially derived from other sources, but it appears for the first time in this book. We chose it after much consideration and debate. The criteria for its selection were clarity, consistency, and ease of use. Though this system will probably not be adopted universally, we do hope that some clear, consistent standard notation is adopted soon. We don't expect that you'll remember all of the details of the notation the first time you read it. It will probably be helpful if you refer back to it from time to time.

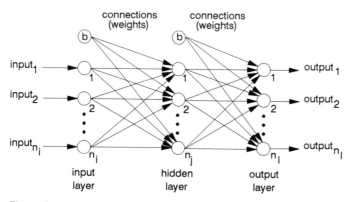

Figure 2-1   Back-propagation network structure.

   The attributes of individual neurodes or connections are represented by lowercase letters with subscripts. The letter i denotes an input, o an output, w a connection weight, and n the number of nodes in a layer. The subscripts i, j, and l refer to the input, hidden, and output layers, respectively. For example, i_i is the input to an input layer neurode, o_j is the output of a hidden layer neurode, and n_l is the number of neurodes in the output layer. (The subscript k is used for the second hidden layer, described and implemented later in the book.)

   Vectors are represented by bold lowercase letters. For example, the input vector to the input layer, consisting of all individual inputs, is represented by $\mathbf{i}_i$ and the output vector of the output layer by $\mathbf{o}_l$.

   We often work with a combination of an input vector and its associated output vector. This means that we know for a given input set what the output set should be. The combination of input and associated output comprises a *pattern vector*, represented by $\mathbf{p}$. The input part is listed first, then the output.

   We typically divide all available patterns into two categories, or sets: a training set and a test set. The subscripts r and s are associated with training and testing, respectively. Thus, for example, $\mathbf{p}_r$ is a training pattern and $\mathbf{p}_s$ is a testing pattern. In both cases, in the presentation to the network, such as the one used in the pattern files for the neural network tool, the input components are followed by the ouput components.

   With the exception of patterns, we'll not use vectors very much. Most of the time we'll deal with the attributes at the individual neurode level because that is the way computer code generally implements the solution to the equations. (Often, the calculations are hidden by library and/or coprocessor routines.)

   Connection weights require two subscripts that represent the sending and receiving layers. For example, the weight of the connection from an input neurode to a hidden neurode is w_{ji}. Note that the receiving neurode layer is the first subscript and the sending layer the second. Though this may seem somewhat counterintuitive, it is the generally accepted way to represent weights and corresponds to the columns and rows in the matrix notation with which weights are sometimes represented.

   Matrices are represented by bold capital letters. For example, the matrix of weights to the hidden layer from the input layer is represented by $\mathbf{W}_{ji}$. As is the case with vectors, we'll use matrix notation very little.

   Three coefficents, which are defined later, are represented by lowercase Greek letters. The learning coefficient is η (eta), the momentum factor is α (alpha), and the error term is δ (delta).

   Later, we describe each of the network elements. We also describe the operation and training of the back-propagation network of Fig. 2-1 by describing what happens at each step. But first, let's look at how input is presented to the network.

Network Input

On the left of Fig. 2-1, inputs are shown coming into the input layer of the network, to a layer of processing neurodes. The set of n_i inputs is presented to the network simultaneously. (In our NNT, which is implemented on a von Neumann computer, we must actually process the data serially.)

These inputs may be a set of raw data, a set of parameters, or whatever we have chosen to represent one single pattern of some kind. The way you choose n_i, the number of inputs you have, depends heavily on the kind of problem you are solving and the way your data are represented.

If you are dealing with a relatively small segment of a sampled raw voltage waveform, for example, you may assign one input neurode to each sampled value. If you are dealing with a relatively large video image or, worse yet, with several images, you may present a value averaged over several pixels to each neurode or present some calculated parameters to the input neurodes.

Beware of the urge to "mix and match" your input data in an attempt to reduce the number of input neurodes. For example, resist the urge to combine parameters before presentation to a neurode. It will be more efficient for you and your computer to allow the network to take a little longer to train successfully, than if it fails to train at all.

For our back-propagation NNT, each input can take on any value between zero and one. That is, the input values are continuous and normalized between the values of zero and one. The fact that we can use continuous valued inputs adds significant flexibility to the NNT.

Does the normalization between zero and one constrain us in any way? Probably not. Whenever we deal with a digital computer system that is receiving input, we are limited by the size of the number we can put in. As long as the resolution of our input data doesn't get lost in the normalization process, we're all right. In the implementation of the back-propagation NNT that we describe here, and for which we present the source code written in C in Appendix A, we use standard floating-point variables, called *float* in C. This type of variable is 32 bits in length and uses 24 bits for the value and 8 bits for the exponent.

We therefore have a resolution of about one part in 16 million, or seven decimal places. So if your data have seven significant digits or less, you'll be OK. Input data from a 16-bit analog-to-digital (A/D) converter requires a little less than five digits of resolution. Most applications seem to require three to five digits of resolution.

Normalizing input patterns can actually provide a tool for preprocessing data in different ways. You can normalize the data by considering all of the n inputs together, normalize each input channel separately, or normalize groups of channels in some way that makes sense. (*Input channel* means the stream of inputs to one input neurode.) In some cases, the way you choose to normalize the inputs can affect the performance of the NNT, so this is one place to try different approaches.

If all your inputs consist of raw data points, you'll probably normalize all of the channels together. If the inputs consist of parameters, you can normalize each channel separately or normalize channels that represent similar kinds of parameters together. For example, if some of your parameter inputs represent amplitudes and some represent time intervals, you might normalize the amplitude channels as a group and the time channels as a group.

Feedforward Calculations

Now that we have a normalized set of patterns, what happens at the input layer? The input neurodes simply distribute the signal along multiple paths to the hidden layer neurodes. The output of each input layer neurode is exactly equal to the input and is in the range 0–1. (Another way of looking at the input layer is that it performs normalization, even though in most NNT implementations this is done prior to presentation of the pattern to the network.)

A weight is associated with each connection to a hidden neurode. Note that each neurode of the input layer is connected to every neurode of the hidden layer. Likewise, each neurode of the hidden layer is connected to every neurode of the output layer.

Also note that each connection and all data flow go from left to right in Fig. 2-1. This is called a *feedforward* network. There are no feedback loops, even from a unit to itself, in a feedforward network. Almost all back-propagation implementations, including ours, are feedforward.

The way that total (net) input to a neurode is calculated and the way that the neurode calculates its output as a function of its net input are dependent on the type of neurode being used in the NNT. For the remaining discussion on back-propagation networks in this chapter, unless we state otherwise, we assume that an additive sigmoid neurode is being used. Most back-propagation NNTs today use the sigmoid neurodes. Unless stated otherwise, all neurodes used in back-propagation NNTs are assumed to be of the additive sigmoid variety.

In the following paragraphs, we present mathematical equations that describe the training and testing/running modes of a back-propagation NNT. They are presented without derivations or proofs. This information can be found in Rumelhart and McClelland [2], especially in chapter 8.

The signal presented to a hidden layer neurode in the network of Fig. 2-1 due to one single connection is just the output value of the input node (the same as the input of the input node) times the value of the connection weight. The net input to a hidden neurode is calculated as the sum of the values for all connections coming into the neurode, as described in Eq. 2-1. Note that this includes the input from the neurode we call the bias neurode, which is assumed to have an output of 1 at all times and is otherwise treated as any other neurode. We'll say more about the bias neurode later.

$$\text{net-input}_j = i_j = \sum_i w_{ji} o_i \qquad (2\text{-}1)$$

The output of a hidden neurode as a function of its net input is described in Eq. 2-2. This is the sigmoid function to which we have been referring. An illustration of the general shape of the sigmoid function appears in Fig. 2-2.

$$\text{output}_j = o_j = \frac{1}{1 + \exp(-i_j)} \qquad (2\text{-}2)$$

As can be seen, the output, after being put through the sigmoid function (also called a "squashing" function), is limited to values between 0 and 1. For a net input of zero to the neurode, the output is 0.5. For large negative net input values, the neurode output approaches 0; for large positive values, it approaches 1.

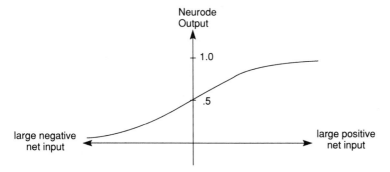

Figure 2-2 Sigmoid transfer function used in back-propagation network.

The nonlinear nature of this sigmoid transfer function plays an important role in the performance of the neural network. Other functions can be used as long as they are continuous and possess a derivative at all points. Functions such as the trigonometric sine and the hyperbolic tangent have been used, but the exploration of other transfer functions is beyond the scope of this book. For more information, refer to Rumelhart and McClelland [2] and McClelland and Rumelhart [4].

Now that the way to calculate the output of each hidden layer neurode has been described, you may be wondering how many hidden layer neurodes should be assigned to a given network. The selection of this number n_j is probably more art than science. It can vary widely according to the application and bears a relationship to the number of statistically significant factors that exist in the input data.

In many cases, if we knew how many of these factors there were, we might be able to write an algorithm and not need NNTs at all. We have found that a reasonable number to start with in many cases can be obtained by taking the square root of the number of input plus output neurodes, and adding a few—which sounds like a recipe for baking a cake, perhaps, but it often works.

If you have too few hidden neurodes, the network probably won't train at all. If you have just barely enough, the network may train but it might not be robust in the face of noisy data, or it won't recognize patterns that it hasn't seen before. Too many neurodes, in addition to taking forever to train, tend to create a "grandmother" network that has memorized everything and, again, doesn't recognize new patterns very well. In other words, it doesn't generalize well. The number of hidden neurodes, along with the values of α and η, are the parameters most often "fiddled with" when trying to get back-propagation NNTs to train successfully.

Once the outputs of all hidden layer neurodes have been calculated, the net input to each output layer neurode is calculated in an analogous manner, as described by Eq. 2-3. Similarly, the output of each output layer neurode is calculated as described by Eq. 2-4.

$$\text{net-input}_l = i_l = \sum_j w_{lj} o_j \qquad (2\text{-}3)$$

$$\text{output}_l = o_l = \frac{1}{1 + \exp(-i_l)} \qquad (2\text{-}4)$$

The set of calculations that results in obtaining the output state of the network (which is simply the set of the output states of all of the output neurodes) is carried out in exactly the same way during the training phase as during the testing/running phase. The test/run operational mode just involves presenting an input set to the input neurodes and calculating the resulting output state in one forward pass.

Generally the number of output neurodes is fairly straightforward to determine (unlike the number of input neurodes!). If you are trying to classify data into one of five classes, you need to assign an output node to each class. Even though you *could* assign one output neurode to monitor two (hopefully mutually exclusive) classes, resist the urge. There are inherent dangers in that approach. For example, what if the two classes aren't as mutually exclusive as you thought? In general, output neurodes cost you relatively little computationally, so be generous with them.

To summarize, during the feedforward calculations, two math operations are performed by each neurode, and the output state, or activation, is obtained as a result. The first is a summation of previous layer neurode outputs times interconnecting weights, and the second is the squashing function.

The squashing function (Fig. 2-2) can be viewed as performing a function similar to an analog electronic amplifier. The gain, or amplification, of the amplifier is analogous to the slope of the line, or the ratio of the change in output for a given change in input. As you can see, the slope of the function (gain of the amplifier) is greatest for total (net) inputs near zero. This serves to mitigate problems caused by the possible dominating effects of large input signals.

Training by Error Back-Propagation

During the training phase, the feedforward output state calculation is combined with backward error propagation and weight adjustment calculations that represent the network's learning, or training. It is this learning process, resulting from the back-propagation of errors, and how it is implemented, that is the secret to the success of the back-propagation NNT.

Central to the concept of training a network is the definition of network error. We need to identify a measure of how well a network is performing on our training set. Rumelhart and McClelland [2] define an error term that depends on the difference between the output value an output neurode is supposed to have, called the target value t_i, and the value it actually has as a result of the feedforward calculations, o_i. The error term is defined for a given pattern and summed over all output neurodes for that pattern.

Equation 2-5 presents the definition of the error. The subscript p denotes what the value is for a given pattern. Note that we implement the error calculation in the back-propagation training algorithm on a neurode-by-neurode basis over the entire set (epoch) of patterns, rather than on a pattern-by-pattern basis. We sum the error over all neurodes, giving a grand total for all neurodes and all patterns.

Then we divide the grand total by the number of patterns, to give an *average sum-squared error* value. This makes sense because the number of patterns in our training set can vary, and we want some standardized value that allows us to compare apples with apples, so to speak. Because the factor of 0.5 is a constant, we usually delete it from our calculations.

$$E_p = 0.5 \sum_{l=1}^{n_l} (t_{pl} - o_{pl})^2 \tag{2-5}$$

The goal of the training process is to minimize this average sum-squared error over all training patterns. Figuring out how to minimize the error with respect to the hidden neurodes was the key that opened up back-propagation models for wide application. The derivation is not presented here; it can be found in chapter 8 of Rumelhart and McClelland [2]. Even their derivation lacks absolute rigor but reviewing it should give you an understanding of where all the equations come from and help make you more comfortable with them.

Remember from Eq. 2-4 that the output of a neurode in the output layer is a function of its input, or $o_l = f(i_l)$. The first derivative of the function $f'(i_l)$ is important in error back-propagation. A quantity called the *error signal* is represented by δ_l for output layer neurodes and is defined by Eq. 2-6.

$$\delta_l = f'(i_l)(t_l - o_l) \tag{2-6}$$

For the sigmoid activation function of Eq. 2-4, the first derivative is just $o_l(1 - o_l)$. In the case of the sigmoid function, we end up with the expression for the output layer error signal, calculated for each output neurode, given in Eq. 2-7.

$$\delta_l = (t_l - o_l)o_l(1 - o_l) \tag{2-7}$$

We want to propagate this error value back and perform appropriate weight adjustments. There are two ways to do this. One way involves propagating the error back and adjusting weights after each training pattern is presented to the network; this option is called *on-line*, or *single pattern*, *training*. The other way is to accumulate the δ's for each neurode for the entire training set, add them, and propagate back the error based on the grand total δ; this is called *batch*, or *epoch*, *training*.

We implement the back-propagation algorithms in our NNT using the second option, batch processing. In fact, Rumelhart and McClelland assumed that weight changes occur only after a complete cycle of pattern presentations [2]. As they point out, it's all right to calculate weight changes after each pattern as long as the learning rate η is sufficiently small. It does, however, add significant computational overhead to do that, and we want to speed up training whenever possible.

Before we can update weights, however, we must have something to update. That is, we must initialize each weight to some value. If you just start with all the weights equal to zero (or all equal to any single number, for that matter), the network won't be trainable. You can see why if you study the equations we present later on weight updating.

It is typical to initialize the weights to random numbers between 0.3 and -0.3. Picking random numbers over some range makes intuitive sense, and you can see how different weights go in different directions by doing this. But why do we pick -0.3 and 0.3 as the bounds? To be honest, there is no better reason than "it works." Most back-propagation NNTs seem to train faster with these bounds than with, say, 1 and -1. It may have something to do with the bounds of the neurode activation values being 1 and -1, which makes the products of weights and activation values relatively small numbers. Therefore, if they start out "wrong," they can be adjusted quickly.

Neural network researchers have recommended a number of variations on the initial weight range. For example, Lee [38] has shown that in some instances initializing the weights feeding the output layer to random values between 0.3 and -0.3, while initializing weights feeding the hidden layer to 0, speeds training. (Initializing all weights feeding the hidden layer to 0 is permissible as long as the next layer up is initialized to random, nonzero values. You can verify this by working through the weight updating equations.) In most cases, however, the random number initialization to values from -0.3 to 0.3 works well and is almost always a good place to start. There are cases for which the bounds of $+/- 0.3$ won't work, and you'll have to pick others, either smaller or larger, depending on your application.

We now look at how to use δ_l to update weights that feed the output layer w_{lj}. To a first approximation, the updating of these weights is described by Eq. 2-8. Here, η is defined as the learning coefficient. It can be assigned values between 0 and 1.

$$w_{lj}(\text{new}) = w_{lj}(\text{old}) + \eta \delta_l o_j \qquad (2\text{-}8)$$

This kind of weight updating sometimes gets caught in what are called *local energy minima*. If you can visualize a bowl-shaped surface with a lot of little bumps and ridges in it, you can get an idea of the problem, at least in three dimensions.

The error minimization process is analogous to minimizing the energy of our position in the bumpy ridgelined bowl. Ideally, we'd like to move our position (perhaps marked by a very small ball bearing) to the bottom of the bowl where the energy is minimum; this position is called the *globally optimal solution*. Depending on how much or how little we can move the ball bearing at one time, however, we might get caught in some little depression or ridge that we can't get out of. This situation is most likely with small limits on each individual movement, which corresponds to small values of η.

We can help the situation by using the "momentum" of our ball bearing. We take into account its momentum (previous movement) by multiplying the previous weight change by a momentum factor that we label α. The momentum factor α can take on values between 0 and 1. Equation 2-9, which is just Eq. 2-8 with the momentum term added, becomes the equation we actually use in our back-propagation NNT to update the weights feeding the output layer.

$$w_{lj}(\text{new}) = w_{lj}(\text{old}) + \eta\delta_l o_j + \alpha[\Delta w_{lj}(\text{old})] \qquad (2\text{-}9)$$

Watch out! We've just thrown another delta at you. This one, $\Delta w(\text{old})$, stands for the previous weight *change*. Stated in words, the new weight is equal to the old weight plus the weight change. The weight change consists of the δ error signal term and the α momentum factor term. The momentum term is the product of the momentum factor α and the previous weight change. The previous movement of the weight thus imparts momentum to our ball bearing, making it much more likely to reach the globally optimum solution.

Keep in mind that we have processing elements called bias neurodes, as indicated by the neurodes with the letter b in Fig. 2-1. These neurodes always have an output of 1. They serve as threshold units for the layers to which they are connected, and the weights from the bias neurodes to each of the neurodes in the following layer are adjusted exactly like the other weights. In Eq. 2-9, then, for each of the output neurodes, the subscript j takes on values from 0 to n_j, which is the number of hidden neurodes. The n_jth value is associated with the bias neurode.

Now that we have the new values for the weights feeding the output neurodes, we turn our attention to the hidden neurodes. What is the error term for these units? It isn't as simple to figure this out as it was for the output neurodes, for which we could intuitively reason that the error should be some function of the difference between the desired output t_l and the actual output o_l.

We really have no idea what the value for a hidden neurode "should" be. Again we refer to the derivation by Rumelhart and McClelland [2]. They show that the error term for a hidden neurode is

$$\delta_h = f'(i_h) \sum_{l=0}^{n_l} w_{lh}\delta_l \qquad (2\text{-}10)$$

As was the case in the output layer, the output of a neurode in the hidden layer is a function of its input, or $o_h = f(i_h)$. The first part of the right-hand term in Eq. 2-10 is the first derivative of this function. For the sigmoid transfer function, this derivative is $o_h(1 - o_h)$, resulting in the hidden neurode error term defined by Eq. 2-11.

$$\delta_h = o_h(1 - o_h) \sum_{l=0}^{n_l} w_{lh}\delta_l \qquad (2\text{-}11)$$

The weight changes for the connections feeding the hidden layer from the input layer are now calculated in a manner analogous to those feeding the output layer:

$$w_{ji}(\text{new}) = w_{ji}(\text{old}) + \eta\delta_j o_i + \alpha[\Delta w_{ji}(\text{old})] \qquad (2\text{-}12)$$

For each hidden node, the subscript i takes on values of 0 to n_i, the number of input neurodes. As before, the bias neurodes are represented in the calculations by the n_ith value.

We now have all the equations (2-7, 2-9, 2-11, and 2-12) to implement back-propagation of errors and adjustment of weights for both groups of weights. We first calculate the error terms for each output neurode using Eq. 2-7, then for each hidden neurode using Eq. 2-11 for each pattern in the training set. We sum the error terms and, after all patterns have been presented once, calculate the weight adjustments as in Eq. 2-9 and 2-12.

There are a few things to keep in mind.

1. Because we are updating using the batch (epoch) mode, the δs given in Eqs. 2-9 and 2-12 are the grand totals (for each neurode) for the entire training set, whereas the δs in Eqs. 2-7 and 2-11 are calculated pattern by pattern and summed after one epoch.
2. Although values for η and α can be assigned on a layer-by-layer basis or even a neurode-by-neurode basis, typically only one value is selected for each in a given implementation. These values are often adjusted in the process of getting a network to train successfully but once chosen, they are usually left alone.
3. When you calculate δs for the hidden layer in Eq. 2-11, the old (existing) weights (rather than new ones you might have calculated

from Eq. 2-9) from the hidden to the output layer are used in the equation. This is really only a potential problem if you decide to update the weights after each training pattern is presented. If you do epoch training, weights aren't updated until all patterns have been presented, so you don't have to worry.

What values do you pick for η and α? The choices depend on your application. Rumelhart and McClelland [2] frequently use values of 0.5 and 0.9, respectively, as a place to start. We have found, however, that for our applications, these values often throw the network into oscillation or saturate the neurodes. (Saturation causes all outputs during training and testing to be about the same value, typically near zero or one.) Saturation occurs when the net input to a neurode is a large value (either positive or negative) and variations in the input thus have little effect on the output. Refer to Fig. 2-2. For our electroencephalogram (EEG) spike detection NNT, discussed in a later chapter, we often have good results with values of $\eta = 0.15$ and $\alpha = 0.075$. Other times, for larger networks, we've used values of 0.04 and 0.02, respectively.

Another parameter you have to experiment with is the number of iterations of the training set needed to give an acceptable average mean-squared error. First, pick a reasonable average mean-squared error value, perhaps 0.04 or 0.05. If you don't train in 1000 to 2000 iterations, you should probably consider adjusting η or α. You might also need to normalize your inputs in some different way. You'll probably have to experiment. Don't be disappointed when your NNT doesn't train successfully the first time. It almost certainly won't!

We'll discuss some of the finer points of adjusting η and α and talk about other systems-related topics in later chapters. See, in particular, Chapters 3 and 4. For now, however, you should have the theoretical basics needed to implement a back-propagation neural network tool.

Running the Back-Propagation NNT

But what about the code? Funny you should ask. Appendix A contains the C source code you need to get the back-propagation NNT we've been discussing up and running.

To run Batchnet, once you have compiled batchnet.c to get an executable file called batchnet.exe, you need to build a run file. The first number in the run file, on the first line, tells Batchnet how many runs are to be carried out. For example, if you are going to train the NNT using a training set and then test it with a test set, the number of runs is 2. Each line following the number of runs contains specifications for one run. Each line gives the names of the input pattern and input weight files, the names of the results and output weights files, the number of patterns to be read, the number of input, hidden, and output nodes, and values for η and α. To run Batchnet, at the system prompt, just type:

```
batchnet runfile.run
```

where runfile.run is the name of your run file.

Included in Appendix A are the files needed to build the executable network code itself and to build the initial random weights input file. Also included are examples of pattern files and a run file. In the source code listing of Batchnet you can see how the four equations 2-7, 2-9, 2-11, and 2-12 are implemented. A diskette with all of the files in Appendix A, plus executable code versions and sample outputs, is available from the authors. The pattern files are taken from real-world EEG parameters as discussed in the case study in Chapter 10. Also on the diskette is a batch file which allows you to run a demonstration, and a brief user's guide.

Chapter 3 (Software Tools) reviews in detail how the code implements the back-propagation architecture we've been discussing. It discusses the in's and out's of general topics such as programming languages versus development environments and also addresses the tricks and techniques needed to make the NNT as general and as fast as possible. But for now, you might want to get started "mucking about" with the code and thinking about your own applications.

The Self-Organization Model

We now present an implementation of the self-organization neural network model which was made famous primarily through the work of Dr. Teuvo Kohonen of Helsinki University of Technology in Finland.

Introduction

This neural network architecture, the self-organization model, is probably second only to back-propagation architecture in terms of the number of applications for which it is being used. The most significant difference between the back-propagation and self-organization models is the fact that the self-organization model is trained without supervision. Remember that we present targets values to the output nodes during back-propagation training. In the self-organization model, we present only the input patterns, and the network organizes (trains) itself.

The best description of the self-organization model is the 1988 edition of Kohonen's book on self-organization and associative memory [22]. A good addition are the notes from Kohonen's tutorial given at the 1989 International Joint Conference on Neural Networks [37]. Caudill's article on the Kohonen architecture, which appeared as part of her series in *AI Expert*, is also an excellent introduction [39], as is the section on competitive filter associative memories in her recent book [40].

As we mentioned in the introduction to this chapter, however, there is no standard definition or implementation of the self-organization model. In fact, there is significantly more variability in how it is implemented than there is for the back-propagation model. We begin by describing the notation and topology of the self-organization model and then describe the procedure for weight initialization and normalization and for input normalization. The training calculations are then reviewed. Finally, we discuss testing and running the network and review the implementation, for which source code appears in Appendix B.

The self-organization model is more biologically oriented than the back-propagation model. One indication of this is that the network is trained without supervision. This is similar to many of the neural cells in our brains, in other words nobody applies electronic stimuli to our neurons to train them to, say, learn to walk or to speak. It seems that the self-organizing feature map implementation described by Kohonen might bear some resemblance to the way some areas of our brains are organized.

Topology and Notation

Self-organization networks, also known as Kohonen networks, consist of two layers: an input layer and an output layer. Each neurode in the input layer is connected to each neurode in the output layer by a connection (synapse) with an associated weight. Although each of the layers can be represented in a variety of ways, each is typically represented as a two-dimensional array of neurodes. Within two dimensions, obviously, the neurodes could be arranged in many ways. Most often, they are arranged in either rectangular or hexagonal arrays.

To facilitate the illustration of layers of the self-organization network model, we now introduce the concept of a *slab* in the context of self-organizing networks. The slab simplifies network diagrams because groups of neurons are represented by one symbol. The concept of the slab is also necessary as we begin to use more complicated network architectures in which there can be more than one slab in a layer, as discussed in Chapter 3.

Functionally, a slab of neurodes is just a collection of neurodes with similar attributes. These attributes include such things as activation function, learning coefficient, and momentum factor. Some attributes have meaning only for certain types of networks. In addition, all neurodes in a given slab receive their inputs from the same source(s) [slab(s) and/or input pattern] and send their outputs to the same destination(s) [slab(s) and/or output pattern].

Figure 2-3 illustrates the concept of a slab. In the figure, the neurodes are arranged in a rectangular pattern. The geometrical arrangement of neurodes in a slab can vary and is dependent on the application. In the self-organization model, a rectangular array is usually used to depict the neurodes in the input slab and is often used for the output slab as well. In the back-propagation model, a slab usually represents a linear array of neurons; one slab would thus represent each layer illustrated in Fig. 2-1.

Another arrangement, the hexagonal array (Fig. 2-4), is also often used to represent the output slab in the self-organization model. The geometry chosen to represent the output slab determines the configuration of the "neighborhood" of each neurode, a subject we address later.

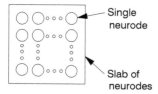

Figure 2-3   Illustration of slab of neurodes.

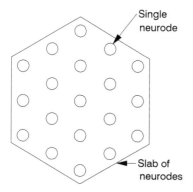

Figure 2-4   Slab of neurodes in hexagonal array.

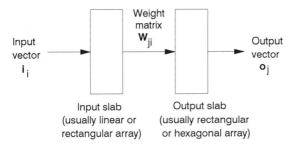

Figure 2-5   Self-organizing (Kohonen) network model.

A simple example of a self-organization neural network model appears in Fig. 2-5. This figure introduces the notation that we use throughout this book for self-organization, or Kohonen, networks. As with back-propagation, we use a notation derived mainly from other sources, but which, to the best of our knowledge, appears for the first time in this book. Clarity, consistency and ease of use were again our criteria for selection. You don't need to memorize all of the notation details the first time you read them. Instead, refer back to them. As before the attributes of individual neurodes are represented by subscripted lowercase letters. The letter i represents an input, o an output, w a connection weight, and n the number of neurodes in a layer. The subscripts i and j refer to the input and output layers, respectively. For example, i_i is the input to an input layer neurode, o_j is the output of an output layer neurode, and n_j is the number of neurodes in the output layer. Using the subscript "j" for the output layer is different than the back-propagation case where "l" is used. In each case, however, "j" refers to the layer adjacent to the input layer.

Vectors are represented, as before, by bold lowercase letters and matrices by bold capital letters. Thus, the input vector to the input layer, made up of all of the individual inputs, is represented by $\mathbf{i}_i$ and the output vector of the output layer by $\mathbf{o}_j$. The weight matrix is represented by $\mathbf{W}_{ji}$, with an individual weight of a connection from an input neurode to an output neurode designated by w_{ji}. The Euclidean distance between an input pattern vector and the weight vector to a particular output unit for the tth iteration of pattern p is represented by $d_{jp}(t)$.

The two-dimensional slab configuration makes it desirable, in some cases, to use double subscripts for neurodes and for the input and output vectors. We use the single subscript version in this chapter, primarily for simplicity.

A learning coefficient that is defined later is represented by the lowercase Greek letter η (eta). A few words of caution are appropriate here. This learning coefficient isn't exactly the same as the one for the back-propagation model. (We discuss that later.) Also, Kohonen used the lowercase Greek letter α (alpha) for his learning coefficient. We chose η for consistency with the back-propagation model. When you see η in this book, you know that it's a learning coefficient, and when you see α, you know it's a momentum term.

Network Initialization and Input

On the left of Fig. 2-5, a set of n_i inputs comes into the input layer of the network. The inputs are presented simultaneously but remember that our computer must simulate this network model by actually processing the items in series.

The number of input neurodes you select depends, as in the case of the back-propagation model, on your specific problem; but there is a different emphasis on how you should think about the input and choose the number of input neurodes. You are more likely to use raw data, and less likely to use precalculated parameters as inputs to a self-organization model. This is because one of the main accomplishments of self-organization is to cluster data into classes, reducing its dimensionality. In other words, the self-organization model often does your parameterization for you. Also, most people working with self-organization models usually normalize each entire input vector. (In the case of back-propagation, we constrained each input to be in the range of 0 to 1, but we set no limit on the magnitude of the input pattern vector, the square root of the sum of the squares of each input component.) For a Kohonen or self-organization network, the general guideline is that each input vector, in its entirety, must be normalized. You can see what this could do to parameterized inputs; it could distort them in unpredictable ways. You could have very carefully calculated parameters, perhaps even normalizing them by constraining their values to lie between 0 and 1, only to have their values changed in unforseen ways during an input vector normalization process.

There are NNT developers who claim that, for some applications, you don't necessarily need to normalize the input vectors. You just have to try training the NNT both ways, normalized and unnormalized, and select the better one. Others argue that for the dot-product calculation (to be described) used to select the "winning" neurode to be meaningful, the input vector must be normalized [40].

There is general agreement about the need to initialize the weight vectors by normalization. What isn't necessarily crystal clear is how best to do it. First, random values are assigned to each weight. We might start, as we did in back-propagation, with random values between -0.3 and 0.3. This isn't how most implementations handle it. One common approach is to initially assign random weight values between 0.4 and 0.6. However, if you inspect the initial illustration of figure 5.16 in Kohonen's 1988 book [22], you see that he initialized his network weights to values between 0.45 and 0.55. If you look at the Pascal code for a program called ToPreM2 which he published with his 1989 tutorial notes, you'll find each weight initialized to a random value between 0.4 and 0.6 [37]. Meanwhile, Caudill, in her article on Kohonen networks, generates initial weight vectors that lie at random locations on the unit circle [39].

The weight vector normalization procedure is done on all of the weights coming to a given output neurode from all of the input neurodes. The most logical way to do this would seem to be to set the square root of the sum of the squares of the weights from all of the inputs to each output to the same value, presumably to 1. The reason we say *would seem* and *presumably* is that various examples of self-organization implementation have normalized weights in different ways. (If you normalize to 1, you save yourself the trouble of taking the square root.) Kohonen's ToPreM2 program uses a value of one-half times the sum of the squares of the weights as the "squared norm" of the weights.

Caudill, on the other hand, normalizes weight vectors in what appears to be a more logical way: dividing each weight vector component by the square root of the sum of the squares of all weight vector components [39]. In this way, the total length of each weight vector from all inputs to a given output is 1. If w'_{ji} is the initial random weight generated in the interval from 0 to 1, then the normalized weight w_{ji} is given by

$$ w_{ji} = \frac{w'_{ji}}{\left[\sum_{i=0}^{n_i} (w'_{ji})^2 \right]^{1/2}} \tag{2-13} $$

Whatever method you choose for normalizing your weight vectors, the next step is to apply input to your self-organization network, and perform the training calculations.

Training Calculations

Now we are ready to look at self organization and introduce the concepts of neighborhood, Euclidean distance between an input vector and a weight vector, and a winner-take-all neurode.

Briefly, the training process consists of presenting pattern vectors from the training set to the self-organization network, one at a time. We select the winning neurode by making a series of calculations after each pattern presentation. We then make weight adjustments, using a neurode neighborhood that shrinks over time and a learning coefficient that also decreases with time. The result is that the values of the weights form clusters that reflect the probability density of the input vectors. When the network has self-organized, and training is complete, neurodes that are topologically near each other react similarly to similar input patterns.

Note that we don't train the network by telling it what the "correct" answer is; we simply present the patterns to the initialized network, over and over, while varying the neighborhood and learning parameters, and the network trains itself by adjusting its weights. We now go through the process in detail. The "neighborhood" is the portion of the output slab (in particular, the neurodes) within a specified topological radius of a given winning neurode.

We must first define the initial size of the neighborhood. All neurodes in the neighborhood of the winning neurode have their weights adjusted. Each iteration of a complete training pattern set is a discrete step in time. Thus, the first pattern set iteration is at t_0, the next at t_1, and so on.

For the moment let us suppose that the neurode in the center of the slab illustrated in Fig. 2-4 is the winner. (We describe later how to perform the calculations to select the winner.) For the first group of iterations, the neighborhood of the winning neurode is relatively large, perhaps large enough to cover all of the output slab. For example, in Fig. 2-4 the initial neighborhood consists of the winning neurode and the 18 neurodes surrounding it. After further iterations, the neighborhood is decreased in size. This smaller neighborhood could consist, in our example, of the winning neurode plus the six neurodes immediately surrounding it. Finally, after another set of iterations, the neighborhood could shrink to include only the winning neurode. The number of iterations between changes in neighborhood size varies appreciably with the application but is often in the range of a few hundred to a few thousand.

Now that you know how to decrease the size of the neighborhood with time, what do you do with the weights of the neurodes inside the neighborhood? (Remember that the weights of the neurodes outside the neighborhood are not changed.) Figure 2-6 illustrates three approaches to weight adjustment. To discuss these functions, imagine that the neurode slab is significantly larger than that of Figs. 2-3 and 2-4, so that the initial neighborhoods can be at least 10 neurodes in diameter.

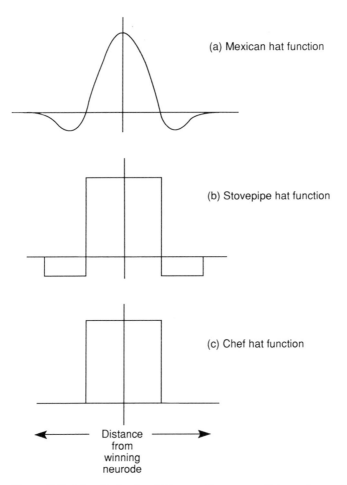

Figure 2-6 Magnitude of weight correction versus distance from winning neurode in self-organizing network.

Figure 2-6a illustrates the Mexican hat function described by Kohonen [22, 37]. The largest weight adjustment, which is positive, occurs for the winning neurode. Somewhat smaller positive changes are made to adjacent neurodes, and still smaller changes to neurodes adjacent and just outside of these, and so on, until at some distance r_0 the weight adjustments go to zero. The weight changes then become slightly negative for a while, finally becoming zero.

The shape of the Mexican hat function is reminiscent of the on-center off-surround excitation pattern observed in some biological systems and implemented by Grossberg in his gain control system for a neuron group (see Chapter 1). Although the Mexican hat function may exhibit biological plausibility, it adds computational complexity to a set of calculations that is usually performed thousands of times while training a self-organization network. Therefore, some applications of self-organization have used the simplified functions.

In the Stovepipe hat function (Fig. 2-6b), identical positive weight changes are made to all neurodes within a radius of r_0 of the winning neurode and identical negative changes to neurodes at a slightly larger radius. Taking the simplification even further, we arrive at the Chef hat function (Fig. 2-6c), in which only identical positive weight changes are made to those neurodes within the r_0 radius. Kohnonen [22, 37] and Caudill [39] each use this extremely simple form of weight correction function when they implement the self-organizing model.

Whichever of the three methods you implement (or perhaps even some other method) to define the neighborhood for weight changes, you now need to know how to pick the winning neurode. This is done by calculating the Euclidean distance between the input pattern vector and the weight vector associated with each output node. The output node with the minimum Euclidean distance is the winner.

The Euclidean distance is the square root of the sum of the squares of the differences between each input vector component and its associated weight vector component. Because we're interested in relative magnitudes and want to conserve computing time, square root calculations are not usually done. The resulting distance calculation is defined as

$$d_{jp}(t) = \sum_{i=1}^{n_i} [i_i(t) - w_{ji}(t)]^2 \qquad (2\text{-}14)$$

where $d_{jp}(t)$ is the distance to neurode j for the tth iteration of pattern p. The winning neurode for the particular iteration of an input pattern is the one with the smallest distance, that is, the smallest value of $d_{jp}(t)$. The calculation of this dimensionless Euclidean distance has meaning because we normalized the input and weight vectors before performing the calculations.

Each weight in the neighborhood of the winning neurode is then adjusted according to Eq. 2-15. The learning coefficient η takes a different form than for back-propagation. First, it usually decreases with increasing iterations (time). Second, it can vary with the distance from the winning neurode, taking on the shape of the Mexican hat function or the Stovepipe hat function, although many implementations for personal computers use the Chef hat function in which η doesn't vary with distance.

$$w_{ji}(t + 1) = w_{ji}(t) + \eta(t)[i_i(t) - w_{ji}(t)] \qquad (2\text{-}15)$$

Equations 2-14 and 2-15 are calculated for each iteration of each pattern presented to the self-organization network during training. Iterations continue until the corrections in Eq. 2-15 become acceptably small.

Do we need to renormalize the weight vectors during or after training, given what we said about the validity of the dot product? No, not as long as the changes to the weight vector components carried out according to Eq. 2-15 are small enough. Keeping them small keeps the length of our weight vectors near 1 (near the surface of a unit hypersphere), and the dot product process remains valid.

Selection of training patterns for the self-organizing network is the subject of much discussion in the literature [22, 37, 40]. It is generally agreed that each category, or classification, to which the network is trained should be represented by examples that are "gold standard" (i.e., right down the center of the category space) as well as by examples that are near the decision surfaces with other categories. Experimentation will probably be required to arrive at the best set of training vectors for a particular application.

Testing and Running

The process of testing the self-organization network is analogous to the process for back-propagation. You present patterns of known classification to the network and use some sort of performance metric to compare network performance with specifications. The patterns used for testing should not have been used during training.

As is the case for training, the patterns used for testing (and, subsequently, during operation of the network) should be normalized. A discussion of neural network performance assessment appears in Chapter 7 (Performance Metrics).

A listing of the source code you need to build, train, and test a Kohonen-inspired self-organization network appears in Appendix B. The source code, with its associated compiled versions, is also on the software diskette available from the authors. A more detailed discussion of the software appears in Chapter 4 (Software Tools).

CHAPTER 3

Systems Considerations

Russell C. Eberhart
Roy W. Dobbins

Introduction

In several other places in this volume, we emphasize that the neural network portion of the neural network tool (NNT), developed to solve a problem, likely comprises a small percentage of the total amount of NNT computer code. Although the neural network code is an absolutely indispensable part of the system, a well-designed NNT represents a systems approach to problem solution. It typically incorporates a number of major subsystems, including preprocessing and user interfaces. In this chapter, we discuss some of the systems aspects of building, testing, and using neural network tools.

We begin by looking at which kinds of problems should utilize NNTs and which are best left to other approaches. Next, we look at "the big picture," which is the overall process of developing a neural network tool once you decide that neural networks will play a role in your system. This systems development process is similar to that used for the development of many software/hardware analysis sytems.

After looking at the big picture, we examine some of its parts. The first thing to do after you decide to use a neural network tool (or any other specific approach) is to develop a specification of the problem. We briefly look at ways, both less and more formal, of system specification development.

We next examine ways to use a neural network most effectively in a neural network tool, that is, how to decide which role the neural network will play and which jobs will be done by other parts of the system.

Perhaps the most important consideration in this area is preprocessing. We discuss the pros and cons of preprocessing in some detail.

A brief look at the trade-offs between NNTs and expert systems comes next. We discuss the strengths and weaknesses of each and briefly look at ways in which they can work together, in anticipation of a later chapter on expert networks, an NNT–expert system hybrid approach.

Finally, we summarize examples of several problem categories to which NNTs have been successfully applied. A few of these examples are described in detail in the case study chapters later in this volume. This chapter should be used more as a road map or guidebook than as a cookbook. Because neural network technology is still in its infancy, there are very few hard and fast rules.

Evaluating Problem Categories

NNTs can provide solutions for a variety of problems. For some of these problems no other ways are known to provide solutions. For another subset of problems, other ways to tackle them may exist, but using an NNT is by far the easiest and/or gives the best results. For still another subset, other methods might work about as well and could be implemented with about the same amount of work. For the last subset, there are clearly better ways to attack the problem than by using NNTs.

It is the objective of this section to give you guidelines on how to evaluate an NNT for use in a particular situation: in other words, how to decide into which of these subsets your problem falls. This evaluation should always be done from a systems point of view. As we plan, we should always strive for the best overall system and the best overall systems performance.

It has been pointed out in this book and by other authors, that the best candidate problems for neural network analysis are those that are characterized by fuzzy, imprecise, and imperfect knowledge (data), and/or by a lack of a clearly stated mathematical algorithm for the analyis of the data. It is, however, important that you have enough data to yield sufficient training and test sets to train and evaluate the performance of an NNT effectively. The amount of data required for training a network is very dependent on the network architecture, the training method, and the problem being addressed. We know of no rigid rules but have found that for back-propagation networks, in general, a minimum of about 10 to a few dozen pattern vectors *for each possible output classification* are often required. Hopefully, in the case of self-organizing networks, you have some rough idea of how many categories might be derived by the network, in which case the guideline of 10 to a few dozen for each possible classification is a place to start. (You also need to factor the estimated number of classifications into how you pick the number of output neurodes, as discussed in Chapter 2.)

The quantity of data required for a generation of test patterns is closely tied to user requirements and to the specifics of the application. The information generated from the testing must satisfy the user that the performance of the NNT is adequately represented in terms of the quantity and distribution of test cases. Also, the statistical methods and specifications used to analyze the results must be meaningful and convincing. For example, if you want to specify the percent correct for each possible classification to a precision of 5 percent, then at least 20 examples of each possible output classification must be present in the test pattern vector set.

Beyond the desirability of looking at problems with fuzzy, noisy, or otherwise questionable data sets and the need for a sufficient amount of data to build the training and test sets, it is difficult to say much more that's useful. You need to accumulate your own experience and generate your own guidelines.

Some things are fairly obvious. Although it is true that neural networks have been trained to do arithmetic operations, such as multiply two numbers, nets do arithmetic relatively imprecisely and inaccurately. You are better off with a calculator or a computer. You'll never use your friendly NNT to balance your checkbook (even assuming it's possible to balance it). Beyond that, perhaps the best advice is that if you're unsure whether or not an NNT might be a viable approach, try it! In general, when compared with more traditional statistical approaches, NNTs are often easier to implement. (This, of course, depends on the problem and your own background. If you are a Ph.D. statistician with lots of computer experience and unlimited statistical analysis capability at your fingertips . . . well, you get the drift.)

If you have a set of input pattern data for which you are pretty sure you know the classification, you can start by trying to train a backpropagation network. If you don't really know what the answers (classifications) should be, or if you feel there may be more than one way to categorize the outputs, you may want to start with some sort of self-organization or competitive learning network structure.

Make sure you have some basic knowledge about NNTs before you start experimenting. Have a pretty good idea what you're doing as you try different approaches, such as experimenting with various network architectures or varying network parameters such as the learning or momentum coefficients. If you get to the point where nothing seems to work, and you are fiddling with network parameters and architectures without knowing what you're doing, like fiddling with knobs on a black box, *STOP!*

Also, you shouldn't necessarily make assumptions about where or how many neural networks will reside in your system or what kind of networks might be used. Before we look at these items, they will be considered in some detail in the next section on system specification. If you do your system specification properly, whether it is "on the back of an envelope" or a formal structured analysis, these issues will be addressed.

As you analyze whether or not an NNT might be useful in your application, keep in mind that a network could appear in one or more locations, in one or more incarnations, and/or in one or more forms. A network could be used for preprocessing data that are handled by an expert system, or a network could be used to analyze parametric data that have been derived from raw data by some algorithms.

If accurately knowing classifications ahead of time is a problem, you might want to operate on the data initially with a self-organization network, such as a Kohonen net, and feed the results to a back-propagation network. Similar network architectures could appear at several places in a system, either as subnetworks (parts of a larger structure) or standing alone. The possibilities are endless, and the message here is merely to keep your mind open as you first consider how to approach the situation.

The Big Picture

When it appears probable that you'll be incorporating a neural network tool into your system, you begin a development process that is similar to the one followed regardless of the specific software/hardware tools to be implemented. Although there are several ways to depict the process (actually there are probably as many ways to depict it as there are systems developers), one way is illustrated in Fig. 3-1. It starts with the system specification activity shown in the upper left-hand corner of the figure and ends with the integration of the neural network tool into the system in the lower right-hand corner.

Once you complete the system specification, two somewhat independent sets of tasks must be done. The tasks arranged horizontally along the bottom of the figure, starting with the selection of training and test data, require significant involvement of the end user(s) of the system. User involvement is required in the selection of training and test data to ensure, among other things, that valid data and results are used to train and test the network. Some user participation in data characterization and preprocessing is often useful. For example, users can pro-

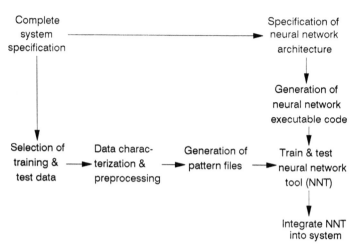

Figure 3-1 Neural network tool development process.

vide insight into which input channels should be normalized together and the best representation of raw data by parameters.

The tasks arranged vertically on the right-hand side of the figure, starting with the specification of neural network architecture, are mainly computer-related tasks and don't require as much participation by the end user(s). An exception is the interpretation of the training and testing results. User involvement is important from the specification of training and testing criteria to the interpretation of the results.

The tasks not discussed elsewhere in this book (primarily those leading up to and including the generation of pattern files) are discussed in the following sections. The generation of executable code is described in Chapters 4 and 5. Training and testing of NNTs are discussed in Chapters 7 and 8. This subject is also covered in several of the case studies.

Developing a System Specification

No matter what you think the final configuration of your system might eventually be, the first thing you need to do is prepare the system specification.

Specifications and Models

The purpose of a requirements specification is to describe a system's behavior so that users can approve the proposed system and developers can understand what they are to design and implement. The specification should describe what a system does, not how it does it.

Systems analysis is one of the most critical activities during systems development because errors and omissions at this stage can have widespread, expensive repercussions later in the project. The product of the systems analysis phase is the system specification. The goal is to document the requirements so that the implementation can be accurately evaluated (have we produced the system we said we were going to?). The specification serves as a model of the proposed system, helping users visualize the system before it is built and the developer validate the system. This is particularly useful to the neural network field, in which we are almost always trying to develop models.

In recent years, CASE (computer-aided software engineering) tools have emerged to support all phases of software and systems development. Tools to support the systems analysis phase are known as *front end* or *upper case* tools; those that support design, implementation, debugging, and testing are known as *back end* or *lower case* tools.

Specifications can range from the informal narrative document to formal executable requirements specifications.

Informal Specifications

The informal English narrative is the least desirable method and is thankfully becoming rarer as better tools emerge. This is not a good specification technique because it is hard to understand, can contain ambiguities, and is extremely difficult to check for completeness and consistency. It is almost impossible for anyone to look at a delivered system and say whether it complies with the narrative specification. Because English is not a formal language, we cannot (currently) use automated tools to analyze a narrative document. Finally, it is difficult to maintain such a specification document as requirements change.

Perhaps the only reason that informal specifications survive has been the lack of CASE tools, but this is changing rapidly as more and more tools become available on PCs and workstations. In the next section, we describe the basic principles of structured analysis, which is easily adaptable to CASE tools and should eliminate narrative specifications altogether.

Structured Analysis

Structured analysis [85] uses a set of tools to produce a structured specification that overcomes most of the preceding problems. The structured specification consists of

Data flow diagrams
Data dictionary
Structured English

as well as other tools for describing the logic of systems, such as deci-sion trees and decision tables. Structured analysis has recently been extended with tools for real-time systems [72, 86], including

Control flow diagrams
State transition diagrams

Structured analysis is a rigorous technique that employs semiformal tools and some informal tools.

Data flow diagrams, for example, are amenable to formal graphical analysis. This is illustrated in Chapter 5, which uses data flow diagrams to depict neural networks and automated tools to generate executable code directly from the graphical structure. Structured English, on the other hand, is rather informal, although it does employ some of the control structures of structured programming, such as:

```
IF ... THEN ... ELSE
CASE ...
DO WHILE ...
```

But the goal of structured English is to describe process logic in a way that can be communicated to (possibly non–computer literate) users. Therefore, more emphasis is placed on human readability than on the capability for automated analysis.

Data flow diagrams model requirements graphically in terms of data flows and processes. Data flows show information and control signals flowing between the system and its environment, as well as between processes (Fig. 3-2). Processes are the active agents of the system, trans-forming the input flows to produce output flows.

Hierarchical Structure

Data flow diagrams are structured as a leveled hierarchy. Figure 3-2 is an example of the context diagram, showing the whole system as a single process and data flows between the system and the environ-ment. The single process in the context diagram is then exploded as in Fig. 3-3, revealing more detail about the system model, with several processes, flows, and data stores. Each of the processes in Fig. 3-3 can in turn be exploded into more detailed diagrams. The decomposition can be continued to an arbitrary level of detail until processes at the lowest level can finally be adequately described using structured English.

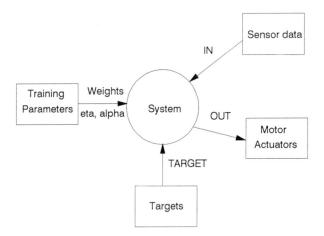

Figure 3-2 Data flow diagram.

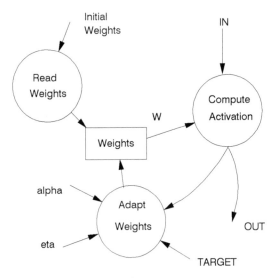

Figure 3-3 Explosion of process system.

This hierarchical structure is a powerful tool for modeling and constructing systems, which is one of the main reasons that structured
analysis has proved to be such an effective technique for describing
systems. Developers and users can focus on any aspect of the system at
the desired level of detail. It is not necessary to look at the lowest level
data flow diagrams, for example, while considering whether the context
diagram accurately reflects the system boundary (division between the

system to be constructed and the environment in which it will operate). Once you are satisfied with the model at a particular level, you can dig into the deeper levels for more details.

The last major tool of structured analysis that we cover here is the data dictionary. Originally used to record only data elements, it is now more broadly defined as a system encyclopedia, a software engineering database that stores data elements as well as specifications for processes and other objects that make up the system model. The system encyclopedia is another tool that adds to the rigor of structured analysis because it allows automated tools to analyze facts about the system model for completeness and consistency.

Formal Specifications

Formal specifications are often written in formal specification languages from which programs can be automatically synthesized and validated [87]. There are two problems with this highly formal approach. First, formal specification languages belong in the realm of mathematics and are incomprehensible to the average user. Second, they have been applicable only to small-scale problems so far and they have not been used yet to describe complete systems of any appreciable size. We are sure that this will eventually happen, but for the moment, rigorous tools such as structured analysis are more useful for system development. That is not to say that certain critical portions of a system could not be specified in a formal language while the remainder of the system is specified informally.

Specification Languages

Programming languages such as C, Ada, and Pascal are formal languages, so why not use such a language as a specification language? Well, for the same reason already stated: How many of your users are also programmers? The main problem with C, Ada, Pascal, and similar procedure-oriented languages is that they are too oriented toward design. It is difficult to state requirements for a system without dropping into details that inevitably relate to design.

Prolog as a Prototyping Language

Prolog, on the other hand, is a declarative language, which suggests the intriguing possibility that it could be used successfully as a requirements specification language, with the additional powerful feature of being able to execute specifications [88,89]. This opens up some fascinating approaches to system development. If you can execute the specification, then you immediately have a prototype, apparently before any code has been written. User and developer can put their heads together and work with the prototype. The prototype not only serves as a working model of the proposed system but at the same time serves as a specification for the implementation.

Of course there's no such thing as a free lunch. In this case the catch is that this prototype may not run anywhere near the speed of the final implementation because of the inherent computation overhead of Prolog, and the fact that the specification is an abstract specification that does not attempt to deal with optimization features that would appear in a typical implementation. This timing problem will be encountered, especially when one is trying to model real-time systems. Database applications would in all likelihood run fast enough. Probably, the prototype could often serve as the final implementation!

Applying Specifications to Neural Networks

"What does all of this have to do with neural networks?" you may be asking. "Why bother with specification and design, if all I want is to get my neural network running to solve my problem?" Well, neural networks have to be implemented as systems, whether we like it or not. We have to analyze the requirements for a given problem and design the most appropriate and cost-effective system to solve that problem. Before plunging into neural networks, you should therefore determine the nature and structure of the system and how (and why) neural networks are going to fit into that system.

Specifications can be applied to neural networks in two ways. First, in specifying the system, the neural network is eventually identified as a possible component (process) of the low-level data flow diagram. This process has several inputs and outputs and a specification of the desired mapping. If the process is to be implemented as an algorithm, the specification takes the form of structured English, decision trees, and so on, as already described. Second, if the process is to be implemented as a neural network, it remains for the neural network to discover the algorithm, and the specification merely states the required performance.

Hierarchical Networks

Hierarchical networks can be specified and constructed, using the tools of structured analysis and design. The hierarchical nature of data flow diagrams and other tools of structured analysis have been described. We could use these tools to model neural networks in which nodes at one level are built from subnetworks. In other words, we can use networks as building blocks for constructing systems.

Specifying Neural Network Architectures

A second way in which specifications are applied to neural networks is stating the required architecture. We give more detail in Chapter 4. At this point it is sufficient to say that the architecture is a specification of the neural network topology, whereas other attributes of the neural network—such as learning rule, activation function, update function, learning and momentum factors, and environment—complete the specification.

An example of the specification of a three-layer back-propagation network follows:

```
slab(node1,48).
slab(node2,6).
slab(node3,1).
connect(node2,node1).
connect(node3,node2).
inputs([node1]).
outputs([node3]).
activation(node1, linear).
activation(node2, sigmoid).
activation(node3, sigmoid).
learning_rule(node2, backprop).
learning_rule(node3, backprop).
update([node2,node3]).
learn(node2, .05).
learn(node3, .1).
momentum(node2, .075).
momentum(node3, .075).
```

This listing, and the meaning of each term, is discussed in Chapter 5, so we won't discuss it here.

Choosing Effective Roles for Neural Networks

Introduction

The system specification, whether done on a napkin or with a formal structured analysis approach, basically produces a detailed description of the requirements for each piece of the system. It also describes how the pieces fit together and work with each other. As discussed in the previous section, however, it can be anything but straightforward to relate the system specification results to specific tools, or hardware/ software modules, that implement the specification.

It is the objective of this section to help you with the implementation of your system specifications by discussing some of the ways to use neural networks effectively in your systems. We first review some of the possible roles and configurations in which networks are found, then focus on the issue of preprocessing.

Network Incarnations and Reincarnations

As was mentioned in the section on system specifications, one or more neural networks may find themselves in your system in a variety of roles. We believe that a useful guideline is to keep your mind as open as possible to different roles and combinations as your detailed system design proceeds.

For example, don't assume that raw data either will or will not be preprocessed before being presented to a neural network for processing. Furthermore, don't assume that a single neural network or, even worse, a single network of a given architecture will be playing a given role. In fact, you may find that you use more than one network, or one kind of network more than once, implemented perhaps as subnetworks of a larger structure. You may even combine different network topologies in a single structure. For example, you may use a self-organizing network to preprocess data, then use the output neurodes of the self-organizing network as input neurodes to a back-propagation network that performs the final classification.

Also, don't be a purist in the sense that you try to make neural networks do everything. We've met some folks who seem to believe that, by golly, if you're going to use networks, then you should do absolutely everything remotely feasible with them. They also seem to think that using any other approach is admitting defeat. Keep in mind that the goal is to design a *system* with optimum performance.

Avoiding Preprocessing Pitfalls

Preprocessing is often one of the most difficult areas we deal with when designing a neural network tool. One of the reasons is that there are several facets to it. For example, there are different *types* of preprocessing. Two examples are normalization and parameterization of raw data. Then there is the question of how it is done: That is, whether a neural network or some other algorithm is used, whether it is done across channels or by individual channel, and whether the normalization transformation is done linearly or by some other method such as gaussian.

In general, one form of preprocessing will be required regardless of the network configuration(s) used in the system and the raw data formats available for input: That form is normalization. Most networks generally require normalized inputs. That is, either the value of each input should always be in the interval between 0 and 1, or the total length of each input vector should be some constant value such as 1; the former is true for a back-propagation network and the latter for a self-organization network. There is disagreement between the degree of adherence to the normalization of inputs for back-propagation, but the authors believe that normalization is good practice for most applications.

Remember that the input layers (slabs) of both back-propagation and self-organization networks (implementation examples are presented in Chapter 2), simply act as distribution points for the input values. The values are passed on to the next layer of the network, altered only by connection weights. In the case of the back-propagation network, values go to a hidden layer; in the self-organization case, they go to the output layer.

For the self-organization network, there is generally little choice in how the normalization is done. Most of the time, each component of every input vector is divided by the absolute value of the total length of the vector. This normalizes the total length of each input vector to a value of 1. If you have any questions about why this is done, you might want to reread the sections in Chapter 2 related to self-organization network inputs. Note that this kind of normalization can have an effect on the relationships among corresponding components of different input vectors.

For back-propagation, the only requirement is that the input to each input neurode should always be in the interval between 0 and 1. As a result, there are several ways of accomplishing normalization, and the method you choose depends on your application.

One situation encountered frequently is when the input data to each neurode of a back-propagation network is raw data from the same source, often representing samples at time intervals. For example, samples from a voltage waveform are taken at a given rate (so many samples per second) and a given number of these samples are presented to the input of the network as a block. In this case, normalization generally should be done across all of the channels uniformly. If you have data that range from a maximum value (Xmax) to a minimum value (Xmin), for example, and Xmin is a negative number, you would first add Xmin to all values, making them range between 0 and Xmax + Xmin. Then you would divide each value by Xmax + Xmin. You now have all values normalized between 0 and 1. It is quite possible, even probable, that you'll find the values of Xmax and Xmin in different channels. That's what we mean by normalizing across channels.

If, however, the input data to a back-propagation network are in the form of calculated parameters, then the situation may be very different. We may, for example, be using several different kinds of parameters as inputs. We could have a mixture of voltages, time durations, and waveform sharpness parameters. Just to make life even more interesting, we could also have some statistical parameters such as standard deviations, correlation coefficients, and chi-square goodness-of-fit parameters. In this case, normalizing across all channels could lead to failure in terms of being able to train a network. It must be emphasized, however, that the other extreme of normalizing on each channel individually can also result in problems. Let's look at why each of these statements is true.

The first case, normalizing across all channels, can result in problems in at least one way. For example, if some of your channels represent a parameter, such as the sharpness of a waveform, that can vary only from, say, -0.1 to $+0.1$, and other channels represent waveform amplitudes that can vary from -50 to $+50$, it's easy to see that the sharpness values will be swamped by the amplitude values after normalization.

A variation of 0.1 unit in each type of channel will result in a variation of 0.001 after normalization. This is probably quite acceptable in the case of an amplitude channel, representing only 0.1 percent of the dynamic range. In the sharpness case, however, the 0.1 variation represents 50 percent of the dynamic range, so it is likely that the precision required to train and test the network's discrimination on the sharpness parameters will be severely hampered.

The second case, normalizing on each channel, has also resulted in difficulties in training networks but it is not as clear why the difficulties sometimes arise. The authors have experienced problems, however, and we'll review an example.

We were training a network with parameters calculated from a biopotential waveform. Two of the parameters were amplitudes, three were widths, and three were sharpnesses. The other parameter was a product slope (an indication of the steepness of the waveform at a point). The unit of measure of the amplitudes was volts; widths were in seconds and sharpnesses in degrees.

When we normalized across all of the channels, the sharpness parameters were swamped out, as described. We then normalized on each channel individually, but the network had difficulty training; sometimes it would, sometimes it wouldn't, and the test set performance was uneven and unpredictable. We then normalized the three width channels as a group. We did the same for the three sharpness channels and the same for the two amplitude channels. Bingo. The network trained and tested well and was robust with changes in network parameters such as eta and alpha.

Why did this help? Theoretically, normalizing on each channel individually should have both positive and negative effects: the positive one being that each channel gets to reflect its dynamic range over the entire interval between 0 and 1 and the negative one being that the relationship between any two channels is lost to the extent of an offset and a multiplicative factor. Supposedly, the network can discover the relationship anyway. Perhaps it might take longer to train the network, but it should eventually train. In this case, however, it seems to have made the training of the network sufficiently difficult that the network's performance was only marginally acceptable.

In the case of the widths, when summed two of them formed the width of a half-waveform between zero crossings; the third was the inflection width, the width between the two points at which the second derivative of the half-waveform changed sign. In the real world of raw data, the sum of the first two widths was always larger than the third width, and each of the first two widths was smaller than the third. These and any other relationships that existed between the two amplitudes or among the three sharpnesses were obscured in the individual channel normalization process.

We therefore suggest, on the basis of this experience and several other similar ones, that you normalize related channels as a group rather than individually, particularly if you are experiencing difficulty training your network with individually normalized channels.

But why, you may ask, normalize at all? Is it *really* required? For self-organization networks, the answer is clearly yes. If you need to understand more, look at the section on self-organization networks in Chapter 2. For back-propagation, the answer is still generally yes, but the situation is a little fuzzier. The input nodes merely distribute the input values to the connections leading to the first hidden layer; and the connection weights, when multiplied by the inputs and summed, provide the input values to the hidden layer. Why would the hidden layer care whether or not the inputs are strictly limited to the range between 0 and 1, particularly when the weights are usually initialized to some relatively small, random values between, say, -0.3 and $+0.3$? The answer seems to be that strict limitation to values between 0 and 1 isn't always necessary, but that normalization is still a good guideline for several reasons. We discussed some of them earlier.

In addition, large input values, particularly when multiplied by a large number of weights (large fan-in), can result in a hidden neurode receiving a very large value as its input. This effectively swamps the hidden neurode, driving it into a condition similar to saturation in an electronic amplifier. (The number of connections coming into a neurode is called its "fan-in value," or just "fan-in.") This saturation makes it difficult to adjust the weights to values sufficiently low to get the neurode into the region where it is effectively doing something. It may take, for example, thousands of iterations rather than hundreds to accomplish the necessary learning because each iteration of weight changes does relatively little to move the neurode out of saturation.

One way to avoid this saturation effect has been suggested by Pineda [53]. This is to divide each initial randomized weight by the value of the fan-in for that layer. At the same time, the value of η for the layer should be divided by the same value. This tends to reduce the saturation of neurodes with large fan-in values and thus contributes to better learning performance by the network.

This is a constructive approach for some problems, but a word of caution is in order. If you have a very large fan-in, such as perhaps 1000, you may get such small values for initial weights after doing the division, and such small values for the individual weight adjustments, that the resolution, or precision, of the weight adjustments approaches the precision limits of your computer, possibly being affected by things such as roundoff error.

If you take this approach, however, it is in our opinion necessary to divide *both* η and the initial weights by the fan-in value. In the case of the initial weights, it is needed to keep the neurodes from saturating right at the beginning. If you don't also divide η by the fan-in, you run the danger of saturating within the first few weight changes anyway, in spite of keeping the initial weights small.

Neural Networks versus Expert Systems

One of the recently acquired tools in the arsenal of diagnostic systems developers is expert systems. In this section, we look briefly at how neural network tools stack up against expert systems. In the process of doing this, we discuss some of the strengths and weaknesses of neural network tools and expert systems and get an idea of instances when each tool might be more appropriate. We also see how, in some cases, they might work together. In Chapter 9, on hybrid systems that include both neural networks and expert systems, we explore ways they can work together in more detail. We call these contraptions *expert networks*.

What are the basic differences between expert systems and neural networks? We begin to explore this topic by defining each:

An *expert system* is a software-based system that describes the behavior of an expert in some field by capturing the knowledge of one or more experts in the form of rules and symbols.

A *neural network* is a computing system that imitates intelligent behavior; it is made up of a number of simple, highly connected processing elements and processes information by its dynamic state response to external inputs.

One of the major problems with expert systems is with the acquisition and coding of the expert knowledge. A related problem is the evaluation of the accuracy and completeness of the encoded knowledge thus acquired. Gaines has published a list of specific problems associated with acquiring expert knowledge [54]. We don't think we can substantially improve his list, so here it is, verbatim:

- Expertise can be fortuitous. The expert achieves results due to features of the situation out of his control.
- Expertise may not be available to awareness. The expert may not be able to transfer his expertise through a critique of the performance of others because he is not able to evaluate that performance.
- Expertise may be inexpressible in language. The expert cannot transfer the expertise explicitly because he is unable to express it, or does not know what needs expressing.
- Expertise may not be understandable when expressed in language. An apprentice may not be able to understand the language of an expert.
- Expertise may not be applicable even when expressed in language. An apprentice may not be able to transfer verbal comprehension of a skill into successful performance of the skill.
- Expertise expressed may be irrelevant. The expert may transfer superstitious behavior learned from random reinforcement schedules.
- Expertise expressed may be incomplete. There may be implicit situational dependencies that make explicit expertise inadequate for performance.
- Expertise expressed may be incorrect. Experts may make explicit statements which do not conform to their actual performance.

There also are some drawbacks to expert systems that are independent of the difficulty in acquiring the knowledge base necessary to implement them. First, they are *brittle*, which means that they are susceptible to degradations in performance from a variety of sources. That is, if you give an expert system incorrect, fuzzy, or noisy data, you are likely to get the wrong answer. Another important aspect is, if you don't think of *all* the rules needed to characterize the knowledge you are representing fully, sooner or later (probably sooner) the expert system will fail.

But you must know by now (unless you started reading the book on this page) that these are precisely the areas in which neural networks shine. You can, within limits, give NNTs some fuzzy, noisy data and still get the right answers. You can even, within limits, lie to them and come out all right. Why, then, even consider using expert systems?

There are several cases when the use of an expert system, or at least something *other* than a neural network tool, is indicated.

An expert system might be a better approach if you don't have enough information (patterns) to train a neural network tool. For example, suppose you are designing a medical diagnostic system that is supposed to diagnose an extremely rare abdominal affliction (only seven cases of whatever-it-is have ever been reported in the history of mankind) as well as to diagnose appendicitis and other relatively common abdominal ailments. It may be that you can train a neural network tool for everything but the rare ailment; then you use a rule-based approach for the rare ailment.

In some applications, using a rule-based system is obviously (at least fairly obviously) the better (and simpler) approach. At the risk of being accused of heresy, it seems to us that using a single rule (one line of computer code) is the better way to solve the exclusive-OR (XOR) problem discussed at length in the neural network literature [2,4,16]. Using a neural network for the XOR problem is sort of like smashing a peanut with an elephant! (The "exclusive-or" problem consists of correctly detecting when one, and only one, of two inputs is "on.")

The final example is user interfaces, those parts of the system that interact directly with the user. It is likely that an expert system, or some other tool such as a procedure written in a structured language such as C++, will do a more efficient job of providing the program shell that handles input and output and provides general guidance to the user.

It should be clear by now that you could build some pretty powerful systems by using combinations (hybrids) of neural networks and expert systems (and other tools, as well). For example, for a medical diagnostic system, you might use an expert system, augmented with C++ functions, to interact with the user and provide the initial query capability that guides the system into the proper general area. A series of neural network tools, consisting of networks and subnetworks, could be used to assist in the diagnosis of the more common ailments, and rule-based systems could come into play for the relatively obscure ailments. Chapter 9 (Expert Networks) will explore these ideas in more detail.

Successful Application Examples

The list of successful applications of neural networks grows constantly. It seems that each time a major conference is held or another issue of a neural networks journal is published, new areas of applications are described.

In this section, we briefly discuss four examples of applications that we've run across in our experience, at conferences, and in reviews of the literature. We chose these examples primarily because of the *motivation* that led to the use of neural network tools in each case, rather than the uniqueness or other attribute of the application. These motivations include feasibility, time, money, and improved system performance.

Example 1

The reliable real-time detection of epileptiform spike waveforms in an electroencephalogram (EEG) is a task that did not seem feasible by other methods. Neurologists, scientists, and engineers had been trying for decades to write an algorithm to analyze EEG waveforms for spikes. Some software had been written, but its performance was not sufficiently accurate for general use. In particular, recent advances in rule-based systems had provided tools for reasonably effective off-line analysis, but a tool for multiple channel on-line analysis was elusive.

It is particularly difficult to apply rigorous analysis techniques to this problem because of a lack of agreement among the expert neurologists as to what constitutes a spike. Training a neural network with examples of waveforms that, by consensus, represented spikes achieved the desired performance. The motivation for applying NNTs to this application could be summed up as *feasibility*. Doing the job as specified just hadn't proven feasible any other way.

Example 2

The second application, a three-layer back-propagation network that forecasts solar flares, was developed at the University of Colorado [55]. This NNT was developed following the development of an expert system called THEO that does the same job.

It turns out that THEO, which involves an OPS-83 production system with about 700 rules, is able to perform as well as a skilled human forecaster. Not surprisingly, the neural net tool, called *TheoNet*, performs even better than THEO. Receiver operating characteristic (ROC) curves were used to measure the performance of each system. (ROC curves and their use are described in Chapter 7.)

The folks in Colorado already had a working expert system. So why did they bother to develop a neural network tool? The answer reflects an important motivation for many applications. The development of the expert system THEO had required more than one man-year of effort and consisted of 700 rules. Even at that, it was heralded as one of the most rapid developments on record of a usable expert system. In contrast, *TheoNet* was developed in less than a week using a simple simulator [55]. There is also a marked difference in performance. The THEO expert system requires about 5 minutes to make a single prediction whereas *TheoNet* needs only a few milliseconds. The motivations here are therefore *time*, *money*, and *system performance*. Although the expert system makes almost as many right answers, it took a relatively long time to develop and takes a relatively long time to get the answers.

This example is not unique. A growing number of NNTs have replaced (or, in some cases, augmented) more costly, slower expert systems. They are being used for modeling, simulation, prediction, and generation of new patterns.

Example 3

Our third example, using an NNT to compose music, also falls into the preceding category. One of the case studies in this volume describes the use of a back-propagation network to compose music. Other network configurations have also been used [56]. Music, like art, appeals to each individual differently. It is relatively easy for each of us to give examples of the kind of music or art that we like, but it is almost impossible, even for a person versed in music theory and computers, to develop a complete set of rules to describe, in the sense of a specification, even a very narrow segment of music. In addition, it is well known that attributes of music that help make it enjoyable are the elements of surprise, variety, and change [56]. Another way of looking at these attributes is that they represent stochasticity, creativity, and nonadherence to rules.

Music composition NNTs can incorporate these attributes while being trained to any chosen style of music, without the need to specify rules for that style. The motivation for using NNTs to compose music, then, in addition to *feasibility*, is *creativity*.

Example 4

Our last example was developed to predict the load on Puget Power and Light's electric distribution system, that is, to predict the amount of power that would have to be generated to meet customer demand. The development of the neural network was motivated by a desire for better predictions than those that were being made by the other two methods being used [57]. The first method was a classical mathematical technique involving regression analyses. The second method was forecasting based on the opinions of an expert.

The development of a neural network tool was facilitated by the existence of a large data base of raw data that could be used to train and test the network and by some folks at the Electrical Engineering Department of the University of Washington who figured they'd like to tackle the job. The result is a standard back-propagation network written in C, with 3–6 input nodes, 5–10 hidden nodes, and one output node (the configuration depends on whether the network is being used for peak, total, or hourly load forecasting); the network originally ran on a Unix-based system at the University of Washington. The final neural network tool, however, is run by Puget Power on an IBM PC. In fact, the back-propagation code in the back of this book has been used to investigate refinements to the original version [57].

So, to summarize, the neural net was developed because existing techniques weren't working well and an adequate database and expertise existed to develop a network solution.

CHAPTER 4

Software Tools

Roy W. Dobbins
Russell C. Eberhart

Introduction

In this chapter, we describe software tools to model, specify and run neural networks on PCs, and examine how a network specification is turned into working code. This chapter concentrates on the low-level programming tools for implementing networks, and the next chapter looks at high-level modeling and specification languages.

Software is needed to run the neural networks, once they've been built. Before presenting data to the network, you have to prepare training and test pattern sets and ensure that the data are properly normalized (if you don't it will surely head off into the ozone). In this chapter, software for standard, off-the-shelf personal computers is described.

Software is also required to adapt to hardware accelerators that are available now or that may become available in the future. We must find ways to make the software flexible enough to support many accelerators. The most popular accelerator is the 8087 math coprocessor chip. We describe this in some detail and point out some general principles that are useful for more exotic coprocessors. Parallel processing architectures are covered in Chapter 6.

What Is Neural Network Software?

Neural network software implements neural networks on a hardware platform. The terms *artificial neural network* and *neural network simulation* are often used to describe the software. These words suggest aspects of other computing fields—AI and system simulation—that create some confusion. We don't use *artificial* because it is already clear that we are implementing electronic, not biological, neural networks; furthermore, we are seeking practical solutions to real-world problems, and we are *not* trying to model the brain (although brain-style processing is a good computational model). We don't use *simulation* because this suggests that you're simulating the neural network, not doing the real one. A software implementation is no more a simulation nor any less real than a hardware implementation.

The Last of the Programmers?

You may get the idea from popular press articles that neural networks require no programming. Programmers had better start thinking about new careers? Not likely. At least not yet. Remember what assembler language programmers were told when high-level languages hit the scene some 30 years ago? That soon there would be no need for assembly language because compilers would generate superefficient code with which you could program a machine to do virtually anything? That hasn't happened yet, but we still get predictions about the imminent demise of assembly language.

Although you can use a given neural network software tool to solve problems, apparently without any further programming (neural networks are sometimes called nonprogrammed adaptive information processing systems), the fact remains that programmers have very active roles to play in developing the field. Someone must implement neural networks on different host configurations.

Many neural network paradigms are known [76], and more remain to be invented. Each paradigm requires careful programming to make it work efficiently (assembly language again). A neural network is much like a module, task, or subroutine in conventional von Neumann style computing. For the network to be useful, it must cooperate with other software. It has to be called, parameters must be passed to it, and it must return a result. This requires a lot of software and system integration effort.

Apart from using hardware assistance to speed up neural networks, there are ways to get more performance out of what we have. After dealing with the basics, we'll look at code generation and optimizing techniques.

Implementing Neural Networks on the PC

In this section, we take a detailed look at how networks are implemented, with examples from back-propagation and self-organizing networks (source code appears in Appendix A). Chapter 2 covered theoretical aspects of back-propagation techniques. Now we show how this can be put into practice on the PC.

Using C and Assembly Language

C is the primary tool for many PC applications, including neural networks. C is the language of choice for writing system software (Pascal, Forth, Modula-2, or other high-level languages can also be used). We won't get into a heated debate about programming languages. From a practical point of view, C is the strongest choice today (tomorrow this could change). C has emerged from the shop floor, and the features in the language are there because they are necessary in a practical language tool.

On the other hand, Pascal was designed for teaching beginning computer science students. Pascal is a fine language for beginners, and many interesting ideas about language design can be learned from it. Some of these, such as structured programming and data structures, are also incorporated into C. Many aspects of the original Pascal language, however, were not intended for hard applications. For instance, no provision was made for in-line assembly language or separately compiled modules; I/O functions are rather primitive. The language has been extended in ad hoc ways to solve these and other problems. The result is that portability has suffered because different implementations are incompatible.

By contrast, C was designed by a single person (Dennis Ritchie [75]), and has matured gracefully from that one standard. Now it holds the title to the most portable language available (well, OK, Forth excluded). Although C is an excellent tool for system programming, it cannot do everything we want. Assembly language is another essential tool in the neural network developer's repertoire, although it is necessary only for a small percentage of the total code. Assembly language is the way to go in order to squeeze the last drop of performance out of neural networks or to do weird things to the hardware. We go into more detail about this when we discuss optimization.

Back-Propagation Networks

The complete C source listing of a working back-propagation neural network appears as Listing 1 in Appendix A. The program can readily be translated to Pascal or other languages. The general flow of the program is shown by the mini C program, which has the same basic structure as the back-propagation program in Listing 1, except that many of the code fragments have been replaced by capitalized comments— a sort of pseudo C, if you like.

```
main()
{
    ALLOCATE STORAGE
    READ INITIAL WEIGHTS AND INPUT PATTERNS

    for (q = 0; q < nInterations; q++)
    {
        for (p = 0; p < nPatterns; p++)
        {
            COMPUTE ACTIVATIONS              /* FORWARD PASS */
            PROPAGATE ERROR SIGNALS          /* BACKWARD PASS */
        }

        ADAPT WEIGHTS                        /* BACKWARD PASS */

        if (sum_squared_error < MinError)
            break;
    }

    WRITE FINAL WEIGHTS
    WRITE OUTPUT ACTIVATION VALUES
    FREE STORAGE
}
```

Figure 4-1   Back-propagation neural network model.

The Three Rs . . .

It should come as no surprise that neural networks are subject to the laws of the three Rs. We start by describing one of the Rs: aRithmetic. You can see that the neural network kernel (the part computing activations) is very computation intensive. The other Rs, Reading and wRiting, take care of getting patterns in and out of the network, a topic we cover in the section on running neural networks.

Iterations . . . Kernel, Brain, or Engine?

As you can see, Fig. 4-1 has an iteration loop, beginning

```
for (q = 0; . . . ; . . .)
```

The program stops when the requested number of iterations has been completed or when the average sum-squared error is less than the required minimum. Both the number of iterations and the minimum error are parameters specified by the user when running the program. This iteration loop is the "real" neural network, or kernel. The rest of the code is there purely to read and write data and do housekeeping. In this section, we discuss the neural network kernel in detail.

Forward . . . and Backward

Each iteration consists of a *forward pass*, in which processing elements compute their activation values, starting at the input layer, and propagate them forward to the next layer, and a *backward pass*, in which error signals are propagated backward through the network, starting at the output layer, and weights are changed to reduce the difference between the desired (target) output vector and the current output vector. To understand the back-propagation rule, it is useful to construct a data flow model, showing the actions of a single processing element (Fig. 4-2). Let's look at the C code to implement these actions.

Computing Activations

Each processing element computes its output or activation as a function of its inputs. Inputs are weighted and (because there are many of them) summed to form the net input to the element. As an example of the computation, look at the hidden layer on lines 231−234 of Listing 1 in Appendix A. The following symbols or phrases are used:

out0   Input vector (the input pattern
                                                vector)

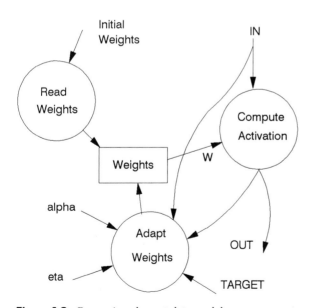

Figure 4-2   Processing element data model.

w1	Weight vector (the weights for the input to hidden layer connections)
w1[h][nInputNodes]	is the bias (stored for convenience as the last element of the weight vector). Bias is the weight of the connection from a unit that is always on. There is one bias weight for each processing element in the hidden and subsequent layers.
sum += w1[h][i] * out0[p][i]	is the sum of the products, over the input and weight vectors. This is called the inner product, a term described in the next section.
p	Index referring to the pattern being processed (all patterns are stored in memory so that they can be rapidly accessed).
h	Index referring to a node in the hidden layer.
i	Index referring to a node in the input layer.
nInputNodes	The number of nodes in the input layer.

The sigmoid activation function is implemented by the C code on line 237 and illustrated in the following statement:

$$out1[p][h] = 1.0/(1.0 + exp(-sum))$$

Other nonlinear, differentiable activation functions can also be used (e.g., arctan and tanh functions), but the sigmoid works well for most applications:

out1	is the hidden layer activation vector.
exp(-sum)	computes the exponential function on the net input calculated as described.

    Vectors and matrices are crucial to neural network implementations; hence, in the following sections, we'll spend a little time showing how vectors are manipulated and stored.

```
for (i = 0, sum = 0; i < N; i++)
    sum += w[i] * out[i];
```

Figure 4-3 Inner product computation

Vector and Matrix Operations

In most neural network implementations, it is necessary to manipulate large vectors and matrices of numbers: We are talking about massively parallel architecture. Activation values and weights are stored and manipulated as vectors. Trying to work this as individual numbers would be about as easy as traveling from New York to Tokyo on a mule. Vectors are especially important when coprocessors are used because you can get a much better performance by giving them whole vectors to crunch all at once, rather than element by element. The *inner product* or *multiply–accumulate* is a typical example of a vector operation. It has the general form shown in Fig. 4-3.

This is discussed in the section on Computing Activations. You can pick out this type of loop several times in the listing (see, e.g., lines 231–234 of Listing 1 in Appendix A). The efficiency of these loops can make a substantial difference to the running time of a neural network, particularly when the number of units is large. The reason is that the loops are computed many thousands of times during a training run. Later we look at ways to make this code as efficient as possible.

Storage Allocation

For neural network implementations, you need *lots* of storage and a good way to manage it. For many real-world applications, the storage needed for the data can become substantial because there are lots of processing elements and even more connections. Storage for nodes must be allocated as shown in Fig. 4-4.

Consider for example, a three-layer network with 192 input nodes, 16 hidden nodes, and 2 output nodes that is used for real-time EEG classification. Assuming 100 patterns are used for training, we get

$$\text{Number of activation values} = 100 * (192 + 16 + 2)$$
$$= 21000$$
$$\text{Number of interconnections} = 2 * (16 + 1) + 16 * (192 + 1)$$
$$= 3122$$
$$\text{Number of bytes of storage} = 8 * (21000 + 3122)$$
$$= 192976.$$

Note that the activation values of all processing elements *for all patterns* are stored. We need to keep these values handy during the learn-

```
Total storage in bytes   =
  number of bytes per item *
  2 * (number of interconnections + number of activation values)

  (note: deltas and delta weights double total storage needed).

Number of activation values   =
  number of patterns * number of nodes.

Number of interconnections =
  number of output nodes * (number of hidden nodes + 1) +
  number of hidden nodes * (number of input nodes + 1)
  (note: bias term adds one connection to each node.)
Number of bytes per item = 4
  (note: uses float numbers:  4 bytes each).
```

Figure 4-4   Estimating storage for neural networks.

ing phase, during which training patterns are repeatedly presented to the network.

For back-propagation learning, we store deltas and delta weights (weight changes) (see Listing 1 in Appendix A, lines 263–266 and 290–295). This doubles the storage needed because for each activation value a corresponding delta is stored and for each weight a corresponding delta weight is also stored. Activations and weights are stored as single-precision floating-point numbers, requiring 4 bytes each. A double-precision floating-point number needs 8 bytes per location, which doubles the amount of storage needed. On the other hand, integer numbers require only 2 bytes each, which divides the storage needed in half. But single-precision integers are probably not sufficiently accurate for training networks. This is a current research issue.

Propagating Error Signals

Previous sections have described the forward pass of the neural network in some detail. Next is the backward pass, in which error signals are propagated backward through the network, starting at the output layer. The error term (or delta) at the output layer, *delta2*, is computed from the difference between the actual output and the desired target values for each node in the output layer, for each training pattern (see line 254 in Listing 1):

$$delta2 = (target - out2) * out2 * (1 - out2)$$

where out2 is the activation vector at the output layer, and target is the target vector (desired network reponse).

The error at the hidden layer, *delta1*, is calculated recursively from the error terms of units in the output layer, using the following formulas (see lines 264 and 266):

```
sum += delta2 * w2
delta1 = sum * out1 * (1 - out1)
```

where `delta2 * w2` is the product of the delta of an output unit and the weight of the link between the hidden unit and the output unit; and `sum` is the error term, derived from all output units to which the hidden unit is connected. Consult lines 251–268 of Listing 1 for the full C implementations of these formulas.

Adapting Weights

The weight changes depend on the propagated error terms. The magnitude of the weight change is controlled by the learning rate constant *eta*. The higher eta is the bigger the weight changes and the faster the network is able to train. However, high eta increases the danger of oscillation. The momentum term *alpha* damps high-frequency weight changes and reduces the risk of oscillation while still permitting fast learning rates.

The change in weight, *dw*, at the hidden to output connections is (line 293 of Listing 1):

```
dw = eta * sum + alpha * delw2
```

where `sum += delta2 * out1` (line 291 of Listing 1) computes the product of the error term at the output layer and the activation values of the hidden layer. This product is summed over all units of the hidden layer. The new value of the weight, w2, is (line 294 of Listing 1):

```
w2 += dw
```

Notice that the value of dw is retained (Listing 1, line 295) for the computation of the momentum term on the next iteration. See lines 285 to 296 of Listing 1 for an implementation of these formulas. Note that the *bias* weight is calculated in exactly the same way as any other weight, as shown on lines 276–283 of Listing 1.

The adaptation of the input to hidden layer weights follows a similar set of rules, as seen on lines 300 to 325 of Listing 1. This completes the description of the kernel for a back-propagation neural network. There are many variations on the basic techniques. For example, you can see in the listing that the backward pass consists of two activities, namely, propagating the error signals and adapting the weights. In our network, the error propagation is done for each pattern presented whereas weights are adapted only after all patterns have been seen by the network. This is called *batch training* (which is why the C program in Listing 1 is called BATCHNET).

Another approach is to complete both backward pass activities at once for each pattern presentation. This technique is called *on-line training* or *interactive training*. One disadvantage of on-line training is the increased computation load, but in some circumstances this overhead may be worthwhile if fewer training iterations are needed to get an acceptable error. An advantage of on-line training is that less memory is needed during training than for batch training.

Kohonen Self-Organizing Networks

The complete source listings for a self-organizing network are presented in Appendix B, Listing 2. The basic flow is summarized in Fig. 4-5.

Compare this to the back-propagation neural network model of Fig. 4-1. There are some significant differences. Weights and input vectors are normalized differently. The components of these vectors are typically initialized in the range 0 to 1 for back-propagation networks, as described in Fig. 4-7. But for a self-organizing network like Kohonen's, it is necessary to normalize the vectors to constant length [22]. This is called Euclidean normalization (see lines 495–510 of Listing 2 for examples). Note that the vectors, rather than the individual elements, are

```
kohonen ( )
{
    ALLOCATE STORAGE
    READWEIGHTS AND PATTERNS

    for (q = 0;   q < nIterations;   q++)
    {
        for (p = 0;   p < nPatterns;   p++)
        {
            COMPUTE ACTIVATIONS
            FIND WINNING UNIT
            ADAPT WEIGHTS OF WINNER AND ITS NEIGHBORHOOD
            SHRINK NEIGHBORHOOD SIZE
            REDUCE LEARNING COEFFICIENT eta
            if (eta <= 0)
            break;
        }
    }
    WRITE FINAL WEIGHTS
    WRITE OUTPUT ACTIVATION VALUES
    FREE STORAGE
}
```

Figure 4-5   Kohonen self-organizing network.

normalized. We'll see how this affects the way in which the network learns. Normalization is also described in some detail by Caudill [39,40].

Only the weights of the winner and the neighborhood of the winner are adjusted whereas, in the back-propagation model, all weights are adjusted. The size of the neighborhood starts off large—typically covering the whole output layer—then the neighborhood shrinks over time until only the winning unit is allowed to learn. The effect of this approach is that initially the whole network organizes itself coarsely according to the distribution of the input patterns [37]. As the neighborhood shrinks, finer adjustments are made only to the units actually responding to the input stimuli.

Because this is an unsupervised learning scheme, there is no error criterion for terminating learning. Instead, the learning coefficient eta is gradually reduced over time, and if it should fall to zero, learning is terminated. Of course this does not imply that the network has been trained sufficiently.

Finding the Winning Unit

After each pattern is presented to the network, the weights are adjusted in the neighborhood of the winner. The winner is the unit (neurode) whose weight vector most closely matches (i.e., has minimum Euclidean distance to) the input pattern vector. This is the reason that the vectors must be normalized. If they are not, the selection of the closest match does not work correctly. See lines 495–510 in Listing 2 of Appendix B for details of computing Euclidean distance between vectors.

What Is This Good For?

To illustrate the use of the Kohonen style self-organizing network, a simple example is given in Appendix B. The data sets are presented to the network to show how it learns to classify patterns statistically into clusters. The data consist of 16 two-dimensional vectors (pattern vectors with two elements in each pattern), but vectors of larger dimension can also be processed by the network. We chose two dimensions because this makes the presentation and display of patterns and weights easier. All of the results are equally valid for higher dimensions.

The patterns are repeatedly presented to the network. After several epochs, some units in the output layer arrange themselves into clusters corresponding to the most frequently occurring patterns; that is, the network responds to the probability distribution of the input data. For example, in our simple data set of 16 patterns, there are 9 instances of pattern a, 4 instances of pattern b, 2 instances of pattern c, and 1 instance of pattern d. The output layer develops four units that respond to these patterns. When an instance of pattern a is presented to the network, unit a responds, when pattern b is presented, unit b responds, and so on.

All other units respond less strongly, but for each presentation, we are interested only in the winner. If you look at the weight vectors, you can see that the winners—a, b, c, and d in our example—have vectors very close to the input pattern clusters. But the weights to other units have hardly learned at all and are not close to any of the input clusters. This is to be expected because only the weights of the winners are adjusted.

Nondeterministic Response

It is important to note that the set of actual units responding to each input pattern is nondeterministic. If you run the example a few times, you can get different results on each run! The units a, b, c, and d can appear at different positions in the output layer on each run. However, there is always the same number of units, four in this case. The units are nondeterministically selected because the weights are randomly initialized. When the first few training patterns are presented, the winning units therefore depend on the random arrangement of weights at that time. Whichever units happen to respond first, it influences the subsequent learning behavior of the network. But the final outcome, the number of clusters, is always the same.

Running Neural Networks

In the previous sections, we showed how a neural network is implemented. We are now ready to feed it some real data and get some answers. This is where the hardest work begins!

Running a neural network involves several activities. The network must be trained on a set of training patterns. Once trained, the network is ready to do its thing. Test patterns or real data are presented to the network and results obtained from the network outputs. But this is oversimplified. Weights must be given initial values when training begins; and once the network has been trained, the final weights must be stored so that the network can be reused many times. Reusing the set of weights means that the network can be run without the need to retrain it each time. When running the network, you need to set parameters to control learning, average sum-squared error, termination criteria, and so on. Finally, the network needs to be monitored by displaying the state of weights and activations.

Getting Data into and out of the Network

Text Files

Text files are attractive for storing data patterns and weights. The main advantage is that they are easy to read (for humans, that is) and easy to edit using word processors or other text processing tools. They are also highly transportable: The numbers look exactly the same no matter what machine they are on. They can be passed around on floppies, printed on a sheet of paper, or transmitted by E-Mail. The disadvantage of text files is that they are rather large. Each datum may take up 10 characters whereas the floating-point binary value only needs 4 bytes.

Importing and Exporting Data

Another advantage of text files is that they can easily be imported into databases and spreadsheets for analysis. You can preprocess data using a spreadsheet and then export that as a text file to the neural network.

Spreadsheets can be used to normalize data, organize training sets, and do virtually any preprocessing required. Spreadsheets are also good for analyzing and graphing the results, doing statistical analyses, and calculating network performance parameters. Spreadsheets can even perform the actual network calculations (for limited size networks), as described in Chapter 12. Similar arguments can be made for the use of databases. Databases can store and record results. It is easy to extract, manipulate, and normalize datasets by means of built-in database tools or quick-and-dirty tools that you write yourself using the fourth-generation languages (4GL) which is provided with most database packages.

A final point about spreadsheets and databases is their ability to exchange data in relatively machine-independent ways. It is possible to transmit spreadsheets or databases over networks between different host computer architectures through dynamic data exchange. This relieves the developer of much of the burden of integrating a neural network into a larger system and presenting the data in the appropriate formats. When developing a neural network tool, it is a good idea to bear in mind how it will be used in a larger system.

Reading Input Patterns

The patterns to be processed by the neural network are read from disk files or other input devices. To speed up training, patterns are read into memory arrays so that they can all be processed at once. Patterns are stored as the activation values of the input layer of the neural network, as shown in lines 183–206 of Listing 1. This does cause some storage problems when the data sets are large. If you run out of storage, you have no choice but to read and process patterns one at a time from the disk. Because of the iterative nature of training, patterns are looked at repeatedly, maybe even thousands of times, before the network is considered trained. Even with all patterns resident in memory, training can sometimes take hours or perhaps days. Presenting patterns from disk is relatively slow, and training may then take days or weeks.

Dealing with the Real World

One must employ different techniques for reading patterns when testing a neural network from those that one employs when running it in real time. In applications, such as signal processing or image processing, you may have to deal with binary data rather than text files. Note that the kernel of Listing 1 deals only with text patterns. That part of the code responsible for reading patterns looks a little different in a real-time system. This must be replaced by code that reads sensory signals directly from the input device and then converts and scales the data as floating-point numbers. Or, the signal conversion can be accomplished by a separate task in a real-time operating system and piped to the neural network task for processing. Typical task data flow is illustrated in Fig. 4-6.

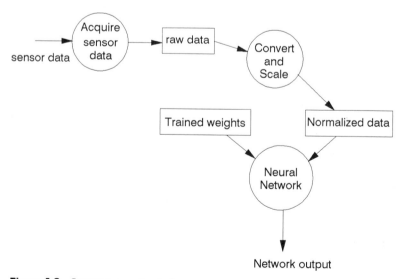

Figure 4-6   Sensor processing tasks.

```
maxval  =  maximum value in the data set
minval  =  minimum value in the data set
range   =  maxval - minval
for (every pattern vector p)
    for (every vector element i)
        pattern[p][i] = (pattern[p][i] - minval) / range
All patterns are now normalized to lie in the range 0 to 1
```

Figure 4-7 Normalizing data.

Normalizing Data

The input patterns, whether text files or binary sensory signals, must be normalized before being presented to the network. The network of Listing 1 assumes that the patterns have already been normalized. It is better not to do normalization inside the network; rather, put this with the preprocessing step. This reduces the size of the neural network code and also keeps things flexible. Often one can normalize patterns in different ways for different runs. Or the preprocessing step, which is application dependent, can in any case normalize the data, so the neural network should not try to normalize again. A typical normalization procedure is given in Fig. 4-7.

Weights

What Goes In Must Come Out

Apart from reading in the patterns to be analyzed, notice that an initial set of weights is read in. The code for this appears on lines 158–181 of Listing 1. Perhaps not obvious from the code is that the bias weights for all hidden and output units are also read at this time. Notice that the read loop has the form:

```
for (i = 0; i <= nInputNodes; i++)
```

Because an array with N components is indexed from 0 to $N - 1$ in C, this read loop reads one weight for each connection from the input layer plus one weight representing the bias. The bias is stored as the $(N + 1)$th term of the weight vector.

When you train a network for the first time, weights are random numbers in the range ± 0.3, or a similar small range. The initial weights file can be written by a random number generator, or the neural network itself can contain a code fragment to do this. In our case, the separate module weights.c (see Appendix A) is run once to generate the required number of weights. When the program is done, the final set of weights is written to the output file. Like the patterns, weights are typically text files.

What Have We Learned?

There are two reasons for writing the weights to a file. First, the set of final weights represents what the system has learned. We want to use these weights when testing the system's ability to recognize or classify new patterns. Generally, the network is trained once on a set of training patterns and then is run several, possibly many, times on the test patterns.

Some people train a large network on a mainframe, then send the weights to a PC, where the network is run. As long as the format of the weights file is agreed upon, this is a very useful technique for transferring *learning* between machines. What one machine has learned through training can be rapidly transferred to another machine running in a totally different environment. This also takes advantage of the fact that for some applications, training is a difficult, computationally intensive task that needs a mainframe or supercomputer to be completed in a reasonable amount of elapsed time. Once trained, however, the neural network can often be operated on a PC with much less computational power. This is because, in test mode, all the network actually does is the forward pass, which requires much less computation than the training mode, in which both forward and backward passes must be completed. Furthermore, in test mode only one iteration is required for each test pattern presented.

Let's Try That One More Time

A second reason for saving the weights at the end of training is to resume training of a network by feeding in the previous set of weights. Normally, the initial weights for an untrained network are small random numbers. Suppose now we want to reuse the weights and make slight adjustments to them to enhance the performance of the network. Rather than starting from scratch with random weights, we want to pick up the weights from where we left off the last time the net was run.

This not only requires far less training but also allows the network to adapt to a changing environment, in which the initial training is perhaps no longer as applicable as it was originally.

How Many Weights?

To fix ideas, suppose we have an architecture consisting of two output units, two hidden units, and four input units; how many weights

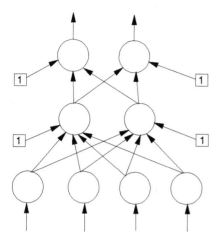

Figure 4-8   Neural net with weights and biases.

OBJECT TYPE	ATTRIBUTES
network	architecture
slab	number of processing elements
	activation function
	learning rule
	learning rate
	momentum factor
processing element	activation value
	threshold

Figure 4-9   Neural network attributes

are required? Refer to Fig. 4-8. Each unit of the output layer has three input connections: one from each hidden node plus a bias term. Similarly, each unit of the hidden layer has five input connections, making a grand total of 16 connections.

Setting Attributes

The attributes of a network are its distinguishing characteristics that describe its form and function. Here is a partial list of some of the attributes needed to construct a working neural network (Fig. 4-9). Many more attributes are needed to model any neural network completely. This topic is discussed in more detail in Chapter 5.

How do we set the attributes of a network? Attributes such as learning rate and momentum factor are parameteric values that can easily be changed on the fly. On the other hand, the activation function is an algorithm, implemented in code, which may not be that easy to change. Generally, rules and algorithms are preprogrammed into the network when the network is specified and built. These cannot (efficiently) be changed without rebuilding the network. Parameters, on the other hand, are easily entered and changed while the network is running.

Average Sum-Squared Error

How do you know if the network is training correctly, and how can you tell how well it is doing? These questions are discussed at length in Chapters 7 and 8. One way is to look at the output nodes and compare them to the target values. The difference between the actual output and the target gives the error at a node for a given pattern (line 345–347 of Listing 1):

```
temp  = target[p][j] - out2[p][j]
error = temp * temp
```

By summing the error over all output nodes for all patterns and taking the average, we get a measure of training performance. The average sum squared error is then (line 352 of Listing 1):

```
error /= nPatterns * nOutputNodes
```

The code monitoring the sum-squared error is on lines 362–364 of Listing 1. When the error is less than the required maximum error (ErrorLevel), training is terminated. The error value is displayed and logged to a file for later analysis (lines 355–360 of Listing 1). Because the error computation takes a finite time and therefore poses some overhead, it is not calculated on every iteration of the network, but only every nth iteration, where n (nReportErrors on line 359 of Listing 1) can be specified at run time.

What's It Doing?

The object of back-propagation is to minimize the average sum-squared error term. It does this by performing a gradient descent in error space. It has been shown mathematically [2, 4, 5] that in most practical cases it stabilizes at the global minimum though there is a small danger of getting stuck or oscillating around a local minimum. A good way to observe these trends is to plot the error graphically against the number of iterations.

Although we use the sum-squared error as the primary indicator of performance, it is sometimes more useful to look at other indicators, such as activation states and weights of the network.

Using Graphics to Observe the Neural Network

In some applications, neural networks have a very large number of processing elements and an even larger number of connections. It is therefore difficult to display the state of the network.

Displaying State of Computation

The neural network state (composed of activation values and weights) can be displayed in many ways. The most obvious is to display a set of numbers representing the activation values of processing elements or the weights of connections (Fig. 4-10). This is not a very useful technique, however (though we have to make do with it if we cannot come up with something better), because humans are not particularly good at working with lots of numbers or perceiving patterns and trends in data.

A better way to represent network state is by using graphics. As you read the examples that follow, remember that this is a current research issue; new understanding of feature representation in biological neural networks is emerging and may help us identify better ways to implement and display these structures in computers. Also, as networks become more ambitious, larger and more sophisticated display methods will have to be invented to deal effectively with the massive amount of data.

A Hinton diagram [2, 4, 5] shows the weights of connections to or from a layer of a network. In the version available on our diskette of neural network software, white rectangles represent positive weights, black rectangles represent negative weights, and the size of a rectangle is proportional to the magnitude of a weight (Fig. 4-11). There are several variations on this scheme. Activation values as well as weights can be displayed. A state value can be represented by colors and fill patterns, not just by black or white intensity levels. Different geometric representations can be used to display multiple layers and their interconnections. For large networks, it may only be possible to display part of a layer at one time.

The network state can be displayed continually as the network runs and can be refreshed on each iteration. However, this may not be a good idea in a production system because the display takes processing time

1.29106	11.2225	3.59078	3.09737	−6.1963	−1.54122
−2.98045	0.934287	−0.798011	−3.74849	−0.0865482	−0.990547
−0.348277	−0.581802	0.180709	...		

Figure 4-10 List of numbers representing weights.

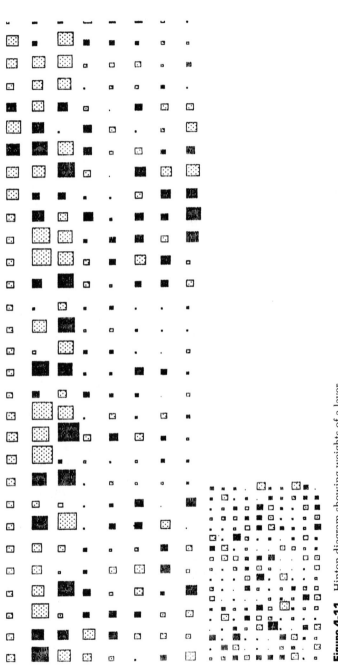

Figure 4-11 Hinton diagram showing weights of a layer.

away from the network. Also, it is not that useful if the network is iterating rapidly, because changes may happen too fast for the human observer to follow. In that case you may want to display network state once every so many iterations, or you may want to suspend the network while the "frozen" state is examined. Another option is to have no real-time display but to examine the state after the network is done.

Implementation Issues

Here we discuss several design issues that should be considered when implementing neural networks.

Interpretation versus Compilation

Many neural network systems that have been reported in the literature or are available on the commercial market use interpreters instead of compilers [2, 4, 5, 78]. This is acceptable on superfast mainframes in which the speed at the central processing unit (CPU) makes up for the interpretation overhead, especially when running "toy" problems requiring relatively few nodes and connections. However, on PCs this approach is not very useful for real-world problems in which many nodes and connections are necessary for effective solutions. In most cases we have to pay a great deal of attention to the run-time efficiency of the code and try to maximize the performance of the available computing resources of the PC. Compilation of the neural network code is one way to help achieve this goal.

One of the main reasons for choosing interpretation is to take advantage of good debugging and software development environments offered by interpreters. Two major examples are Lisp and BASIC. Lisp is well established in the AI world and is an obvious candidate for hosting a neural network environment. However, Lisp is usually run on large mainframes or special purpose Lisp machines. It is too slow and memory hungry to be useful as a neural network implementation language for PCs.

Compilers now typically come with excellent integrated development environments, including mind-blowing debugging tools that largely eradicate any advantages that interpreters might have had in the past. This is illustrated in the section on debugging neural networks. The CaseNet development environment demonstrates how you can have a high-level, graphical, user interface with no sacrifice in speed. This gives you the best of both worlds: the user friendliness and flexibility of the interpretive environment coupled with the speed and efficiency of compiled code. It needs only a few seconds to compile and run the neural network from the specifications. It is therefore possible to have a highly interactive environment whereby the user can rapidly experiment with different neural network models.

Optimizing the Code . . . How to Make the Network Scream!

Why Optimize?

A hairs breadth often differentiates success from failure. The white-water experience is a good example. Anyone who has ridden the white waters of some wild river by kayak can appreciate that a matter of a few inches to the left or right of a rock can be crucial. If you go three inches to the left, the rock deflects your kayak down a smooth, safe path; if you go a few inches to the right, the sharp nose of the kayak is deflected the other way, to send you plummeting down a fatal cataract! With respect to neural networks, we mean that paying attention to fine detail in just a small portion of the code, can move you from a (unoptimized) system that fails to work satisfactorily to one that performs the task in an acceptable amount of time.

Optimizing Compilers

Wouldn't it be nice if all we had to do was hand our lousy programs to the optimizing compiler and have it figure out the best code? Optimizing compilers are steadily improving and are now generating respectable code. This is no easy job on the 80x86 based architecture! Perusing the back issues of popular technical journals, one can observe that compiler writers have made substantial progress in code quality over the past few years. See Walter Bright's article [74] for an excellent introduction to compiler optimization. Unfortunately, compilers haven't yet reached DWIM (Do What I Mean) optimization level. It *is* necessary, therefore, to write fairly decent code if you expect reasonable performance. Generally, compilers are good at optimizing things such as code fragments, register allocation, and loops, but it is still up to you to decide on the gross structures and algorithms of the solution. A good example from our back-propagation neural network code is that input patterns are stored in memory during training. Although this is a minor detail in terms of number of lines of code, it makes orders of magnitude difference to the network's performance because referencing a pattern vector in memory takes microseconds whereas getting it from disk could take milliseconds or more.

Generating Machine and Assembly Language Code

When have we hit the wall with optimizing compilers and when is it time to dust off the assembly language programmer's manual?

This is a difficult question to answer because compilers keep getting better (even as we write). At the moment, if you look at the code generated by a compiler, it is possible to squeeze a bit more speed out of it by some hand optimization. Optimizing trades off space against time: the faster the code the more space it takes up; the smaller the code the slower it runs. For neural networks, the space taken up by the code is quite tiny. We therefore want the most speed we can have without much concern for code space. To do this, you need a programming language tool that allows you to embed in-line assembly language statements. Without this you would have to call external functions each time you wanted to drop into assembly language. This negates the advantages of assembly language because a function call carries some overhead (push and pop parameters, save and restore registers).

Memory Limitations

The amount of storage needed to run a neural network is governed by the size of the executable code plus the size of the network (number of interconnections). A rule of thumb for estimating storage requirements is given in Fig. 4-4.

To speed training, patterns are read in *once* from the input device and stored in memory. An alternative, *much slower*, method is to repeatedly read the patterns from disk for each presentation to the network. Clearly, both techniques are valid. The trade-off is space against time. Storing all patterns simultaneously in memory is the faster method but it demands more storage. On the other hand, keeping patterns on disk is slower but uses less storage space. On machines with 32-bit addressing, such as the 80386, it's possible to use more sophisticated virtual memory techniques to run large networks. In this case the ultimate limit on network size is the speed of the processor.

Static versus Dynamic Storage

The simplest way to declare matrices for activation values and weights is with statements such as those in Fig. 4-12.

The weight vector w1 is a *static* variable. Storage is reserved for it when the program is loaded and remains in effect until the program exits to DOS.

```
#define NHIDDEN 16      /* number of hidden units */
#define NINPUT  192     /* number of input units  */

/* matrix input to hidden weights */
float w1[NHIDDEN][NINPUT];
```

Figure 4-12 Static storage of weights.

So What's the Problem?

This simple scheme has two problems. First, the size of w1 is fixed.
Each time you want a different number of output, hidden, or input
units, you have to edit the source code and recompile the program. The
source code must be available to the user, which poses a problem for
neural network developers in distributing their code. Users want to experiment with different sized networks without getting into programming. They should be able to enter the sizes of layers as parameters.

A second problem is that neural networks are memory hungry: 192
Kbytes were needed for weights and activation values for the example
we gave earlier. Total storage of twice this number, and more, is quickly
reached with bigger networks. This does not work on MS-DOS based
systems because of the 64-Kbyte segment limit imposed by the Intel
8086 architecture (bless their hearts for complicating our lives). Although PCs can have 640 Kbytes of storage or more, a matrix bigger than
64 Kbytes cannot efficiently be handled on the 8086. The architecture
of the microprocessor is based on segmented addressing. Each segment
is accessed via a segment base register and a 16-bit offset, limiting the
segment size to 64 Kbytes. Systems based on 80386 or 68000 microprocessors, which have a large linear address space, do not suffer from the
fixed length segment problem. On these systems, the simple static
model could therefore be used to define large arrays. However, the need
for variable sized arrays still applies, so dynamic storage is necessary
to take care of this, as explained in the next section.

Dynamic Storage for Vectors and Matrices

Dynamic arrays use storage most effectively and solve the problems
encountered with static arrays. Dynamic array sizes can be variable and
limited only by the amount of physical memory available. A vector is a
one-dimensional array, and a matrix is two dimensional. The C language directly supports one-dimensional arrays only. A matrix is declared as an array, with each element being an array.

How do you define a dynamic rather than a static array? The statement

```
float *w1;
```

declares w1 to be a pointer to a float value. In C there is no distinction between a pointer to a single element and a pointer to an array. Both are simply pointers (though the draft ANSI C standard does have stricter type checking, whereby these pointers would be regarded as different types). *w1 can be viewed as pointing to a single float value, or it can be viewed as pointing to an array of float values. When considered as an array, we can refer to the *i*th element as w1 [i]. In this case, w1 *looks* just like an array declared, for example, as

```
float w1[10];
```

However, the difference is that no *storage* has been set aside until we explicitly allocate it by using a call like

```
w1 = (float *) calloc(10, sizeof(float));
```

which allocates storage for an array of 10 float cells from the heap and sets w1 to point to that array.

Suppose we want a two-dimensional matrix. This could be declared, for example, as

```
float w1[10][20];
```

How do we make this a *dynamic* variable-sized matrix? In the static declaration, w1 is an array of 10 rows by 20 columns. To implement it, we need an array of 10 elements, where each element is a *pointer to* an array of 20 float elements. But for a variable-sized matrix, we don't know in advance what the actual size is going to be, so we want an array of unknown rows by unknown columns. This can easily be handled in C as follows. The statement

```
float **w1;
```

says that w1 is a pointer to ... a pointer to ... a float value; in other words, w1 is a doubly indirect pointer. Confused? You are not alone. After the second level of indirection, as far as I'm concerned, all pointers go off into the ether. I found that a diagram showing little boxes with arrows coming from other little boxes worked wonders for my understanding. Figure 4-13 shows how to visualize a two-dimensional matrix.

4. Software Tools

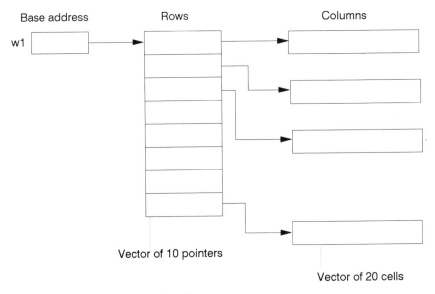

Base address   Rows   Columns

Vector of 10 pointers

Vector of 20 cells

Figure 4-13 Two-dimensional matrix.

To allocate storage for the two-dimensional matrix w1, we have to first allocate an array of 10 pointers (the rows), then allocate arrays of 20 float elements (for each of the columns). The statement

```
w1 = (float *) calloc(10, sizeof(float *));
```

sets w1 to *point to* an array of 10 cells, each cell holding a *pointer* to a float value; and the statement

```
for (i = 0; i < 10; i++)
    w1[i] = (float *) calloc(20, sizeof(float));
```

sets each element of w1 to point to an array of 20 float cells. The element in the *i*th row and *j*th column is referred to by w1[i][j], just as it would be for the static array. Therefore, once storage has been allocated, references to the array need not be aware of the particular storage allocation technique used. This makes for easy transparent use in programs.

What Does This Dynamic Storage Scheme Buy You?

We've solved both of the problems inherent to static storage. The size of w1 is no longer fixed (each time the program is run, we can specify different dimensions using variables, not just the 10 × 20 of the static case). Moreover, w1 can now be much bigger than 64 Kbytes because it is segmented. In Fig. 4-6, the array of pointers is defined as one segment, and each row of floating-point numbers is a segment. Each of these segments can be up to 64 Kbytes in size, so the total size of the w1 matrix can be very large. For full details on storage allocation, look at Listing 1 in Appendix A, lines 442–488.

Do You Really Need Floating Point?

Notice that in Listing 1, the back-propagation neural network is implemented in floating-point arithmetic. Is it possible to represent weights and activations as integer (or fixed-point) numbers? Or going the other way, is floating-point sufficiently accurate? Don't we perhaps need double-precision floating-point representation? There are two things to consider: dynamic range and number of significant digits. Floating point wins on both counts.

So why not just use floating point and be done with it? Speed. Also storage space. A neural network using integer arithmetic would be *much* faster on the PC than one using float, even with a math coprocessor. Representing network state with integer numbers takes up half the memory needed with floating-point numbers. Figure 4-14 compares some float and integer operations.

Making the Most of Coprocessors

In this section we discuss the 8087 math coprocessor for the PC. This is the cheapest math accelerator for the PC (although some ask why math coprocessors still cost $150—$450 when the cost of the microprocessor chip is way below that).

Most programmers never have to bother with the idiosyncrasies of the 8087 instruction set: It is much simpler to have the compiler take care of the details. However, the brave souls implementing code for embedded systems cannot afford this luxury. Arguably, the neural net-

	float	int
Word size (bytes)	4	2
192-16-2 Network (Kbytes)	192	96
Add (clock cycles)	85	2
Multiply	97	21
Divide	198	25
Store to memory	6	3

Figure 4-14 Comparing float and integer operations.

work developer belongs to the latter species. We therefore take a look at the 8087, bearing in mind that the principles can be extended to other math coprocessors.

In spite of the glowing terms in which optimizing compilers were described earlier, treatment of the math chip by some compilers is rather shoddy. One benefit of debuggers is that you get to view the compiler's generated code. It is clear from this that substantial improvements in speed can be achieved in neural network performance by optimizing just the 8087 code. To illustrate this, consider the *inner product* operation we looked at earlier (Fig. 4-3). The assembly language output of a certain C compiler is shown in Fig. 4-15.

Apart from the fact that the C code, which consisted of just two lines, has exploded to more than 30 lines of assembly language code, several operations are unnecessarily repeated each time through the loop. For example, the value of sum is computed by the coprocessor and stored in memory. The statements

```
FLD   . . .
FSTP  . . .
```

are unnecessary because the value of sum is needed only within the 8087 coprocessor and can be held in the internal stack. There is no need to store and load it from memory each time around the loop. Another example is that the contents of the variable called h don't change anywhere in this loop (h is loop invariant); therefore, it is a waste of time to compute repeatedly the address of the vector w1[h]. If the dimension of the vector is large and if this inner product is repeated many times within other loops in the system, the unoptimized code can begin to contribute significantly to degrading the neural network performance.

Debugging Networks

There are two major aspects to debugging networks. The first is the network architecture or paradigm used. If you select the wrong architecture, the network will not train correctly. Debugging network architectures is briefly discussed in Chapter 8. This level of debugging is largely a matter of treating the network as a black box and observing its performance.

The second aspect of debugging is the implementation. Does the code implement the chosen neural network correctly? In this section we consider this second problem. We need to take the network apart and examine its anatomy intimately by looking at the actual machine instructions in the implementation.

```
; for (i = 0;  i < nInputNodes;  i++)
      mov   word ptr [bp-378],0              ; i = 0
      jmp   short L66                        ;
; sum += w1[h][i] * out0[p][i];
      L65:
      mov   ax,di                            ; h
      shl   ax,1                             ;
      shl   ax,1                             ; h << 2
      les   bx,dword ptr DGROUP:_w1          ; w1
      add   bx,ax                            ; w1 + h
      les   bx,dword ptr es:[bx]             ; w1[h]
      mov   ax,word ptr [bp-378]             ; i
      shl   ax,1                             ;
      shl   ax,1                             ; i << 2
      add   bx,ax                            ; w1[h] + i
      FLD   dword ptr es:[bx]                ; w1[h][i]
      mov   ax,word ptr [bp-376]             ; p
      shl   ax,1                             ;
      shl   ax,1                             ; p << 2
      les   bx,dword ptr DGROUP:_out0        ; out0
      add   bx,ax                            ; out0 + p
      les   bx,dword ptr es:[bx]             ; out0[p]
      mov   ax,word ptr [bp-378]             ; i
      shl   ax,1                             ;
      shl   ax,1                             ; i << 2
      add   bx,ax                            ; out0[p] + i
      FLD   dword ptr es:[bx]                ; out0[p][i]
      FMUL                                   ; w1[h][i] * out0[p][i]
      FLD   dword ptr [bp-402]               ; sum
      FADD                                   ; sum += w1[h][i] * out0[p][i]
      FSTP  dword ptr [bp-402]               ;
      FWAIT                                  ;
      inc   word ptr [bp-378]                ; i++

      L66:
      mov   ax,word ptr [bp-378]             ; i
      cmp   ax,word ptr [bp-368]             ; i < nInputNodes
      jl    L65                              ;
```

Figure 4-15 Assembly language code generated for INNER PRODUCT.

The excellent debugging tools available with C compilers are useful in testing and verifying the correct operation. It is possible to step through the program and examine its state at any point. The contents of variables and registers can be examined or changed at breakpoints in the program. This way you can quickly find out what is going on and correct the code.

Another approach is to place *assert* statements in the code at critical checkpoints. An assert statement is embedded in the program to verify a given condition at that step of the computation. This can ensure, for example, that a number is within the allowable range expected by the program. If the condition fails, the program executes an error routine and exits. Assertion checking can reveal bugs that otherwise lurk in the woodwork. Such bugs may show up only when unusual combinations of patterns are presented.

CHAPTER 5

Development Environments

Roy W. Dobbins
Russell C. Eberhart

Introduction

In this chapter we discuss neural network development environments for personal computers and describe one such environment, CaseNet [9], in detail. In the previous chapter, we examined the basic tools for implementing and running neural networks on PCs; now we explore ways to extend these principles to higher level, more powerful modeling tools. We incorporate ideas from artificial intelligence, simulation, and software development into neural network development environments.

Because neural networks are evolving so rapidly, we can do no more than take a snapshot of current events as they flash past. Several research directions are simultaneously influencing the evolution of development environments:

1. Researchers are inventing new neural network models and need to experiment with these models. The process of implementing models should be rapid and efficient, if we are to progress effectively in the neural network field.
2. Scientists and engineers are inventing new hardware neural network chips or coprocessor boards and need to integrate them with software systems.
3. Powerful artificial intelligence (AI) languages and environments are increasingly available on small, cheap computers [71]. Such tools can be used as the basis for neural networks, allowing us to build on established principles.

Neural Network PC Tools

4. Software development environments for personal computers, including graphics and computer-aided software engineering (CASE) tools [79], enable these traditional software tools to evolve toward intelligent development environments for neural networks. We expect to see a fusing of AI, software tools, and other approaches, which will make neural network development more powerful.

Although these influences make for some dynamic, exciting events to come in the world of neural networks, we expect that the principles of environments as we see them today will endure and be useful for some time before they are eventually replaced by newer and better developments in neural networks. We can think of environments as being the "second wave" of neural network research. The first wave is the development and analysis of neurobiological and engineering models. The second wave is the refinement and implementation of these models by using software and hardware tools.

What is a Neural Network Development Environment?

A neural network development environment has most of the features developers have come to expect in software development environments for PCs such as:

- Editors
- Compilers
- Interpreters
- Linkers
- Library managers
- Debuggers
- Spreadsheets
- Databases
- Graphics
- Word processors
- Communications

These tools will be integrated into the development environment so that neural network software can be developed easily. But, in addition, neural network development environments should share something in common with AI—simulation and modeling packages that do the following:

- Provide languages and tools to model systems
- Specify dynamics
- Run experiments
- Acquire sensory data

- Transmit motor signals
- Analyze results
- Display and graph results

A neural network development environment should incorporate these concepts and adapt available tools to the needs of neural networks.

Let's see what characteristics such an environment should have. After defining the "ideal" neural network development environment, we look at several state-of-the-art environments for PCs.

Desirable Characteristics of Development Environments

A development environment, whether for production software, AI, or neural networks, should strive to include the following key characteristics:

- Easy to use
- Powerful
- Efficient
- Extensible

We now consider how these characteristics apply to neural networks.

Easy To Use

A neural network environment should be a user friendly system for specifying and executing network models. The user interface should support both novice and advanced users. It should be easy for the novice to become familiar with the system. The software should be menu driven, with context-sensitive pop-up help screens and other user interface features that make it easy to learn and use. At the same time, it should support the advanced user in accomplishing more complex tasks. This is what developers have come to expect as a minimum capability of any software development environment. The user interface should be simple and intuitive, allowing the researcher to think and work entirely in terms of neural network models, without being distracted by idiosyncrasies of operating systems or computer hardware implementations of the models.

Powerful

Using the environment, you want to choose from predefined neural network paradigms or specify the attributes of new neural network models; execute a network; monitor and control the network; transfer patterns and weights into and out of the network; couple the network via pipelines to other processes (including other neural networks); display the state of the network; and set learning and operating parameters. The environment should be powerful enough to allow you to do these things.

Efficient

Neural networks demand that we use computers as efficiently as possible. Large neural networks require enormous amounts of computation, which may preclude them from being run on less powerful personal computers. However, some problems can be solved on PCs if we extract all their available processing power. We must eliminate badly structured code. Because of the iterative nature of neural network solutions, every microsecond of execution time, summed over thousands of iterations and thousands of processing elements, can make a substantial difference to a network's response and overall training time.

Similar arguments apply to the use of storage. Neural networks require large amounts of storage, and memory is always a precious resource, no matter how many megabytes you have. The trend toward more powerful development environments requires sophisticated and memory-hungry software. Hence, there is a need to be as efficient as possible in use of storage.

Efficiency also applies to coprocessor targets. Even if you have a superfast multimegaflop parallel processor in your PC, you still have to make it work effectively, especially in transferring information between processors, because parallel systems are typically limited by communications channel bandwidth.

Moreover, neural network applications are often embedded in large real-time multitasking systems, and the neural network process itself may claim only a small fraction of available computation time while other tasks in the system consume the rest. So, even in a large, powerful computer system, there is a demand for optimized code.

Extensible

For a system, extensibility means that it is able to do things not foreseen when it was originally designed and built. A simple example is the ability to define new procedures or functions that are made available as primitive constructs.

In neural networks, extensibility means being able to define network primitives that allow you to build new types of networks that are not possible without those primitives. We cannot predict what kinds of networks may be needed in the future and have to provide the mechanisms to handle this uncertainty. Extensibility is one of the key features of AI languages such as Lisp and Prolog [70]; similar techniques are needed for neural networks.

Why a Development Environment?

For many applications of neural networks, there is a need to explore different network architectures and paradigms. For example, in the electroencephalogram (EEG) spike and seizure detection work [9], we were entering uncharted waters and therefore wanted to try several radically different approaches. Generally, to do this kind of experimentation, a neural network must be hand coded and debugged for each new application. Many researchers are faced with the problem of developing their own neural network software, and the time spent on this activity detracts from the actual application modeling and simulation.

An environment can solve these problems by making it quick and easy to build a new network model, experiment, and get immediate feedback, so that the results of a proposed model can be evaluated. A development environment is needed in experimental situations in which you want to try new ideas. The environment should support a rich set of tools for monitoring, debugging, and controlling the network. If these tools are not readily available, then we either have to hand code them from scratch or do without them. An environment can also provide libraries of previously tried and tested paradigms, in the form of reuseable modules. An environment for the PC, supported by standard interfaces, allows researchers to exchange models, tools, and utilities.

To identify the needs for a neural network development environment, it is useful to look at the possible stages of neural network development that a particular researcher might go through in arriving at a solution. We think there are roughly three phases of evolution:

- Hand-coded neural network
- Neural network paradigm library
- Generalized neural network model

Hand-Coded Neural Network

We call the first stage the hand-coding phase (Fig. 5-1). To solve a particular problem, the researcher must select a paradigm and then hand code the implementation on the computer to arrive at a system. We don't address the issue of whether this solves the problem or whether it is an optimal solution. We assume that the researcher has made an intelligent choice of paradigm and that the only question is

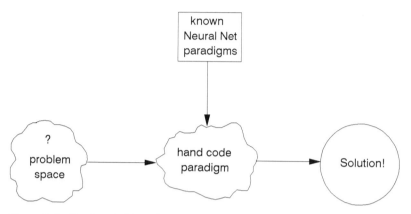

Figure 5-1   Hand-coded neural network.

how to go about getting it implemented on a computer. This develop-ment phase is characterized by the material in the previous chapter on neural network software, in which we built a back-propagation neural network from the ground up.

Neural Network Paradigm Library

The second stage in the evolution of neural network development is the use of a neural network paradigm library (Fig. 5-2). The neural net-work developer makes available a set of useful paradigms, from which the researcher selects the most appropriate paradigm to solve the prob-lem, and a neural network implementation is automatically built. It is thus easy for the researcher to implement a neural network solution for a given problem because someone else has already done the work in developing the library. By selecting a paradigm, the user is in effect extracting a code skeleton from the library and filling slots with code fragments to implement variable attributes of the network (e.g., number of slabs). The work on CaseNet I, described later in this chapter, is an example of this development phase.

Generalized Neural Network Model

The third stage in neural network evolution is the use of a general-ized neural network model (Fig. 5-3). It allows the researcher to visu-alize and build any conceivable network, not just those that have been defined as paradigms in the library. Neural network models are also discussed in some detail in this chapter.

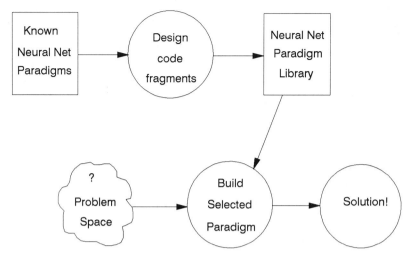

Figure 5-2 Neural network paradigm library.

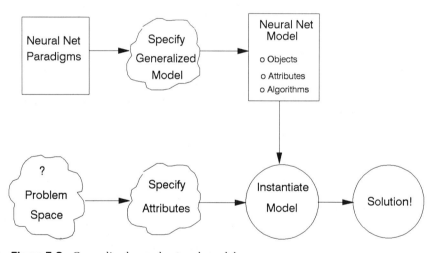

Figure 5-3 Generalized neural network model.

Introduction to Network Modeling Languages

The role of language in specifying networks is important. Without a language you cannot formally or rigorously specify anything. A formal language for describing neural networks is needed to evaluate and re-produce research results.

To date, no such language has emerged. This is not at all surprising, considering that some conventional low-level programming languages have taken a decade or more to become widely accepted as standards. For example, the C programming language had been defined and used as a practical tool by the early 1970s but did not gain wide acceptance for at least 10 years. Emergence of high-level languages for describing neural networks is therefore likely to take some time. Let's consider the chief characteristics of such languages.

Neural networks can be described at roughly three language levels:

- High-level specification languages
- Intermediate-level parallel processing languages
- Low-level conventional programming languages

Specification Languages

At the highest level, a network can be described by using a specification language. You specify the network architecture, activation function, learning and update rules, as described in the later section on specifying neural network models. At this level, the network is specified in terms of its attributes, without describing implementation details. This level is the most abstract. The notation is compact and easy to read. We are saying *what* the neural network looks like without cluttering the description with implementation details. The specification is declarative not procedural. It can and should also be formal so that the network model can be analyzed and validated. It is desirable to be able to generate neural network implementations automatically from the specification. This is not the most important feature, though it is certainly a bonus.

Examples of languages that could be used are Prolog [70], Lisp, and high-level requirements specification languages [87, 91]. This theme is explored in some detail later in this chapter.

Parallel Processing and Object-Oriented Languages

At an intermediate level, we have parallel processing languages and object-oriented languages for implementing neural networks. Typically, these are general-purpose languages with constructs for dealing with parallel processing concepts such as tasks and matrices (examples are Ada, ANSPEC, occam, and C + +). Parallel processing languages are appealing because they can easily express the concurrent actions needed in neural networks. Object-oriented languages allow definition of general neural network classes, from which new network types can be derived [92].

Conventional Programming Languages

Finally, at the lowest level, we have conventional programming languages. Here you are completely on your own. You have to build the network from the ground up. Problems such as parallel tasks, matrix manipulation, graphics, and file I/O must all be taken care of, though you may get some help from function libraries. We have flexibility, but the details involved (many of which have nothing to do with neural networks) make the software difficult to work with. It is not easy to deduce what the program is supposed to do or what kind of neural network model it is by looking at the code. A typical model at this level (BATCHNET. C) is described in detail in the previous chapter (typical examples are C, Pascal, and native code assembler).

A Brief Survey of Neural Network Modeling Languages

Unlike development environments, there have been very few language implementations for neural network applications. This is to be expected in a field that has only recently attracted widespread interest. Because a language is an abstraction of a subject area, it takes time to formalize and generalize concepts so that they can be expressed in a consistent way. It is much easier to roll up your sleeves and start hacking a neural network model that "works" than it is to come up with a formal specification of the model that is general enough to be used in a broad range of situations.

AXON (HNC, San Diego, CA)

AXON is a neural network definition language with features found in von Neumann languages such as C or Pascal, augmented with functions for handling vectors and other neural net specifics.

ANSPEC (SAIC, San Diego, CA)

This is an actor-based language for specifying neural networks. The specification is translated into an intermediate virtual level where the simulated system is tested, then compiled for a particular target system—for example, SAIC's Delta Floating Point Processor. Actors are more suitable for modeling large-scale multiprocessing systems than the fine-grained interactions of PDP. There is a semantic gap here. In specifying a neural network model, you have to think in terms of actors, then visualize how that can be mapped onto the desired neurodelike structures. What is needed is a higher level language more directly suited to specifying neural networks.

Specifying Neural Network Models

In the previous section, we looked at language tools for describing and implementing neural networks. We now show how these tools can be used to specify generalized neural network models.

What is needed to specify a neural network model? Figure 5-4 lists the objects and attributes of a network. The diagram is presented as a tree structure showing relationships between attributes. It is intended to serve as a framework for further discussion and to stimulate discussion of neural network models and the tools needed to specify them. Our approach to modeling neural networks is based on *information modeling*, as proposed in [73]. An information model describes objects, attributes of objects, and relationships between objects. Information modeling has proved to be valuable as an analysis tool in databases, expert systems, real-time process control systems and many other applications. It is also a promising tool for describing and formalizing neural network models.

The graphical model of Fig. 5-4 can also be written in text form as a set of predicates, as in Fig. 5-5. This is another way of expressing the same idea (see [73, p. 28] for the notation used). Figure 5-5 is a formal representation of the abstract model, which we will show later in this chapter to be easily translated using Prolog into working code. For the moment, we are concerned with a simple model for specifying networks. These networks can be implemented on a variety of target machines, using the abstract specification. In this way neural networks can be formal, portable objects.

Each predicate in Fig. 5-5 corresponds to an object in Fig. 5-4. For example, the statement

```
model(architecture, update_rule, environment).
```

says that there is an object called model that has several attributes, called architecture, update_rule, and environment. Other statements that follow this in Fig. 5-5 describe the characteristics of these attributes. We can describe a complete model and establish a vocabulary for talking about neural networks.

Further details are needed to complete the descriptions of objects such as backprop_algorithm, activation_timing_rule, and learning_timing_rule in Fig. 5-5, but the principles are similar. The resulting specification can be as detailed as you care to make it. For example, the backprop predicate can be specified down to the level of the learning equations.

Relationships between objects and attributes can be structured in several ways to reflect different model types. For example, some people may regard update rule as an attribute of slab, not of network and activation

Neural Network Model:
- Architecture
    - Slabs
        - Processing elements
            - Activation values
            - Thresholds
            - Local storage
        - Activation functions
        - Learning rule
            - Learning algorithm
            - Learning rate
            - Momentum factor
    - Bundles
        - Source slab
        - Destination slab
        - Connectivity
        - Connection Weights
- Update rule
    - activation timing rule
    - learning timing rule
- Environment
        - Input rule
        - Output rule
        - Event rules

Figure 5-4   Neural network attributes.


```
model(architecture, update_rule, environment).
architecture(slabs, bundles).
slab(processing_elements, activation_function, learning_rule).
processing_element(activation_value, threshold, local_store).
activation_value.
threshold.
local_store.
activation_function(sigmoid).
learning_rule(backprop).
backprop(backprop_algorithm, learning_rate, momentum_factor).
backprop_algorithm.
learning_rate.
momentum_factor.
bundle(source, destination, connectivity, links).
link(weight).
weight.
update_rule(activation_timing_rule, learning_timing_rule).
activation_timing_rule.
learning_timing_rule.
environment(input_rule, output_rule, event_rule).
input_rule.
output_rule.
event_rule.
```

Figure 5-5   Neural network predicates.

function as an attribute of processing element, not of slab. But the goal is to develop a model that is sufficiently general and powerful to be able to describe any neural network. For more details on information modeling consult [73].

Let's briefly discuss some of these attributes and see how they could be used to construct a generalized neural network model.

Specifying Network Architecture

Network architecture is a specification of the slabs in a network and the bundles of interconnections between slabs. Architecture also describes how a neural network is coupled to its environment, including the number and ordering of input nodes and output nodes.

A *slab* is a group of processing elements that share the same activation function and learning rule, and have similarly ordered connection topologies. Individual processing elements in turn have attributes such as activation values and thresholds. Similarly, a *bundle* is a group of connections between elements of slabs, and individual connections have attributes such as weights (Fig. 5-6).

Neural networks composed of several layers are adequate for many applications, but the layer concept is too restrictive to allow us to experiment with new architectures. A slab, on the other hand, is a more convenient and more general concept. We can build more powerful networks out of slabs than out of layers. Slabs are connected in order to achieve the processing interactions needed for a specific network

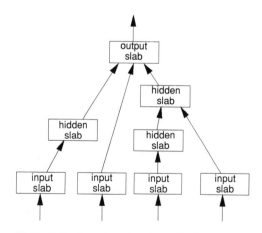

Figure 5-6   Generic network architecture.

model. Using slabs, we can construct any imaginable network topology, whereas, with layers, we are restricted to ordered layers of elements.

Activation Functions

The *activation function* is an algorithm for computing the activation value of a processing element as a function of its inputs and the weights or connection strengths. Because processing elements are grouped into slabs, it is more common to assign the same activation function to all elements in a slab rather than to individual elements.

Learning Rules

The *learning rule* is an algorithm for adjusting the connection weights. For example, back-propagation uses the generalized delta rule. Because the learning rule is an attribute of slab, the rule specifies the learning behavior of the slab. The rule typically adjusts the weights by using information, such as the activation values of processing elements. With this scheme all processing elements of a slab apply the same learning rule, but different slabs could have different learning rules.

Specifying the Environment

To be useful, a neural network must interact with some environments. Objects in the environment provide sensory inputs to the neural network and receive motor signals from it. The environment must be specified in detail and all input/output flows from the neural network defined [72]. For more on this topic, see Chapter 3.

Not only do we have to describe how the neural network is coupled to the environment, but we also have to describe the behavior of the environment. One could expect the environment to have attributes that specify rules for producing the input signals and rules for processing outputs. To complete the environment model, a specification of events is also needed.

Update Rules

Update rules have been described as rules for specifying when processing elements apply their activation functions. This is not a complete model of reality, however. Accordingly, attributes for update rules must include timing for learning rules too.

Neural Network Paradigms

A paradigm is a particular choice of network attributes—architecture, activation and learning rules, update procedure, and so on—that exhibits a certain type of behavior (see Fig. 5-4). Back propagation is a paradigm because it implies a certain set of attributes, for example, the architecture and the learning rule. A paradigm is a "canned" set of choices for all attributes. You can invent a new paradigm by putting together a set of attributes that completely define the intended behavior of the network.

A Brief Survey of Neural Network Development Environments

In this section we look at some development environments, focusing on those that run on the PC. However, some systems that don't run on PCs offer a glimpse of what future PC environments might evolve toward. The systems reviewed have a considerable range in capability, from simple ones with a single predefined neural network type to comprehensive systems that allow you to create your own neural networks.

Disclaimer: The following is not an exhaustive list of environments, nor is it a detailed account of every feature. We present highlights from a few environments that reflect the state of the art. New environments are most certainly going to be developed before this book appears in print, and some currently available environments have been excluded. This does not imply that one package is better than another. To the best of our knowledge, the information presented is accurate at the time of going to press. However, new releases may substantially alter the capabilities of the packages presented.

Plexi (Symbolics, Inc., Burlington, MA)

This is a comprehensive and powerful system, which is not surprising because of the underlying Lisp machine. It has many useful features to support both the advanced user who wants to experiment with new models and the novice user who wants to use predefined networks. It takes full advantage of the high-resolution bit-mapped display in providing a graphical user interface. This is an expensive system that is not available for the PC, but it's the one to look for in the future as a model for PC environments.

The graphical network editor allows you to represent architecture by clicking on layer icons and connecting layers via bundles. Network behavior can be observed with several graphical tools, including Hinton diagrams, graphs, and scatter plots. Attributes can be specified for learning rules, activation functions, update rules, and so on, but default values are also provided. The package includes several standard network paradigms and allows you to define your own. This package lets you do almost anything with neural networks. However, you must be a Lisp programmer to take full advantage of it. Also, if you use any with the exception of the canned paradigms or default parameters, you need to fully understand the implications. This is a sharp tool, but you should know how to handle it.

Neuroshell (Ward Systems Group, Frederick, MD)

While it may be at the other end of the spectrum from Plexi (in power, flexibility and price), Neuroshell is nevertheless a useful, straightforward system for running neural network applications. With this package, which incorporates a built-in back-propagation model, you can be up and running your application very quickly. It is simple to use and is backed up with some insightful examples that you can walk through and experiment with. The version of the software we saw has a nice utility for viewing the results graphically. Trends and relationships between factors can be seen by plotting the data in several ways.

NEURALWORKS PROFESSIONAL II
(Neuralware Inc, Pittsburgh, PA)

This comprehensive but expensive package, with a graphical user interface, gives you a lot of flexibility to create networks and choose from a large range of predefined network types, and to specify parameters such as the number of layers and number of nodes. The network is shown on the graphics screen with each individual neurode and each individual link. This makes the screen look rather busy. The network architecture can be edited on the graphics screen. You can train or test the network using standard format binary or ASCII files or user-written C functions to preprocess the data. You can choose instruments to display outputs while the network runs, using several formats including strip charts and histograms, while probes let you look inside the network at weights, hidden activations, Hinton diagrams, and so on.

NETSET II (HNC, San Diego, CA)

This package runs on the PC under Microsoft windows. NETSET uses small, graphical icons representing objects, laid out left to right on the screen connected by arrows.

NETSET has a nice way of presenting a system level data flow diagram. You model your system by graphically drawing icons, such as databases, pipes, Dynamic Data Exchange, data transformers, neural nets, and graph display devices. You connect these objects with 1–1, or 1–many relationships, with arrows depicting the direction of information flow.

Having drawn the system data flow diagram, you then specify the details of the processes, including layouts of data files, data types of each field, and predefined formats such as DIF and dBASE III+. To specify a neural network object, you choose from 19 canned neural network paradigms.

A nice feature is the idea of "styles," which are user-defined instances of any of the objects at any level. You can define a style, even the whole application system, and save it with a name for reuse.

N-NET 210 (AI Ware, Cleveland, OH)

This system is limited to two built-in proprietary algorithms for supervised and unsupervised learning. The development system allows you to set parameters for your application, train, and test the network. It does not support a graphical environment.

The "process" concept, allowing several networks to be linked, is rather neat, but an automatic connection between processes is not currently done. You edit a process object (neural network) in a text window and enter the names of the input and output files that it reads from and writes to. The C library allows you to embed neural networks in other applications.

CaseNet: A Neural Network Development Environment

Anatomy of CaseNet

CaseNet is a development environment for PCs developed by the authors [9]. Various general-purpose parallel processing system simulators have been proposed that have generally been interpretive systems requiring large-scale or special-purpose processors, such as Lisp machines to achieve reasonable performance. Although such simulation systems may be useful for some applications, they have not been usable on personal computers.

A large class of problems can be effectively solved on personal computers, provided that the neural network software is well structured and reasonably well optimized. The CaseNet approach is to generate highly optimized machine code from the user's network specifications in order to maximize the performance of the available computing machinery [9].

A second problem with the simulators that has been proposed is that they are language driven, presenting a complex command language that takes time to master and use effectively. Instead, CaseNet provides a graphical interface that allows the user to draw the network architecture on a graphics screen and enter network attributes from menus on the screen. The network graph, together with the attributes attached to the nodes of the graph, form the network specification, from which executable code is automatically and quickly generated.

To achieve these goals, CASE and neural network code generation tools are used to translate the specified neural network model into executable code. This section describes the basic CASE tools and mechanisms used by CaseNet to automate neural network generation. Examples are given that illustrate typical applications using back-propagation networks, a paradigm well suited to EEG and similar classification or recognition applications. Other types of networks, in particular Kohonen's self-organizing models, are being incorporated into the development environment.

CaseNet, as described here, is in use to generate working neural networks in EEG spike and seizure detection [9] and other applications. Ways to optimize code for numeric coprocessors are under development. Once debugged, the code generator can reliably and quickly generate different kinds of network architecture to suit researchers' needs. This approach can easily be extended to radically different neural network paradigms. CaseNet is currently being extended to address the generalized network model described in Fig. 5-4.

CaseNet Components

The CaseNet system consists of four major sets of tools: the network definer, the analyzer, the code generator, and the compiler. Figure 5-7 illustrates the CaseNet system components. The network definer is a graphical network editor for drawing the desired network architecture. The editor (CADSYS) and postprocessor (NETPARSE) translate the user's graphics into a formal representation (NET.DEF). The analyzer validates this network definition and extracts essential network attributes. The code generator parses the network definition and emits code fragments (*.G files). The compiler builds the executable network from the code fragments and a generic network skeleton (NETGEN.C and NETGEN.H). The results of each phase of the network translation of

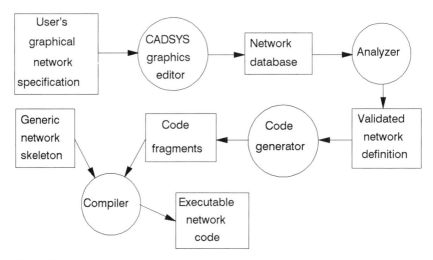

Figure 5-7 CaseNet components.

Fig. 5-7 are available as intermediate files, which the advanced user can edit to customize or optimize any level of the network. The novice or ordinary application user does not have to fiddle with these files.

These tools are described in detail in the following sections, with examples of use.

Graphical Network Editor

Graphical Network Specification

The architecture of a generic neural network can be defined graphically by using a few simple concepts (see Fig. 5-6). CADSYS is a data flow diagram editor that is used to build a graphical executable model of the neural network. To define the network, the user places slab icons on the graphics screen with simple mouse commands and connections between slabs by drawing directed arrows. The diagram is annotated with the slab identifiers and number of units (Fig. 5-6). With CADSYS you can easily edit the diagram by adding, deleting, and moving objects with the mouse.

CADSYS stores the data flow diagram as a set of relational database files. The diagram consists of processing elements (slabs) and connections between elements. The files are stored in the network project directory. The database files store information about the graphical representation of the diagrams, the objects appearing on the diagram (slabs), and relationships between objects (connections). Let's see how the parser uses these files to produce a formal definition of a network. For more information about the structure and content of the database files, consult the CADSYS user's guide [83].

Network Parser

The database parser NETPARSE translates the relational database representation of the network graphics drawing into the formal neural network definition. The parser predigests the database on behalf of the analyzer because the files contain information that is not relevant to neural network architecture. Also, the database files are not particularly easy to work with. Hence, the job of the parser is to present the network relationships in a more readable way.

An example of the resulting specification for a three-layer backpropagation network follows:

```
slab(1,48).    connect(5,1).    inputs([1,2,3,4]).
slab(2,48).    connect(5,2).    outputs([6]).
slab(3,48).    connect(5,3).
slab(4,48).    connect(5,4).
slab(5,16).    connect(6,5).
slab(6,4).
```

The statement

```
slab(id, number of units).
```

creates a slab with a unique identifier and number of processing elements. The identifier is used to specify the slab in any further computations. The set of slab() statements is a complete specification of all nodes in the network. The predicate

```
connect(destination, source).
```

establishes a path from the source slab to the destination slab. The set of connect() statements specifies all connections in the network. The analyzer uses these facts to check that the network has no cycles or isolated nodes, necessary conditions for feedforward networks [2,4,5]. The predicates

```
inputs(list of input slabs).
outputs(list of output slabs).
```

create connections from the neural network to the outside world and specify the order in which inputs are attached to processing elements (in cases that have more than one input slab).

NETPARSE is a dBASE III+ program [80], compiled using Clipper [81]. It uses the following database files as input:

PROCESS.DBF List of processes indexed by process id. Defines all processing elements in the network. Because the network is leveled, we need the subset of primitive processes only from this. This is the actual set of slabs that comprise the neural network.

FDFLOWS.DBF List of flows; defines all connections between processing elements of the network. Indexed by flow name for generating ordered I/O lists.

FDIAGRAM.DBF List of objects on the diagram indexed by diagram id. Defines all diagrams in the leveled set. The top level (context) has id = 0. Lower levels have id of the exploded process from the higher level. Primitive (lowest level) processes have no entries in this file.

Network Definition Algorithm

The algorithm currently has four passes. This could probably be made more efficient if a better language than dBASE III+ were used (or maybe I'm just a hacker, overlooking the way things should be done). But each pass through the database extracts some relevant attribute of the network and generates a set of completed predicates. Note that this is a fairly dumb translation (lack of sophistication of dBASE III+ cited) and does very little analysis of the network—definitely a case of garbage in, garbage out. If you, the user, have drawn nonsense on the graphics screen, you will get nonsense predicates out of the parser. It is left to the Prolog analyzer (to be described in the next section) to make some formal sense out of the network definition.

Pass 1. Generate the Slab() Predicates

Search PROCESS.DBF for all primitive processes. For each primitive process, prints the predicate

```
slab(id, size).
```

where id is the process id and size is the number of units in the slab.

Pass 2. Generate the Connect() Predicates

Search PROCESS.DBF for all primitive processes, as before. For each primitive process, search FDFLOWS.DBF (in flow id sequence) for all flows with the process as its destination and print

```
connect(id, sourceid).
```

where id is the destination process id and sourceid is the id of the source process.

Pass 3. Generate the Learn() Predicates

Search PROCESS.DBF for all primitive processes as in pass 1. For each primitive process, prints the predicate

$$learn(id, eta, alpha).$$

where id is the process id, and eta and alpha are numbers in the name field. If any lexical or syntax errors are detected in the name field, the predicate is omitted (causing selection of default values at runtime for eta and alpha).

Pass 4. Generate the Inputs() and Outputs() Predicates

Search FDFLOWS.DBF (in name sequence). For each flow, if the source is a primitive process and the destination is an external entity, adds the process to the list of outputs; or if the process is the destination and the source is an external, adds the process to the list of inputs. Prints the list of inputs and outputs as the predicates

```
inputs([list of input processes]).
outputs([list of output processes]).
```

Note that the flows are processed in name sequence so that the user can specify I/O ordering by annotating the diagram.

Network Analyzer

The analyzer and code generator NETGEN are automated tools, written in Prolog, to validate the network definition (NET.DEF) and generate executable code. The analyzer and code generator are analogous to compilers for conventional programming languages. Usually the first pass of the compiler is the syntax analyzer. If the user's program is syntactically correct, an internal representation of the program is constructed and handed to the second pass, which is the code generator. Although it's bundled as one program, we discuss it as two separate tools for convenience. In this section we describe the analyzer; the code generator is described in the next section.

The analyzer is passed the file NET.DEF, the network definition file (generated by NETPARSE). The analyzer checks that a valid (syntactically correct) neural network architecture has been defined. Two important facts are that all nodes are properly connected and, for a feedforward network, that there are no feedback cycles. These facts are easily established using Prolog. To search all slabs of the network and check that each slab is connected, the predicates

```
connected(X, X).
connected(X, Y) :- connect(X, Y).
connected(X, Y) :- connect(X, Z), connected(Z, Y).
```

define the transitive closure of the connect() facts in the database to recursively determine connections in the network.

The analyzer detects cycles by using the connect() facts to visit all slabs in the network, as in the predicates

```
cyclic(X, Visited) :- member(X, Visited).
cyclic(X, Visited) :- connect(X, Y), cyclic(Y, [X | Visited]).
```

The search is performed depth first, starting at the output layer.

Note that the words *node* and *slab* are often used in this section to mean the same thing. The word *layer* is also often used interchangeably with *slab*. Strictly speaking there are no layers, but the term *input layer* is taken to mean a slab or several slabs that have direct connections from the outside world.

fanin(X, L). constructs the list L of fan-in slabs for the slab X. This rather simple predicate is crucial for the analysis of neural networks because fan-in to a node is needed in computing connectivity as well as traversing the network.

inputlayer(X). identifies X as an input layer if it is a member of the inputs() list.

outputlayer(X). identifies X as an output layer if it is a member of the outputs() list.

hiddenlayer(X). X is a hidden layer if it is neither an input layer nor an output layer.

The network validation is by no means bullet proof. For example, there is currently no check for the existence of hidden layers (mandatory for the back-propagation paradigm). However, this can be defined quite easily in Prolog, in terms of the hiddenlayer(X) predicate just described.

Errors in Network Definition

If NETGEN detects an error, it prints an error message and quits. Possible error messages are

Network has isolated nodes. One or more nodes in the network are improperly connected to neighboring nodes. Each node in the network must be connected via some path from the input layer through to the output layer.

Network has cycles. Feedback paths are not allowed in a feedforward network. Paths through the graph from input layer to output layer must be strictly feedforward.

Experiences in Using Turbo-Prolog

Prolog is ideally suited to processing recursive data structures such as the network graph. It is much more difficult (but not impossible) to do the same thing in other languages such as C. Prolog is also ideal for parsing and syntax analysis tasks required now. Much more sophisticated processing can easily be added when demanded, without a change in philosophy. This is difficult to do with lower level languages such as C. Turbo–Prolog [82] has an excellent environment for testing and debugging the analyzer. It is thus relatively easy to develop and maintain the analyzer as it evolves.

Network Code Generator

The code generator parses the validated network definition and emits C code fragments (*. G files). Each code fragment corresponds to a particular net task:

alloclay.g   Dynamic storage allocation for net layers
deflayer.g   Define names of net layers
deltahid.g   Compute deltas of hidden layers
deltanet.g   Compute delta of net output layer
freelaye.g   Free dynamic storage for layers
netout.g   Iterate network
readpats.g   Read patterns into network
readtgts.g   Read targets
readwts.g   Read weights
sumerror.g   Compute sum squared error
weights.g   Compute change of weights
writenet.g   Write network output layer
writewts.g   Write weights

NETGEN redirects I/O to the appropriate *.g file before invoking the code-emitting predicate, closes the file afterward, and goes on to the next code emitter, and so on until all code fragments have been completed. Individual code emitters can easily be debugged without I/O redirection by calling the predicate directly in the Turbo–Prolog interpreter. The generated code can then be viewed interactively on the screen.

Each C code fragment consists of a (small) generic code skeleton with several uninstantiated parameter slots. The Prolog code generator unifies the parameters with the particular network architecture being defined. Typical parameters are

X, Y   name of the slab, fan-in slab
N, M   size of the slab, fan-in slab

For example, the parameterized code fragment for the "iterate net" task is

```
float sum = BiasX[i];
for (j = 0; j < N; j++)
  sum += wX[j] * outY[p][j];
outX[p][i] = 1 / (1 + exp(-sum));
```

Code Generation Predicates

For each of the net tasks just described, there is one code generation predicate.

definelayer. emits storage names for the net layers. Generates different code, depending on if the node is an input, hidden, or output layer. For example, an input layer requires only the outX matrix; all other layers require in addition the deltaX, biasX, deltabiasX, wX, and deltawX matrices, and output layers also have an associated target matrix.

alloclayer. emits dynamic storage allocation code for the net layers. Generates allocation statements for each matrix named in definelayer.

readweights. emits code that reads weights from a file into the weight vectors for all layers except the input layer. Other vectors such as deltawX and deltabiasX are initialized to zero.

readpatterns. emits code that reads patterns from the pattern file into the input layers. The database fact, inputs (), specifies the order in which data are read into the input layer.

readtargets. emits code that reads target values from the pattern file into the target vector.

iteratehidden. emits code to iterate the hidden and output layers of the network. This is the forward pass of the neural network computation algorithm.

Probably the most complex group of predicates in the program, consisting of the iteratehidden predicate with three versions of arity

0/1/2 and the auxiliary predicate sumin. It is conceded that this is in all likelihood a bad Prolog hack, but it does the job! These are the issues that iteratehidden must address:

Depth-first traversal of the network to discover all output and hidden nodes. The ordering is important because the fan-in to a node must be computed before the activation function of the node. This is elegantly achieved by Prolog's inherent search techniques!

deltanet. emits code that computes the deltas at the network output layer. This is the beginning of the backward error pass of the back-propagation algorithm.

deltahidden. emits code that computes deltas at the hidden layers of the network. It's a close contender to iteratehidden for the title of most complex predicate! Like iteratehidden, this must traverse the network in the "proper" order. Because this is a backward pass, it does a *breadth-first traversal* through all hidden nodes. This ensures that the deltas at the fan-in to a node are computed after the deltas of the node itself (opposite order to that used by iteratehidden).

iterateweights. emits code that computes weights at all internal connections in the network. This is the undefeated holder of the title of simplest predicate generating the most complex code. The predicate is simple because it needs only to discover hidden nodes of the network, which is trivial for Prolog. It then emits a tremendous amount of code at each node for the weight computation.

sumsquarederror. emits code that computes the sum-squared error at the output layer of the network.

writeweights. emits code to write the weight vectors to a file in the same order used by readweights. Weight files can therefore be re-used to restart the network for retraining or testing.

writenet. emits code that writes the values of the output layers to a file.

freelayer. emits code to free dynamic storage for net layers. Restores memory to what it was before alloclayer was called. This is needed for reinitializing the network for another training or test session.

Network Compiler

This tool compiles the network using a generic network skeleton that has slots for net tasks. Each slot is filled by a code fragment for a net task. The network is compiled directly by a C compiler or native code assembler. The same principle can be used for virtually any type of neural network architecture. This exploits reusability because code skeletons can be written, optimized, and debugged once, then used many times in different applications.

The back-propagation neural network is derived from BATCHNET. C (see Appendix A). Each slot consists of a

```
#include "fragment.g"
```

statement, where fragment.g is the name of a code fragment for a net task (see the earlier section on code generation predicates).

The final outcome is a compiled .EXE program . . . , the executable neural network code.

Compiling the Neural Network in C

NETSHELL. C, NETSHELL. H, and the *. g files are compiled directly by Turbo C [82], Microsoft C [84], or compatible MS-DOS C compilers. Consult the user's guide for more detail about setting up the compiler environment. Note the following restrictions:

Memory model must be compact, large, or huge because of the large data arrays needed for (all but the tiniest) neural networks.

80286/80287 hardware is desirable but not essential. These switches can therefore be changed without loss of generality. For most practical applications however, the speed of the 80286/80287 is necessary.

Note that it is equally easy to generate 80x86 assembly language instead of C or to optimize code fragments in other ways.

CHAPTER 6

Hardware
Implementations

D. Gilbert Lee, Jr.

Corollary to Murphy's Law
  New computing power will be completely overwhelmed within five minutes of coming on line.

Because neural network research is still in its infancy there are very few specific guides one can use when solving a problem using a neural network. One must empirically adjust many parameters (size of hidden layer(s), learning rates, and even paradigms) before the problem is solved. If the neural network is part of a product, one may not have the leisure to develop the neural network on the platform that is ultimately used in production. It may be necessary to spend more money initially for a hardware platform on which neural networks can be more quickly modified and trained than would be possible using the platform intended for final production. Although they are certainly not the ultimate platforms for speed, several coprocessor boards exist today that plug into an IBM PC or Macintosh. These boards provide significant increases in speed over the original computer at relatively low cost.

Coprocessor boards are not new. Third-party vendors that provide coprocessor boards have existed since personal computers first became available. Shortly after the Motorola 6502 microprocessor-based Apple][computers became available, it was possible to buy a plug-in board that contained the Zilog Z80 microprocessor [114]. This allowed a person to use programs on the Apple that were orginally developed for computers based on the CP/M (control program/microcomputer) operating system. Today it is possible to obtain cards that fit into the IBM PC that contain complete UNIX computers based on the 68000 or the 32032 processors. For these cases the coprocessors have their own operating systems, requiring the user to learn a new set of commands. The host processor typically operates transparently as a I/O server (screen, keyboard, and disk interfaces).

A different type of coprocessor card available now is characterized by one or more high-speed digital signal processors with large amounts of memory. These coprocessor boards do not use their own operating system. The host system is used to edit, compile, and download programs onto the coprocessor card. Some cards such as the SAIC Delta II and the HNC Anza Plus are marketed for use with neural networks. These systems, costing $U.S. 10,000 and up, provide software with the boards to allow the implementation of several neural network paradigms. Others, such as the Mercury cards and Transputers, are marketed for a variety of numerical or digital signal processing applications.

Transputers are particularly intriguing to use with neural networks since they are designed for parallel processing. The transputer has the advantage of having a low start-up cost ($U.S. 3000 for a single transputer with 1 Mbyte memory, motherboard, and compiler) and the disadvantage of somewhat less capability than other more expensive coprocessor cards. This computational deficit can be overcome, however, with the addition of more transputers. This chapter concentrates on the use of transputers both individually and in parallel. First, we discuss the transputer's features. Second, every trick in the book is used to optimize the matrix–vector multiply operation (if you are going to spend the extra money on hardware, you might as well go all the way). Then, we discuss a group of programs that implement a neural network that can be run in parallel to as many transputers as you have available. Finally, a short case study involving the recognition of ships using neural networks is presented.

The Transputer

Transputers are a relatively unique technology for parallel processing. The Inmos Ltd. makes several types of transputers of various speeds and capabilities. The T800 model has both an internal 32-bit integer processor and an internal 32-bit floating-point unit (Fig. 6-1). The 20-MHz version of the T800 can perform computations at rates up to 1.5 million single-precision (32-bit) floating-point operations per second (faster than the 68020/68881 and 80386/80387 processor combinations

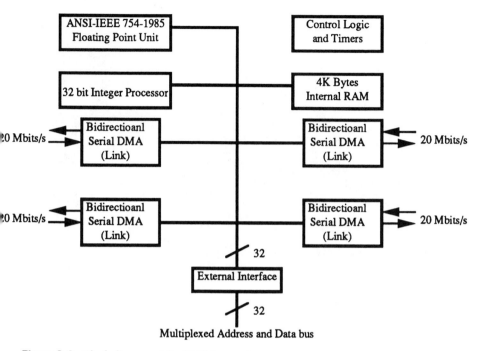

Figure 6-1 Block diagram of the T800 transputer.

available in present day PCs). The device has 4 Kbytes of internal RAM and supports an external 32-bit address space and 32-bit wide data. It contains special communication hardware (serial DMA channels called *links*) that allow many transputers to communicate and work in parallel with each other. The device also provides a couple of timers and hardware-supported multitasking. All of these features mean that the transputer can provide a very powerful platform for implementing numerically intensive applications.

Inmos–SGS Thomson and several other vendors have developed a series of products that ease the use of transputers with PCs. Each Transputer comes on a small daughter board called a TRAM (Fig. 6-2). The TRAMs, which have varying amounts of memory, plug into a motherboard for a specific computer bus. So far, motherboards exist for the IBM PC, Apple Macintosh II, VME, and Eurocard buses. Depending on the amount of memory with which the TRAMs are configured, up to 10 TRAMs will fit onto a IBM PC motherboard. With the variety of hardware products available, it is possible to configure a transputer-based system with just the right amount of memory and processors for the problem being considered.

Figure 6-2   Transputer Modules (TRAM) on an IBM PC AT TRAM motherboard. Shown
are modules from two manufacturers. The unit on the left has 1 MByte RAM and the unit
on the right has 2 MBytes of RAM. The motherboard can hold up to five TRAMs of
this size

Interprocess Communications

To understand what distinguishes the transputer from other general-
purpose processors and makes it suitable for parallel processing, one
must understand how it handles communications between processes
and multitasking [115]. Communications between processes are handled by using the same instructions whether the communication is between two local processes or between processes located on two adjacent transputers. Thus, the programmer does not have to decide
whether or not two processes will reside in the same processor while
code for the processes is being written.

   Communications are performed using one-way channels. In theory
the only way for a process to access data that originates from another
process is through a channel (you can get around this if you want to).
This is certainly true if the processes reside on different transputers
because transputers do not share memory space.

   If the channel is to exist between two processes on adjacent transputers, then the channel is implemented using a point-to-point hardware
link. Each link can either transmit or receive a serial stream of data at
20 Mbits/sec. There are four pairs of links (half of each pair for transmitting, the other for receiving) on the T800. A transputer can therefore
be attached to a maximum of four other transputers at a time.

Although individual links are capable of only 1.7 Mbytes/sec throughput (2.4 Mbytes/sec when both links are used simultaneously), the aggregate communications band with of an array of transputers is phenomenal. For example, if all the links of 16 transputers were connected, over 76 Mbytes/sec of data could be transmitted. Transputers can be connected in any arrangement desired (e.g., pipes, rings, meshes, trees, or hypercubes). This is in contrast to multiprocessors with shared communications buses that can handle only so many additional processors before bus contention problems become significant.

If the channel is to exist between two processes in the same processor, it is implemented using a single memory location. This location serves as a flag for the microcode that implements the communications instructions.

Communications are always synchronized. This means that when one process wants to communicate with another, it must wait until the other is ready. If there are two processes (whether local or across adjacent transputers) and only one is ready to communicate, the one that is ready is suspended. When the second process involved in the communication becomes active and is ready to communicate, the data transmission is performed. The first process is then allowed to continue. It does not matter whether the first process that wants to communicate is transmitting or receiving.

Multitasking

Multitasking is managed by a microcoded scheduler. The transputer supports two levels of process priority: high and low. Processes are either active or inactive. Two lists (one for high priority and one for low priority) of the active processes are maintained by the scheduler. During operation the scheduler runs all active high-priority processes one at a time until they all are waiting for communications or for a user-specified time delay to be completed. Then the process at the top of the low-priority list executes for one time slice (approximately one millisecond) or until it becomes inactive as a result of having to wait for a communication to take place or for having to wait for programmed time delay to be completed.

Inactive processes do not require attention (i.e., time) from the scheduler. When a communication is completed or the programmed time delay has expired, then the inactive process is added back to the list of active processes waiting to execute.

In summary, the use of the internal channels and the multitasking scheduler allows a single transputer to support several concurrently running processes. The use of the external channels extends the concurrency across multiple transputers.

Programming Languages

Several languages exist to support the transputer either individually or in parallel configurations. Occam was the original language developed for the transputer and is supported by Inmos–SGS Thomson. This language appeals to computer language purists for its strong data typing and the cleanness with which multitasking, multiprocessing, and intertask I/O are supported. Having a C and assembly language background (and no formal training in occam programming), I have found programming in occam to be somewhat frustrating. I have also found myself being disappointed at the speed of the code that the IMSD705A occam compiler generated. I do understand, however, that more recent versions of the compiler have better code optimization. For programmers with a Pascal or Ada programming background, occam may be the most appropriate language when using the transputer.

Other languages for which compilers exist for the transputer include FORTRAN, C, Pascal, and Ada. These compilers have extended the language or provided additional libraries of routines to support all the features of the transputer. Some vendors, realizing the availability of the transputer's computational power, actually perform the compilation using the transputer instead of the native processor.

The particular C compiler that I have been using, developed by Logical Systems Inc., provides functions to support communications and multitasking. One of the features I like best about the C compiler over the occam compiler is that the C compiler generates a human readable, assembly-language source file that is then used as input to the assembler. This means that I can see exactly what code the compiler is generating. I can then use the in-line assembly language support provided by the C compiler (also available with the occam compiler) to optimize those sections of the code that need it.

Optimizing the Matrix-Vector Multiply

The key to gaining high performance with transputers is to make sure that both on-chip processors are operating as efficiently as possible and to spread the computations as evenly as possible around the available transputers. With regard to the first point and neural networks, the biggest benefits from operating efficiently occur during the matrix–vector multiply operation that is at the heart of most neural network simulations. The following discussion describes how to program the transputer to get the best performance during the matrix–vector multiply operation for a fully connected neural network.

In the discussion of the matrix–vector multiply operation presented in Chapter 4, data within the input, weight, and output arrays were accessed using indices (Fig. 6-3a & b). One of the reasons for using this

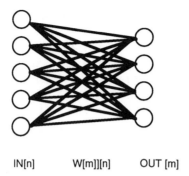

IN[n]   W[m]][n]   OUT [m]

Figure 6-3a   Arrays required for matrix–vector multiply.

```
IN[n]     values for input nodes
W[m][n]   values of weights
OUT[m]    values for next layer nodes
          for(i = 0; i < m; i++)
          {
             OUT[i] = 0;        /* Initialize sum */
             for(j = 0; j < n; j++)
             {
                OUT[i] = OUT[i] + (IN[j] * W[i][j]);
                /* Multiply and Accumulate */
             }
          }
```

Figure 6-3b   C code fragment showing straight forward implementation of Matrix–Vector Multiply.

```
IN   pointer to the n values for the input nodes
W    pointer to the m x n values of weights
OUT  pointer to the m values for next layer nodes
        for(i = 0; i < m; i++)
        {
           *OUT = 0;                         /*Initialize sum */
           IN = address of first input node
           for(j = 0; j < n; j++)
           {
              *OUT += *IN++ * *W++);
              /* Multiply and Accumulate */
           }
           OUT++;                            /* Move to next node */
        }
```

Figure 6-3c   C code fragment showing implementation of Matrix-Vector Multiply using pointers.

method is to overcome the 64-Kbyte segment boundaries found in the address space of the INTEL 80x86 processors. The transputer, however, has no problem accessing data anywhere within its 32 bit address space and can have arrays as long as needed. This sets the stage for dispensing the indices entirely and accessing the data from the arrays using pointer arithmetic only.

To use only pointer arithmetic, the data for the weight matrix must be organized within the memory in a very specific manner. All the weights for a next layer node must be arranged consecutively within memory. Then the weights for the next node are arranged consecutively, etc. Now, instead of calculating an offset into the weight matrix using indices for each weight, we can increment a pointer to access each weight sequentially (Fig. 6-3c). With this approach on an 8-MHz IBM PC/AT with 80287 and using *very small arrays*, I achieved 9800 multiply-accumulates/sec (MAC/sec). On a 20-MHz Compaq 80386 with 80387, I got 65,000 MAC/sec. On the latter system, this was almost 5000 MAC/sec more than with the approach using indices.

Now, the same exercise on the 20-MHz T800 transputer, using the approach with indices, produces a rate of 184,800 MAC/sec. With the pointers I achieved 276,900 MAC/sec. This, however, is a mediocre performance considering the advertised performance of 1.5 Mflops. Given that a single multiply–accumulate operation executes two floating-point operations, the transputer should be getting around 750,000 MAC/sec. What's going on?

Because the matrix–vector multiply is performed with floating-point numbers, it is crucial that the floating-point processor runs continuously. The transputer's architecture is designed so that the integer processor can be calculating the addresses for the next set of operands at the same time that the floating-point processor is performing a multiply or an add. This is accomplished by interleaving the integer processor instructions with the floating-point processor instructions. Because the C compiler generates an assembly language source file, I can see how efficiently it uses the two processors. By using the in-line assembly language capability of the C compiler, one can replace the original C instructions with appropriately arranged assembly language instructions. In practice, this turns out to be only six or seven assembly language statements for a multiply–accumulate instruction.

Additional improvements in speed can be obtained by using two of the transputer's features to the best advantage: The first is how the transputer creates constants, and the second is the availability of high-speed internal RAM [116]. Because so few operations occur per iteration through the matrix–vector multiply loop, a significant proportion of time is used to increment the index and test for exiting the loop. To

get around this situation, it is possible to "open the loop" by enlarg-
ing the code within the loop to perform several multiply/add calculations before the loop is taken (Fig. 6-4). This approach improves performance (to varying degrees) no matter what processor is being used. In
fact, the fastest code implementation (assuming any noncaching processor) would open the loop up all the way, so that no looping was
required. This is unrealistic for all but the smallest of neural network
topologies because of the memory space that would be required for the
instructions.

By how much, then, should the loop be opened up? This can be
determined by taking advantage of how the transputer works with
constants.

The fastest executing instructions are a byte long and use one nibble
to indicate the instruction and a second nibble for a constant. Thus
constants between 0 and 15 are easily handled in 1-byte instructions. If
larger numbers are required, then the transputer "builds" them a nibble
at a time (also using a byte-long instruction). The instruction associated

```
IN   pointer to the n values for the input nodes
W    pointer to the m x n values of weights
OUT  pointer to the m values for next layer nodes

    nr = n-(n%4);              /* Determine remainder */

    for(i = 0; i < m; i++)
      {
      *OUT = 0;                           /* Initialize Sum */
      IN = address of first input node
      for(j = 0; j < n%4; j++)
        {
        *OUT += (*IN * *W)        /* Multiply and Accumulate */
           + (*(IN+1) * *(W+1))   /* Multiply and Accumulate */
           + (*(IN+2) * *(W+2))   /* Multiply and Accumulate */
           + (*(IN+3) * *(W+3));  /* Multiply and Accumulate */
        IN += 4;
        W += 4;
        }
      for(j=0; j < nr; j++)       /* Use normal approach */
        {                         /* for the last few */
        *OUT += *IN++ * *W++;     /* Multiply and Accumulate */
        }
      OUT++;
      }
```

Figure 6-4 C Code Fragment showing how the Multiply Accumulate loop can be
opened up (in this example by 4). The assembly language code increments I and W on
the fly instead of adding 4 at the end of the loop.

with the last nibble necessary to form the desired constant also executes the desired operation on the constant (e.g., load, store, etc.). As
an example, if you need a number between 256 and 4095, then three
nibbles are needed (with an additional nibble instruction for each, i.e.,
a total of 3 bytes). Of course, for each additional nibble needed, another
clock cycle is used.

Therefore, it would be good to open up the loop by 16. This requires
only one nibble (and therefore one instruction) to access each operand
needed. To make the code usable for a neural network of any size, regular loop code is added after the opened-up loop code to handle the
situation when the number of nodes is not evenly divisible by 16.

We can also obtain improved speed by taking advantage of the transputer's internal RAM. Most compilers use this internal RAM for stacks
and workspace pointers, but there is nothing wrong with directing the
compiler to set aside space within the internal RAM for a small routine
or two. Instructions and data found in this area (4 Kbytes) require only
one clock cycle for retrieval. Given that the less expensive TRAMs use
external memory requiring 4 clock cycles for accessing and that so
much time is spent performing the matrix–vector multiply, it makes a
lot of sense to use the internal RAM to increase the simulation's performance. It's too bad that we can't get the arrays in there also.

Now what are we up to? Using the hand-optimized assembly language to maximize the floating-point unit operation, and opening the
loop by 16 to minimize the loop instruction overhead, I got around
675,000 MAC/sec. When I placed the code in the internal RAM, the
speed improved by another 50,000 MAC/sec to over 725,000 MAC/sec.
Now we're talking! Appendix F has the actual code for the matrix–
vector multiply. The appendix also has the code for performing the
tranposed vector–matrix multiply needed during the error correction
phase of the neural network simulation. This code is not quite as efficient as the first but is still able to perform at a rate of over 700,000
MAC/sec.

Before I finish with the discussion on optimizing the matrix–vector
multiply operation, I'd like to present some occam compiler results.
After several telephone conversations with friends who are much more
skilled in occam than I, I was able to coax approximately 560,000 MAC/
sec out of the transputer. This was without using the in-line assembly
language capability (which I never figured out) and without using internal RAM. No doubt the performance figures achieved with the C
compiler can also be obtained with the occam compiler.

Finished! We have eked every last bit of speed out of the transputer.
This code can be used with both on-line and epoch training. Just take

your code that has been written for the PC and modify it to insure that the data for the weight matrix are arranged correctly. Otherwise, in general, code written for the IBM PC using the Turbo C compiler from Borland International or the Microsoft C compiler can be compiled by the Logical Systems' C compiler with little or no modification.

Using Transputers in Parallel

So far, only a single-transputer approach to simulating neural networks has been considered. If you want to process more data and/or process the data in as short a time as possible, then parallel processing with transputers can provide the needed performance. The true potential of transputers is best realized when two or more are used together to solve a problem. The underlying hardware architecture, with its multitasking and synchronized communications capabilities, almost completely eliminates the programming hassles associated with controlling several tasks concurrently.

Processor Farms

Once you decide to implement a problem on several transputers, it becomes important to achieve as great an increase in performance as possible by distributing the computational workload as evenly as possible among the processors. Not every problem benefits in the same way by parallel processing. Certain algorithms fit more naturally into a parallel implementation than others. Ideally, we seek to find a computational algorithm that, when applied to parallel processors, increases linearly in performance as the number of processors is increased. One computational algorithm is a *processor farm* [117]. In a processor farm, one processor serves as the *farmer* and the remaining processors serve as *workers*. The worker processors execute identical code. The farmer processor sends packets of data to each worker. When a worker finishes with the data that it has been given, the farmer retrieves the results and sends a new packet of data. This farming process continues until the problem is completed. Some image processing tasks can be easily accommodated with a processor farm where each worker processes a different section of the image. This approach is probably the most appropriate for using multiple transputers to simulate neural networks in a production environment. Each worker runs a complete neural network simulation. As new data come in, the farmer sends them to the next available transputer. When the results become available, the farmer retrieves them and sends them back to the host.

Pipelining

Although it makes sense to use a processor farm once the weights are known, it is not as appropriate for training. An algorithm called pipelining is a better approach in a training situation. This algorithm can be mapped onto a network of transputers in such a manner that any number of transputers can be used in a particular training session, with almost linear improvement in speed for every transputer used. The computational algorithm has been described by Pomerleau et al. [118] for use with the Carnegie Mellon University Warp machine (a very expensive systolic array processor) and by Chong and Fallside [119] for the transputer.

The algorithm uses a group of processors that are arranged in what is called a pipeline (Fig. 6-5). The main concept of a pipeline is that each processor receives intermediate results and/or data from its upstream neighbor, processes the data, and then sends its results/data to its downstream neighbor. For best results, the computational approach should try to perform communications in parallel with the computations. Also, the amount of work that each processor performs should be the same. In this way no processors have to wait for another processor to finish before they can continue with the next stage of the processing.

For neural network simulations on an array of transputers, the computational approach is to send a subset of the exemplar vectors to each pipe processor and then pipe the weights and the weight corrections through the pipeline. Each pipe processor has a complete copy of the neural network's nodes and the input and output values for each exemplar vector for which it is responsible. The weights are stored and

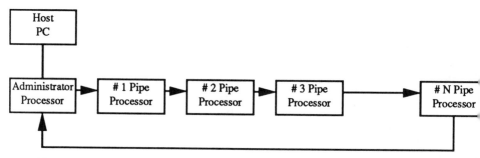

Figure 6-5 Processors arranged in a pipeline.

modified at one end of the pipeline in an administrator processor (typically another transputer). The administrator processor is connected to the host PC and to the first and last processors in the pipeline. It gets the topology and exemplar and test vectors from the PC (typically in files) and then uses this information to configure the pipe processors.

When all the pipe processors have their specific exemplar vectors and a copy of the neural network nodes, the administrator processor sends a copy of all the weights down the pipeline. When a pipe processor receives the weights, it immediately sends them to the next processor downstream. In parallel, it begins to use the weights to perform a forward pass through the neural network for each of the exemplar vectors that it has. The pipe processor then compares the calculated output values with the exemplar output values and calculates an error value, which it then sends back to the administrator processor. The administrator node receives the error values from all the pipe processors and determines if the total error for all the exemplar vectors meets the desired criteria.

If the error is low enough, the administrator processor transfers the weights back to the PC and runs through any test vectors that have been supplied. If the error is too high, the administrator sends a message to all the pipe processors instructing them to calculate a change of weights based on their individual exemplar vectors. The administrator processor then sends an empty array down the pipeline. When a pipe processor receives the array, it adds the change in weights that it has calculated to the array and then sends it downstream to the next pipe processor.

When the administrator processor gets the array back it has the sum of all the changes for each weight based on all the exemplar vectors. The array is then multiplied by the necessary learning rate constant and then added to the previous changed-weight vector (which has been multiplied by the desired momentum constant) to produce a new changed-weight vector. The administrator then creates a new set of weights by adding the present weight vector to the new changed-weight vector. The whole process begins again with the administrator node sending the new weights down the pipeline.

Programming the Transputers

To implement the pipelined neural network simulation on the transputers requires only three programs, no matter how many processors are involved.

The first program (ADMIN) is the administrator processor program; it interfaces to the host PC and to the pipeline, and is responsible for:

1. Retrieving the topology of the neural network to be simulated from the host;
2. Transmitting this information down the pipeline so that each pipe processor can configure itself;
3. Retrieving all the exemplar vectors from the host;
4. Transmitting evenly divided subsets of the exemplar vectors to each pipe processor;
5. Transmitting the weights into the pipeline;
6. Getting error measurements from each processor in the pipe;
7. Determining whether the total system error is below a user-specified value;
8. If necessary, instructing the pipe processors to calculate the change in weights;
9. Sending an empty weight-change array downstream;
10. Collecting the filled weight-change array from the pipe processors;
11. Using the host (i.e., user) supplied momentum and learning rate constants along with the weight-change array to calculate a new weight vector;
12. Looping back to step 5;
13. Saving the weights when training is complete; and
14. If necessary, running test vectors on the trained neural network and collecting statistics.

The second program (PIPE) is run on all of the pipe processors, and is responsible for:

1. Receiving and retransmitting the topology of the neural network;
2. Setting aside enough space for the weights and its own exemplar vectors;
3. Reading and storing its own exemplar vectors;
4. Receiving and retransmitting any exemplar vectors destined for processors downstream;
5. Receiving and retransmitting the weights;
6. Using the weights to calculate the output for the neural network for each of its exemplar input vectors;
7. Comparing the neural network calculated outputs with the exemplar output vectors and calculating an error value;
8. Transmitting its error value downstream;
9. Receiving and retransmitting any error values produced by upstream processors;
10. Receiving and retransmitting any instructions with regard to the necessity of performing the backward pass through the network;

11. If necessary, using the output errors from all of the exemplar vectors to calculate the changes in the weights;

12. Receiving the weight-change array from upstream, adding the locally calculated changes, and transmitting the array downstream; and

13. Looping back to step 5.

The third program (TAIL) is run on the last transputer in the pipeline in parallel with a copy of the PIPE program. Unlike the other processors that used the hardware DMA channels (links) to transfer data from one processor to the next, the PIPE and TAIL programs on the last processor communicate with each other over a memory channel. The memory channels operate identically to the hardware channels as far as programming is concerned. This means that the last PIPE program is identical to the PIPE programs on the other processors.

The TAIL program primarily serves to transmit information coming out of the pipeline back to the administrator processor and to do some garbage collection. When the neural network topology information reaches the last pipe processor, there is nowhere to send the data to. Because all the PIPE programs are identical, the last PIPE program tries to send the data on anyway. The TAIL program receives the topology data and just lets it sit in a buffer that will be written over later with other unnecessary data. The weights that are transmitted down the pipeline are likewise garbage collected. The error values are, however, sent back to the administrator processor, as is the weight change array.

Each of the differently used processors has a *harness* program associated with it. The harness programs specify whether specific channels are hardware or memory channels and which programs (ADMIN, PIPE, or TAIL) are to be run together. If desired, the TAIL program could be run on the same processor as the ADMIN program instead of with the last PIPE program. Likewise, if space allows it, a copy of the PIPE program could also be run on the administrator processor. However, to maintain load balance, it might be necessary to reduce the number of exemplar vectors that this first PIPE program processes.

Finally, a short configuration file (used by the network loader program supplied by the vendor) must be written to indicate which program is to run on which transputer. The network loader is responsible for resetting all the transputers and loading each one with its specific program. From the file, the network loader can tell which transputers and which links a program must be transmitted through before the program arrives at the transputer that it is to be ultimately run on.

What is the best approach to writing three programs that are to work and communicate together across multiple processors? Start out by writing the communications software. Think through the communications requirements for each program. Then write the code for all three programs to support a few of the requirements. As an example make sure the topology information is successfully transmitted down the entire pipeline.

As a debugging aid, when the topology information reaches the TAIL program, have it send a short message to the ADMIN program as an indicator that the communications are working. If there are problems, try running the ADMIN and TAIL programs without the PIPE program. If the problem goes away, the programming mistake is in the PIPE software. If the problem remains, then have the TAIL program send everything it receives back to the ADMIN program where it can then be printed.

Build up the programs by adding additional communications activities until all of the communication requirements have been implemented. Make sure to try the software with pipelines of several lengths. Only after all the communications are working should one begin adding the number-crunching software. Ideally, this software has had most of its bugs worked out ahead of time in a program that was running on only one transputer. In all likelihood, the computing sections of a batch update simulation program written for a conventional processor will require little modification for use in a multiple transputer environment. Again, check the software using pipelines of different lengths.

This approach does not make use of any debuggers. Figuring out what is happening on an array of transputers when things are going wrong can be very trying. In this example, only the transputer program that is directly connected to the host processor (ADMIN) can print information to the screen. All the other processors must communicate with the host computer indirectly through the ADMIN program. This means that to display data from a remote processor, the programmer must supply code to handle the transmission for all of the intermediate processors along the way. If one is debugging code on a remote processor, this approach requires tampering with the communications code of the intervening processors; and that in itself may produce more bugs.

Fortunately, vendors are now providing operating environments for the transputer that implement message-handling protocols. With some of the protocols a communications process runs continuously in parallel with the application program. Any time that data must be sent to another transputer, the application program uses a vendor-supplied function or a memory channel to pass the data to the communications process. This process then adds a header to the data and sends the message out the appropriate link. The transputer receiving the message uses the header information to determine whether the message is intended for another transputer or for itself. If necessary, the process forwards the message to another processor. Otherwise, the process strips the header off the message and sends the data through a memory channel to the appropriate application process. Although this scheme slows the application programs it can make programming communications simpler.

More importantly, these communications processes can provide a means for debugging remote transputers. Even though the application program may have stopped on a remote processor because needed data have not been communicated to it, the communications process can still send and receive messages. One of those messages can be an instruction to read a particular memory location or register and send the data back over a link to the host computer.

Discussion

In practice, the very clean approach just described may require modifications due to the limitations of available memory. The topology of the neural network, the number of test vectors, and the available transputer memory resources determine how the transmission of the weights is managed. In most situations, the weights are transmitted by the administrator transputer and stored locally on each of the processors in the pipeline. During the error correction phase of the training cycle, each processor generates a set of changes for the weights. These changes are then sent back to the adminstrator where they are all added and then any momentum and learning rate adjustments are made. This approach requires few or no parallel processes running within each transputer.

If however, the network is very large and there are memory constraints on the processing nodes, it may be necessary to break the weights into packets (say all the in-bound weights for a hidden unit) and send them sequentially down the pipeline. The PIPE program then calculates all the partial sums for each exemplar vector that it can with the data in the packet. When all the weights for one layer have been received, the activation function is calculated for each unit. This approach allows a larger neural network to be simulated than the previous approach, and/or more exemplar vectors to be used in each processor.

How efficient is a multiple transputer system? Figure 6-6 shows how the two approaches to managing the transmission of the weights fared with different topologies and different numbers of exemplar vectors. The first program uses the first approach of transmitting weights with no parallel processes on the processors, save the last transputer in the pipeline, which has both the PIPE program and the TAIL program. The second program uses packets for the weights and double and triple buffering of the data, so that one packet can be received while another one is both transmitted and used for computations. Typically, two or three

Topology and Processor Count		Number of Vectors Processed			
		20	80	320	1280
16:64:16	1				1
	4				0.98 0.95
256:64:16	1			1	
	4			0.92 0.96	0.98 0.97
4000:10:5	1	1			
	4	0.45 0.75	0.83 0.82		

Figure 6-6 Neural Network Simulation Performance for Various Topologies, Processor Counts, and Vector Counts. Values indicate how efficiently each transputer runs in a multiple transputer topology with respect to a single transputer implementation. Performance has been normalized for each topology with respect to one processor. Both the approach of transmitting all the weights at once (nonitalicized) and the approach using multiple transmissions of packets of weights (italicized) are presented.

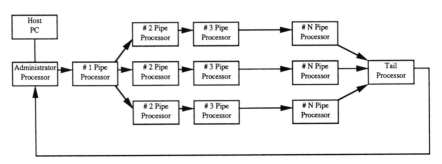

Figure 6-7 Processors arranged in a multiple pipeline.

processes run in parallel at any given time. No doubt, neither program is as efficient as it could be. It is clear, however, that as long as the number of test vectors is large, both approaches perform respectably. The second program can be as fast or faster than the first for larger neural network topologies. Pomerleau reports obtaining 17 million connections per second with a basic Warp machine with 10 processors. Using the same computational algorithm on a set of 10 transputers would yield approximately 7 million connections per second. Given the expense of the Warp machine ($U.S. 350,000), the transputer implementation is much more cost effective.

A variation of the pipeline that has higher efficiency is multiple pipelines (Fig. 6-7). The ADMIN processor connects to three pipelines, each containing the same number of PIPE processors. The TAIL processor collects the results from each pipeline and communicates back to the ADMIN process.

I would be remiss not to mention that there are other approaches to dividing a neural network simulation among many transputers. As an example, [120] describes how each transputer can manage the processing needed for a subset of the nodes being simulated. Other researchers [121, 122, 123] have used transputers with neural network paradigms other than back-propagation.

Mini Case Study: Ship Image Recognition

This section describes a neural network experiment that takes advantage of the capabilities of the transputer(s). The use of transputers was motivated by the size of the data set being worked with and the speed with which different learning rates and momentums could be analyzed. The purpose of the experiment was to study how well a neural network can distinguish among images of different ships that are viewed from various angles [124]. In the process, the effects of different starting conditions and different learning techniques were also examined. The experiment did not attempt to address the very important image recognition issues of lighting variation and obstructed views. Thus the approach used in this experiment is more appropriate for recognizing objects on a conveyor belt.

Description of Ship Image Preprocessing

Four ship models were used in this experiment. The models are made by a company in Austria and show the ships from the waterline up. They are very accurate and are all 1:1268 scale. During the photographing session each ship was placed on a $10\frac{1}{2}$-inch diameter rotating platter. The platter is marked in 5° increments to allow precise orientation of the ships with respect to the video camera. The camera was located 31 feet away from the platter giving a scaled distance of approximately 7.5 miles. The ship models and camera are at the same height, thus producing sea-level pictures of the ships. A black and white video camera with a 70 to 210 zoom lens was used. The camera introduces a 6:5 aspect ratio to the viewed object. The pictures were 40 × 100 pixels in size.

Because this was a preliminary experiment, pictures were collected for each ship only from 90° starboard to 0° (bow) in 10° increments. To make up for the lack of more pictures, the starboard pictures were flipped to produce simulated port pictures. Given the symmetry of most ships across the bow–stern axis, this was not considered too great a short cut. The camera was aimed so that the ship waterline was always at the very bottom of the picture. The zoom lens was used to adjust the image of the ship so that the bow and stern just touched the sides of the

Figure 6-8   Video image of ship.

picture, or so that the waterline of the ship and the masthead touched
the top and bottom of the picture. Figure 6-8 presents an example of
the pictures. From 0° to 30°, the top-to-bottom axis is the longest axis
on the ship images and is used to frame the boat. At angles greater than
30°, the bow-to-stern axis is the longer, and vertical features in the images remain in the same position from picture to picture.

Neural Network Training Description

The pictures were processed using an IBM PC/AT with a transputer
coprocessor card containing five T800 transputers. The neural network
simulation was written in the C language to run on the T800s. The
learning paradigm studied was the generalized delta rule algorithm described by Rumelhart, Hinton, and Williams [125]. Both on-line and
batch updating of the weights were studied. Only one transputer was
used for on-line training, and all five transputers were used for batch
training. The neural network has fully interconnected input, hidden,
and output layers. The input layer contained 4000 units (one for each
pixel). The output layer contained a unit for each ship to be classified
(4). The number of units in the hidden layer was varied, starting with
50 and working toward smaller sizes. A momentum of 0.5 and a learning rate of 0.15 were used for all on-line simulations. For batch processing, 0.9 for momentum and 0.5 for learning rate were used. The weights
could be initialized in two ways. The first method creates random values (± 0.3) for all the weights. The second (similar to Leung and Zue
[126]) sets the first layer of weights (W_{ji}) to zero and the second layer of
weights (W_{kj}) to random values (± 0.3).

Originally, the 4000:50:4 neural network was trained on one exemplar from each ship at 60°. This angle was chosen because it was approximately halfway through the range of angles for which the images
of the ships are framed by the sides of the picture. The number of starboard image exemplars was then increased (and the neural network
retrained) until the neural network when tested could successfully recognize all the ships. The number of hidden units was then decreased to
determine how well smaller networks could learn. Training was

stopped when the values of the outputs were within 0.05 of the desired results for all exemplars.

After the neural network was successfully trained on a group of exemplars, it was tested by presenting the starboard and then the simulated port picture at every angle for each ship. The output unit with the largest value from the two presentations for a particular angle was considered to be the response of the network.

Results

The neural network simulations recognized the ship images under varying conditions. As a minimum the networks needed to train on images of the ships at 0°, 20°, 30°, 60°, and 90°. With this amount of training data, the networks could successfully train with a hidden unit layer as small as 3 units and as large as 50 units (largest configuration manageable). As might be expected, because the networks had been trained only on starboard images, they tested miserably with the simulated port images. The output values from the port image tests were small enough so that the corresponding starboard image test would determine which ship was actually being presented.

The best results with the on-line weight updating occurred when the momentum term was 0.5 and the learning rate was 0.15. When batch weight updating was used, the network trained more quickly using a momentum term of 0.9 and a learning rate of 0.5. Many training sessions were required to determine the best parameter values. Being able to simulate the neural network on the transputer(s) contributed significantly to determining the parameters in a reasonable period of time.

Several hundred neural network simulations were performed to see how the initialization of the weights affected training speed and final performance. A random number was used to randomly initialize the W_{kj} weights between ± 0.3. A training simulation was then run with the W_{ji} weights initialized to zero. Ten additional simulations were then made using the same initial W_{kj} weights but with the W_{ji} randomly initialized between ± 0.3. Neural networks with hidden layers containing 3, 10, 20, 30, 40, and 50 hidden units were tested. It was found that initializing the W_{ji} layer weights to zero improved both the learning rate and the performance of the neural network. Only occasionally did a simulation using randomly generated W_{ji} weights outperform a simulation using zeros for the initial W_{ji} weights.

A simple argument can be made for these better results. During training, the zero initialized W_{ji} weights that contributed to the successful learning of the exemplars merely have to increase in magnitude with the correct sign. Some (many?) of the randomly initialized W_{ji} weights must be reduced in magnitude and possibly flipped in polarity to pro-

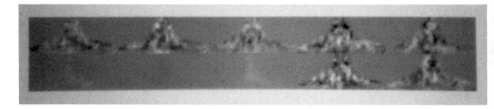

Figure 6-9   Input layer to hidden layer weights.

vide the proper contribution to learning the exemplars. Because there are so many weights in the first layer, during learning some of the "poorly" initialized weights are compensated by other weights. One can argue that when new test data are presented to the network, the compensating weights may be unable to "cover" for the poorly initialized weights, thus resulting in incorrect results. It is still necessary to have random values for the second layer of weights (layer connected to the output nodes) in order for the network to converge [125]. Figure 6-9 shows a graphical image of the contribution to a hidden unit of each first layer weight. The zero initialized weights are nonzero only for those pixels that were needed to learn the exemplars. By looking at images of the W_{ji} weights for each hidden unit, it is also possible to roughly estimate the number of hidden units that are necessary.

Summary

When push comes to shove, adding parallel processing power in an organized fashion can be beneficial. The back-propagation simulation of neural networks maps very nicely into a parallel processing environment. Although other parallel processing platforms are available, transputers represent a solution that can be obtained with modest means and will be useful for projects other than simulating neural networks.

Vendors

Companies advertising transputer TRAMs and/or language compilers for use with the transputer:

Inmos–SGS Thomson   Levco
1000 Aztec West   6181 Cornerstone Ct. East
Almondsbury   Suite 101
Bristol BS12 4SQ   San Diego
UK   California 92121
                                           USA

Multis Corporation
99 Willie Street
Lowell
Massachusetts 01854
USA

MicroWay, Inc.
P.O. Box 79
Kingston
Massachusetts 02364
USA

Computer Systems Architects
950 North University Avenue
Provo
Utah 84604
USA

Logical Systems
P.O. Box 1702
Corvallis
Oregon 97339
USA

3L Limited
Peel House
Ladywell
Livingston EH54 6AG
Scotland

Sension
Denton Drive
Northwich
Cheshire CW9 7LU
UK

Transtech Devices Ltd.
Unit 17, Wye Industrial Estate
London Road
High Wycombe
Buckinghamshire HP11 1LH
UK

Companies advertising neural network software using coprocessor cards and IBM PC compatible computers:

SAIC
10260 Campus Point Dr.
San Diego
California 92121
USA

HNC
5501 Oberlin Drive
San Diego
California 92121
USA

Companies advertising neural network software for transputers and Apple Macintosh II computers:

Neurix
Suite 2200
One Kendall Square
Cambridge
Massachusetts 02139
USA

CHAPTER 7

Performance Metrics

Russell C. Eberhart
Roy W. Dobbins
Larrie V. Hutton

Introduction

Most of the time, measuring how well a system is performing is relatively straightforward. We simply specify what percentage of correct answers are obtained in a test or operational situation and compare that with the specification that was established beforehand. Another approach is to see how well a system does with respect to some specified tolerance. The situation is seldom this simple, however, when we must measure the performance of neural network tools.

In this section, we examine some of the issues related to measuring how well a neural network tool is doing. This is, unfortunately, not a subject that has been treated extensively in the literature, so in some cases, we adapt techniques that have been applied in related areas to measuring performance. A number of issues related to measuring neural network tool performance are reviewed. For example, we look at the importance of specifying the sizes and number of iterations of training sets and the selection of test sets. We also discuss the selection of the "gold standards" against which performance is measured and the role the decision threshold level can play in determining system performance.

The performance measurements we discuss include the relatively simple measure of the percent correct, the average sum-squared error measure, receiver operating characteristic (ROC) curve measurements, measurements based on ROC curve parameters (recall, precision, sensitivity, specificity, etc.), and the chi-square goodness-of-fit metric. We see that the specific measure chosen depends on the type of system we are using and on other, somewhat more loosely defined parameters, such as the level of technical sophistication of the system end user.

Percent Correct

Because it is, at least on the face of it, the simplest, we start with describing the measurement of neural network tool performance by measuring the percent correct obtained in a particular situation. This is simply the percentage of all of the answers obtained that were judged to be correct according to some gold standard.

In discussing the calculation of percent correct, we introduce some of the issues that must be attended to regardless of the type of performance measurement tool(s) chosen. First, we look at the issues of selecting the gold standards and the test and training sets.

Neural network tools are generally used for some type of pattern recognition, or classification, or associative memory application in which a complete pattern is obtained from a partial, fuzzy, or noisy one. The issue of selecting the gold standard examples for training is important in these cases. (For some applications of neural networks the concept of percent correct is not particularly useful, such as in the composition of music; other measures, or metrics, are then used.)

At least two issues are associated with the selection of gold standards, both for training sets and testing sets. The first is the classification itself, and the second is the selection of a representative pattern set. A third issue to be addressed, which encompasses the first two, is selecting the person(s) or process used to designate the gold standards.

Relative to the first issue, it is sometimes straightforward to specify the classification of the items, or patterns, in the training and testing sets. For example, if the neural network tool is being used to classify printed versions of individual letters of the alphabet, such as A, B, and C, there should be no disagreement about which letter is which. On the other hand, some classification tasks can be more difficult. For example, in the classification of biopotential waveforms, such as electrocardiograms and electroencephalograms, the meaning of waveform can be a matter of opinion among experts. In the case of a neural network system to detect epileptiform spikes (described later), the average overlap in identification of individual spike waveforms was only about 60 percentbetween any two of the six neurologists who evaluated the records.

It is therefore important to obtain agreement beforehand on the classification process and the classifications themselves and to state both clearly when presenting any performance measurement results. In this step, it is extremely important to get the active participation of the end users of the system (such as the neurologists in the case just mentioned).

Given that classifications can be made and agreed to, the next job is usually the selection of the "representative examples" for the training and testing sets. This is an area in which much development work is currently being done. We can give you guidelines but few hard rules.

The examples selected for the training and testing sets, in addition to being agreed to by the experts as representative of the class, must be distributed over the class being represented. That is, the examples should not all be ideal, or textbook, examples of the pattern, with pattern vectors "right down the middle" of the classification. Rather, they should include patterns that, though clearly belonging to the identified class, are somewhat borderline, having attributes that place them near a decision surface with another class or classes. This is particularly important for cases, such as the biopotential waveform analysis, in which human perception is involved and opinions, though generally in agreement, may vary from expert to expert. Kohonen [22,37] and Rumelhart and McClelland [2] have discussed and demonstrated the need for using training/testing patterns near decision boundaries. We suggest that you refer to their work if you want more information on this aspect of pattern selection.

The designation of the person(s) or process used to identify the gold standard patterns is very important. Too often, engineers and programmers working on a project take it upon themselves to do this identification. This tendency should be avoided. It is important to involve the end users of the system in this process. Although the engineers and programmers can provide the end users with information regarding the technical constraints within which the system must operate, it should be left to the users, as much as possible, to provide the pattern designation, or at least the process for the designation. This is particularly important in areas such as biomedical engineering: Medicine must drive engineering, not the other way around.

Once one has made the classifications of testing/training patterns, the selection of representative samples, and the selection by expert end users of the process to be used in designating the gold standards, the calculation of percent correct is relatively straightforward. There is still, however, the issue of how to select the set of patterns used for training and testing, and how to interpret the different values of percent correct obtained for the testing and training sets.

The issue of interpreting error values for training and testing is discussed elsewhere in this volume, but we mention here that it is important to use different sets of patterns for training and testing. It's not fair to test a neural network tool with the same set of patterns used to train it! Furthermore, you may want to rotate training and testing patterns through the available patterns. That is, you can select a given set of patterns for training one time and a different set another time. Likewise, you can use different pattern sets for testing at different times. It is best to look at the performance of your neural network tool with these changes, if possible.

You should generally select a training set with about the same number of patterns for each classification. That is, if you have three output neurodes, each of which becomes active for a particular pattern classification, it is probably a good idea to have a training pattern set with about one-third of the total number of patterns from each classification. This is, for some people, counterintuitive.

An intuitive argument can be made that the numerical distribution of patterns should reflect the probability distribution of the classes. For example, if we are training a neural network tool with two output nodes and if one of the classes appears in the real world 20 percent of the time, then we might think that 20 percent of the training cases should be drawn from this class (and 80 percent from the other class).

Better network performance usually results, however, if, in the case just described, 50 percent of the patterns are selected from each class, regardless of the probability distribution. In fact, the authors have seen cases in which allocating the percentage of classes of patterns according to probability distributions has resulted in a complete failure to train the network.

What are some of the limitations of percent correct? As one example, consider the following situation. College scholarship winners were predicted accurately by our neural network tool 90 percent of the time last year (the training set) on the basis of SAT scores. Scholarship nonwinners were accurately predicted 60 percent of the time. This year (the testing set), only 85 percent of the scholarship winners were predicted accurately and only 55 percent of scholarship nonwinners were predicted accurately. However, overall ability to predict improved.

Is this possible? The answer is, yes. Suppose that half of the training set last year consisted of scholarship winners. The overall performance was $(90 * .50) + (60 * .50) = 75\%$ correct. Now, suppose that the testing set this year was composed of 70 percent scholarship winners. The performance was, therefore, $(85 * .70) + (55 * .30) = 76\%$ correct. Thus, overall predictive accuracy went up even though the predictive accuracy on the individual criteria went down. It might be noted that part of this "problem" is due to the fact that the proportions of instances of the categories (i.e., those who were scholarship winners) were unequal in the training and testing sets. (The world does not come packaged with equally representative databases.)

The example shows that percent correct can be misleading if it is the only method of evaluating performance. In the example, we might have chosen a network trained on the second set of data over one trained on the first set of data, even though the two networks may have been identical. The following sections describe performance metrics that are often used in place of percent correct.

Average Sum-Squared Error

As we discussed in Chapter 2 (Implementations), the goal of network training when using the back-propagation algorithm is to minimize the average sum-squared error. The average sum-squared error is obtained by computing the difference between the output value that an output neurode is supposed to have, called t_1, and the value the neurode actually has as a result of the feedforward calculations, called o_1. This difference is squared, and then the sum of the squares is taken over all output nodes. Finally, the calculation is repeated for each pattern in the testing or training set, as applicable. The grand total sum over all nodes and all patterns, multiplied by 0.5, is the total error E_t:

$$E_t = 0.5 \sum_l \sum_p (t_{pl} - o_{pl})^2 \qquad (7\text{-}1)$$

The total error is then divided by the number of patterns to yield the *average sum-squared error.*

There are a couple of things relative to average sum-squared error that you might want to take into consideration. They relate to being able to compare results. First, the original definition of average sum-squared error made by Rumelhart and McClelland [2] includes the multiplier 0.5, as discussed in Chapter 2. Many implementations ignore this factor of 0.5, but you need to be aware of how the error term is implemented in your neural network tool and in any one in which you are comparing results.

Second, the error term is summed over all output neurodes. This is also the way it is defined by Rumelhart and McClelland [2]. A potential problem is that if you happen to be trying various network configurations with different numbers of output neurodes, the average sum-squared error may not accurately reflect the performance of the network.

You could, for example, train a network with one output neurode to a given error, then find the error increase when you train essentially the same net with several output neurodes. The performance of the network as measured by percent correct may have increased at the same time as the average sum-squared error (per pattern) increased. You therefore need to keep in mind that average sum-squared error, as it was originally defined, means that it is averaged by dividing by the number of patterns in the training or test set, not that it is averaged on a per neurode basis. You probably will, for most applications, want to compute the error on a per-neurode basis by dividing the average sum-squared error (per pattern) by the number of output neurodes. We will call this the *average per-neurode sum-squared error*.

Because the average per-neurode sum-squared error is primarily used in conjunction with the back-propagation algorithm, when used as a performance metric it is generally used with the back-propagation model. There is no reason, however, why it can't be used with other models, such as the self-organization model, as long as the correct values of the output neurodes are known.

It should be cautioned that the average sum-squared error measure (whether per pattern, or per neurode and per pattern) may not adequately measure the network performance in some instances. For example, depending on the value selected for the threshold in a back-propagation model, the average sum-squared error may not accurately reflect the neural network tool performance.

The threshold value is the number, between 0 and 1 for a sigmoid activation function in a back-propagation model, above which an output neurode is considered to be on and below which it is off. The most common value selected for the threshold is 0.5, but for some applications a different value, such as 0.8 or 0.9, may be more appropriate.

Let's look at a couple of cases in which the values of the average (per pattern) sum-squared error are somewhat misleading. Assume we have only one output neurode (so the error is also a per-neurode error), 10 patterns in our pattern set, and a threshold value of 0.5. Also assume that for five of the patterns the output neurode should be on and for the other five it should be off.

If the values of the output neurode for the on patterns are always 0.6 and for the off patterns always 0.4, then, with the threshold value of 0.5, the network is classifying all 10 patterns correctly and is thus performing perfectly, based on the percent correct. The average per-pattern (and per-neurode) sum-squared error is [10(0.16)]/10, or 0.16.

Now consider another case, in which the output neurode has a value of 0.9 for all on patterns and 0.1 for all off patterns except for two, in which it has a value of 0.6. Thus, it is getting 8 of the 10 patterns correct, so the percent correct is 80 percent, which is less than the previous case. The average per-pattern sum-squared error, however, is [8(0.01) + 2(0.36)]/10 = 0.08, only one-half of the value in the previous example in which the network exhibited perfect performance.

For cases in which the threshold is a value such as 0.5, it may be more appropriate to calculate the average sum-squared error based on values (or a single value) other than 0 and 1. With a threshold of 0.5, for example, it may be more meaningful to calculate an error value only for those neurodes that are on the incorrect side of the threshold and to use the threshold as the desired value.

In the first of these two examples, then, this threshold-based average sum-squared error is 0 whereas in the second case it is [2(0.01)]/10, or 0.002. This method of error calculation seems to provide a more realistic picture of the network performance in the examples chosen.

Normalized Error

A problem with the average per-neurode sum-squared error is that it is corrupted by the target variances of the output neurodes. It would therefore be ideal to have some error metric that is independent of these variances.

For those of you who are not statisticians and like us, have forgotten most of what little statistics you ever knew, a brief discussion of variance may be helpful. For more information, you should refer to a book on statistics, such as the one by Roscoe [51].

Variance is defined as the average of the squared deviations from the mean. It is often referred to as the mean square. Two slightly different versions of the variance exist: the population variance and the sample variance. Although there is some disagreement about which should be used in descriptive statistics, we'll work with the population variance. In practical applications of neural network tools, there is very little difference between them.

The population (target) variance for a single output neurode is represented as σ_1^2, and the equation for the target variance is given in Eq. 7-2, where μ_1 is the population (target) mean, or the average of a given output neurode's target values for all of the patterns, and p is the number of patterns. The standard deviation, by the way, is just the square root of the variance, or the root mean square (rms), therefore the standard (target) deviation for a single output neurode is represented as σ_1.

$$\sigma_1^2 = \frac{\sum_p (t_{1p} - \mu_1)^2}{p} \qquad (7\text{-}2)$$

An error measure that removes the effects of target variance and yields an error value between 0 and 1 for all networks regardless of configuration has been proposed by Pineda [53]. This error measure involves the calculation of a quantity defined in Eq. 7-3 that Pineda calls E_{mean}, which is the sum of squared deviations of the target values about the target mean. Note that, for a given training pattern set or test pattern set, E_{mean} remains constant.

$$E_{mean} = 0.5 \sum_l \sum_p [t_{lp} - \mu_l]^2 \qquad (7\text{-}3)$$

Now, the *normalized error* E_m is defined as the total error E_t, defined in Eq. 7-1, divided by E_{mean} defined in Eq. 7-3.

$$E_n = \frac{E_t}{E_{mean}} \qquad (7\text{-}4)$$

As Pineda explains, E_n is particularly useful for back-propagation networks because, regardless of network topology or the particular application, a back-propagation network learns relatively easily the pattern represented by the average target values of the output neurodes. This is a sort of "worst case," in which the network is "guessing" the correct output to be the average target value, and results in a value of E_n of 1.

As the patterns are learned, the value of E_n moves toward 0. The speed depends on the network architecture and application.

 A word of caution is appropriate here. Think about what would happen if you had an output neurode in your network that never changed value. Every target value would be equal to the mean value μ_l, and E_{mean} would be 0, making the normalized error infinite. This situation isn't as farfetched as it may seem. On more than one occasion, the authors have trained a network with several output neurodes using only a partial training set (i.e., one that didn't contain one or more of the output classifications). For the missing classifications, of course, the corresponding output neurode values were zero.

There are at least two ways to deal with this situation. You can remove the neurodes that don't change value, or you can calculate the normalized error on a per-neurode basis, discarding the "infinite" values (you'll have to divide by something other than zero, such as E_{mean} + .000001 to avoid a divide-by-zero error).

One way of looking at the normalized error is that it reflects the proportion of the output variance that is due to error rather than the architecture (including the initialized random weight values) of the network itself. Overall, we believe that this error measure may be, in many cases, the most useful one for back-propagation neural network tools.

Receiver Operating Characteristic Curves

Another way to measure the performance of a neural network system is with receiver operating characteristic (ROC) curves. For some generalized applications, these curves are called relative operating characteristic curves. The use of these curves dates back to the 1940s, for electronic communications systems and the field of psychology. More recently, the use of ROC curves has been described useful for measuring the performance of diagnostic systems, including those that use expert systems and neural networks [42–50].

ROC curves provide a means to quantify the accuracy of an automated diagnostic system by comparing the decisions, or classifications, of a system, such as one that includes a neural network tool, with a gold standard. ROC curves are particularly valuable tools when they are used with neural network systems because the results obtained are not sensitive to the probability distribution of the training/test set patterns or decision bias.

The curves can be generated and compared qualitatively with little regard for their statistical attributes. Over the past few years, however, the use and interpretation of these statistical attributes have become increasingly popular. For example, the calculation of (and understanding the meaning of) the area under the curve has become a common way of evaluating system performance.

An ROC curve is generated for, and reflects, the performance of the system for one given result such as a particular diagnosis. It indicates how well the system did, compared with a gold standard, in making a given diagnosis or making a given decision. The ROC curve thus represents the performance of one output neurode. The discussion that follows focuses on the use of the one-neurode curve, but the use for multiple-output neurode cases is reviewed in the literature [49, 50].

For a given decision, indicated by a given output neurode, four possible alternatives exist. These are illustrated in Table 7-1, which illustrates the contingency table used in the definition of ROC curves.

The first alternative is a true positive decision (TP), in which the positive diagnosis of the system coincides with a positive diagnosis according to the gold standard. For example, the system may have identified the presence of an epileptiform spike waveform that was also identified by a neurologist. The second is a false positive decision (FP), in which the system made a positive diagnosis that was not included in the gold standard; this would mean that the system identified a waveform as a spike waveform the neurologist did not. The third possibility is a false negative decision (FN), in which the gold standard made a

Table 7-1 Contingency table used in ROC curve definition

		"Gold standard" diagnosis	
		Positive	Negative
System diagnosis	Positive	TP (true positive)	FP (false positive)
	Negative	FN (false negative)	TN (true negative)

positive diagnosis that was not made by the system. This is analogous to the neurologist identifying a waveform as a spike but the system failing to do so. The fourth possibility is a true negative decision (TN), in which both the gold standard and the system indicate the absence of a positive diagnosis (neither the neurologist nor the system identifies a waveform as a spike).

The ROC curve makes use of two ratios involving these four possible decisions. The first ratio is TP/(TP + FN), which is generally called the *true positive ratio;* it is also called, for some applications, the *sensitivity.* The second ratio is FP/(FP + TN), generally called the *false positive ratio.* Because the ratio TN/(FP + TN), generally called the *true negative ratio,* is also called the *specificity,* you can see that the false positive ratio is the same thing as (1 − specificity). We discuss sensitivity and specificity in more detail later.

The ROC curve is a plot of the true positive ratio versus the false positive ratio. When applied to the performance of neural network tools, the curve is usually obtained by plotting points for various values of the threshold, then connecting the points with either line segments or a smooth curve. A typical way to proceed is to plot points for a number of threshold values, for example, 0.1, 0.2, . . . , 0.9. To plot the points for true positive ratio versus false positive ratio, each of the four possible decisions must be calculated for each chosen value of the threshold.

Another way to plot the ROC curve is to use actual output neurode values obtained for a training or test set. A given output neurode is typically trained to respond with either a 1 or a 0, depending on the input pattern. When the set of patterns is actually presented to the network, whether it is the last iteration for the training set or the one and only iteration for a test set, the neurode typically responds with numbers close to but not equal to 1 or 0 for most patterns. A few patterns may result in values scattered in between.

The idea is to use the output values, rather than fixed values of the threshold, as the "break points" for calculating the ROC curve. Again, the values for each of the four possible decisions must be calculated for each value of the output neurode.

Figure 7-1 illustrates a hypothetical case involving two configurations of a neural network tool that result in the two ROC curves shown. The curve representing the configuration of NNT2 better reflects overall system performance than that of NNT1. The dotted line drawn along the major diagonal where the true positive and false positive ratios are equal represents the situation in which no discrimination exists. In other words, a system can achieve this performance solely by chance. When the curve follows the left vertical and upper horizontal axes, the system is discriminating perfectly. In this case, for all values of false positive ratio, the true positive ratio is one.

From this brief discussion, we can see that the ROC curve has two attributes: It always lies above the major diagonal, and it always is monotonically increasing in value from left to right. This discussion also implies that a single-value performance measure of a system might be obtained by measuring the area under the ROC curve. This is, in fact, currently the preferred measure of system performance using the ROC curve.

Note that the total area of the graph is one square unit, and the area under the ROC curve is just the proportion of the entire graph area lying

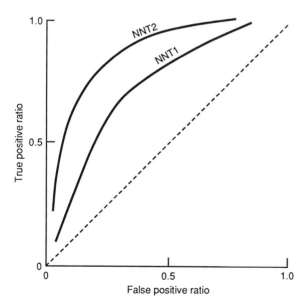

Figure 7-1   Examples of ROC curves.

beneath the curve. Also note that the area under the curve is always between 0.5, the area under the diagonal when no discrimination exists, and 1.0, the area corresponding to perfect performance.

There are two main ways to calculate the area under the ROC curve. One is to generate a smooth curve through the points and calculate the area under it. An easier way is to connect the points with straight line segments, and calculate the area under it using the *trapezoidal rule*. The trapezoidal rule simply means taking the average of two adjacent values of the true positive ratio (*y*-axis values) and multiplying by the corresponding false positive ratio interval along the x axis, then adding all of these individual segment areas together to get the total area.

It should be obvious that an ROC curve requires some minimum number of points if a reasonably smooth curve is to be plotted or if the area under a curve constructed of straight line segments between adjacent points is to have meaning. Generally speaking, an absolute minimum of 5 points should be used to construct a smooth curve, and 9 or 10 will give a reasonably fine-grained structure from which to calculate an area from straight line segments.

We can use the information represented by an ROC curve in a number of ways. For example, the shape of the curve can give you an indication of the sensitivity of the system performance to the threshold value. As another example, the shape of and area under the ROC curve may reflect changes in network parameters (such as eta and alpha in a backpropagation network) or training regimens (such as the number of training epochs) more sensitively than other performance measures such as percent correct.

Other parameters and measurements associated with the ROC curve might prove to be useful to you in your applications. The standard error, for example, can help assess the reliability of the calculation of the area. The discussion of these items is beyond the scope of this book, but a number of references are available if you are interested in pursuing the subject [43, 48–50].

Recall and Precision

There are several ways of looking at the performance of a neural network system that use the four possible decisions defined in the contingency table (Table 7-1) and in the definition of ROC curves. One way is the use of metrics that have been familiar in the fields of expert systems and databases: recall and precision [35, 36].

Recall is the number of positive diagnoses correctly made by the system, divided by the total number of positive diagnoses made by the gold standard. This is defined in the discussion on ROC curves as the true positive ratio and provides an indication of the relative number of false negatives.

Precision is the number of positive diagnoses correctly made by the system, divided by the total number of positive diagnoses made by the system. In the parlance of Table 7-1, this is TP/(TP + FP), and it provides an indication of the magnitude of false positives.

As you can see, precision and recall are just another way of looking at the four quantities in the table; they "cut" the data in a different way than the sensitivity and specificity parameters. Which metric you use will depend heavily on your application and end users. The authors found that recall and precision were a metric of choice when developing an epileptiform spike detection system for use by neurologists. In that application, the number of true negatives had relatively little meaning, and the precision metric provided more meaningful information than specificity.

Other ROC-Related Measures

The object of this section is to present four other performance metrics from the contingency table (Table 7-1), that can often be more informative for characterizing network performance than percent correct and are easy to compute.

Sensitivity [TP/(TP + FN)] is the likelihood that an event will be detected given that it is present. It is likely to be especially important when it is critical that an event be detected. For example, the detection of AIDS is important because its consequences are severe.

Specificity [TN/(TN + FN)] is the likelihood that the absence of an event will be detected given that it is absent. For example, the absence of a "blip" on a radar screen is likely to be an important event: a downed airliner, for example.

Positive predictive value [TP/(TP + FP)] is the likelihood that a signal of an event is associated with the event, given that a signal occurred. This is an especially important statistic when it is imperative that a signal be paid attention to. For example, support staff always pay attention to a signal spike in an EEG, especially if the spike has a high probability of being associated with the corresponding signal of interest.

False alarm rate [FP/(FP + TN) = 1 − specificity] is the likelihood that a signal is detected (falsely) given that a nontarget event occurred. It is easy to see where the name came from.

Each of these statistics can be computed at each output location in a multiple-output neural network. If the outputs are mutually exclusive, the criterion for correctness is based on the winning neurode having the largest value, not on its merely being above 0.5. If the output neurodes are not mutually exclusive, then a criterion of 0.5 can be used.

Examples of the former, with mutually exclusive categories, might be mammal, fish, or bird. In such a case, only one can be considered correct. An example of a nonmutually exclusive categorization might be output nodes that indicate the presence of properties: warm-bloodedness, breathes air, and so on. Assuming in both cases that the input vector is a list of primitive features for an animal, the latter case clearly could contain instances of multiple correct categories (many animals are both cold-blooded and breathe air).

Chi-Square Test

At least one of the preceding neural network performance metrics will probably work whenever you know what the results are supposed to be. For example, in a pattern classification situation, if you know which classification the network is suppose to choose for each case, it's easy to tell how well the network is doing its job. Depending on the specific application, you can calculate the percent correct, recall and precision, or some other measure. What do you do, however, if you don't know what the "right" answers are? This situation isn't as farfetched as it might seem at first glance.

If you remember, in Chapter 1 we outlined four main application areas for neural networks. The fourth area described was different from the other three in that no classification was involved. Instead, it involved the generation of structured sequences or patterns from a network trained to examples. The composition of music, based on training to a given music style, is one example of this area. Another example is the simulation of some process, such as a biological process, which can be described statistically. In this general class of applications, we may not know what the specific result should be in each case, but we may have an idea of what the statistical distribution of results should look like. A useful measurement tool we can use in many such cases is the chi-square test.

The chi-square test examines the frequency distribution of all of the categories (or answers, or classifications) that it is possible to obtain from a particular network system. That is, it looks at how often each category is expected to occur versus how often it actually occurs. The expected frequency of occurrence for a particular category is defined as E, and the actual (observed) frequency of occurrence for that category as O.

The activation values of output neurodes don't directly enter into the chi-square test. Only the frequencies of occurrence of the output patterns do. Of course, the threshold value chosen plays a role in the selection of the winning output pattern, so the output values play an indirect role. The values themselves, however, don't enter into the chi-square calculation.

The chi-square test is used to determine whether a given set of output categories, when compared with an expected distribution, has a variance from probability or a predefined expectation greater than would be expected by chance alone. The equation for chi-square is

$$X^2 = \frac{\sum_{i=1}^{n} (O_i - E_i)^2}{E_i} \tag{7-5}$$

where n is the number of categories. We now outline the calculation and interpretation of the chi-square test. For a detailed explanation, you can refer to any of the several well-known books on statistics [51].

Remember that we are interested in the frequency distribution of the output patterns. If you have four output neurodes in your application, and the neurode with the largest output indicates the output classification ("winner take all"), then $n = 4$, and the calculation is relatively straightforward.

Assume that, in any test set of 50 patterns, the expected frequency distribution of classifications is 5, 10, 15, and 20, respectively, for neurodes 1–4. Suppose that for one 50-pattern test set, we get a distribution of 4, 10, 16, and 20 for nodes 1–4, respectively. Then chi-square for this first test set, as calculated by Eq. 7-5, is 0.267. Suppose, for a second test set, that we get a distribution of 2, 15, 9, and 26 for nodes 1–4, respectively. Chi-square for this second test set, calculated by Eq. 7-5, is 8.500.

Now that we have calculated values, we must decide how many degrees of freedom the system has, which corresponds to the number of frequency distribution values required to uniquely determine the entire set of values, given the total number of tests is known. In our case, if we know the frequencies of occurrence for any three of the four output nodes, we can calculate the fourth, given that the total number is known. Thus, there are three degrees of freedom. (In general, if there are n output nodes, each representing exactly one possible classification, then we can say that there are $n - 1$ degrees of freedom.)

Now, refer to chi-square distribution tables. Along the row corresponding to three degrees of freedom, under the probability of 0.950, you'll find the value 0.352; under probability of 0.05 is the value 7.81. The results for the two test sets can now be interpreted.

For the first test set, we can say that the hypothesis of no difference between the expected and obtained distributions (sometimes called the null hypothesis) is sustained at the 0.95 level. Stated another way, no significant difference between the two distributions exists with a probability exceeding 95 percent. (It is over 95 percent probable that the differences are due solely to chance.)

For the second test set, the null hypothesis is rejected at the 0.05 level. In other words, there is a greater difference between the two distributions than would have been expected by chance, with a probability less than 0.05 that the difference was due to chance.

Now that we've briefly reviewed how to use the chi-square test, a few comments are appropriate. First, note that the chi-square test measures the performance of the entire network system at once, that is, all of the output neurodes. Remember that the ROC curve was designed to analyze one output neurode at a time. The other side of that coin, however, is that you must correctly determine how many output combinations you have. For example, in a music composition situation, you could have, say, 20 output neurodes: 14 that represent note values such as C and F♯, and 6 that represent duration times such as quarter notes and half notes. In this case, there would be up to $14 \times 6 = 84$ possible combinations. In the expected distribution, there may be fewer than 84 if some combinations don't occur. You'll have to decide how to handle these combinations with zero expected frequencies if you obtain them because you'd have to divide by zero if you were to apply the chi-square test strictly. You may also have a problem finding chi-square distribution tables with more than about 30 or 40 degrees of freedom.

It should be obvious that if you are using a neural network system for modeling or simulation, you want the chi-square test to yield the smallest value feasible. In other words, you want the differences between the modeled and the modeling systems' outputs to be so small that it is attributed to chance.

It would not be surprising if new learning algorithms were developed for neural networks that replaced the back-propagation algorithm for modeling and simulation applications. These algorithms could be based on the minimization of chi-square values for the network as a whole, rather than minimizing error values summed over individual nodes.

CHAPTER 8

Network Analysis

Vincent G. Sigillito
Russell C. Eberhart

Introduction

We regard artificial neural networks as tools. Like any other tool, their use can provide satisfactory results if they are the right tool for the job and if they are used in a proper way. One purpose of this chapter is to suggest some ways in which neural network tools can be analyzed. We suggest some analysis methods that are easy to implement and will be helpful to those who are exploring neural net solutions.

It is not enough that a neural network can be trained to solve a problem of interest. The question invariably arises: "How does the network do it?" In other words, what problem-solving strategy did the network discover for solving the problem of interest? Unfortunately, there are no strict guidelines for performing a network analysis, but in this chapter we discuss some approaches that we believe are sufficiently generic and can be used generally. Because feedforward neural networks use their hidden nodes to form internal representations of the map that the network learns, much of the discussion on network analysis will be spent on understanding how the network uses its hidden nodes.

This brief chapter cannot provide all you need to know to decide which network architecture provides the most appropriate tool for a job. We use supervised feedforward networks in our examples because they are the most widely used network architecture and are most likely to be useful to you.

Network Analysis

Introduction

Relatively few discussions in the neural network literature treat their analysis, but three of the best are Gorman and Sejnowski [140], Sejnowski and Rosenberg [145], and Lehky and Sejnowski [146]. The first two use a hierarchical clustering technique of Johnson [147].

Gorman and Sejnowski discuss an approach for interpreting the patterns of weights among neurodes (processing units) that are matched to structures in the training signals (sonar returns from different but similarly shaped objects). The Euclidean distance between each pair of weight-state vectors was computed and then the hierarchical clustering technique was applied. Each resulting cluster was a set of training signals whose weight-state vectors were similar to each other. Cluster centroids were then computed by averaging the signal vectors over all members of each cluster. The cluster centroids comprised a set of distinct patterns that could be ordered along the dimension defined by the response of the hidden unit. This dimension was interpreted as a signal feature that the hidden unit had learned to extract.

Sejnowski and Rosenberg used a similar technique to analyze the hidden units in their seminal work on NETtalk, a network that converts English text to phonemes. Their clustering analysis showed that the most important distinction discovered by the network was between vowels and consonants. Further, within these two groups the clustering produced distinctly different patterns: for the vowels the most important variable was the letter whereas for the consonants the clustering was based more on the similarity of their sounds.

We now illustrate useful approaches to the analysis of neural networks with two detailed case studies.

The Divide-by-Three Problem

This problem involves teaching a network to output a 1 when its input (an 8-bit binary number) is divisible by 3 and to output a 0 otherwise. Because 8 bits can represent integers in the range 0–255, the problem can be restated as that of determining when an integer between 0 and 255 (given its binary representation) is divisible by 3. This is a hard problem for a network because it has many exclusive-OR-like relations that must be solved. In fact, like the exclusive-OR, none of the eight input bits is correlated to the output (target)—the correlation coefficients are exactly 0.

A network with five hidden neurodes was used in the experiment.

Although this network did not learn the map perfectly (it incorrectly classified the numbers 85 and 170 as divisible by 3), it learned 254 of the 256 pairs correctly. We decided to analyze the network at this point to determine how it got the 254 pairs correct and, just as important, why it missed two. Later we comment on the inability of our network to learn the classification task exactly.

The network had eight input neurodes, corresponding to the eight bits of the input representation, five hidden neurodes and one output neurode (1 = divisible by 3; 0 = not divisible by 3). The weights at the end of training are shown in Tables 8-1 and 8-2. Table 8-1 gives the connection weights from the five hidden neurodes and the bias neurode to the output neurode. Notice that the bias weight is +4.4, so the network outputs a +1 (divisible by 3) unless shut off by large negative activations coming from the hidden neurodes.

Table 8-2 shows the weights from the eight input neurodes and bias neurode to the five hidden neurodes. The columns in Table 8-2 are indexed by the power of 2 that the corresponding input node represents in the binary representation. A striking feature of this table is that the connection weights to a given hidden neurode are (approximately) equal in magnitude but alternating in sign. This regularity is not likely to be a chance happening and must therefore be indicative of the learning strategy used by the network.

Table 8-1 Weights from the five hidden neurodes and the bias neurode to the output

$i = 1$	2	3	4	5	Bias
-12.0	$+9.2$	$+9.4$	$+3.4$	-10.0	$+4.4$

$$W_{ij}$$

Table 8-2 Weights from the eight input neurodes and the bias neurode to the five hidden neurodes

i	$j =$ 7	6	5	4	3	2	1	0	Bias
1	-5.0	$+5.0$	-5.0	$+5.0$	-5.0	$+5.0$	-5.0	$+5.0$	-3.0
2	$+2.5$	-2.5	$+2.5$	-2.5	$+2.5$	-2.5	$+2.5$	-2.5	-5.5
3	-2.6	$+2.6$	-2.6	$+2.6$	-2.6	$+2.6$	-2.6	$+2.6$	-6.0
4	-1.4	$+1.2$	-1.4	$+1.2$	-1.4	$+1.2$	-1.4	$+1.2$	-2.3
5	$+5.0$	-5.0	$+5.0$	-5.0	$+5.0$	-5.0	$+5.0$	-5.0	-2.4

$$W_{ij}$$

To help discover this strategy, we examine the behavior of the hidden neurodes to find out when they output a 1, when they output a 0, and when they output intermediate values. For this, it is convenient to introduce the following notation: For a given input, let n_e denote the number of even indexed bits that are 1 and n_o denote the number of odd indexed bits that are 1. Thus, for the number 115, the input is 01110011 $= 2^6 + 2^5 + 2^4 + 2^1 + 2^0$. Therefore, $n_e = 3$ (because of 6, 4, and 0) and $n_o = 2$ (because of 5 and 1). Tables 8-3 and 8-4 are constructed by using this notation and taking into account the bias weight to each neurode. From these tables it is clear that if $n_e = n_o$, the network outputs a 1 (i.e., the input is divisible by 3) because the net input to the output node is 4.4 due solely to its positive bias weight. Let's examine what the network has learned.

An example of a number whose binary representation satisfies $n_e = n_o$ is 204 ($= 11001100$ binary). By its binary representation we see that $204 = 2^7 + 2^6 + 2^3 + 2^2 = 128 + 64 + 8 + 4$. Now 128 mod 3 = 2; 64 mod 3 = 1; 8 mod 3 = 2; and 4 mod 3 = 1. Thus, the remainders upon dividing by 3 are 2, 1, 2, and 1. Because these remainders add to 6, which is divisible by 3, then the number 204 is divisible by 3.

Examination of the 86 numbers in the range 0–255 that are divisible by 3 shows that 70 of these have the property that $n_e = n_o$ in their binary representations. It is thus clear why the network picked up so strongly on determining when $n_e = n_o$. However, the relation $n_e = n_o$ is a sufficient but not necessary condition for divisibility by 3. How did the network learn to handle the remaining 16 inputs that are divisible by 3? To determine this, examine Tables 8-3 and 8-4 to see what other relationship between n_e and n_o results in the network outputting a 1.

The only other condition is when either $n_e - n_o \geq 3$ or $n_o - n_e \geq 3$. For example, take the case $n_e - n_o = 3$. Then the outputs of the five hidden neurodes are 1, 0, 1, 0.5, and 0. Using Table 8-3 we find that the input from the hidden neurodes to the output neurode is $-12.0 + 9.4 + 3.4(0.5) = -0.9$, which is more than compensated for by the positive bias weight of 4.4. Likewise, for $n_e - n_o = 4$, the input from the hidden neurodes to the output neurode is 0.8. Thus, in both cases, the output neurode outputs a 1, indicating divisibility by 3.

To gain some insight into what the network has learned, consider the number 213 ($= 11010101$ binary), for which $n_e - n_o = 3$. This number can be represented as $128 + 64 + 16 + 4 + 1$. The remainders of these numbers upon dividing by 3, are 2, 1, 1, 1, and 1, respectively. Because they add to 6, which is divisible by 3, 213 is divisible by 3. Eight of the 16 numbers in the range 0—255 satisfy $n_e - n_o = 3$, and eight satisfy $n_o - n_e = 3$, accounting for all of the numbers that are divisible by 3.

Table 8-3 Total (net) input of hidden neurodes as a function of n_e and n_o

Hidden neurode	Total (net) input
1	$5 * (n_e - n_o) - 3.0$
2	$2.5 * (n_o - n_e) - 5.5$
3	$2.6 * (n_e - n_o) - 6.0$
4	$1.2 * n_e - 1.4 * n_o - 2.3$
5	$5 * (n_o - n_e) - 2.4$

Table 8-4 Output of hidden neurodes as a function of $_e$ and n_o

Condition	Hidden neurode	Output
$n_e = n_o$	1	0
	2	0
	3	0
	4	0
	5	0
$n_e > n_o$	1	1
	2	0
	3	0.0 if $n_e - n_o = 1$
		0.4 if $n_e - n_o = 2$
		1.0 if $n_e - n_o \geq 3$
	4	0.0 if $n_e - n_o = 1$
		0.2 if $n_e - n_o = 2$
		0.5 if $n_e - n_o = 3$
		1.0 if $n_e - n_o = 4$
	5	0
$n_e < n_o$	1	0
	2	0.0 if $n_o - n_e = 1$
		0.4 if $n_o - n_e = 2$
		1.0 if $n_o - n_e \geq 3$
	3	0
	4	0
	5	1

But our network also outputs a 1 when either $n_e - n_o > 3$ or $n_o - n_e > 3$. There are only two numbers that satisfy these inequalities, 170 (= 1010100 binary) and 85 (= 01010101 binary). Neither is divisible by 3, and each is misclassified by the network.

In effect, the network has learned three rules.

Table 8-5 Weights from six hidden neurodes and bias neurode to the output neurode

$i = 1$	2	3	4	5	6	Bias
17.4	20.4	17.9	8.3	-19.3	45.8	-5.7
			W_{ij}			

Table 8-6 Weights from the eight input neurodes and bias neurode to the six hidden neurodes

$j = 7$ i	6	5	4	3	2	1	0	Bias
1	-4.2	$+4.7$	-4.2	$+4.7$	-4.2	$+4.7$	-4.2	$+4.7$	$+14.7$
2	-10.4	$+10.1$	-10.4	$+10.1$	-10.4	$+10.1$	-10.4	$+10.1$	-21.5
3	$+5.7$	-6.0	$+5.7$	-6.0	$+5.7$	-6.0	$+5.7$	-6.0	-13.4
4	-6.5	$+5.8$	-6.5	$+5.8$	-6.5	$+5.8$	-6.5	$+5.8$	-10.9
5	$+6.4$	-6.5	$+6.4$	-6.5	$+6.4$	-6.5	$+6.4$	-6.5	-5.2
6	-1.0	$+1.0$	-1.0	$+1.0$	-1.0	$+1.0$	-1.0	$+1.0$	-1.7
				W_{ij}				

Rule 1 is correct: An 8-digit binary number is divisible by 3 if $n_e = n_o$.
Rule 2 is only partially correct: An 8-digit binary number is divisible
   by 3 if abs$[n_e - n_o] \geq 3$ (the correct relationship is abs$[n_e - n_o] = 3$).
Rule 3 says that if rules 1 and 2 are not satisfied, then the number is not
   divisible by 3.

This network never did learn rule 3 correctly.

The weights for a network with six hidden nodes that did learn the divide-by-three classification correctly are shown in Tables 8-5 and 8-6. It is worth noting that finding this solution required 1.28 million presentations of the training set. The reader will find it instructive to analyze the network's solution. (*Hint:* an 8-bit binary number is divisible by 3 if and only if abs$[n_e - n_o]$ mod 3 = 0.

Other Considerations

Additional insight is obtained by treating the weights as the components of a vector and examining how the error, the percent correct, the length of the weight vector, and the angle that the weight vector makes in weight space vary with the number of presentations of the training set.

The weight vector $\mathbf{w}$ has dimension N, where

$$N = (n_i + 1) \, n_h + (n_h + 1) \, n_o$$

This expression takes into account the $n_h + n_o$ bias terms which are expressed as learnable weights. The angle made by the weight vector must be measured with respect to a reference vector that we chose, arbitrarily, as the unit N-dimensional vector

$$\mathbf{s} = \frac{(1, 1, \ldots, 1)}{N^{0.5}}$$

Then the angle theta θ is

$$\theta_{w,s} = \arccos\left(\frac{\mathbf{w} \cdot \mathbf{s}}{\|\mathbf{w}\|}\right)$$

Figure 8-1 gives the angle of $\mathbf{w}$ with respect to $\mathbf{s}$, the length of $\mathbf{w}$, the error, and the percent correct as a function of the number of presentations of the training set for the divide-by-three problem. During the first 1100 iterations, the percent correct is constant at approximately 67 percent (the net is classifying all inputs as not divisible by 3 and hence is correct $\frac{2}{3}$ of the time); the error is also essentially constant; and the length of the weight vector is very slowly increasing.

The angle $\theta_{w,s}$ is changing more rapidly. Our interpretation is that, though nothing seems to be happening based on vector length, error, and percent correct, in reality a lot is going on: The system is converging on the *direction* (in weight space) along which a solution lies. Notice that during the first 1000 presentations, $\theta_{w,s}$ varies from 125° to approximately 115°.

During the next 200 presentations, $\theta_{w,s}$ changes from 115° to 95°, and this latter value remains essentially unchanged thereafter. During this change in $\theta_{w,s}$, vector length grows rapidly, the error drops precipitously, and the percent correct jumps from 67 to 95 percent. What has happened is that the network has learned the rule that if the number of even bits that are on equals the number of odd bits that are on in the binary representation of a number, then that number is divisible by three. Of the 86 numbers in the range 0–255 that are divisible by 3, 71 satisfy this rule.

Between 1200 and 1400 presentations of the training set, $\theta_{w,s}$ is essentially constant, the length of the weight vector continues to increase rapidly, the error decreases further, and the percent correct jumps to another plateau at 97 percent. This is the regime in which the network learns the (only partly correct) rule that if the number of even nodes that are on exceeds the number of odd nodes that are on in the binary

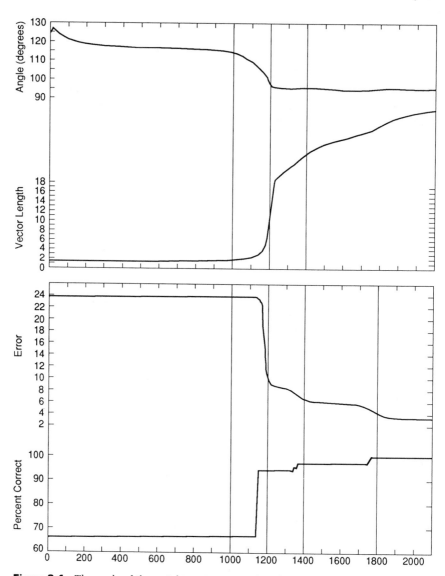

Figure 8-1   The angle of the weight vector, vector length, mean-squared error, and percent correct for the divide-by-three problem, all versus the number of training set presentations.

representation by 3 or more, then the number is divisible by 3. (The correct rule is that the number of even nodes that are on must exceed the number of odd nodes that are on by exactly 3.)

As training progresses, $\theta_{w,s}$ remains essentially constant, and the length of the weight vector continues to increase, but at a slower rate, until somewhere between 1600 and 1700 iterations the network learns the rule (again only partly correct) that if the number of odd nodes that are on exceeds the number of even nodes that are on in the binary representation by 3 or more, then the number is divisible by 3. When this partly correct rule is learned, the percentage jumps to the new plateau at 98 percent.

The Square-within-a-Square Problem

This is a simple problem that is used to illustrate clustering methods for hidden neurode analysis. In this problem a square S, defined by $S = \{x, y \mid 0.2 \leq x \leq 0.9; 0.1 \leq y \leq 0.8\}$, is embedded in the unit square. Given 150 points randomly selected from the unit square (Fig. 8-2) the network is trained to output a 1 if $(x, y) \varepsilon S$, otherwise it outputs a 0.

To analyze how the hidden neurodes were used by the network to solve this classification problem, the output O_i of each of the hidden neurodes for a given (x, y) input pair was mapped into one of five bins:

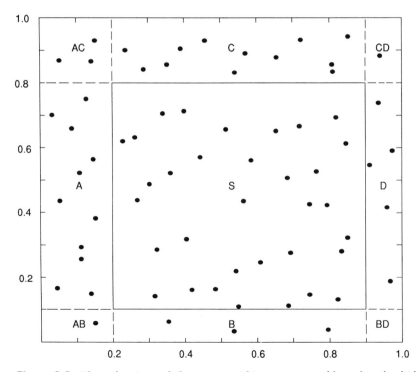

Figure 8-2 The subregions of the square-within-a-square problem that the hidden nodes learned to represent. The dots indicate some of the points of the training set.

$0 < O_i < 0.2$; $0.2 \leq O_i < 0.4$; $0.4 \leq O_i < 0.6$; $0.6 \leq O_i < 0.8$; and $0.8 \leq O_i < 1.0$. These bins were denoted by 1, 2, 3, 4, and 5, respectively.

In the network used, there were four hidden neurodes. If, for example, for a given (x, y) input pair, the outputs of the hidden neurodes were 0.998, 0.010, 0.015, and 0.750, then this would be represented by the vector $(5, 1, 1, 4)$. Doing this for all (x, y) pairs used in the training set resulted in the observation that there was a vast preponderance of five vectors: $(1, 1, 1, 1)$, $(5, 1, 1, 1)$, $(5, 5, 1, 1)$, $(5, 1, 5, 1)$, and $(5, 1, 1, 5)$.

When they were related to the (x, y) pairs that produced them, it was found that (x, y) pairs in region A (Fig. 8-2) resulted in vectors of the type $(1, 1, 1, 1)$, those within the square S produced vectors of the type $(5, 1, 1, 1)$, those in region B produced $(5, 1, 5, 1)$ vectors, those in region C produced $(5, 5, 1, 1)$ vectors, and those (x, y) pairs in region D produced $(5, 1, 1, 5)$ vectors. Thus, each hidden neurode acted as a boundary detector: The first hidden node detected crossing the left boundary of the center square, the second hidden neurode detected its top boundary, the third hidden neurode detected crossing its bottom boundary, and the fourth hidden neurode detected crossing its right boundary.

Input pairs in the corner regions produced the expected combination vectors. For instance, an input pair in the top right-hand area of the region AB would produce one of the vectors $(4, 1, 4, 1)$, $(3, 1, 4, 1)$, $(4, 1, 3, 1)$, or $(3, 1, 3, 1)$.

The solution the net developed was easily discovered by looking at the weights from the hidden neurode to the output neurode along with the output node bias weight. The output node had a large negative bias weight. The weight from the first hidden neurode [this neurode was on when $(x, y)\varepsilon S$] was large and positive and was approximately twice the absolute value of the output neurode's bias. The weights from the other three hidden neurodes were all negative.

Thus, to allow the net to output a 1 required a large output from the first hidden neurode and relatively small outputs from the other three. The network had one condition for all $(x, y)\varepsilon S$, that is, a $(5, 1, 1, 1)$ pattern was produced by the outputs of the hidden neurodes. In effect the solution found by the network was: check to see if $(x, y)\varepsilon S$; if so, output a 1; otherwise output a 0. Not profound, perhaps, but clearly parsimonious.

Distributions of Hidden Neurode Activity Levels

The use of a back-propagation neural network tool to determine surface curvatures from images of simple geometrical surfaces is discussed by Lehky and Sejnowsky [146]. As part of their work, they analyzed the distribution of activity levels for hidden neurodes.

Following the training, they presented the 2000 images used to train the network and plotted histograms of each hidden neurode's activity levels, in 10 equal increments from 0 to 1. They found that the histograms tended to be divided into two groups: those with a unimodal distribution (one maximum) and others with a bimodal distribution (two maxima).

Upon comparison of the hidden neurode activation level distribution with the performance of the network, they concluded that neurodes with the unimodal distribution were primarily detecting orientation or amplitude (i.e., sensing the magnitude of a continuously changing parameter). The neurodes with bimodal distributions, on the other hand, seemed to be detecting features or making either/or decisions (i.e., sensing an on/off binary parameter).

This kind of analysis, used in your application and with your network architecture, could provide insight into how the network tool is functioning.

Analyzing Weights in Trained Networks

When calculated parameters have been used as inputs in a back-propagation network (see the EEG spike detection case study in Chapter 10 for an example), it is sometimes possible to gain some understanding of the network's strategy by examining the weights and weight patterns after training is complete. In general, if a given input neurode has weights of relatively high magnitude fanning out from it to the neurodes of the hidden layer, then that parameter may play a relatively important role in the network decision-making process. You should exercise caution, however, before reaching any conclusions from the weight magnitudes. The distribution of input values and how normalization of those values was done can have an impact on your interpretation. If the magnitudes of normalized inputs to a given input neurode are sufficiently large, then it is more likely that large fan-out weights from the input neurodes will be meaningful. If, however, because of input normalization or some other reason, the input magnitudes are small, it is less likely that significance can be attached to the weight magnitudes.

Relation Factors

Relation factors reflect the strengths of the relationships between individual input neurodes and individual output neurodes. They are discussed in detail by Saito and Nakano [35]. Relation factors can sometimes represent information similar to rules in expert systems.

Two main kinds of relation factors are used to analyze neural network performance. We refer to them as relation factor one and relation factor two.

Relation factor one is the effect of a given input on a given output when all other inputs are constrained to be zero. The effect is calculated by subtracting the value of a given output with all inputs set equal to zero from its value with the one specified input set equal to one. With n_i input neurodes and n_l output neurodes, there are a total of n_i times n_l relation factor ones.

Relation factor two takes into account the fact that the effect of a given input on a given output differs with varying input value combinations (input patterns). Relation factor two measures the average effect of a given input on a given output over a set of input patterns.

For the set of patterns, relation factor two is calculated as follows. First, calculate the change in an output neurode's value when a given input neurode is switched from one to zero while all other input neurodes have the value defined by the first input pattern. For the same input neurode, repeat the calculation for each pattern in the set. Then, add all of the changes together and divide by the number of patterns. This gives you a value for relation factor two for a given input–output neurode pair. Now repeat the process for each of the remaining input neurodes.

Then repeat the entire process for each output neurode. Again, there are n_i times n_l relation factor twos.

An example of using relation factors could occur when you have a partial set of inputs available and you would like your system to be somewhat "intelligent" about what input it asks you for next. For example, if you have a medically related neural network tool that distinguishes between appendicitis and general abdominal pain, you can use a variation of relation factor one to decide which symptom to enter next.

Just present the partial set of symptoms you have so far to the network, and, one by one, set each of the remaining input neurodes to one. The neurode that causes the largest differential to occur between the appendicitis output neurode and the general abdominal pain output neurode corresponds to the symptom you enter next.

The fact that this example seems to bear some resemblance to an expert system should give you some insight as to why the distinctions between expert systems and neural networks are fuzzy and are getting fuzzier! You'll find even more discussion along these same lines in Chapter 9.

Expert Networks

Maureen Caudill

What animal has black-and-white stripes like a zebra, the build of a large antelope, fur like chocolate-brown velvet, a long neck like a giraffe, and a blue tongue? Give up? If you had an expert zoologist to help you with this question, you might easily have answered "an okapi." Without such assistance and lacking a visit to one of the very few zoos in the world that include okapis in their collections, you most likely could not answer it—or else you believed the question was a trick one.

An expert is someone who knows more about a particular field than the average person. Notice that an expert does not have to know more about everything than an average person, only more about some particular thing. This is one of the traps that people commonly fall into: Just because a person is an expert in, say, biophysics does not mean that he or she necessarily knows more than your next-door neighbor about gardening. In fact, because of the time and attention experts must devote to staying current in their own fields, they may very well know much less than your neighbor about keeping aphids off your roses.

So an expert is someone who has exceptional knowledge or skill within a limited field. The range of information over which the expert excels is usually called his *knowledge domain*—literally, the territory over which he rules as expert.

Having valuable expertise available at a moment's notice is something that business and industry have always needed. But because gaining expertise takes time and effort, human experts are nearly always a relatively scarce resource. In the past 10 years or so, artificial intelligence (AI) researchers have developed tools and techniques that permit human experts to automate their experience and thus make their skills available when they are not present. Systems that provide these skills are called *expert systems*, systems that can apply specific domain expertise to hard problems. These systems arose from the belief of their developers that experts apply their knowledge to a problem in a highly rational fashion. Like other AI tools and techniques, expert systems attempt to reason their way to a solution. Let's see how they work.

Rule-Based Expert Systems

What is an expert system? At a minimum, the system has three parts, shown in Fig. 9-1. First, it has a collection of rules, called the *rule base* (in analogy to a database of facts). This rule base consists of a number of specific rules, generally called *production rules*, that are usually in the form of conditional statements: *If* it is raining outside, *then* take your umbrella to work with you. Because of this nearly universal format, the rules are also sometimes called *if–then rules*. The first half of each rule (the *if* clause) expresses a condition which, if true, indicates that it is appropriate to perform the action expressed in the second half of the rule (the *then* clause). This rule base is at the heart of the operation of the expert system.

A second major part of an expert system is the collection of facts and beliefs the system currently knows about its domain of expertise. Sometimes these are embedded in the rule base along with the production rules, and sometimes they're contained in a separate *knowledge base*. No matter where they are stored, however, they perform the necessary function of embodying the system's current understanding of the state of the world—or at least that part of the world the system is dealing with. Also notice, by the way, that this knowledge base contains not only facts but also beliefs. Beliefs are pieces of information that the expert system has reason to believe are true but that may actually be false. For example, "the sky is blue today" is a fact; "the sky will be blue tomorrow" is a belief, based on the system's knowledge of weather forecasting. Beliefs can arise in several ways. The system may have certain beliefs built into it, particularly if it's dealing with problems that are not black-and-white issues, such as diagnosis of medical problems. Often, however, beliefs arise because the system developed them during its attempts to solve a problem. The system literally deduces that some things are probably true. We will talk more about this later.

The third part of an expert system, the *inference engine*, makes the whole thing work. The inference engine is the active portion of the expert system. It performs (at least) two key functions: First, it matches the current state of the world against the conditional clauses of the rules in the rule base to generate a list of matching rules; second, it selects one or more of these matching rules to "fire," or execute the action clause. Performing this action will presumably change the state

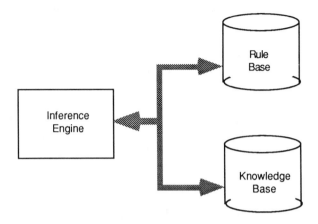

Figure 9-1 An expert system consists of rules in a rule base, facts and beliefs in a knowledge base, and an inference engine that operates on both.

of the world in some fashion, so the inference engine starts the cycle all over again. The inference engine's cycle of "observe the world, match the rules, fire a matching rule" is the expert system equivalent of the digital computer's "fetch an instruction, execute the instruction, store the result" operational cycle.

An inference engine *infers* the correct answer from the rules and facts that it knows. It can work in any of several ways and is most often distinguished from other inference engines by how it reasons its way through a problem. Generally, this reasoning falls into two categories: forward chaining and backward chaining.

A forward-chaining system reasons from the current state of the world forward to the final result. This is useful for problems in which we don't know what the answer should be; a good example of this is the medical-diagnosis expert system, which knows a patient's symptoms and test results but initially has no idea what the correct diagnosis will be. Based on these known details, it asks for additional information, more test results, and so on, until it has narrowed its diagnosis to a small range of possible causes. Thus, it reasons from what it knows— the symptoms—to deduce what illness could be causing these symptoms and to generate what it does not know: the diagnosis.

A backward-chaining system reasons from the known, desired result backward until it reaches the current state of the world. Once it has done this, it knows what to do to change the current state of the world to achieve the desired final state. A good example of the use of a back-ward chaining system is in path planning. Suppose that we want to travel to the Capitol Building in Washington, D.C. As is typical for this kind of problem, we know where we want to go, we just don't know exactly how to get there from where we are. One way to solve this prob-lem is to begin by considering the transportation means that terminate at the Capitol Building (rather than by beginning with all the transpor-tation means that leave where we are now). Suppose we decide on a taxi to achieve that final step; we then need to figure out how to take a taxi, which might result in specifying an arrival at National Airport. From there we figure out how to get to National Airport, and so on. Backward chaining works very well when the final outcome is known, but the path or method to take to achieve that outcome is not known.

Some expert systems use both kinds of reasoning. Such systems for-ward chain from the current state while simultaneously backward chaining from the desired final state. When the forward chain of rea-soning intersects with the backward chain of reasoning, a path that leads from the current state to the final state has been found. Depending on the problem to be solved, this can be more efficient than using either form exclusively.

As mentioned earlier, expert systems deal with facts, but unlike more traditional computer programs, they also deal with beliefs. This means that the system has to have a way of coping with opinions about the world. In most cases, human experts are expected to offer advice even when not all the facts are known about a particular situation; it is one of the characteristics of a human expert that she can do so and generally be correct. If an expert system is to fill the same role as the human expert, it must have a similar ability to draw upon its experience and understanding to deal with situations that are only partially specified. How is this done?

Uncertainty in data, which is the essence of something that is only *believed* to be true instead of *known* to be true, is one of the most dif-ficult things an expert system builder must deal with. There is no single solution to this problem as yet; much depends on the specific problem domain to be solved by the expert system. One way that has worked well in certain cases is to assign a "certainty factor" to all facts in the knowledge base. The certainty factor is a measure of how strongly a particular fact is believed to be true. For example, if the fact is that lead is denser than water, the certainty factor would be 1.0—this fact is cer-tainly true. On the other hand, if the fact is that the sky will be clear this afternoon, the certainty factor might be only 0.7—it is likely to be true, but we cannot be absolutely sure. And if the fact is that the earth is flat, the certainty factor might be 0.0 because it is certainly false. (Apologies are extended to members of the Flat Earth Society.) An expert system that implements certainty factors must spend a great deal of effort making sure that the factors truly represent the system's current understanding of the world around it. For example, if the system observes that the sky is indeed clear this afternoon, it must update its certainty factor to 1.0 because that is now a known fact.

Dealing with certainty factors can be extremely complex, particularly when the problem does not lend itself to conclusive tests of truth or falsity. For example, suppose the problem is one of diagnosing a disease. The patient's symptoms and test results may indicate that there are four or five possible causes, ranging from the likely (a very high certainty factor) to the rare (a low certainty factor). But just because a particular disease is rare does not mean that this particular patient doesn't have it, only that it is less likely. The problem is that medical tests, like most everything else that has to do with biological systems, are neither perfectly accurate nor perfectly foolproof. The results of a particular medical procedure almost never come back with a definitive answer, just as the identifying symptoms of a particular disease are never numerically precise. As a result, adding more facts to the knowledge base by performing more tests on the patient may or may not help. And how should the new test data be incorporated into the existing knowledge anyway? Suppose Test A has a result that, by itself, would offer a 40 percent certainty that the patient has a particular disease; also suppose that Test B has a result that separately indicates a 60 percent certainty of the same disease. Does this mean that the patient is 100 percent certain to have the disease? No, it does not; certainty factors cannot be simply added together. Figuring out ways to deal with this kind of situation in a consistent and reasonable manner that is appropriate to the problem at hand is critical to the success of implementing certainty factors in an expert system.

Sometimes expert systems do more than reason things out on the basis of given rules. Some more sophisticated expert systems can actually change the rules they operate under, on the basis of their experience with previous problems. This ability to infer, to develop new rules as they go along, makes such systems much more powerful than other expert systems. Systems that can modify the facts and beliefs in their knowledge bases and change the rules in their rule bases can learn from experience and become even more expert at their tasks.

Rule-based expert systems have become a staple in industry in recent years. They have several advantages over other techniques for problem solving. First, they provide a logical, symbol-processing approach to solve problems that are inherently cognitive. By this we mean problems that inherently have rules that can be used in developing a solution. Such problems can best be solved by taking a rational approach that works its way through the known rules to find a solution. Because this is precisely how an expert system works, it is easy to understand why they are so useful for such problems. A good example is diagnosing problems, whether medical or otherwise. When trying to determine the cause of a symptom, often the safest approach is to work through all known possible causes carefully, eliminating those that do not apply to the current situation. Because expert systems, unlike humans, never forget anything and always reason carefully, they can be of great assistance for such tasks.

A second reason expert systems are so useful is that they nearly always provide thorough explanations of what they do. If an expert system asks for more information, perhaps a particular test result in the case of a medical diagnostic system, the user can query the system to find out why it wants the requested information. The system can respond with a good explanation, such as "If the red blood cell count is greater than a particular value, it will eliminate beriberi as a possible cause for the patient's symptoms." In addition, the expert system can explain how it arrived at its final decision. Generally the system keeps track of every rule that is fired and can reproduce the exact chain of reasoning that it used to produce its answer.

Almost every expert system built today has such explanatory capabilities built in, which can be essential for the system to be accepted by users. Most people are reluctant to accept the word of a computer as law; they want an explanation of why the system states that a particular answer is correct. This is especially true when a system is first introduced; time and usage eventually make the user more trusting, but the expert system literally has to prove itself to its users. Having the ability to explain what it is doing has proved to be a tremendous boon.

Many useful commercial expert systems have been developed, and the number is growing steadily. In spite of their successes, however, rule-based expert systems are not a panacea. They have weaknesses as well as strengths. Let's consider what those weaknesses might be.

The first is the difficulty of finding an expert to help with building the system. There may not be an available person who can be clearly identified as having superior expertise in the field. The area of stock-market analysis is a good example of this. Although many people are called experts, their approaches and tactics are often diametrically opposed, and their success rates may be only average, or even below average. As a result, if one tried to build an expert portfolio manager using a rule-based system, the expertise embodied would reflect only the expertise of the particular person being used as expert, including that person's weaknesses as well as his knowledge. The success rate of this expert system would be, at best, no greater than that of the original expert.

A second problem is hidden here as well: A rule-based system designer generally has a very difficult time if more than one expert is used or if the experts involved disagree. As can easily be imagined in cases like a stock portfolio manager system, experts will probably have different opinions on what rules should go into the rule-based system. This kind of situation can be difficult or even impossible to straighten out. Thus, rule-based systems are usually built on the skills of a single expert, rather than embodying the talents of a panel of experts. This can be a significant limitation when there is no clearly superior expert to call on.

Suppose the system designer has selected the single, well-recognized expert in the problem domain and that person has agreed to assist in developing a rule-based system. Is all well now? Unfortunately the answer is no. The human expert may not be able to express the rules he uses to solve the problem in any coherent way. This is very interesting, in fact, because when expert systems were first being developed and this phenomenon was first encountered, it was widely assumed that the reason the human experts didn't clearly articulate the rules they used was that they held a deep-seated fear of being replaced by the rule-based expert. As a result, so the theory went, the experts would consciously or unconsciously sabotage the rule-extraction process to save their jobs and personal reputations. Knowledge engineers, the builders of expert systems, sometimes actually tried to trick the experts into revealing the appropriate rules to include in the rule base. As experience with this phenomenon became more widespread, however, developers eventually realized that the real reason experts couldn't articulate the rules they used to solve their problems was simply that they didn't use clearly defined rules. A human expert does not necessarily—does not usually, in fact—reason out the answer to a problem. Because the expert does not use explicit rules to solve the problem, she cannot articulate them for the system developer. This can make the process of writing the appropriate rules a next-to-impossible task.

There are still more potential problems. Because the expert system can deal only with situations that it is told about, the system designer has to build in rules to handle nearly every possible contingency, just as a traditional programmer must do when writing a computer program. As a result, a large expert system can contain thousands or tens of thousands of rules. This often means that the rule base becomes unmanageable, and even unmaintainable, unless the developer is extremely careful when it is built. Unanticipated additions to the rule base as the expert system's capability is further refined can result in a tangle of rules that becomes difficult or impossible to understand and check for completeness and accuracy. As with any large software project, size and complexity can mean unexpected and undesirable behavior in the final system.

Still another potential pitfall is dealing with the certainty factors often found in an expert system. As was pointed out earlier, if one test indicates a 40 percent certainty that something is true, and another indicates a 60 percent certainty that it is true, it does not follow that it is 100 percent true. Yet it generally isn't clear exactly how such factors should be combined to provide consistent and reasonable estimates of how sure the system should be of each belief.

One more unfortunate characteristic of rule-based expert systems is that they exhibit a trait called the *mesa effect*, a term that refers to the shape of their performance graph. A chart of a typical rule-based system's performance relative to the scope of the problem domain usually shows consistent and fairly high performance levels throughout its area of expertise, until it moves even slightly outside the area of its known problem domain. If given a problem that is even a bit outside this area, the rule-based system's performance drops sharply to near-zero levels. It is as though the system stepped off the edge of a high mesa and tumbled to the ground far below. In other words, although the system can handle an appropriate problem, if the problem is new or outside its knowledge domain, the system's response is likely to be just so much babble. Worse, a rule-based system usually has no means of detecting when it is near the edge of a mesa; it does not know that it doesn't know about the problem. It is usually up to the user to determine whether the system's response makes sense for each problem, but this puts the demand for expertise back in the lap of the human user.

To summarize, the rule-based expert system approach works very well when the problem has a reasonably accessible set of rules, with a clearly identified expert who is available to help build the system. However, this approach stumbles when the problem cannot be easily solved with known rules or when multiple experts disagree on how to solve it. Furthermore, rule-based approaches can suffer from poor maintainability and verification problems if the problem is complex. And the user may have to be sure that the problem given to the system is within its domain of expertise because the mesa effect can result in nonsense answers if the problem is inappropriate.

But rule-based systems are not the only way to get automated expertise. What if we use neural networks?

Expert Networks

How would we build a neural network expert, an *expert network* in other words? And when is it appropriate to take this approach rather than the more traditional rule-based approach? Let's consider the first question and then see if the answer to it sheds some light on the second.

Neural networks can be used in several ways to build an expert network. The simplest is by building a fuzzy cognitive map, originally developed by B. Kosko at USC. The term *fuzzy cognitive map* refers to the use of fuzzy mathematics in building an expert network that can handle the expertise of multiple experts. Because you may not be familiar with fuzzy math, let's take a moment to review the basics.

Fuzzy Mathematics

Fuzzy math is used to deal with situations that are not clear-cut and precise. We begin by reviewing what a fuzzy set is. You may be familiar with the basic concepts of set theory: A set is a collection of items. Each distinct item in the set's universe is either a member or not a member of the set. Two sets intersect if they have at least one item that exists in both sets. The union of two sets is a set that contains all objects in either set. And the complement of a set is the set that consists of all objects *not* in the original set. For example, suppose the universe consists of the planets in the solar system. We can define a set A that contains the planets {Mercury Venus Earth Mars}. (The curly brackets {} are traditionally used to identify members of a set.) Set B might contain the planets {Mars Jupiter Saturn Uranus}. The intersection of sets A and B is the set {Mars} because it is the only planet in both A and B. The union of sets A and B is the set {Mercury Venus Earth Mars Jupiter Saturn Uranus}. The complement of set A is the set {Jupiter Saturn Uranus Neptune Pluto}.

This works very well for objects as definite as planets. After all a planet is a tangible thing that is either present or absent. But what if we want the set of all people who like astronomy? If we take a poll of a group of individuals, most likely we would get a variety of responses ranging from "I hate astronomy" through "It's an okay subject" to "It's my favorite subject." The problem is how to identify this vague continuum of responses in a set notation.

The solution to this is to use fuzzy sets. A fuzzy set is one in which the membership of an individual entity in the set is a matter of scale. Just as a person can "sort of" like something or "kind of" dislike something, a fuzzy set permits its members to be partial and incomplete participants. Using the example of people who like astronomy, we might poll four people and construct a fuzzy set that represents each person's membership in the likes-astronomy set:

likes astronomy: {0.5/Alice 0.8/Bob 0.1/Charles 0.9/Doreen}

Here the notation uses a fraction on the scale of 0 (hates astronomy) to 1.0 (loves astronomy) to indicate each individual's relative membership in the set. The individual concerned is identified by a slash and his or her name so that there can be no confusion. Suppose we also poll these same individuals on how much they like English literature. We might get the following responses:

likes English = {0.4/Alice 0.1/Bob 0.9/Charles 0.2/Doreen}

To find the set of people who like both astronomy and English, we would normally take an intersection (those individuals who are present in both sets). This is the equivalent of performing a logical-AND operation, by the way, because the result will be individuals who comply with both "likes astronomy" and "likes English." In fuzzy sets, however, it is not obvious exactly how we should take an intersection. It turns out that it is quite simple: We compare each individual's likes-astronomy membership with that person's likes-English membership. The intersection is the *minimum* of those two memberships. In our example this would be

likes astronomy AND English = {0.4/A 0.1/B 0.1/C 0.2/D}

(The names have been abbreviated to initials here for easier notation.)

Similarly, if we want to find the fuzzy set membership of those who like at least one of astronomy and English, we would normally take the union of the two sets. This is the same as performing a logical-OR operation because the result will be those who like either astronomy or English or both. In fuzzy sets, this is done by considering each individual's membership value in the two sets and taking the *maximum* membership as the union. Specifically, this results in the following fuzzy set:

likes either English or astronomy: {0.5/A 0.8/B 0.9/C 0.9/D}

Finally, we can construct the complement of a fuzzy set: for example, the set that represents those individuals who *don't* like English. The likes-English set uses a 0.0–1.0 scale to represent how much each person likes English. To find out how much that person doesn't like English we simply subtract his or her likes-English ranking from the maximum value of 1.0; the result is how much that person dislikes English. In the example, the result is

doesn't like English: {0.6/A 0.9/B 0.1/C 0.8/D}

Fuzzy set theory is basic to applying fuzzy logic to problems. By combining the operations for intersection, union, and complementation (negation), the whole array of logical operations can be constructed for use with fuzzy sets and relationships. The advantage that fuzzy sets offer over more traditional probability operations is that the specific numbers chosen are not especially important; what is important is their relative ordering. For example, as long as "I hate astronomy" is assigned a lower score than "It's an okay subject," fuzzy sets will work out properly. It really doesn't matter how much lower or higher the responses are scored as long as they are properly ordered. This has tremendous practical advantages. In many cases, a human expert can consistently order a response set, even when she feels quite uncomfortable about assigning specific numerical values to its members. Given a consistent ordering, it is often possible simply to assign integer values to the responses, beginning with 0 for the lowest and continuing until all receive a ranking.

As was mentioned before, rule-based expert systems often have trouble dealing with certainty factors consistently. One excellent use for fuzzy logic is to provide a reasonable and consistent way of combining certainty factors in an expert system. Although standard probability theory could be used instead, the probabilities assigned are likely to be arbitrary even when assigned directly by the expert. Furthermore, probability theory requires much more complex mathematical operations (multiplication, combinations, and factorials) than fuzzy set operations, which rely almost exclusively on *max*, *min*, and simple subtraction.

But how can we use fuzzy logic to build an expert network? There is one excellent and simple example of a fuzzy logic network, and that is the fuzzy cognitive map. Let's consider how it works.

Fuzzy Cognitive Maps

A fuzzy cognitive map is one of the easiest expert networks to build. It has interesting advantages over the more traditional rule-based systems, particularly in its ability to deal with multiple experts, even when they

Table 9-1 Factors affecting used car sales, sample grid

	High sales	Union raises	Safer vehicles	Govt. rules	Foreign competition	Lower prices	Better design	High profits	Happy buyers	Good gas mileage
High sales	—	0	0	0	0	0	0	0.8	0	0
Union raises	0	—	0	0	0	-0.6	0	-0.8	0	0
Safer vehicles	0.4	0	—	0	0	-0.6	0	-0.4	0.4	-0.2
Govt. rules	0	0	0.9	—	0	-0.8	0.4	-0.6	0.6	0.4
Foreign competition	-0.5	-0.4	0.2	0	—	0.6	0.6	-0.8	0.4	0.6
Lower prices	0.8	-0.4	0	0	-0.2	—	-0.2	-0.4	0.8	0
Better design	0.4	0	0.4	0	0	0.4	—	0.4	0.6	0.2
High profits	0	0.4	0	0	0.6	-0.6	0	—	-0.2	0
Happy buyers	0.8	0	0	-0.2	-0.4	0	0	0	—	0
Good gas mileage	0	0	0	-0.2	0	0	0	0	0.6	—

disagree. In addition, because no explicit rules need to be articulated, the development time for a fuzzy cognitive map is dramatically less than for a rule-based system.

A fuzzy cognitive map sets up a series of nodes, each of which is a fuzzy set. Each node represents a particular concept or object that is relevant to the problem. Weighted, directed connections among the nodes represent causal relationships among the concepts or objects; the weights represent the relative strengths of the causal relationships. A positive weight means the source node causes the destination node to increase in significance or become more powerful; a negative weight means the source causes the destination to decrease or become less powerful.

If a fuzzy cognitive map followed standard AI approaches, it would be implemented by performing a graphical search through the cognitive map; because it is more like a neural network, the fuzzy cognitive map receives a stimulus and then allows the resulting activity to resonate through the nodes of the map until an equilibrium is reached. Let's take a moment to see how one is built.

Suppose we want an expert system that deals with the automobile industry and new car sales. This is, of course, a very complex issue with many factors that affect the number of new cars sold in any given time period. There is no single, recognized expert in this field though a number of people have expertise, so developing a rule-based system is not feasible. We must take a more innovative approach. A fuzzy cognitive map is an ideal choice in this instance.

The first step in building the map is to ask each of our panel of experts to identify the key factors that affect the number of new cars sold in the United States. This is a task that an expert can usually do fairly easily. Next we build a blank grid like that shown in Table 9-1 and ask each expert to fill in the relationships in the grid. These relationships reflect how much the expert feels the factor at the head of the row causes the factor for that column. For example, the expert filling out this sample grid felt that *High sales* (the first-row factor) was a strong cause for *High profits* (column 8). The expert can list his opinion of the relative strength of the causal link in words such as *very much* or *has a slight effect on* without indicating a numerical relationship. Notice that in the table several of the causal relationships are expressed as negative values; these indicate that the factor tends to repress another factor. For example, in the second row, the factor *Union raises* tends to reduce the factor *High profits*, and this is expressed by a negative value. Again, because the expert does not have to quantify anything, it is usually easy for him to fill in such a table.

Once the expert has given his qualitative estimates on the possible causal relationships, the system developer turns these into fuzzy weights. This is easier to do than you might think. We simply list all the verbal responses that the expert uses to describe the causal relationships between factors and order them from least intense to most intense. For example, one possible ordering might be {has no effect on, has a slight effect on, has some effect on, affects, affects strongly, is a direct cause of}. We do a similar ordering for any negative causal expressions as well. If there is any doubt as to the correct order, the expert can usually clarify things. Once the order is determined, we assign fuzzy values to each expression in the range 0.0 to 1.0 (for positive links) and 0.0 to −1.0 (for negative links). Surprisingly, it doesn't matter what the exact values are for this, as long as they retain the relative order of the expressions. In this sample, we might assign the fuzzy values of {0.0, 0.2, 0.4, 0.6, 0.8, 1.0} for each of the positive-link expressions. The numbers in Table 9-1 are the fuzzy numbers for this expert's opinion.

Once this grid is filled out, we no longer need the expert to help us develop the fuzzy cognitive map. Because the expert was never asked to articulate any rules, his participation in the development of the system is both easier and less time consuming than for a rule-based system. In addition, his information—assuming he does a thoughtful job in filling out the grid—is more likely to be an accurate reflection of his understanding of the problem.

For simplicity, let's assume for the moment that we are using only a single expert for this problem. What happens next? We construct a directed map like that shown in Fig. 9-2, with a node representing each factor in the grid and links that connect nodes that have nonzero weights in the matrix. Negative links are shown with gray arrows in the illustration, and positive links are shown with black arrows. The weight matrix of links is as shown in Table 9-1. If we want to do this in a computer simulation or in hardware, this directed map is implemented as a Hopfield network, with each neurode in the map representing one of the factors in the table, and each connection weight representing the corresponding value shown in the table. Once we have built this network of nodes and links, the fuzzy cognitive map is complete.

It may be complete, but how do we use it? In effect, the fuzzy cognitive map is a model of the expert's view of the way the car-buying world works. Suppose we want to know the effect of increasing foreign competition on the system. Using the network implementation of the map, we force the *Foreign competition* node to be very active. This causes inhibitory signals to be sent to *High sales*, *Union raises*, and *High profits*. It also sends positive signals out to *Safer vehicles*, *Lower prices*, *Better design*, *Happy buyers*, and *Good gas mileage*. Each of these

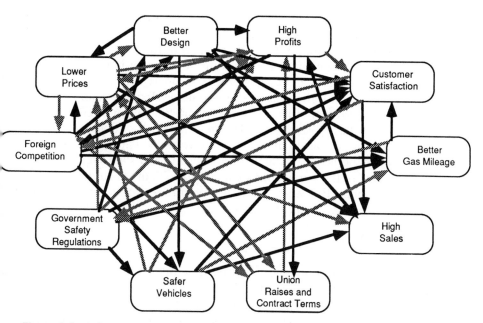

Figure 9-2 A fuzzy cognitive map. Negative causal relationships are shown by gray arrows, positive ones by black arrows.

nodes then becomes active to a greater or lesser degree and sends its signals to the nodes with which it has causal relationships. This results in a brief period of chaotic activations, followed eventually by a stable cycle of activity. The nodes that are involved with this stable activity cycle reflect the long-term effects of increasing foreign competition.

In this example, we used only a single expert's model to make the fuzzy cognitive map. But suppose we have a group of experts who may or may not agree with each other. How do we deal with this? It is simplicity itself with a fuzzy cognitive map. We first poll all the experts about the relevant factors to include in the grid. All factors mentioned by the experts should be included. Then the blank grids are given to the experts as before. To combine the resulting matrices into a single grid, we perform a fuzzy union operation on each grid element. In other words, if three experts indicate that the effect of *Safer vehicles* on *High sales* is 0.4, 0.6, and 0.2, respectively, the value used in the final fuzzy cognitive map is the fuzzy union of (0.4, 0.6, 0.2), or the value 0.6. Everything else is done as before.

We can even deal with experts with greater and lesser credibility by multiplying their factors by a "believability" factor before combining them with other experts' opinions. And if we have an expert who is extremely knowledgeable about certain factors and not others, we can use differing believability factors on different parts of his grid, as appropriate, before combining it with other expert opinions.

Kosko's fuzzy cognitive map is a kind of half-way house between a rule-based system and an expert network. It deals with high-level concepts as nodes and links, just as a rule-based system does, and yet it is built and operates more like a neural network than a rule-based system. And though it has close ties to a Hopfield network, it does not implement a learning rule as do most neural networks. It is particularly good when many experts of varying believability and skills are available, and it avoids most of the knowledge extraction problems of rule-based system development. But we can also use neural networks directly as an expert network. Let's look at one example.

An Expert Bond-Rating Network

Nearly any mapping network can be used as an expert network, including back-propagation networks, counter-propagation networks, and madalines. Even categorizing networks such as the Kohonen feature map can be used as an expert network with a bit of pre- and postprocessing. Let's see how we might do this.

Consider the problem of rating bonds. Companies that want to borrow money often submit an application to bond-rating agencies, such as Standard and Poor's, which consider the relative merits of the company's application and offer expert opinion on the worth of the bond. These expert opinions are translated into ratings, such as AAA or AA or BBB which investors then use to decide whether or not to purchase the bonds. The rules that determine whether a bond will receive a particular rating are difficult or impossible to write down because every application is unique and has its own particular situation. In other words, there is no good mathematical model of how to rate bonds, nor is there a single, well-recognized expert at this task. As a result, bond rating is not a good candidate for a rule-based expert system.

In 1988, Soumitra Dutta and Shashi Shekhar, two researchers from the University of California at Berkeley, developed a neural network system for rating bonds. Their system demonstrates the effectiveness of neural networks in this and similar problems. Let's see how they built it.

The bond rating system consisted of straightforward back-propagation networks. Dutta and Shekhar collected 47 applications to Standard and Poor's for a AA bond rating, along with the Standard and Poor's final decision on each one. These data were split into two groups and used as training and test data for the network. Thirty of the applications

Table 9-2 Input data for bond-rating neural network

Variable	Definition
1	Liability/(cash + assets)
2	Debt proportion
3	Sales/net worth
4	Profit/sales
5	Financial strength
6	Earning/fixed costs
7	Past 5-year revenue growth rate
8	Projected next 5-year revenue growth rate
9	Working capital/sales
10	Subjective prospect of company

were used for training and the other 17 for testing the network. From each bond application, they took 10 data items, shown in Table 9-2.

Notice that all of the data items chosen by the researchers except variables 8 and 10 are objective, verifiable facts. Only the projected growth rate and the subjective prospects for the company are opinions. Note also that the researchers checked the statistical correlations among all 10 of the variables and determined that all such correlations were very small; in other words, the value of variable 8 had little or nothing to do with the value of any other variable and served as a poor predictor of the probable value of any other variable. As a result, all 10 variables are considered independent variables. In essence, the researchers defined a 10-dimensional vector in which each of the 10 elements were orthogonal to each other. This is one key to getting a good training result.

Dutta and Shekhar trained two groups of back-propagation networks to this problem. One network group used a 10-element input pattern; the other received only the first six variables of the input vector: The revenue growth history and projection, the working capital/sales value, and the company prospects data were omitted. In each case, the network merely had to decide whether each bond application was to be awarded a AA rating. Because there is a range of possible ratings, a sliding linear scale was used for the final rating output (A, AA, AAA, etc.). They also used networks of two, three, and four layers to determine the optimum size for this problem. Of concern to us here is their three-layer network, the traditional back-propagation choice.

Their results are illuminating. With the 10-element input pattern, the three-layer network was able to learn extremely well. It correctly classified 100 percent of the rejected applications in the training set and accepted 92.3 percent of the applications that Standard and Poor's actually accepted. Its only errors in the training set were a 7.7 percent chance of predicting a rejection when the bond was actually accepted. With the test set of new cases, the network was about as accurate at predicting acceptances as rejections, with approximately an 83 percent accuracy record overall. (In case you're wondering, the results with both the two-layer and the four-layer networks were similar.)

The three-layer network that received only the first six input pattern variables did not perform quite as well, as might be expected because it had fewer data to work with. This network was able to learn only about 77 percent of the accepted cases and 82 percent of the rejected cases in the training set. However, its performance in the test set was almost identical to that of the 10-element network, with about an 80 percent accuracy overall.

There are a couple of interesting things about this project. One is that the researchers compared the neural network's performance with that of statistical regression analysis, a tool often used in financial applications. They did both 10- and 6-element regressions of the training data, using the resulting coefficients to categorize the test data. In all cases, the regression analysis had an overall accuracy of about 64 percent, significantly lower than that of any of the neural networks they used. Further, they found that the total error in the regression approach was about an order of magnitude higher than that of the neural network. These regression results are comparable to those of other researchers using regression on similar problems.

Another interesting point was that the neural network model never predicted a rating that was more than one rating level off the actual final rating for that application. In contrast, the regression analysis often suggested ratings that were several categories away from the Standard and Poor's rating for that bond. Apparently, when the regression was wrong, it was very wrong. In a sense, this is similar to the mesa effect of a rule-based system: If the system is outside its area of expertise, the output might not be much better than a random guess.

The researchers who built this system did a lot of things right. They selected an interesting problem with available training and test data. They carefully chose the input values to be independent variables and restricted the size of the input set to a reasonable dimensionality. (This was especially important because they were working with software simulations of neural networks and thus had to be concerned with overall computation time.) They compared their neural network results with those of more traditional techniques to determine which offered the best performance for this problem. They also experimented with different architectures and network sizes to find the best results for this problem.

More than being an example of a simple problem solved carefully and well, however, this bond-rating system also demonstrates that a neural network expert system can do more than just learn a set of data. If that were all a network could do, it would serve as a nice associative memory system, but it would not be useful as an expert network. This bond-rating system demonstrates the ability of a neural network to generalize from specific examples to more general principles. This notion of generalization is essential if networks are to perform expertly in problem-solving domains.

Generalization means that when a network learns a collection of training cases, for whatever problem, what the network is really learning is not the specific examples but the general principles that control or determine the answers to those examples. In other words, the network does not merely memorize cases but extracts the relevant features that distinguish the examples and absorbs those features. Furthermore, it does so without being told what the critical features are; the training process permits the network to determine *for itself* what characteristics are key determining ones. This is not meant to imply a consciousness or intelligence in the network, but it does mean that we need to consider how knowledge is contained in an expert network.

Knowledge in an Expert Network

We have seen that neural networks can be used for expert system applications, which means that during the training process they must have learned something; they must have obtained some knowledge about the problem that they did not have before. In particular, we have seen that the network generalizes the cases it is shown during training to construct a model for decision making. Can we somehow extract that knowledge from the expert network to confirm that it is correct?

The answer to this question is yes and no. It is possible to figure out what the network knows, but it is not necessarily easy to do so. Recall that during training, the network typically modifies only the weights on the connections among its neurodes. Certainly we can easily get a printout of the values of all those weights; but does knowing that the weight between the sixth neurode in the input layer and the twelfth neurode in the middle layer is 0.546 tell us anything about why a particular person's mortgage insurance was accepted? Of course it doesn't. Yet somehow the network had the knowledge buried in it to make that decision. Where is all that information?

The knowledge and rules that the network works by are contained not in individual weights and connections but in the overall pattern of weights and connections. With a bit of effort, we can inspect the pattern to discover how the network makes its decisions. Let's assume we are working with a trained, three-layer network. Convention tells us that the input layer distributes the input data pattern to the middle layer, the middle layer acts as a collection of feature detectors to determine the features present in the input pattern, and the output layer generates an appropriate output response based on the features detected by the network. (Obviously, more complex connection schemes will modify this global vision of the network's operation, but the principles remain the same.) One of the first things we might like to do is figure out what features the middle layer looks for in the input pattern.

We can deduce the middle layer's feature-detection scheme by looking for weights on connections from the input layer that are exceptionally strong. Strongly positive weights leading from a particular input neurode to a middle-layer neurode probably mean that that input value is especially critical to the feature detected by that middle-layer neurode. By checking the weights on all the connections leading to a particular middle-layer neurode, we can come up with a pretty good idea of what it will take to make that feature detector fire. Notice, however, that not all weights will be positive. A strongly negative weight implies that the middle-layer neurode is looking for the *absence* of a signal coming in along that connection rather than the presence of a signal. Thus, features consist of both the presence and the absence of incoming signals.

Let's consider an example. Suppose we train a back-propagation network to recognize images of the letters *A*, *B*, and *C* and then check its middle-layer neurodes to see what features it uses. First, we might guess that distinguishing features of the letter *A* are the angle at the top of the letter, the diagonal lines that make up the sides, and the open bottom of the letter. We could check for middle-layer neurodes that react strongly when they receive inputs corresponding to each of these characteristics. Chances are, we would find at least one neurode in the middle layer that responds strongly to each of them. There might be one that has strong incoming net signals when the angled top appears in the input pattern, another that has strong net input signals when one or the other diagonal lines appears, and another that responds strongly when there is no incoming signal from the bottom of the letter.

(By the way, it is also possible that the neurode that responds to a diagonal line may also respond strongly to a curve at the right hand side of the letter or some other feature. This will be especially true when the number of feature-detecting neurodes in the middle layer is small. In such cases it is up to the output layer neurodes to sort out the overall pattern of features detected to decide on the correct output. This is why a middle layer that is too small can make training more difficult.)

In spite of this general agreement with our predictions, we would probably find that the exact features we expect are not used by any of the neurodes in the middle layer. There is no reason why the network has to solve any problem the way a person would, and in general neural networks do not do so. The features chosen are usually similar to ones a person might use, but they are not likely to be exactly the same. The implications of this are important: It means that when we build an expert network, we should expect it to have expert-level performance, but we should not expect it to achieve that level of performance in the same way a person would. In particular, we should not assume that the features and generalizations that the expert network develops during its training are the only way to solve the problem; they are only *a* way— ideally an effective way—to solve the problem.

Expert Network Characteristics

How good are expert networks in general? The fact is that expert networks can be very, very good indeed. They often are much more cost effective to generate and easier to maintain than a rule-based system because they are built entirely from training examples; thus they do not need a lengthy, costly, and often frustrating knowledge-extraction process in which a human expert tries to articulate rules that he may or may not actually use in solving the problem. Instead, expert networks are simply given training examples derived from known solutions.

Often the development time for an expert network solution is an order of magnitude (or more!) less than for a rule-based system. Because no human expert need be identified, nor must the examples derive from a single person's decisions, the resulting system can often be built with less impact to the company or operating group involved. Even if human experts disagree with each other, the network can be trained to offer an amalgamation of their total knowledge, rather than sticking to one person's opinion exclusively. Furthermore, because there is no conglomeration of rules to handle exceptions and specific cases, the expert network can be far more cost effective in maintenance than a rule-based system. Complex rule-based systems of thousands of rules can be enormously difficult to expand or maintain; a neural network needs simply to get a new training course to extend its abilities.

Even better, because the network learns generalizations from the examples it is trained with, it is much less susceptible to the mesa effect than a rule-based system. As we saw with the bond-rater, even when the network is wrong, it can give a reasonable answer; a rule-based expert behaves much more like the regression analysis system, in that when it is outside its area of expertise, its answers may be nearly meaningless. The neural network's superior performance at the edges of its knowledge domain is the result of using training examples from which the network can generalize rather than articulated rules from people.

But expert networks have their problems as well as their successes. Some of these arise from the fact that neural network technology is only beginning to be developed. For example, successful expert networks must be limited in scale to networks that can be reasonably implemented today. This means that if development is as a software simulation, the network must be kept quite small. If parallel processors or accelerator boards are used, the network can be considerably larger. And if commercial neural network chips are available the network must be within the capabilities of the chips. Rule-based systems generally have few limitations of size because the technology for implementing them is fairly mature; the technology for implementing neural networks is still in its infancy.

A second limitation of expert networks is that the trained network's capability is limited by the effectiveness with which the training data is chosen. In the bond-rating network discussed earlier, we noted that the researchers had carefully analyzed the available data and determined those parameters that were independent of each other. In the actual bond application, many more possible numbers were available for input, but the developers were careful to eliminate those that depended on (i.e., were highly correlated with) other values. This attention to detail is necessary when building an expert system. A careless choice of input data parameters or a poor choice of training examples can mean a network that learns and performs poorly. The expert network developer must understand the network architecture and how it works, and also must have a good understanding of the problem to be solved.

These difficulties are important but not severe. It is not terribly restrictive, after all, to expect a problem domain to be kept within reasonable bounds or to insist that system builders do their jobs carefully and thoughtfully. However, other considerations may make an expert network a poor choice in a particular instance.

Suppose, for example, that the problem is one for which we have very few examples. How can we train a network on, say, half a dozen cases and expect it to generalize properly? Generalization demands a significant number of different examples. If the number of cases is too small, all the network can do is memorize them. This means that the network's opinion on a new example may or may not have much relevance. In such cases, it is much better to use a rule-based system in which specific rules can be laid down to govern decisions and solutions.

An even more critical problem with an expert network arises when the network's decision must be used by a human being. People are not noted for their willingness to accept the word of a computer without question. In fact, most people, particularly when faced with a new system, will demand an explanation of the reason for the decision to reassure themselves that the machine's choice is a good one. The problem here is that a neural network cannot explain itself.

Consider how a generic neural network operates. An input stimulus pattern causes neurodes in the input layer to become active and to transmit their activity over the connections to the middle layer. The resulting stimulus pattern, modified by the varying weights along those connections, causes some combination of the middle-layer neurodes to become active in turn. They then transmit their activity over another set of weighted connections to an output layer. Just as in the middle layer, the stimulus pattern that arrives at the output layer is modified by the weights on the connections and causes the output layer to generate a still different pattern, which is the network's response to the original stimulus. Nowhere in this operation is there any central control; each neurode in the network operates as an isolated device, neither knowing nor caring what other neurodes are doing. The individual neurodes do not store information; the network's knowledge is encoded in the pattern of weights and connections in the network, not in the neurodes. And the operation of the neurodes in terms of computing an output for a given input pattern is totally independent of the specifics of the problem the overall network is solving; the same neurodes can solve the bond-rating problem, an image-processing problem, or a robotics problem. Even the weights on the connections are generic strengths that appear to have little relevance to the problem domain. Nowhere in the network is there anything that can be pointed to as a rule or a fact or even a statement of the problem itself. Neural networks may be effective, but they can also be inscrutable.

Hybrid Expert Networks

If people are to rely on the opinions of expert network advisors, they must have some reassurance that the network knows what it is talking about, providing that reassurance is difficult with a pure network solution. What can be done about this?

As it happens, providing expert networks with an explanation capability is an active research issue today. There are several possible ways of doing it; so we'll have to wait to see which of these eventually becomes the solution of choice. Nearly all of them, however, combine an expert network with some other system, thus they can all be classified as hybrid systems of one sort or another. Let's consider a few of them.

Explanation by Confabulation

If we assume that the biggest drawback to an expert network is its inability to explain its reasoning, one solution is fairly obvious. We could build an expert network to solve the problem and also build a simple rule-based system in parallel. The expert network would be used for general decision-making operations, and the rule-based system would do nothing until the user asked for an explanation of the network's operation. At that time, the rule-based system would be given neural network's input data and final decision. It would then use backward chaining to construct a line of reasoning to link the network's input to its output. This would act as the network's "reason" why it responded as it did. In essence, the rule-based system would "confabulate" or rationalize the neural network's decisions as necessary. Although the network did not actually use the resulting line of reasoning to develop its output, it would give the user a justification of the response.

The disadvantage of this approach should be obvious: It requires the developer to build two solutions to the same problem. And of course, the rule-based system has to be complete enough to be able to satisfy users with its explanations. The duplicate efforts required for this approach seem too much for a reasonable solution to the problem of explanation. On the other hand, some argue that this is much closer to the way people really operate than we would like to think.

Rule Extraction

Another possibility is to somehow extract the rules used by the expert network and use them as the basis for a rule-based system, which then has its own explanation capability, of course. This may prove to be an excellent approach for cases in which there is no expert, or the expert cannot effectively articulate the rules used, or multiple experts exist. The procedure would be to train a neural network with examples and let it learn to generalize them. Then a reverse-engineering procedure would be done on the trained network to determine what features and rules it used to make decisions. Such reverse engineering, though not a trivial process, has been done many times on research networks. Once this process is complete, the developer uses these rules and features to build a more traditional rule-based system. Like other rule-based systems, it would have full explanation capabilities built in.

This approach also involves building two kinds of solutions, but because training and reverse-engineering the neural network can be cheaper in time and money than doing a difficult knowledge-extraction process (especially if no expert is available!), it can result in an overall costs savings compared with building the rule-based system from scratch. Also, some advances are currently being made in the area of rule extraction from trained neural networks, so this process can be expected to become easier as time goes on. Furthermore, it allows the final system to handle exceptional cases with few examples much better than might happen with a simple neural network approach.

True Hybrid Expert

Another way the problem can be resolved is to combine neural networks and rule-based systems into a single hybrid system. There are many possibilities. For example, some aspects of a problem may lend themselves to a rule-based approach whereas others may be more amenable to a network-based approach. In such cases, a categorization front end could be used to determine the best solution tool. This might be an expert system or a neural network. One such hypothetical system is shown in Fig. 9-3.

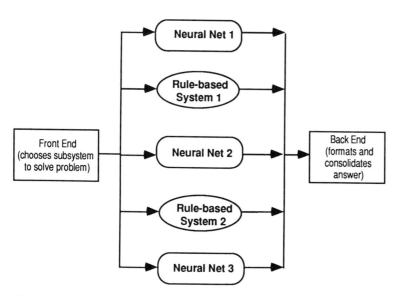

Figure 9-3 A hybrid expert network system. The front end selects the subsystem to handle each problem; the back end formats and consolidates partial answers from each subsystem.

The front end shown in the figure might be a rule-based system or a neural network, depending on the particular problem domain. It might also break an especially large problem into smaller pieces and allocate those to the various support subsystems for parallel solutions. The back end would combine the outputs of the subsystems, format the result, and generate the final answer. Although the networks involved could still not give explanations for their individual actions, a top level explanation based on how the problem was allocated to the various networks and rule-based systems involved would be immediately available.

These are just a few of the ways that expert networks and rule-based systems can be combined. Others exist and are being tested. Rule-based experts have advantages and disadvantages just as neural network-based experts do; the very best way of getting around the weaknesses of each, while retaining their strengths, is almost certainly going to be by combining the two approaches. Rule-based systems are fundamentally rational, logical, and reasoning. Network-based systems are more reactionary (in the sense of reacting to stimuli). They do not reason a problem to its final solution but simply offer a reaction to an input, like a knee jerk is a reaction to a rap on the kneecap. We might even say that rule-based systems are cognitive whereas networks are "instinctive" in some sense. Just as people need to have both their rational, thinking capabilities and their instinctive, emotional ones, it should be expected that a true expert network will also have to have both sides.

CHAPTER 10

Case Study I: Detection of Electroencephalogram Spikes

Russell C. Eberhart
Roy W. Dobbins

Introduction

This chapter comprises a case study of the application of neural network tools to solve a real-world problem: the identification of spikes in a multichannel electroencephalogram (EEG) signal. Some explanation of why the problem is important to solve is presented; for a more complete discussion, you can refer to Eberhart et al. [9], from which much of the material in this chapter is derived.

Although understanding the problem is important, it's more important to understand how the problem was approached and solved. The problem of EEG spike detection is probably analogous to many interdisciplinary problems that must be solved by teams of engineers, programmers, scientists, physicians, and so on. In approaching such problems, it is usually impossible for each member of the team to understand all the details of each aspect, or discipline. For example, an engineer or computer scientist cannot understand all of the ramifications of the medical aspects of electroencephalography. Likewise, it is generally a waste of time for the doctors to try to learn all about implementing neural network tools.

It is important, however, to keep priorities straight. For example, in this case as in all biomedical applications, it is very important to understand that medicine drives engineering, not the other way around. It is easy for engineers and computer scientists to forget this sometimes! The work described in this chapter was a collaborative effort among scientists, engineers, and physicians at The Johns Hopkins University Applied Physics Laboratory (JHU/APL) and the Department of Neurology at The Johns Hopkins Hospital (JHH/ND). The overall goals of the effort, which is still underway as this book is being written, are to provide on-line (real-time) detection of EEG spikes and the detection and prediction of epileptic seizures.

This chapter focuses on the spike detection part of the work, and after discussing the goals and objectives, it reviews the signal preprocessing steps required prior to pattern presentation to an NNT. The application of computer-assisted software engineering (CASE) tools in the development of automated techniques for NNT code generation has resulted in CaseNet, which is described in a previous chapter. Finally, results are reported from single and multichannel spike detection systems.

Goals and Objectives

The presence of EEG waveforms identified as spikes usually indicates some sort of abnormal brain function. The polarity and amplitude patterns of the spikes often provide information on the location and severity of the abnormality, possibly including information such as whether or not seizures are focal (focused in one small volume). This information is then used by neurologists when deciding on corrective measures.

The EEG spike detection system is being developed for use in the four-bed epileptic monitoring unit (EMU) at The Johns Hopkins Hospital. Various versions of the system should also be suitable for use at many facilities that continuously monitor EEG signals. The EMU typically admits patients whose epileptic disorders have proven unresponsive to standard forms of treatment, including medication. It is currently estimated that there are over 200,000 persons in this category in the United States alone. These patients usually stay in the EMU for one to two weeks. EEG recordings are taken for each of the patients around the clock, from up to 64 electrodes per patient. Most of the time, these electrodes are placed on the scalp, but sometimes a custom-designed grid of electrodes is placed directly on the brain, under the skull, in a surgical procedure. (Notice that hospitals don't call them *operations* any more; nowadays they are *procedures*.) The electrodes, whether attached to the scalp or implanted under the skull, are removed prior to the patient's discharge from the hospital.

Because of the around-the-clock acquisition of data and the data rate of 200–250 samples per second from each channel, a very large quantity of data is being handled. Depending on the number of channels being collected and the data rate, on the order of 10–100 Mbytes of data per hour are being recorded for each patient.

The accurate interpretation of the data is critical. Many patients in the EMU will have serious corrective measures taken by the neurologists, including removal of a piece of their brain. Under such conditions, the information provided to the medical staff must be complete and accurate.

Interpretation of the multichannel EEG data must currently be done manually and is therefore labor intensive. We're talking about high-priced labor because it involves large amounts of time from qualified neurologists. The primary goal of the spike detection effort described in this case study is to provide faster on-line analysis of data.

A secondary goal is to investigate the feasibility of reducing the amount of data that must be recorded from each patient. If the recording process can be triggered by abnormal EEG patterns, the quantity of normal data that is recorded can be greatly reduced, leading to significant reductions in data acquisition, storage, and analysis. This secondary goal is also achievable in the nearer term because the spike detection system can probably be used on-line as a data-recording "switch" before it is routinely used on-line as a spike detector.

Two other methods can reduce the amount of data recorded. One is to parameterize the data, recording only calculated parameters instead of raw data. Nine spike parameters are currently being calculated for each candidate spike, and 16 context parameters that could possibly be used for seizure detection and prediction are calculated for each time window of raw data. The other method is to use neural networks for data compression, providing information in a way that the original data, whether raw or parameters, can be reconstructed. Both of these methods will be discussed further.

Design Process

As is the case in the development of most systems, the design process is iterative. On one hand, choices must be made relative to the preprocessing and characterization of the raw EEG data. For example, are raw data presented unprocessed to the network, or are waveforms that represent possible spikes detected and centered prior to presentation? Or is even more preprocessing done and only certain calculated parameters of the possible spike presented to the network?

On the other hand, choices must be made relative to the neural network training algorithms and architecture. For example, is supervised learning better than unsupervised? Once the training supervision question is answered, what specific network architecture is likely to yield the best results, given the design constraints, which include capability of on-line analysis? How should the parameters associated with the learning algorithms be set?

As you can see, the preprocessing and characterization of the raw EEG data have an effect on the implementation of the specific neural network architecture and vice versa. Many of the initial decisions made for this project involved intuition as well as logic; this will probably be the case for many, if not most, applications of neural network tools.

In addition to the circular, iterative nature of the design, two long-term goals are guiding and providing additional constraints to the system development and implementation process. Each step in the system development is being examined to assure that the attainment of these two goals is being facilitated.

The nearer term goal is that the real-time multichannel spike/seizure detection and analysis system be relatively inexpensive to implement. Remember that one of the premises of this book is that you shouldn't need a supercomputer to solve many of the useful problems that can be addressed with neural network tools. The current objective is that the system's cost be no more than about $10,000 and that it use readily available hardware, such as an 80386-based microcomputer. Simple and inexpensive transputer modules, such as the T800, which offer significant speed enhancements, are also candidates for inclusion with an 80286 platform; the cost objective could still be met.

The longer term goal is that the system design support the development of ambulatory (portable) devices for spike/seizure detection. This could be important for a significant fraction of the estimated 200,000 persons in the United States whose epileptic disorder is unresponsive to traditional treatment and who would benefit from advance warning of seizures.

System Specifications

The definition of system specifications is an important step in any system development. In many (possibly most) cases, it is not difficult to specify what results must be obtained for the system to be performing successfully. This is not, however, straightforward in the case of some aspects of an EEG spike detection system. In fact, it seems that many medical applications of neural network tools present special challenges to system design. For a more complete discussion of system specifications, see Chapter 3.

Some specifications can be arrived at fairly readily. For example, a multichannel real-time capability is currently being interpreted as meaning that the final system should be able to analyze at least eight channels of information on-line and provide an indication of any spike within one second of its occurrence. It has also been agreed that the system could require training for each patient. A goal of the system development is that the training time, if required, be minimized. Because patients generally stay in the EMU for one or two weeks, a training time on the order of an hour or two is probably acceptable.

Two other specifications are harder to define. First, what constitutes a spike? Are there measures or calculations that can be applied that definitively specify which waveforms are spikes and which are not? Second, once spikes have been defined, what constitutes successful system performance? What are acceptable levels of false positives and false negatives?

Answers do not yet exist for either question. The most practical answer to the question of what consititutes a spike is that spikes are defined by qualified neurologists. No precise mathematical definition is known to the authors. In fact, each of the six neurologists marked the records used for this study differently. Grappling with attempts to characterize spikes and seizures has led the authors to paraphrase what George Bernard Shaw said about economists: You can lay all of the neurologists in the world from end to end and never reach a conclusion. In the records referred to in this paper [9], of all the events marked by one or more of the neurologists as spikes, about 60 percent of them were marked by four or more. It was decided to define those events marked by four, five, or six neurologists as *spikes*.

The question of what constitutes successful system performance was even more difficult to address. After discussions with hospital staff, it has been decided that, at least initially, the system is considered successful if it detects at least 80 percent of the spikes as just defined. In addition, success requires that no more than 20 percent of the events identified by the system as spikes be false positives, or nonspikes (identified by none of the neurologists). The concepts of recall and precision, discussed later, are being used as measures of success.

It is almost certain that answers to both of these questions will evolve as the work continues. In fact, the system development effort itself will probably contribute to this evolution. In particular, the inclusion of waveforms identified by one, two, or three neurologists in the training process for the NNT will require careful consideration of what these waveforms constitute: "possible" spikes, "probable" spikes, or other.

Background

Significant progress had been made in the area of EEG data acquisition and analysis by the staff of The Johns Hopkins Hospital Neurology Department (JHH/ND) prior to the current project effort involving the JHU Applied Physics Laboratory (JHU/APL). For example, EEG data were routinely being digitized and stored in a format readable by IBM PC/AT and workalike computers. Also, a powerful and flexible method of displaying the data on an AT or workalike computer, the JHMI Spike Viewer, had been developed and tested [14, 15]. As part of the development of the Spike Viewer, software was written that calculates various parameters for each waveform identified as a potential spike. These parameters include such measures as amplitude, width, and sharpness [15].

Prior to the start of the current project, JHH/ND staff had written software using various combinations and weights of these parameters. Although the current version yields unacceptably high numbers of false positives and false negatives to be used as a standalone spike detector, a simplified version of the software plays an important role as a preprocessor in the current project, as described later. Further development of the JHH/ND software is continuing in parallel with the NNT development.

Also started prior to the current work was a collaborative effort between JHU/APL and JHH/ND to develop a seizure detection methodology using autoregressive analysis of raw EEG data. This effort has been expanded to include the use of back-propagation and autoassociative networks. Preliminary results are encouraging, and results will be published.

Data Preprocessing and Categorization

As this project developed, it became evident that the system design effort consisted of two main areas. The first is the preprocessing and categorization of the raw data that is required prior to its presentation to a neural network for training or testing. The second is the development and implementation of the neural network analysis tools and the associated data manipulation. This split was probably due in a large part to the division of effort between JHH/ND and JHU/APL, with the hospital taking primary responsibility for the first area and JHU/APL for the second. Accordingly, this case study divides the reporting of the interim project results into these categories.

Looking back at how we put the project together, it seems now that it might have been better to define this division of effort up front. As is the case with many interdisciplinary projects involving more than one organization, however, this work was started on a shoestring budget, and the division of effort evolved instead of following a comprehensive program plan. In addition to the tenuous budget, the effort possible at one place or the other waxed and waned according to the time the investigators had available to work on the project. Much was accomplished after hours and at home.

The raw EEG data were obtained from patients in the EMU at the Johns Hopkins Hospital. Recordings were done with a scalp electrode arrangement called a *bipolar montage*, with locations referred to as the *10/20 system*. For information about how electroencephalograms are recorded, including the names for the various electrode locations on the scalp, you can refer to a source such as chapter 7 in Stern et al. [18].

Eight channels of EEG were digitized and used for the first stages of this project. Some of the eight-channel records consisted solely of bipolar channels, but most included reference channels. Bipolar channels originate from electrodes placed closer together, typically a few centimeters apart, and they are usually "daisy chained." Reference channels are, as the name implies, tied at one end to a reference electrode and generally span a significant portion of the scalp. Again, a good source for more information is chapter 7 in Stern et al. [18].

The portions of records that were preprocessed and used to train and test neural network tools were reviewed, and the locations of spikes marked, by six physicians qualified to interpret EEGs. These neurologists marked only the location in time of the spikes. Marking was done by each neurologist on a separate copy of the record, so no one knew what any other had done. A JHH/ND staff member then used the marked paper copies of the record, the JHMI Spike Viewer, and the IBM AT-readable raw data files to prepare spike files (which we call SPK files). These files are a compilation of all six hand-marked paper records and include information on the time of the spike event, the number of doctors that identified that particular event as a spike, nine parameters calculated from the spike waveform, and 16 context parameters that are calculated from the two-second window of raw data surrounding the spike [14, 15].

The JHH/ND staff member who prepared the SPK files selected the specific channels that represent the spike waveform for each spike. These selections were reviewed by a JHU/APL staff member, and in some cases additional channels were selected as examples of an identified spike event. These selected examples were used only for the initial work with single-channel neural network tools. A real-world spike event is considered an across-the-channels event in the case of the multichannel spike detection system and is represented by the time marked by the physicians.

Three main possibilities were initially considered for performing spike detection using a neural network tool as part of the analysis system. Each was evaluated keeping in mind that the goal is to implement a system that can eventually be used for on-line (real-time) multichannel analysis.

The first possibility examined was the analysis of raw data using a sliding window (a window of a fixed time width, sliding with time). For example, given that a spike is at most about 200 milliseconds (msec) in width, the sliding window approach using a 250-msec window would require about 20 iterations per second of the neural network to ensure that the spike waveform is entirely inside the window at some time.

Twenty iterations per second of the neural network is feasible but it results in a significantly higher computational load than other approaches. In addition, the training of the network is more difficult than with other approaches because relatively narrow (50–100 msec) spikes must be accurately detected no matter where they are located within the window. This dictates a large training set and a lengthy training process. Because of these drawbacks, the development of this approach was discontinued.

The second possibility examined is to preprocess the data so that candidate spikes are identified and presented, centered in the time window, to the neural network for analysis. This approach results in a lower overall system computational load.

A version of the JHH/ND software designed for spike detection, described previously, is being used to identify candidate spikes. This software isn't sufficiently accurate to act as a standalone spike detector. If we "turn the screws" too far in one direction, too many real spikes are missed, even though the number of false positives is acceptable. Turning the screws too far in the other direction results in an unacceptably high number of false positives.

The software parameters are set for the second of these two situations so that the number of false negatives (the number of spikes identified by at least four physicians but not by the software) is as low as possible.

At the same time, some effort is made to minimize the ratio of false positives (candidate spikes that are not real spikes) to spikes. The candidate spike file is then compared with the SPK file by a scoring program, and three files are produced: a file containing those candidate spikes that match spikes in the SPK file, a file containing false negatives, and a file containing false positives. The false positive file (FPS file) is used as the nonspike file for training and testing the neural network part of the system.

The level of false negatives currently being obtained using the JHH/ ND software for preprocessing is 2 percent or less. For the single-channel results reported later, no false negatives were obtained (zero percent). The ratio of false positives to spikes is generally between 2.0 and 3.0. Because the occurrence of spikes in the records analyzed so far averages about one spike event per second, the computational load on the neural network tool is about three or four computational iterations per second for real-time analysis.

Note that the preprocessing software we are using does a better job of spike detection at a ratio of false positives of 2.0–3.0 than most commercially available software sold specifically for spike detection. It is not uncommon to get a false positive ratio of 5–10 with the commercial software.

Data are taken at two rates in the EMU, and data taken at both rates are being used in this project. This variation in data rates is not uncommon whether you are dealing with medical data acquisition or some other source, and the neural network tool must be able to handle differences such as this, within reasonable limits. Most patient records at The Johns Hopkins Hospital EMU are taken at 200 samples per second, but some are taken at 250 samples per second. A 240-msec window results in 48 and 60 raw data points for each candidate spike, respectively, for the two data rates.

An approach involving preprocessing to find candidate spikes yielded promising results, and its initial implementation is discussed later.

Another approach makes use of the fact that, in addition to identifying the time of the waveform center, the JHH/ND software being used to identify candidate spikes calculates nine parameters for each candidate spike waveform. These nine parameters (for each channel), rather than raw data, are presented to a neural network. This increases the computational load on the preprocessing stage but significantly reduces the computational load on the neural network because only nine input nodes per channel are required, instead of 48 or 60. Promising results have been obtained from this approach in both single-channel and four-channel implementations. The single-channel case is discussed later.

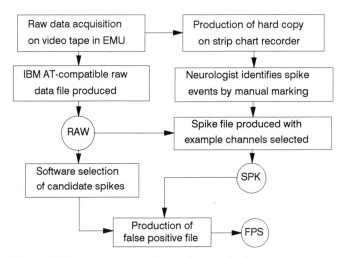

Figure 10-1   Data preprocessing and categorization.

A summary flow chart of the data preprocessing and categorization, as it was initially done, is presented in Fig. 10-1. The three file types used as inputs to the neural network pattern generation software discussed next are the raw data files (RAW files), the spike files (SPK files), and the false positive files (FPS files). Two forms of spike-related data are thus initially chosen and processed for presentation to neural network tools. The first is raw data, digitized to 12 bits of precision. Each candidate spike is represented by either 48 or 60 data points in each channel and is centered in a 240-msec window. The second is a set of nine spike parameters calculated for each candidate spike in each channel. For each form, a set of neural network pattern generation software has been developed to produce pattern files suitable for neural network input from the RAW, SPK, and FPS files.

In the case of raw data input, a catalog program is used to select events with the desired status values from the SPK and FPS files for a given record. Target values for the output nodes of the neural network are specified for each selected status. For example, the SPK files that have been identified by four, five, or six neurologists have been assigned status values of four, five, and six, respectively. These status values are assigned the output neurode target values of 1, 0. The nonspikes from the FPS files have been assigned the status value of 200 and have been assigned output target neurode values of 0, 1. Separate catalog files are built for training and testing.

In the case of the single-channel spike detection system, the catalog files include information on the time of the center of the waveform (spike or nonspike), the channel identification, and the target values. All occurrences in all channels of the statuses selected appear in the catalog files for single-channel networks. Only one occurrence per spike or nonspike appears in the catalog files for four-channel networks.

A pattern generation program then runs the catalog file against the raw data file to generate a raw pattern file. The pattern file contains, for each spike or nonspike in the single-channel case, either 48 or 60 values for the raw data points and the two target values. In the four-channel case, the pattern file contains, for each event, either 192 or 240 values for the four raw data points and the two target values.

For the single-channel case of spike parameter input, a parameter program is used to build a file that is a combination of the subset of the SPK and FPS files containing only data from the selected channel. The parameter program also assigns target values for each example selected.

A program called the "extraction" program is then used to select only the nine spike parameters for the channel, deleting the time, channel number, status, and context parameter information. The output of the extraction program is a "parameter" pattern file containing, for each spike or nonspike, nine values for the spike parameters and the target values.

For the four-channel case of spike parameter input, the parameter pattern file generation software uses the four-channel raw data catalog file as the key to event times in the raw data file. A parameter calculator function then computes each of the nine spike parameters for each channel designated. Each parameter must be provided for each spike and candidate spike event, whether or not an identifiable waveform exists in a particular channel. This requires the use of default values for parameters when no waveform with the required characteristics is detected by the parameter calculator in that channel.

For the particular back-propagation network architecture we use, all pattern files must contain only values between zero and one. All pattern data, whether raw or parameter, are thus normalized before being placed into the pattern file. The normalization of the data is discussed in the section on test results. The way normalization is done, particularly in the case of the parameter pattern files, has a significant effect on the trainability and testability of the networks.

A summary flow chart for the preparation of pattern files and running of the neural network tool appears as Fig. 10-2. Note that the software that generates parameter pattern files for the four-channel network is de-

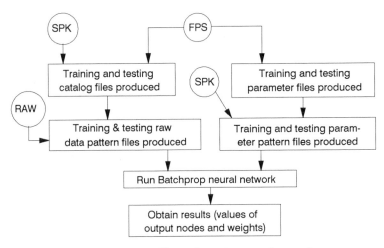

Figure 10-2   Forming pattern files and running neural network.

rived from catalog files. Several general neural network architectures were investigated for analyzing the data, including some that perform unsupervised learning (categorization), and others requiring supervised training [2, 21, 22]. The architecture selected for initial implementation is the back-propagation neural network with a version of the delta learning algorithm [2].

A number of computer programs exist that can implement this type of network on IBM ATs and workalikes. It became apparent early in this project, however, that the relatively large number of nodes and relatively large training and testing sets made most of these programs difficult or impossible to use: Problems were encountered with computer memory management and speed of execution.

The first approach we took was to write a customized program in C, which we named Batchnet because it implements a back-propagation network in a sort of batch processing mode on the PC. (Batchnet is covered in detail in the discussion on back-propagation in Chapters 2 and 4.) It is worthwhile, however, to review how we used Batchnet in the early stages of the EEG spike detection project. The use of Batchnet was essentially the same regardless of the type of model used (single-channel raw data or parameter, or four-channel raw data or parameter). The raw data version for four channels was more involved only because of the pattern file sizes.

To train and test a spike detection configuration using Batchnet, a number of files and parameters must be provided. The files needed are the executable version of Batchnet, a weights file, training and testing pattern files, and a run file in which several parameters and files are specified. Some attention must be paid to which executable version of Batchnet you use because different versions have been compiled that do or do not require an 80x87 coprocessor and do or do not require an 80286 or 80386. Each option, if available, increases the speed of execution, so the version that takes advantage of the maximum performance capabilities of the computer system should be used.

This is particularly important in the case of the 80x87 coprocessor. Its presence, and using code that takes advantage of it, can often mean an increase in speed (decrease in training time) of a factor of three or four when working with Batchnet. Otherwise, the coprocessor functions must be emulated in code. Throughout the development of the spike detector, machines were used that had either the 80286 or the 80386 processor and had the appropriate coprocessor. Training times with the coprocessor ranged from about 15 minutes in the case of the single-channel parameter model to several hours for the four-channel raw data model. The lack of a coprocessor would have made training times for the larger models difficult to live with.

The weights file was generated using weights.exe. The source code for this program, weights.c, appears in Appendix A with the source code for batchnet.exe, batchnet.c. The default setting for the maximum range of the random numbers, which is from -0.3 to 0.3, was used.

Because the weights program needs to know how many weights to generate, you specify the network configuration at run time, in addition to telling the program where to send its output. A typical run time command line for a single-channel parameter pattern version is thus "weights 9 4 2 >b:parm1ch.wts." This says to run weights for a network with nine input nodes, four hidden nodes, and two output nodes, and put the results in a file named parm1ch.wts on drive B.

Training and testing pattern files are built as described in the discussion of Batchnet in Chapter 2. In the case of the nine-parameter one-channel pattern file, each pattern consists of nine values for the input nodes normalized to values between 0 and 1, two target node values of either 0 or 1, and an ID field. You can use the ID field to keep track of a pattern source; it helps provide a sort of pattern audit trail.

The run files are also described in Chapter 2, and you can see how they are built and what goes in them by looking in Appendix A. We typically use 80–100 patterns in a test set, almost evenly divided between spike and nonspike patterns, despite there being many more nonspikes than spikes in the real world of EEG monitoring. Dividing between spikes and nonspikes about evenly usually gave us better network performance. We generally threw any patterns left after building our training sets into the test sets, so the test sets often contained many more nonspikes than spikes.

We usually set the maximum number of iterations to 1000, though we sometimes used as many as 1500. We fiddled a good bit with the values of the learning factor, eta, and the momentum factor, alpha, but often wound up with 0.15 and 0.075, respectively, for single-channel work, and 0.04 and 0.075 for four-channel models.

As we continued to develop neural networks for spike (and seizure) detection, the need to explore different network architectures and paradigms became obvious. With our standard Batchnet model, the network code had to be revised and debugged for each change in structure and each new application. Although Batchnet offered us flexibility in some areas, such as being able to change eta and alpha on the run line for each trial, we were still locked into the standard three-layer backpropagation model. We wanted to be able to construct feedforward network architectures of arbitrary structure and to be able to vary eta and alpha on a slab-by-slab basis. The time required for what was often significant code revision began, we felt, to detract from our work.

As a result, we began to apply computer-assisted software engineering (CASE) tools to develop automated techniques for neural network tool generation. The result is CaseNet. With CaseNet, a user is able to graphically specify a network architecture from which executable code is automatically generated. CaseNet is described in detail in Chapter 5, and the reader is encouraged to review the material presented there. Here we only point out the differences between the uses of CaseNet and Batchnet that pertain to this spike detection project.

The most significant difference is the ability to specify arbitrary feedforward architectures for a network. Connections from slab to slab can cross, skip layers, and so on, as long as they feed forward. (See the example of a generic CaseNet architecture in Chapter 5.) Note that there can be a number of slabs side by side in what might be called a layer. The concept of a layer gets a little fuzzy, however, when the network topology allows connections to skip from a slab to any slab further forward in the network.

Another significant CaseNet difference is that eta and alpha are now attributes of a slab and can be specified on a slab-by-slab basis. It is also possible to specify them in the run file for any slabs for which they are not specified on the graphical network specification. Other than these differences, the executable code generated by CaseNet is used in a similar manner to Batchnet. The pattern and run files are the same except that the run file usually doesn't specify eta and alpha.

Test Results

The neural network tool used for the single-channel case of raw data input patterns consists of either 48 or 60 input nodes (corresponding to 200 and 250 samples per second, respectively), eight hidden nodes, and two output nodes. The single-channel network used for initial testing with spike parameters consists of nine input nodes, four hidden nodes, and two output nodes.

The ability of CaseNet to implement customized network architectures was utilized in the four-channel work. Two of the structures implemented for the four-channel spike detection system are depicted in Fig. 10-3. Figure 10-3a is a fairly standard three-slab network, analogous to a three-layer back-propagation model with one hidden layer. Figure 10-3b is a "channelized" version of a network that is analogous, in many ways, to a four-layer network with two hidden layers.

In each case, the output nodes are designated to be used for indicating a spike (as identified by four or more of the six neurologists) and an "almost spike" (as identified as a candidate by the EMU software but not by any of the neurologists). It is anticipated that a third output node may eventually be added that indicates a spike as identified by one to three of the neurologists.

Initial testing was carried out on single-channel data from each of two channels for one patient's record, and one channel from a second patient's record. Data from channel three was used for patient F5; channel one and channel two data were used for patient F1. These tests are designated as Run 1, Run 2, and Run 3, respectively, for parameter pattern runs, and Runs 4, 5, and 6, respectively, for raw data pattern runs.

For the initial one-channel testing, each network was trained with a

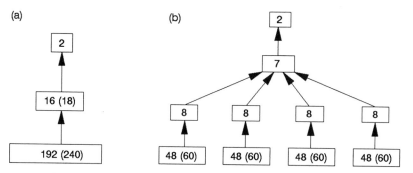

Figure 10-3 CaseNet architectures for two raw data network versions. Numbers of nodes are shown for data sampled at 200 samples/sec for patient F5 and, in parentheses, at 250 samples/sec for patient F1.

Table 10-1 Summary of single-channel results[a]

| | | Training set | | | | | Test set | | | | |
Run	Net type	SPK #	ALM #	Avg. sum-sq. error	Recall	Precision	SPK #	ALM #	Avg. sum-sq. error	Recall	Precision
1	Param.	40	40	.003	1.0	1.0	23	103	0.0054	1.0	0.96
2	Param.	40	40	.045	1.0	0.95	39	131	0.205	1.0	0.63
3	Param.	50	50	.041	0.96	1.0	50	106	0.222	0.88	0.77
4	Raw dta	40	40	.0012	1.0	1.0	22	103	0.212	0.95	0.64
5	Raw dta	40	40	.0032	1.0	1.0	38	131	0.194	0.97	0.74
6	Raw dta	50	50	.0009	1.0	1.0	50	106	0.274	0.94	0.76

[a]For all runs, eta = 0.15 and alpha = 0.075.

230

set of either 40 (Runs 1 and 2) or 50 (Run 3) spikes as identified by four or more of the six neurologists (node 1 trained "on") and the same number of nonspikes not identified by any of the neurologists (node 2 trained "on"). The learning parameter eta was set to 0.15 and the momentum factor alpha to 0.075. In Runs 3 and 4, 2000 training iterations (epochs) were used; 1000 were used in Runs 1, 2, 5, and 6. In each case, the single-channel networks successfully trained with an average sum-squared error of less than 0.05.

Test sets were then presented, consisting of all remaining spikes (identified by four or more neurologists) and all remaining nonspikes (not identified by any neurologists). A parameter in the software that identifies nonspikes was set so that false negatives were minimized and false positives were held to about 2–3 nonspikes for each spike.

Test results for the six single-channel runs are presented in Table 10-1. Previously defined metrics named *recall* and *precision* are used to measure system performance [35, 36]. *Recall* is the number of spikes identified correctly by the system, divided by the number of spikes identified by the neurologists (SPKs). *Precision* is the number of spikes identified correctly by the system, divided by the total number of spikes (which includes false positives) identified by the system. It is generally agreed among the neurologists at Johns Hopkins that recall is more important than precision, but no quantitative relative weights have been identified.

To help you interpret Table 10-1, we give a review of the results for Run 2. The training set for Run 2 contained 40 spikes and 40 nonspikes. The system correctly trained on all 40 spikes (recall = 40/40) but incorrectly identified two nonspikes as spikes in the training process (precision = 40/42). During testing, all 39 spikes were correctly identified (recall = 39/39), but 23 nonspikes were incorrectly classified as spikes (precision = 39/62).

For both training and testing, the average sum-squared error is the sum over all patterns of the square of the desired output minus the obtained output, divided by the number of patterns. The sum-squared error is calculated for the last training epoch (after all training is complete) for the training set and after a once-through forward propagation for the test set.

The results of the single-channel tests were reviewed with neurologists at JHH/ND, and the performance of the system was judged to be adequate for practical use if extended to multiple channels. It is, in fact, superior to any algorithm known to the authors for EEG spike detection.

These encouraging results suggested the development of a multi-channel version of the NNT spike detection system. To be a useful tool for the clinician, an on-line spike detector must evaluate a minimum of

Table 10-2 Summary of four-channel raw data CaseNet results[a]

Patient	Net of figure	Training set				Test set			
		SPK #	ALM #	Recall	Precision	SPK #	ALM #	Recall	Precision
F1	1a	50	50	1.0	0.98	82	133	0.93	0.89
F1	1b	50	50	0.98	1.0	82	133	0.93	0.82
F5	1a	39	41	0.95	1.0	25	63	0.96	0.96
F5	1b	39	41	0.95	1.0	25	63	0.96	0.92

[a]For all runs, eta = 0.04 and alpha = 0.02.

four channels simultaneously and must be able to take into account both bipolar and reference channels. The network configuations used in the four-channel neural network tool are illustrated in Fig. 10-3. Training and testing pattern files were built in a manner analogous to those for single-channel operation, with a few differences. For example, the catalog file for the multichannel neural network tool has only one time mark for each spike event, rather than one for each channel spike element.

Data from the same patients as in the single-channel case were used for the four-channel neural network tool. For patient F5, the four channels selected were 2, 3, 6, and 9. The first three channels are bipolar and channel 9 is a reference channel. (See the description of bipolar and reference channels earlier in this chapter.) For patient F1, the channels selected were 1, 2, 4, and 5; all four are bipolar.

For patient F5, for a waveform to be considered as a candidate spike, from which the false positive and nonspike files are built, the waveform must appear in at least one of the bipolar channels as well as in the reference channel. For patient F1, the candidate spike waveform must appear in at least two of the bipolar channels. These requirements are meant to mirror what the neurologist does when reading an EEG record. Typically, a candidate spike waveform in a bipolar channel must be corroborated by its appearance in a reference channel or in another bipolar channel before it is considered valid.

Results of spike detection on four channels simultaneously are summarized in Table 10-2. Results listed are obtained using raw data pattern files. The recall and precision metrics were defined previously. To help you interpret Table 10-2, we give a review of the first run for patient F5, which used the network topology of Fig. 10-3a.

The training set has 39 spikes and 41 nonspikes; the test set has 25 spikes and 63 nonspikes. With eta equal to 0.04 and alpha equal to 0.02, the network was trained to an average sum-squared error of 0.036 in 1000 epochs. For the training set, recall is 0.95 and precision is 1.0; values for the test set are both 0.96. The performance is thus significantly better than that required for practical application.

Work is currently proceeding on testing four-channel spike detection NNTs using parameter pattern files, extending the four-channel testing to other patients, and implementing other network architectures suggested by the slab orientation permitted by CaseNet. Several nonsymmetrical network topologies designed to handle network flow for reference channels in a different way from that for bipolar channels are under consideration. Although the results are promising, much remains to be done before a real-time system goes on-line at The Johns Hopkins Hospital EMU.

Acknowledgments

This work was supported by JHU/APL Independent Research and Development funding. The active participation of Bob Webber, Ph.D. at The Johns Hopkins Hospital made this work possible. The guidance of Ronald Lesser, M.D. and the assistance of Dale Roberts at The Johns Hopkins Hospital are gratefully acknowledged. The coding and consulting contributions of Chuck Spaur at JHU/APL are also appreciated.

CHAPTER 11

Case Study II: Radar Signal Processing

Vincent G. Sigillito
Larrie V. Hutton

Introduction

This case study describes how a feedforward neural network with hidden layers was taught to classify radar returns from the ionosphere into two categories: those that are suitable for further analysis (referred to as "good" returns) and those that are not suitable (referred to as "bad" returns). The good radar returns are used to study the physics of the ionosphere at the E and F layers (100–500 km altitude).

Separating the returns into the appropriate categories requires a trained person. Because of the large volume of returns that need to be categorized, it is a time-consuming, tedious task. Our goal was to produce a neural network based classification system that would perform the task at the level of a human expert.

Signal classification and interpretation have proved to be fertile areas for neural network applications. For instance, Gorman and Sejnowski [106, 107] have successfully used multilayer feedforward networks to discriminate with high precision between sonar signals from a mine and a similarly shaped rock. In the area of medical signal classification, Boone et al. [108] demonstrated that neural networks can perform as well as trained human experts in detecting certain nodules in radiological data. Lapedes and Farber [109] demonstrated the use of neural networks to predict points in highly chaotic time series. Further application of neural networks to signal processing can be found in Lippmann's [110] seminal introduction to neural computing.

Neural Network PC Tools

Description of the Radar Facility

The Applied Physics Laboratory of The Johns Hopkins University operates a number of facilities dedicated to collecting data about small-scale structures in the high-latitude ionosphere. Three such facilities now exist: at Schepperville, Quebec; at Halley station, Antartica; and at Goose Bay, Labrador. We will focus on the latter facility where the data used in this case study were collected.

The Goose Bay radar station consists of 16 broadband (8–20 MHz) transmitting and receiving antennas. Several features of this installation make it particularly suitable for the remote sensing of high-latitude ionospheric events. An important consideration, for example, is the frequency of the transmitting signal. If returns are to be realized from the ionosphere, the frequency cannot be too high because signals in the very high-frequency (VHF) range (30–300 MHz) and ultra high-frequency (UHF) range (300–3000 MHz) are essentially unaffected by changes in ionospheric events. Even at the lower end of the VHF range, the signal is likely to be lost from the E region of the ionosphere because the incident wave must be almost normal to the magnetic region of interest. Thus, at the higher regions the transmitted signal is restricted to a very narrow angle of operation. Because returns in the 3–30 MHz high-frequency (HF) region are refracted by the ionosphere toward the regions of interest, the frequency of the transmitted signals was kept within that range.

The radar installations at Goose Bay are coherent scatter radars, which are sensitive to fluctuations in plasma density. Thermal fluctuations, which are of relatively low energy, are responsible for incoherent scatter. The perturbations that underlie coherent scatter are amplified well above the thermal level by the action of plasma instabilities. Consequently, high power levels are not required in order to collect signals generated through a coherent scattering process.

The targets, free electrons in the ionosphere, have small cross sections of the order of 10^{-30} square meters (m^2). A typical density of electrons would be of the order of 10^8 per m^3, and the total volume could be as large as 10^6 m^3. Additionally, because the backscattering process is coherent, the backscattered signal is proportional to the square of the density. The signal-to-noise ratio is in the 10–20 dB range but can be as large as 50 dB. A detailed analysis of the backscattering process can be found in Walker et al. [111].

Operation of the System and Data Collection

We now give a simplified version of the operation of the radar system. Our discussion is necessarily incomplete, but it does capture the essential features needed to understand the input to the neural network. A detailed description of the radar system is given in Greenwald et al. [112], and a detailed description of the data analysis procedures can be found in Baker et al. [113].

The radar operates by transmitting a multiple pattern to the ionosphere. The receiver is turned on between pulses, and the target velocity is determined by measuring the phase shift of the returns. If we denote the received signal from the pulse at time t by

$$C(t) = A(t) + iB(t)$$

then the autocorrelation function (ACF) R is given by

$$R(t, k) = \sum_{j=0}^{16} C(t + jT)C^*[t + (j + k)T]$$

where T is the pulse repetition period, k indicates the pulse number, and $*$ indicates complex conjugation.

For the Goose Bay radar, k lies between 0 and 16. From the ACF a number of physical parameters can be derived, most importantly the Doppler velocity of the target. For a target moving with constant velocity, the phase of the ACF shows a shift proportional to the lag k.

Figure 11-1 shows typical ACFs received by the radar. The two parts of each curve, real (dark) and imaginary (light), correspond to the complex ACF that results from the complex electromagnetic signal. The ACFs in the left-hand column are those of good returns, the ACFs on the right-hand column are those of bad returns. The radar at its current operating mode produces 300 returns every minute year round. Because of the large volume of data, much work is required to weed out bad ACFs prior to further data analysis.

Goals and Objectives

We were not directly concerned with analyzing the signals in terms of what they measured or in assessing the nature of the objects that were being investigated. Rather, we were interested in teaching neural networks to correctly classify the returns as worthy of further analysis or not.

Classifying the large number of returns has required a person that, by virtue of experience and training, was able to make the proper classifications. Using such experienced people for manual classification is not good use of their time. If they could assist in the design of a relatively automated system, their time could be used more productively.

Although we were not subject to the same constraints as someone who was developing an on-line medical monitoring system or a real-

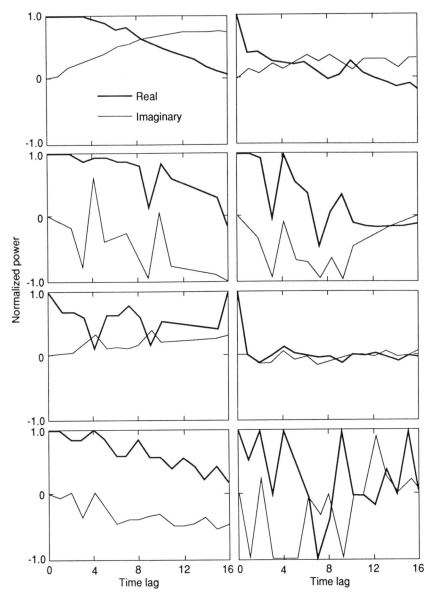

Figure 11-1 Typical ACFs. The four pairs of curves in the first column are good returns, the four pairs in the second column are bad returns. The darker lines represent the real part, the lighter lines the imaginary part.

time signal detection system, we still wanted to develop a system that was fast, easy to use, and, most essentially, accurate. One problem often encountered in such systems is that the accuracy of the system is measured as a function of how a human being (in this case, our radar expert) classifies the object. Because that necessarily introduces the possibility of error (experts are fallible), it was not clear how we should grade our classification system. The problem is that if the expert inadvertently makes a mistake, the neural net will attempt to incorporate the error during training, and this will impair its later performance on new data. Obviously, the system can do no better than the human if the human is the criterion against which errors are assessed. Nevertheless, it seemed reasonable to use the human expert as our gold standard.

Thus, our primary objective was to create a system that classified radar returns as well as our human expert. Although it would be desirable in a complete system to automate the preprocessing of the radar signals in such a way that they are ready for the final network to classify, we'll focus here on the neural network development and assume that all signal preprocessing has already been performed. The process we discuss is not a description of the steps involved in producing a formal product or service. Rather it is a description of problems encountered as we attempted to develop our radar classifier. The process of finding solutions to these problems is intended to be more informative than the solutions themselves.

The Design Process

When we first began using networks, we realized that a number of practical issues were not addressed satisfactorily by any of the reference texts. Even though we had some experience with neural network applications, we still had to contend with those same questions: How do we represent the data to the network? How many hidden nodes do we need (indeed, is a hidden layer necessary)? How do we choose the training set and the test set? What tools are available that might help us see how well we could predict the classification without a neural net approach? Putting the last question in a slightly different form, did we need a neural net to perform the radar classifications at all? How might we justify the use of this tool, which skeptics still consider too esoteric.

It would be tempting to say that the network parameters were chosen "after careful analysis" and to present the final "design" decisions (number of hidden nodes, splitting the database into training and test sets, learning rates, etc.), but this would be less than candid and neither interesting nor helpful. We'll present our case without excessive use of hindsight.

Representation

Our original data came to us after they had already undergone a considerable amount of preprocessing. In the subset of the data shown in Fig. 11-2, the g and the b on the first line indicate whether the corresponding return was good or bad. (The other entries on the first line of each set were not used in our analyses and therefore they are not important for our purposes.) The next five lines are the actual input data: 17 pairs of complex numbers, which served as inputs to the neural networks. The input values have been normalized to lie between -1 and 1 (more on normalization in the next section). The corresponding target values were also handled internally: The b values were converted to 0 and the g values to 1.

Normalizing the Data

Normalizing the dataset is often an important step in intelligent preprocessing of the database. Choosing the appropriate transformation can make a significant difference in how easy it is to interpret the results. In our case, the data had already been normalized by the time we received them, and we restricted our analyses to those values and to the particular normalization procedure that had been used. Each value in each pattern of 34 values had been divided by the largest value in that particular pattern vector.

Normalization is important for a number of reasons. It is easier, for example, to interpret the weights from the input vector to the hidden layer (or to the output layer if no hidden layers are present) if the inputs are normalized first. Of course, feedforward neural networks can pro-

```
g 1987   9 30  0   3    0 beam =  0 range =   3 power =      5638. auto-correlation
        1.00000     0.00000      0.99539  −0.05889     0.85243     0.02306      0.83398  −0.37708
        1.00000     0.03760      0.85243  −0.17755     0.59755  −0.44945        0.60536  −0.38223
        0.84356  −0.38542        0.58212  −0.32192     0.56971  −0.29674        0.36946  −0.47357
        0.56811  −0.51171        0.41078  −0.46168     0.21266  −0.34090        0.42267  −0.54487
        0.18641  −0.45300
b 1987   9 30  0   3    0 beam =  0 range =   7 power =      2374. auto-correlation
        1.00000     0.00000      1.00000  −0.18829     0.93035  −0.36156       −0.10868  −0.93597
        1.00000  −0.04549        0.50874  −0.67743     0.34432  −0.69707       −0.51685  −0.97515
        0.05499  −0.62237        0.33109  −1.00000    −0.13151  −0.45300       −0.18056  −0.35734
       −0.20332  −0.26569       −0.20468  −0.18401    −0.19040  −0.11593       −0.16626  −0.06288
       −0.13738  −0.02447
```

Figure 11-2 Sample of the training set data. Two returns (ACFs) are shown. The first line of each return indicates the expert's classification as good (g) or bad (b), followed by the date and other information not used by the networks. The next five lines are the 17 real and imaginary pairs of the ACF. Note that they have already been normalized to the range $[-1, 1]$.

cess input signals over any real range. However, normalizing the input data facilitates comparisons with other networks and helps to give the researcher a feel for what the network is doing. Generally speaking, normalization means that the same (usually linear) transformation is applied to all the elements of a particular column in the data set (corresponding to a particular position in the input vector), and possibly to the entire data set, or to all the signal components within a particular signal vector. Usually the transformation remaps the input variables to the range 0–1 or, as is the case here, to the range −1–1. Linear transformations on the input data should not have a large impact on the network's performance, so linear transformations on the input data should be chosen for ease of interpretation.

The target values (here we mean the correct classification, good or bad, not the radar target) could have been encoded by using one output node to indicate *good*, and another for *bad*. However, the second node was a redundant predictor, so nothing would have been gained by using two output nodes. (We discovered this empirically on another problem. The weights that developed for the no node were exactly the same as those that developed for the yes node, but with all signs reversed. In retrospect, of course, this is easily predictable.)

Choosing the Number of Hidden Nodes

Unfortunately, there are no theoretical guidelines for determining the number of hidden nodes to use on a given application. Thus, at first we tried 0, 5, 10, and 15 hidden nodes. A maximum of 15 was chosen because experience with other applications had shown that the number of hidden nodes required was usually less than half of the number of input nodes. It quickly became apparent that nets with hidden nodes had significantly improved performance over those with no hidden nodes but that network performance was somewhat insensitive to whether we used 5, 10, or 15 hidden nodes. In fact, initial experiments indicated that (on average) nets with 5 hidden nodes slightly outperformed nets with 10 and 15 hidden nodes. Finally, to more closely determine the optimal number, we also tried nets with 3 and 8 hidden nodes.

Choosing Training and Test Sets

If we had had access to an analytic solution (such as a mathematical formula) to classify our returns, we would have availed ourselves of it. Unfortunately, the more usual situation is that real-world problems do not have analytic solutions or, if they exist, we may not know what they are. The goal in such cases is often pragmatic: Develop a solution that does the best job possible of predicting an output from a set of corresponding inputs. In radar classification there is a further requirement: The solution must generalize to new data. That is, the network should be as valid for returns on which it was not trained as it is for returns on which it was trained.

Because we needed to test the ability of the networks to generalize, we split our database of 350 returns into 200 training cases and 150 test cases. The 200 training cases were comprised of 101 good cases and 99 bad cases. The test set was split into 123 good and 27 bad cases (for no particular reason; those were the cases that remained after the training set data were pulled out). The reasons for the particular split are threefold. First, we wanted an approximately equal number of training and test-set data. Second, we wanted to have an equal number of good and bad returns for training. The third reason was for historical reasons, but still important: the particular split had been used in a previous study and would therefore facilitate comparisons with the earlier work.

Results and Discussion

A Preliminary Analysis

The analysis appropriate for our radar classification system is certainly going to differ from the analysis required by your particular application. Our analysis should still be general enough to be useful, however.

Before starting the neural network approach to the classification problem, we asked ourselves whether it is really necessary to use neural networks to solve the problem. Commonly available statistical tools that are quick and easy should be tried first. In this particular case, a multiple-regression analysis was an appropriate first choice and was helpful in two ways: If the regression analysis solved the classification problem, we would be spared the time and expense of developing, running, and analyzing a neural net that might be only marginally superior. If the regression analysis was inadequate, then the results of that analysis would give us a baseline to assess the performance of the neural network approach.

The multiple-regression analysis correctly classified 87.5 percent of the training set and 91 percent of the test set. This was not adequate, particularly in light of the fact that 82 percent of the test set could have been classified correctly simply by saying *good* without exception. (Recall that 123 of the 150 returns in the test set were classified as good by our expert.)

The Neural Network Analysis and Results

As mentioned previously, the networks were trained using a set of 200 returns: 101 good returns and 99 bad returns. Networks with 0, 3, 5, 8, 10, and 15 hidden nodes were used. For each number of hidden nodes, we carried out experiments with 10 different networks (i.e., 10 sets of random starting weights), and performance characteristics were based on average performance over the 10 networks. This allowed us to get a more accurate picture of how network performance varied with the number of hidden nodes because, for 5–15 hidden nodes, network performance was almost as sensitive to initial starting weights as it was to the number of hidden nodes used.

Training and testing were interleaved: We trained each network for 50 presentations of the entire training set, saved the weights and measured performance on the test set, and then repeated the train/test cycle. This cycle was continued until each network had seen the training set 1000 times. In all cases it was clear that network performance on the test set was optimized after 100–400 training presentations. Thereafter, there was a slow but consistent decrease in test set performance as training continued (Fig. 11-3.)

This seems to be a curious state of affairs at first, but upon reflection it is readily explained. With increased training the network learns to

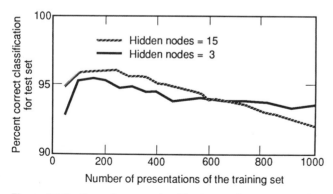

Figure 11-3 Percent correct classification on the test set as a function of the number of presentations of the training set for networks with 3 and 15 hidden nodes.

exploit more and more of the features in the training set as it relent-
lessly refines the weights to reduce the mean error. But if there are
features in the training set (say, due to noise) that are not typical of the
whole population (i.e., training set plus test set), then performance on
the test set degrades even as performance on the training set improves.
This raises another question: How do you determine when to stop training? We don't believe there is a best answer to this question. We chose
to test past the point of optimal performance and to report our best
performance with an indication of average and worst case performance.

We'll refer to the network with no hidden units as a perceptron and
those with hidden units as multilayer feedforward networks (MLFNs).
It is well known that MLFNs can learn more complex mappings than
perceptrons [2]. We used perceptrons to give us a basis for quantifying
the additional power obtained by using hidden nodes in this problem.
It should be noted that if the output node of the perceptron simply
outputs its input, then the output error to be minimized in the training
process is

$$E = \frac{1}{2} \sum_{p=1}^{n_p} \left(T^{(p)} - \sum_{j=1}^{n_{j+1}} w_{1j} o_j^{(p)} \right)^2 \qquad (11\text{-}1)$$

where $T^{(p)}$ is the target (here the correct classification: good or bad) associated with the pth input; $o_j^{(p)}$ the output of the jth input unit when
the pth input is clamped to the input layer; w_{1j} the strength of the connection between the jth input unit and the single output unit; n_i the
number of input nodes; and n_p the number of training input/target
pairs.

Equation 11-1 is identical to that which is minimized when a linear
regression is applied to the training set. The weights w_{1j} correspond
exactly to the regression coefficients. The only difference in the two
approaches is that the weights w_{1j} are found by an iterative steepest-
descent method (i.e., back-propagation) rather than by inverting a correlation matrix as is done to determine the regression coefficients.
Thus, the perceptron calculation, in effect, duplicated the regression
analysis. However, an interesting finding is worth mentioning here. Initially, the multiple-regression program consistently produced a divide-
by-zero error. Eventually we figured out why: The second row and
column of the correlation matrix was zero because the second input
variable, the imaginary part of the ACF for zero time lag, was always
zero. Therefore, the correlation matrix was singular, which caused the
divide-by-zero error when the program attempted to invert the correlation matrix. The problem was solved by deleting that row and column.
On the other hand, the perceptron calculations were not affected by the
problem. Weight changes during training are proportional to the output

of the input nodes. Because the output of the second node is always zero, the weight from this node did not change during training. The moral of the story is twofold. (1) Check your data. (2) The perceptron approach had an advantage in this problem; it simply learned to ignore the second node because its values were uncorrelated with the output. The network (perceptron) solution was more robust.

Results

Figure 11-4 shows learning curves on the training set for the perceptron and for an MLFN with five hidden nodes. The perceptron used a linear transformation for its activation function (i.e., the identity function). All MLFNs used this sigmoid transformation $(1/1 + e^{-x})$. It can be seen that the learning curves begin at values of approximately 50 percent correct and move to above 80 percent correct after 25 presentaions of the training set. Both networks have nearly reached their final values by 100 presentations. The lower curve represents the perceptron, which eventually converged to 87.5 percent correct. The top curve represents an MLFN with five hidden nodes. It, and the other MLFNs used in this study, eventually converged to 99.5–100 percent correct. It is clear that the MLFNs are superior to the perceptron in learning the classification task.

The superiority of the MLFNs over the perceptron becomes more apparent when they are each tested using the data in the test set. Recall

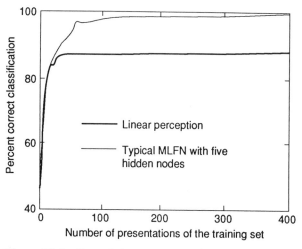

Figure 11-4 Network learning curves for the perceptron (dark curve) and a typical MLFN with five hidden nodes (light curve).

that the test set was composed of 150 returns, of which 123 were good and 27 were bad. (Bad returns were much less common in the data than were good returns.) The linear perceptron correctly classified 90.67 percent from the test set. The MLFNs averaged greater than 96 percent correct, with a range of 94–98 percent. Figure 11-5 shows the worst case; the best case; the average over 10 different starting networks for 3, 5, 8, 10, and 15 hidden node MLFNs; and a one standard deviation band around the average.

Further analysis showed clear differences in sensitivity and specificity of the various network types. Sensitivity is a measure of accurately detecting a good return when a good return was in fact present (as defined by the gold standard). The sensitivity of the perceptron was 95.9 percent (it correctly classified 118 out of 123 good returns); and sensitivity for the best MLFNs was 100 percent. Specificity is a measure of how well the networks correctly classify bad returns. The specificity of the perceptron was only 66.7 percent (it correctly classified 18 out of 27 bad returns) and for the best MLFNs it was 88.9 percent (24 out of 27 correctly classified). The worst MLFN had a sensitivity of 100 percent and a specificity of 66.7 percent. Thus, the worst MLFN did as well as the best perceptron.

The results are captured in the receiver operating characteristics (ROC) curves of Figs. 11-6 and 11-7. These curves show the hit rate

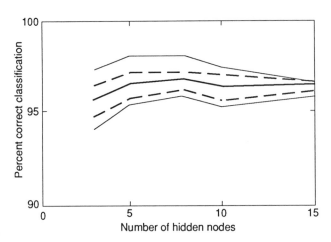

Figure 11-5 Percent correct classification of MLFNs on the testing set as a function of the number of hidden nodes. The middle curve is an average of results for 10 MLFNs with different initial weights. The dashed lines on either side of the average are 1-standard-deviation bands. The light curves indicate the best and worst performance of the 10 networks for 3, 5, 8, 10, and 15 hidden nodes.

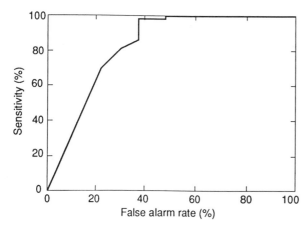

Figure 11-6   Sensitivity versus false alarm rate for a perceptron. False-alarm rate is the probability of predicting a good return when a good return is not present. Sensitivity is the probability of predicting a good return when a good return is present.

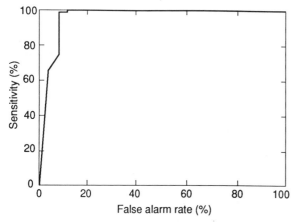

Figure 11-7   Sensitivity versus false alarm rate for the best MLFN. False alarm rate is the probability of predicting a good return when a good return is not present. Sensitivity is the probability of predicting a good return when a good return is present.

(sensitivity) as a function of the false alarm rate (one minus the specificity). Figure 11-6 is the ROC curve for the perceptron; Fig. 11-7 is the ROC curve for the best MLFN. It is clear that the ROC curve for the MLFN is far closer to that of a perfect discriminator than the curve for the perceptron (see discussion on ROC curves in Chapter 7). These conclusions are amplified in Figs. 11-8 and 11-9, in which sensitivity, specificity, proportion of variance accounted for, and percent correct are shown as a function of the good/bad threshold value. Figure 11-8 is for the perceptron; Fig. 11-9 is for the best MLFN. It is particularly notable that, for a threshold of 0.5, the MLFN accounted for 83.8 percent of the output variance while the perceptron accounted for only 49.1 percent.

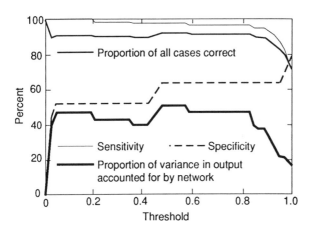

Figure 11-8   Sensitivity, specificity, proportion of all cases correct, and proportion of variance in output accounted for by the network as functions of the good/bad threshold. These results are for the perceptron.

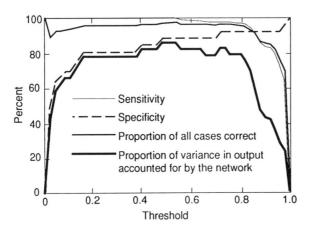

Figure 11-9   Sensitivity, specificity, proportion of all cases correct, and proportion of variance in output accounted for by the network as functions of the good/bad threshold. These results are for the best MLFN.

Conclusions

We have demonstrated that classification of radar returns is a task for which neural networks are very well suited. Furthermore, neural networks with hidden nodes substantially outperform those without hidden nodes. The improvement in performance extends to both sensitivity and specificity measures: MLFNs outperformed perceptrons, and perceptrons performed as well as a multiple linear regression analysis in discriminating between good and bad returns.

The difference between a proof-of-concept experiment as described here and a product that can be used routinely for data analysis is still large. For instance, we trained and tested our networks on data from a single night. When the networks were tested on data from the next day, performance (measured in percent) dropped to the mid to high 80s. This was not unexpected because of the large variations that occur in the ionosphere from night to day. But it does point out that further work must be done to take into account diurnal (and seasonal) variations in the ionosphere if one is to produce a usable product. However, we are confident that we have demonstrated that neural networks can perform the classification tasks at the expert human level of performance.

We said in the introduction that signal classification, discrimination, and interpretation are fertile areas for neural network applications. We also believe that the same is true for the much wider area of data reduction, preprocessing, selection, and classification. We expect that neural networks will play an increasing role in these areas as the need to automate aspects of the processing of large numerical databases becomes inevitable.

We should also mention something about the amount of computation required. To train a network with 34 input nodes, 10 hidden nodes and 1 output node, with 1000 presentations of the training set and by testing after every 50 presentations, required 8 min and 50 sec on a SUN 3/260 with a floating-point accelerator. The comparable time for a COMPAQ 286 with an 80287 math coprocessor was 42.2 min and for a NEC 386 with an 80387 math coprocessor was 19.8 min. Thus, a project of the magnitude of that described here is feasible to carry out on most PCs.

Acknowledgments

It is a pleasure to acknowledge the contributions of Dr. Kile Baker and Mr. Simon Wing, both of the Applied Physics Laboratory. Dr. Baker helped us understand the operation of the radar facility and, along with Simon Wing, acted as one of the expert classifiers. Mr. Wing came up with the idea for this project when he heard about neural networks in a course on artificial intelligence taught by one of the authors (VGS). Simon accumulated the data, performed many of the initial experiments, and as just mentioned, was one of the gold standards. It is no exaggeration to say that the project would not have happened without him.

CHAPTER 12

Case Study III: Technology in Search of a Buck

Thomas Zaremba

Introduction

The purpose of this chapter is to share my experiences, which may be of some value if you accept the challenge of trying to outwit your fellow man in the game of grasping for speculative profits. Because you're reading a book on the use of neural network personal computer tools for solving practical problems, I'll assume you have some interests other than making money. Personally, I can't think of any such interests, but the editors want me to try. So, in addition to describing in some detail a particular type of technical market analysis and showing how it applies to the game of trading options on futures contracts, I'll be addressing some other issues in less detail: issues related to the choice of neural network technology for developing market analysis models and the use of the Excel spreadsheet program on an Apple Macintosh personal computer for implementing those models. (I'm assuming that the reader has an understanding of neural network technology and the Excel spreadsheet program.)

This chapter deals with speculation through trading commodity futures contracts and options on commodity futures contracts. Some people think that speculation is simply one of the unfortunate excesses of capitalism and free markets, that it is nothing more than a euphemism for gambling and has no legitimate economic purpose. It is true that speculation shares with gambling similar levels of risk, excitement, and reward. Speculators even use the slang of gamblers. Although both activities involve the acceptance of risk for the opportunity to make money, there is one important difference that sets speculation apart from gambling: The risks and rewards of gambling exist only because there are willing participants (gamblers). Speculation deals in sharing the risks and rewards of producing and marketing goods and services in a free market economy; these risks and rewards are systemic and would exist even if speculators did not exist. However, evidence demonstrates [93] that the existence of speculators, sharing market risks and rewards, tends to enhance price stability in an economy. Reasonable price stability is a necessary economic and social good. Now, doesn't it make you feel better to know that if you decide to become a speculator you will be contributing to the greater good while having as much fun as a gambler?

Well, if speculation isn't exactly gambling, is it investing? Yes, in the same way that entering an auto race and picking up a quart of milk at the store both involve driving a car. It is a matter of degree. Speculators, just like other investors, must have skills in forecasting the direction of prices in the market in which they invest and in timing their entry and exit from that market. But for speculators, these skills, especially timing, must be more highly tuned. In addition, speculators must be willing to make a greater commitment of their personal time to manage their "investments." They must also possess the psychology of competitors to cope with the substantially higher risks involved in speculation and to let them sleep at night.

The rewards of speculation can be substantially higher than those of more conventional forms of investing. However, for most small speculators they are not. Studies and anecdotal information indicate [93, 94, 96, 98] that most small speculators, like us, lose most of the time. No matter how good our market forecasting skills or timely our information may be, our excessive fear and greed, accentuated by our modest financial wherewithal, cause us to do foolish things at precisely the wrong times. In other words, professional traders tend to win and amateur traders like us tend to lose because we beat ourselves. It follows that if we can overcome our worst instincts, do what most of the pros are doing, and avoid what many of our fellow amateurs are doing, we can improve our odds. That's what we are going to set about and that's the motivation for the neural network based market models described in this chapter.

Markets to Watch and Markets to Trade

If we are going to speculate, we need to know which markets to analyze and which markets to trade. Ideally, the answers would be the same.

Because the premier speculative markets deal in commodity futures contracts, it seems reasonable that we should analyze and trade these markets. These markets are very liquid, timely market data is readily available, and the transaction costs are relatively modest. Unfortunately, in these markets the ante is substantial and the risks are, for practical purposes, unlimited. Small traders either may not be able to ante up for this game or, worse, they may not be able to stay in the game when the stakes get too rich for their blood, even if they have a winning hand (i.e., a position that would be profitable if they could give it a little more time).

Commodity futures contracts are a leveraged substitute for a physical commodity that can be bought or sold on a cash market. A number of commodities are covered by futures, including grains, meats, and other foodstuffs; wood, fiber, petroleum and petroleum products, and precious and industrial metals; foreign currencies, interest-rate instruments, and stock market indices. A futures contract is a binding obligation to buy or sell a specific grade and quantity of a commodity at a specified future delivery date. At the termination of the contract, the contract is settled either by a cash payment from the seller to the buyer equal to the value of the commodity on the cash market or by the delivery of the commodity itself. Before termination, the value of a futures contract is established by open-market trading. A contract's open market value is a function of many variables, including the cash market price of the commodity, the net opinion of traders on the future supply and demand picture for the commodity, the time remaining until the contract's delivery date, and the current level of emotion in the market.

Futures traders can open positions by buying contracts or by selling contracts they do not already own. Traders are said to be *long* the contract if they are the buyers or *short* the contract if they are the sellers. No money actually changes hands at the instant of the sale. Both the buyer and the seller set aside in accounts a security deposit, known as the *margin*. This margin deposit ensures their performance on the terms and conditions of the futures contract. The size of this deposit is typically small relative to the actual value of the contract. Each dollar that the futures trader puts up in margin deposits may control 10 or more times that value of the actual commodity: hence, the highly leveraged nature of this investment vehicle. The balances of the buyer's and seller's margin accounts vary inversely as the market value of the futures contract fluctuates. Due to the leverage involved, these fluctuations in account balances can be substantial enough so that a buyer or seller may be required to replenish a margin deposit. A request to replenish a trader's margin account is known as a *margin call*. Profits and losses on futures contracts are most often realized by *offsetting* a position rather than by settlement. Offsetting a position simply means that the traders who are long sell contracts or traders who are short buy sufficient contracts to eliminate their positions. After offsetting a position, the traders realize a profit or a loss by having their margin deposits returned plus or minus any change in the futures contract value and minus transaction commissions.

The margin deposit requirements, though relatively modest, and the unlimited financial risks of trading commodity futures contracts may be unsuitable for the very small speculator. For this trader the options on commodity futures markets may be a better place to trade. Options are a defined risk substitute for commodity futures contracts. Basically, the performance of an option is tied to its associated futures contract because the owner of an option has the right to buy or sell that futures contract at a specific price (the option's *strike price*) on or before a specific date (the option's *expiration date*). An option giving the owner the right to buy is called a *call*, and one giving the right to sell is called a *put*. If the owner chooses not to exercise the right or not to trade the option on or before the specified date, the option expires worthless. Before expiration, the value of an option is determined by open-market trading. The buyer pays the seller a price that reflects this valuation at the time of the sale. Generally, the value of a call increases while the value of a corresponding put decreases when the underlying futures contract increases in price. Conversely, when the underlying futures contract decreases in price, generally, the value of a call decreases while the value of the corresponding put increases. The time remaining until expiration also affects the value of an option. Profits on options are most often realized by selling the option before expiration, not by exercising the option. Losses on options are most often realized by letting them expire, not by selling. Profits or losses due to selling options are equal to the closing price minus the opening price and transaction commissions. Losses due to expiration are usually total and equal the opening price and transaction commissions.

Options are a good alternative speculative vehicle for the small speculator because they offer defined risk with unlimited reward potential. But how can that be? Options are a substitute for futures contracts and futures are highly leveraged. Option buyers can't lose any more money than the initial cost of the option, but futures traders can lose more than their initial margin deposits. They can lose substantially more. They have both unlimited reward and unlimited risk potential. It would seem that options buyers have a better deal than futures traders. In reality, they don't. Because options are substitutes for futures contracts, someone is absorbing the unlimited loss potential. That someone is the option writer. Unlike option buyers, who buy and then sell options that they already own, option writers sell options that they don't already own. They believe that the options they sell will expire worthless, and they will then have a profit equal to the proceeds of their sales. Option writers must maintain margin deposits to ensure their performance of the terms and conditions of the options should the market move against them. To encourage them to undertake what at first appears to be a dubious position, they are paid a substantial price, or *premium*, by the buyers for the length of time the writers undertake the market risks. The longer the time the writers are asked to bear the risk, the greater the premium they're paid.

Even with the premiums that option buyers pay the writers, the limitation of risk allows small speculators to establish and maintain speculative positions that they might otherwise be unable to do directly in the futures markets. These option positions tend to track the price moves of the futures contracts on which they are based (which, incidentally, are the price moves our market models forecast). If the option premiums are viewed as being too high, there are multiple option positions known as *spreads* (the simultaneous purchase and sale of an equal number of puts or calls with different strike prices or expiration dates) that partially offset the cost of opening a position—if speculators are willing to forgo some of their profit potential. If the cost of spreads is considered too high, then they should not speculate. In speculation, as in most human activities, there is no such thing as a free lunch. For additional information on futures, options on futures, option strategies, trading options and the management of risk capital see [93, 98].

Futures Market Forecasting

Experts differ, but most analytical techniques developed to assist the trader in the forecasting of futures market prices fall into two categories, fundamental and technical.

Fundamental analysis involves the integration of many factors affecting the future supply of, and demand for, a particular commodity. From this process of integration, the analyst develops an estimate of what the future true value or real price of the commodity should be if supply and demand were in balance. He reasons that if current prices differ from his estimates, then the future direction of prices should tend to eliminate that difference. He then develops a forecast of the behavior of the futures market based on the expected movement in the underlying commodity prices. Fundamental analysis consists of a collection of often complex and subtle, knowledge-and-information-intensive market forecasting skills. These skills tend to be very commodity specific. The information used by the fundamental analyst is often hard to come by. A significant weakness of fundamental analysis is that it focuses only on issues of supply and demand and does not take market psychology into account, which is an equally important driver of futures prices. Put simply, fundamental analysis deals with the logical side of futures markets but not the emotional side.

Technical analysis involves the study and interpretation of a futures market itself to forecast the direction of prices in that market. Technicians, who are traders using technical analysis, believe that what they need to know to develop a forecast can be determined from the accurate evaluation of historical market data. The technician's forecast is based on recognizing patterns in these data and related market price behavior. He believes that price changes are not random or at least not totally random; over time, predictable trends and cycles are in evidence. He reasons that if current patterns in market data tend to match historical patterns, then the future direction of prices should tend to match the direction of prices that followed earlier occurrences of those historical patterns.

Technical analysis encompasses a variety of forecasting models from the simple to the complex. These models are often applicable to a number of structurally similar markets involving widely differing commodities. Much of the information used by the technician is readily available. Most importantly, unlike fundamental analysis, technical analysis deals with both logical and emotional drivers of price in a futures market. In fact, the predictable trends and cycles that make technical analysis viable, particularly for shorter term speculative purposes, are probably largely due to market psychology.

Unfortunately for the technician, historical market data can be evaluated in an almost infinite number of ways, some of which may be better than others. Also, as mentioned previously, the viability of technical market analysis depends on the recognition of predictable trends and cycles. The fact that these trends and cycles change or evolve can cause the technician no end of grief if his models do not adapt.

Historical Futures Market Data

Historical futures market data as used by technicians to characterize the past behavior of a market usually consist of three populations of data: futures prices, market volume and market open interest.

The definition of futures prices is obvious. However, in considering market price action over a period of time, the dispersion and skewness of prices about a central measure (average price) is important. Price *dispersion* (the degree of spread of prices about an average price), measured as the variance or standard deviation of the population of prices, measures a market's volatility. *Volatility* is simply the amount that futures prices fluctuate in a given time period. Price *skewness* (the degree of asymmetry of prices about an average price) measures whether a market is trading in an area of price *resistance*. The resistance may be due to either a fundamental or an emotional factor influencing prices at their current levels. *Market volume* is simply the number of futures contracts traded during a specified time period. It is a measure of a market's activity. *Market open interest* is the number of all long or short futures contracts in a market that have neither been offset nor settled. It is a measure of a market's liquidity.

Some technicians contend that price, volume, and open interest can't adequately define past futures market behavior. They contend that these data must be supplemented with data that capture the sentiment or mood of a market. Capturing market sentiment involves measuring the opinions or actions of market traders. Accurately measuring the opinions or actions of traders requires data on the numbers of traders in a market, the size of their positions, their commercial interests in the underlying commodity, their knowledge and experience, and their financial strength. The technicians who value sentiment data believe that market analysis models that incorporate such data should be able to make useful inferences about the direction of prices from the sentiment of various groupings of traders. Those technicians that discount the value of supplemental data do so primarily because they believe that most useful sentiment data are not readily available, distinct, or timely enough to be of value. There is also some debate on how the data should be interpreted. Because much of the sentiment data is not as readily available, distinct, or timely as price, volume, and open interest, there has been a decided lack of models developed to exploit it fully.

One important source of market sentiment data can be developed from detailed breakdowns of long and short open interest held by various classes of traders in the various futures markets. These breakdowns represent the market commitments of traders in these markets. Analyzing these commitments gives the technician a sense of the overall activity, market share and numbers of traders represented by specific groupings of traders within each market. In these breakdowns of open interest, traders are usually grouped by the size of their positions and as either speculators or hedgers. For this purpose a *speculator* is defined as a trader who has no commercial interest in the commodity underlying the futures contracts he is trading whereas a *hedger* is defined as a trader who is directly involved in the production or consumption of the underlying commodity. A hedger is generally thought to be trading futures contracts to reduce his risk of future adverse price moves in a commodity vital to his business. He is trying to add a degree of certainty to his business and avoid losing money. A speculator is trading futures to make money. He is accepting the risk offered by the hedger for the opportunity to profit. It is often postulated that because hedgers are in effect isolated from most futures price fluctuations because of their commodity inventories, they tend to take a longer term view of a market. They are more likely to position themselves based on a forecast for the direction of futures prices driven by their intimate knowledge of the supply and demand factors related to the underlying commodity. In contrast, speculators, exposed to greater financial risk, tend to take a shorter term view of a market. They are more likely to take positions based on their technical analysis of market action and psychology.

Unfortunately, this description is too simplistic. In some markets, to a greater or lesser degree, traders defined as hedgers are in essence speculating. They are trading at levels beyond any reasonable hedging requirement. Therefore, useful information that might be determined by comparing the activities of hedgers and speculators may be somewhat obscured. In addition, although data are available that describe the commitments of "large speculators" and "large hedgers" separately, no source of data gives a distinct breakdown of the current commitments of all speculators and hedgers in a specific market. The available data lump the commitments of "small speculators" and "small hedgers" together into a separate class of "small traders." This lumping of the data compromises its value and makes useful comparisons more difficult. Nevertheless, useful comparisons of speculator and hedger activities, though not perfect, are possible because the majority of hedgers are large hedgers and the majority of speculators are small traders. In addition, the data do support a distinct comparison of the activities of large speculators and large hedgers.

Several other useful comparisons and observations can be made. For example, by adding the commitments of the large speculators and large hedgers together and following the changes in this total from month to month, the analyst can get a measure of what a group, which we'll call professional traders, is doing. This grouping represents a minority of traders by number but often a majority of the outstanding contracts. In the futures markets the net activities of this group are balanced by those of the small traders, a group we'll call amateur traders. The results of a number of studies [93, 94, 95, 96, 97] give us useful insight into the characteristics and performance of these two groups and a sense of the value of tracking and comparing their activities. As groups, over time, amateur traders lose money and professional traders, particularly large speculators, make money. Amateur traders seem to initiate and terminate trades haphazardly. They seem unable to manage risk capital intelligently. They often assume they can beat the odds too easily, and they play to the hilt too readily. They invite ruin in a game that does not relinquish gains without consistent hard work. As individuals, a few amateur traders may be successful and join the ranks of the professional traders, but most stop trading after losing enough money or running out of excuses. The dropouts are quickly replaced by eager rookies. Therefore, as a group, due to the turnover, their knowledge and experience base is limited. Professional traders usually continue to trade for some time and gain knowledge and experience in the process.

Amateur traders tend to rely on *chasing* (trend following) strategies [148] and on the advice of others. On the other hand, professional traders generally rely on *tracking* (countertrend) strategies and follow their own hard-won knowledge and experience. Amateur traders, following chasing strategies, buy after prices start to move up and sell after prices start to move down. In other words, they buy into strength and sell on weakness. Professional traders, following tracking strategies, buy after prices start to move down and sell after prices start to move up. In other words, they buy on weakness and sell into strength. In the long run, futures markets tend to be *trading markets* (trendless or trending in the short term) rather than *trending markets* (trending in the long term), which tends to reward those following tracking strategies. Even trending markets have breaks and strong reversals that reward traders following tracking strategies. In the final analysis, in the high-risk game of speculation, the many (small traders) will tend to lose to the few (large traders). The experienced, usually better financed professional traders have more favorable odds of success than the inexperienced, usually undercapitalized amateur trader.

Because the small trader group represents the vast majority of traders by number, following the changes in their commitments from month to month can give the analyst a sense of the developing opinion of the majority of traders on the future direction of prices. The opinions of traders are useful for assessing the balance of emotional forces in the market. In other words, opinions often lead to action and action is reflected in market prices. The direction of prices tends to increase the strength of the prevailing market opinion, which in turn leads to further action. That cycle of opinions leading to actions that are reflected in market prices can, under the right circumstances, develop into a definite trend in market prices. That trend can continue until extremes of opinion lead to unreasonable actions. Unreasonable actions are not rewarded in the marketplace. Unreasonable (almost frenzied) actions inevitably result in a break in the price trend. This break is due to the exhaustion of the pool of uncommitted or not fully committed traders at market tops and bottoms (i.e., there is no one to sell to at a higher price at a top or there is no one to buy from at a lower price at a bottom).

Often, the stronger the trend the greater the break. An astute technician, wise in the ways of market psychology, might recognize developing price trends and impending breaks from changes in the commitments of small traders.

As we have seen, a number of potentially useful comparisons and observations can be made from the commitments of futures market traders. Underlying this usefulness is the fact that at various times in various types of markets various groups of traders demonstrate consistently higher levels of success (or failure) at profitably positioning themselves. Although it is true that some of the behavior of traders is too short term in nature to be detected in month-to-month comparisons, some of it is not. It follows that if we could construct market models based on consistently good or bad trader behavior, our models might demonstrate an ability to forecast futures prices with favorable odds of success. Such models have been built and initially tested. These models use, as input, measures of average monthly futures price, price volatility, and measures of market sentiment developed from the commitments of futures market traders. The models analyze the month-to-month levels and changes in these inputs in a historical context. They then output estimates of average monthly futures prices for the subsequent month. However, before describing these models in more detail, I'll describe specific sources for their input data.

Sources of Market Model Data

The weekly futures price data used by the market models are readily available from a number of sources such as *Barron's*, *The Wall Street Journal*, and probably your local newspaper. The market sentiment data used are not as readily available. The only source of which I am aware is the Commodities Futures Trading Commission (CFTC). The CFTC is an agency of the U.S. government that regulates the trading of futures contracts and options on futures contracts. The CFTC publishes a variety of reports and handbooks of interest to the trader and market analyst. The publication of particular interest to us is the *Commitments of Traders in Futures Report*. This monthly report, which is available directly from the CFTC for a modest subscription fee, provides end-of-the-month data on the commitments of traders in futures markets. (Previous copies of the report are usually available at large public and university libraries. Subscriptions may be obtained by writing to the CFTC, Office of Communication and Education Services, 2033 K Street, N.W., Washington, D.C. 20581.) The report includes a breakdown of long and short open interest for reportable and nonreportable positions of market traders in every significant futures market. The reportable positions are further broken down into hedging and speculative positions. In addition, the report also provides several other pieces of potentially useful data such as a breakdown of the number of long and short speculators and hedgers with reportable positions and the percentages of open interest held by the market's largest traders.

For each futures market the CFTC defines a reporting level. Any trader whose futures position exceeds that level is classified as a *reportable* and is monitored by the commission. These levels represent relatively large positions in their respective markets. For example, the current reporting levels for the gold, S&P 500, and treasury bond futures markets are 200, 300, and 500 contracts, respectively. In the previous section we called those holding reportable positions large traders or professionals. By definition any trader's position below the CFTC reporting level is classified as *nonreportable*. Because the CFTC also tracks total open interest in each market and because the total of all long open interest equals the total of all short open interest, the commission can derive long and short open interest in nonreportable positions. For our purposes we have called those holding nonreportable positions as small traders or amateurs. The CFTC collects and disseminates much more data on the nature of large traders. Unfortunately, they do not collect nor can they derive equivalent data on small traders. As mentioned previously, the type of data provided by the CFTC does not give a total or distinct picture of the entire market, but it can provide significant insight into the evolving behavior of traders.

Futures Market Model Description

Three separate market models were constructed. These models are identical in structure and differ only in the input data that are supplied to each. The markets modeled are the International Monetary Market's S&P 500 Stock Index Futures market, the Chicago Board of Trade's Long Term U.S. Treasury Bond Futures market and the Commodity Exchange Incorporated's Gold Futures market. (Accurately modeling these markets would not only give the investor a sense of the probable direction of prices in these futures markets but would also tend to act as leading indicators for stock markets, interest rates, and inflation, respectively.) These models each require five inputs per month presented four months at a time. For each of the markets modeled, three of the monthly inputs are based on CFTC supplied data and two are based on weekly futures market prices from *Barron's*.

The three sentiment inputs for each market model are derived from CFTC-supplied data. These inputs represent the end-of-month net commitments of large speculators, large hedgers, and small traders in each

STOCK INDEX FUTURE, S&P 500 - INTERNATIONAL MONETARY MARKET
COMMITMENTS OF TRADERS IN ALL FUTURES COMBINED AND INDICATED FUTURES, OCTOBER 31, 1989

	TOTAL	REPORTABLE POSITIONS								NONREPORTABLE POSITIONS	
		NON-COMMERCIAL				COMMERCIAL		TOTAL			
		LONG OR SHORT ONLY		LONG AND SHORT (SPREADING)							
		LONG : SHORT :		LONG : SHORT :		LONG : SHORT :		LONG : SHORT :		LONG : SHORT	

(S&P 500 INDEX X $500.00)

OPEN INTEREST	TOTAL	NON-COMM LONG	SHORT	SPREAD LONG	SPREAD SHORT	COMM LONG	COMM SHORT	TOTAL LONG	TOTAL SHORT	NONREP LONG	NONREP SHORT
ALL	126,768	4,579	22,125	1	1	95,817	66,966	100,397	89,092	26,371	37,676
OLD	117,195	4,204	21,499	1	1	89,182	60,624	93,387	82,124	23,808	35,071
OTHER	9,573	375	626	0	0	6,635	6,342	7,010	6,968	2,563	2,605

CHANGES IN COMMITMENTS FROM SEPTEMBER 29, 1989

	TOTAL	NON-COMM LONG	SHORT	SPREAD LONG	SPREAD SHORT	COMM LONG	COMM SHORT	TOTAL LONG	TOTAL SHORT	NONREP LONG	NONREP SHORT
ALL	3,512	-5,012	1,375	-130	-130	9,827	-7,450	4,685	-6,205	-1,173	9,717

PERCENT OF OPEN INTEREST REPRESENTED BY EACH CATEGORY OF TRADERS

	TOTAL	NON-COMM LONG	SHORT	SPREAD LONG	SPREAD SHORT	COMM LONG	COMM SHORT	TOTAL LONG	TOTAL SHORT	NONREP LONG	NONREP SHORT
ALL	100.0%	3.6	17.5	0.0	0.0	75.6	52.8	79.2	70.3	20.8	29.7
OLD	100.0%	3.6	18.3	0.0	0.0	76.1	51.7	79.7	70.1	20.3	29.9
OTHER	100.0%	3.9	6.5	0.0	0.0	69.3	66.2	73.2	72.8	26.8	27.2

NUMBER OF TRADERS IN EACH CATEGORY

NUMBER OF TRADERS	TOTAL	NON-COMM LONG	SHORT	SPREAD LONG	SPREAD SHORT	COMM LONG	COMM SHORT	TOTAL LONG	TOTAL SHORT
ALL	132	7	21	1	1	73	57	81	78
OLD	132	7	21	1	1	73	57	81	78
OTHER	12	1	1	0	0	6	4	7	5

CONCENTRATION RATIOS

PERCENT OF OPEN INTEREST HELD BY THE INDICATED NUMBER OF LARGEST TRADERS

	BY GROSS POSITION				BY NET POSITION			
	4 OR LESS TRADERS		8 OR LESS TRADERS		4 OR LESS TRADERS		8 OR LESS TRADERS	
	LONG :	SHORT :	LONG :	SHORT	LONG :	SHORT :	LONG :	SHORT
ALL	19.3	21.4	30.0	31.3	18.6	18.7	28.1	26.9
OLD	18.3	20.5	29.5	29.4	17.8	18.3	28.8	26.9
OTHER	61.7	68.6	73.2	72.8	61.7	68.6	73.2	72.8

Figure 12-1 Stock index future, S&P 500: A typical page from the CFTC Commitments of Traders in Futures Report.

market. Figure 12-1 is a typical page from the CFTC *Commitments of Traders in Futures Report*, in this case a breakdown of the S&P 500 futures market for October 31, 1989. There are five values (highlighted) that must be extracted to calculate the three sentiment inputs for this market. Figure 12-2 is a subset of the Excel CFTC Data Worksheet. The full worksheet, too large to be shown here, contains all of the data extracted from the monthly CFTC reports and is used to calculate the sentiment inputs for all three market models. The subset of the worksheet shown in Fig. 12-2 contains only S&P 500 market-related data from October 31, 1986 until January 31, 1990.

	1	2	3	4	5	6	7	8	9
107									
108									
109	International Monetary Market's S&P 500 Index Futures Market								
110									
111									
112		Total		Reportable Positions			End of Month Net Commitments		
113		Open	Non-Commercial		Commercial		Large	Large	Small
114	Date	Interest	Long	Short	Long	Short	Speculator	Hedger	Trader
120	31-Oct-86	138,262	2,073	14,064	98,680	79,657	-4.34%	6.88%	-2.54%
121	28-Nov-86	144,347	6,604	11,023	90,516	76,634	-1.53%	4.81%	-3.28%
122	31-Dec-86	95,433	3,117	5,708	58,122	57,665	-1.36%	0.24%	1.12%
123	30-Jan-87	107,929	5,298	15,903	65,264	48,591	-4.91%	7.72%	-2.81%
124	27-Feb-87	123,021	8,025	14,834	71,448	60,247	-2.77%	4.55%	-1.79%
125	31-Mar-87	97,673	5,697	13,928	57,375	48,404	-4.21%	4.59%	-0.38%
126	30-Apr-87	121,860	6,113	12,887	73,444	71,298	-2.78%	0.88%	1.90%
127	29-May-87	128,356	5,893	16,594	80,651	73,617	-4.17%	2.74%	1.43%
128	30-Jun-87	109,452	6,577	7,390	69,160	66,860	-0.37%	1.05%	-0.68%
129	31-Jul-87	115,389	2,146	9,398	80,843	57,287	-3.14%	10.21%	-7.06%
130	31-Aug-87	129,539	6,272	9,432	72,965	77,235	-1.22%	-1.65%	2.87%
131	30-Sep-87	114,182	6,553	5,560	67,758	73,091	0.43%	-2.34%	1.90%
132	30-Oct-87	152,340	6,582	4,678	116,409	114,490	0.62%	0.63%	-1.25%
133	30-Nov-87	139,887	1,965	10,961	99,404	92,815	-3.22%	2.36%	0.86%
134	31-Dec-87	107,973	1,588	6,927	84,897	75,209	-2.47%	4.49%	-2.01%
135	29-Jan-88	118,583	4,116	8,619	87,778	82,130	-1.90%	2.38%	-0.48%
136	29-Feb-88	122,741	4,196	7,119	85,627	82,107	-1.19%	1.43%	-0.24%
137	31-Mar-88	110,129	6,494	16,871	79,258	64,510	-4.71%	6.70%	-1.98%
138	29-Apr-88	116,738	4,588	9,909	86,386	76,530	-2.28%	4.22%	-1.94%
139	31-May-88	134,175	3,512	9,975	94,041	87,333	-2.41%	2.50%	-0.09%
140	30-Jun-88	98,175	3,404	5,006	67,123	66,538	-0.82%	0.30%	0.52%
141	29-Jul-88	114,248	5,558	3,139	80,354	80,562	1.06%	-0.09%	-0.97%
142	31-Aug-88	119,496	2,592	3,312	83,504	79,568	-0.30%	1.65%	-1.35%
143	30-Sep-88	114,434	3,943	8,433	83,842	76,115	-1.96%	3.38%	-1.41%
144	31-Oct-88	125,869	3,655	7,398	89,101	76,566	-1.49%	4.98%	-3.49%
145	30-Nov-88	141,766	5,402	10,287	97,920	88,673	-1.72%	3.26%	-1.54%
146	30-Dec-88	120,511	5,723	8,974	90,038	86,784	-1.35%	1.35%	0.00%
147	31-Jan-89	139,535	8,524	7,249	96,430	100,185	0.46%	-1.35%	0.89%
148	28-Feb-89	135,398	2,203	12,257	100,117	81,484	-3.71%	6.88%	-3.17%
149	31-Mar-89	134,158	6,133	16,911	106,171	84,938	-4.02%	7.91%	-3.90%
150	28-Apr-89	136,181	7,499	13,820	96,393	86,993	-2.32%	3.45%	-1.13%
151	31-May-89	140,287	6,984	12,328	89,927	85,274	-1.90%	1.66%	0.25%
152	30-Jun-89	110,764	6,137	16,758	80,387	64,660	-4.79%	7.10%	-2.30%
153	31-Jul-89	122,096	10,724	11,848	79,687	80,857	-0.46%	-0.48%	0.94%
154	31-Aug-89	135,826	11,463	21,279	87,450	81,618	-3.61%	2.15%	1.47%
155	29-Sep-89	123,256	9,591	20,750	85,990	74,416	-4.53%	4.70%	-0.17%
156	31-Oct-89	126,768	4,579	22,125	95,817	66,966	-6.92%	11.38%	-4.46%
157	30-Nov-89	124,470	6,628	22,625	83,065	63,356	-6.43%	7.92%	-1.49%
158	29-Dec-89	107,195	8,418	15,795	70,312	64,079	-3.44%	2.91%	0.53%
159	31-Jan-90	117,579	3,442	17,029	85,388	67,162	-5.78%	7.75%	-1.97%

Figure 12-2 A subset of the CFTC Data Worksheet.

To illustrate the function of the CFTC Data Worksheet, a brief explanation of Fig. 12-2 is offered. The five values extracted from Fig. 12-1 are entered into Fig. 12-2 next to the appropriate date in row 156. The worksheet then calculates the October, 1989 net commitment model inputs, as shown in Columns 7, 8, and 9 of Row 156. Figure 12-3 describes the cell formulas for the calculated cells on the subsetted CFTC Data Worksheet. The full worksheet uses similar formulas to calculate sentiment inputs for the T-Bond and Gold futures market model. The net commitment measures calculated are basically the monthly differences of long and short contracts held by a trader group expressed as a percentage of the total long and short open contracts [96]. Because the net commitments of the three trader groups within each market must equal zero, the net commitments of small traders equals the inverse of the sum of the other two net commitment measures.

For each model, the two monthly price-based inputs are derived from weekly closing futures prices for the most widely held futures contract in that particular futures market. Figure 12-4 is a subset of the Excel Weekly Price Index Worksheet. The full worksheet, too large to be shown here, contains all the data extracted from *Barron's* and is used to calculate the price inputs for all three market models. The subset of the worksheet shown in Fig. 12-4 contains S&P 500, T-bond, and gold futures market-related data from October 10, 1986 until August 7, 1987.

To illustrate the function of the Weekly Price Worksheet, a brief explanation of Fig. 12-4 is offered. The values extracted from *Barron's*, which represent changes in the weekly closing prices for the most widely held S&P 500, T-bond and gold futures contracts, with the exception of the October 10, 1986 entries, are entered into columns 2, 3, and 4 of Fig. 12-4. *Most widely held* means the contract that currently has the highest open interest. The values entered on October 10, 1986 are the actual closing prices for the most widely held contracts that day. These values become base prices of the indices of futures prices shown in columns 6, 9, and 12. Because specific futures contracts expire, it is necessary to construct indices of futures prices that consistently represent the overall change in their respective market prices over a time period of several years. Using the changes in prices for the most widely held contracts every week as bases for the calculations of the indices is a compromise, but it seems like a reasonable one. Figure 12-5 describes

Cell Range	Formula
R120C8:R159C8	= (RC[-4]-RC[-3])/(2*RC[-5])
R120C9:R159C9	= (RC[-3]-RC[-2])/(2*RC[-6])
R120C10:R159C10	= -RC[-2]-RC[-1]

Figure 12-3 Calculated Cell Formulas from the CFTC Data Worksheet

	1	2	3	4	5	6	7	8	9	10	11	12	13	14
					End of Month	S&P 500 Futures			T-Bond Futures			Gold Futures		
			Weekly Closing Prices		Date	Price	Monthly Centered	Monthly Centered	Price	Monthly Centered	Monthly Centered	Price	Monthly Centered	Monthly Centered
	Date	S&P 500	T-Bond	Gold	Adjustment	Index	Mean	Deviation	Index	Mean	Deviation	Index	Mean	Deviation
5	10-Oct-86	235.10	96.19	434.50		100.00			100.00			100.00		
6	17-Oct-86	2.85	-1.63	-12.30		101.21			98.31			97.17		
7	24-Oct-86	-0.20	1.34	-13.00		101.13			99.71			94.18		
8	31-Oct-86	6.95	2.19	-3.70	0.00	104.08	103.07	1.75	101.98	100.44	1.59	93.33	94.19	1.97
9	7-Nov-86	1.20	-1.78	5.10		104.59			100.13			94.50		
10	14-Nov-86	-0.60	1.84	-11.80		104.34			102.05			91.78		
11	21-Nov-86	-0.45	1.50	-19.50		104.15			103.61			87.30		
12	28-Nov-86	3.80	0.06	12.10	0.00	105.76	105.30	1.23	103.67	103.35	0.73	90.08	89.82	1.63
13	5-Dec-86	3.30	0.00	-1.90		107.17			103.74			89.64		
14	12-Dec-86	-4.95	0.06	2.90		105.06			103.67			90.31		
15	19-Dec-86	0.85	0.94	0.00		105.42			104.71			90.31		
16	26-Dec-86	-1.05	0.50	-2.80	0.60	104.98	106.97	3.15	105.23	105.32	0.92	89.67	91.69	1.91
17	2-Jan-87	-0.95	-0.34	11.00		104.57			104.87			92.20		
18	9-Jan-87	12.75	1.69	3.50		110.00			106.63			93.00		
19	16-Jan-87	7.20	-0.47	9.80		113.06			106.14			95.26		
20	23-Jan-87	2.60	-0.75	-12.00		114.16			105.36			92.50		
21	30-Jan-87	4.85	-0.69	-0.20	0.00	116.23	116.45	2.93	104.65	105.22	0.69	92.45	92.58	1.69
22	6-Feb-87	7.05	0.84	-1.50		119.23			105.52			92.11		
23	13-Feb-87	0.85	-1.03	-6.70		119.59			104.45			90.56		
24	20-Feb-87	3.60	0.81	8.00		121.12			105.30			92.41		
25	27-Feb-87	-2.10	1.13	-1.30	0.00	120.23	121.42	1.64	106.47	105.87	0.97	92.11	91.77	0.74
26	6-Mar-87	7.65	-0.13	0.40		123.48			106.34			92.20		
27	13-Mar-87	-1.85	0.44	-2.80		122.69			106.79			91.55		
28	20-Mar-87	8.60	-0.09	1.30		126.35			106.69			91.85		
29	27-Mar-87	-2.45	-0.97	16.90	0.40	125.31	125.10	2.21	105.69	104.12	2.79	95.74	95.08	2.87
30	3-Apr-87	6.10	-1.94	-3.60		127.90			103.67			94.91		
31	10-Apr-87	-10.05	-3.06	12.80		123.63			100.49			97.86		
32	17-Apr-87	-4.50	-0.47	10.60		121.71			100.00			100.30		
33	24-Apr-87	-7.95	-4.66	18.20	0.80	118.33	121.58	2.14	95.16	97.25	2.22	104.49	103.10	2.49
34	1-May-87	8.95	2.25	-6.00		122.14			97.50			103.11		
35	8-May-87	4.75	0.41	-2.80		124.16			97.92			102.46		
36	15-May-87	-7.30	-3.34	19.50		121.05			94.44			106.95		
37	22-May-87	-5.55	0.56	-11.60	0.40	118.69			95.03			104.28		
38	29-May-87	7.65	2.69	-14.50	0.00	121.95	122.52	3.21	97.82	96.78	2.00	100.94	103.07	2.52
39	5-Jun-87	3.80	-0.41	2.80		123.56			97.40			101.59		
40	12-Jun-87	8.85	1.75	0.10		127.33			99.22			101.61		
41	19-Jun-87	4.90	0.06	-10.20		129.41			99.29			99.26		
42	26-Jun-87	1.85	-1.00	1.40	0.40	130.20	129.41	1.17	98.25	99.04	0.46	99.59	99.50	0.82
43	3-Jul-87	-3.80	1.09	-1.30		128.58			99.38			99.29		
44	10-Jul-87	2.50	-0.28	-2.80		129.65			99.09			98.64		
45	17-Jul-87	5.45	0.03	3.30		131.97			99.12			99.40		
46	24-Jul-87	-4.60	-2.53	5.20		130.01			96.49			100.60		
47	31-Jul-87	9.90	-0.28	9.60	0.00	134.22	134.70	4.23	96.20	97.13	1.28	102.81	100.57	1.35
48	7-Aug-87	4.95	-0.06	-10.30		136.32			96.13			100.44		

Figure 12-4 A subset of the Weekly Price Index Worksheet.

Cell Range	Formula
R5C6:R48C6	= SUM(R5C2:RC[-4])/R5C2*100
R5C9:R48C9	= SUM(R5C3:RC[-6])/R5C3*100
R5C12:R48C12	= SUM(R5C4:RC[-8])/R5C4*100
R5C7:R48C7	= IF(OR(RC7=" ",R[3]C[-1]=" "),
R5C10:R48C10	" ",RC7*AVERAGE(R[-1]C[-1]:R[3]C[-1])
R5C13:R48C13	+(1-RC7)*AVERAGE(R[-2]C[-1]:R[2]C[-1]))
R5C8:R48C8	= IF(OR(RC7=" ",R[3]C[-2]=" "),
R5C11:R48C11	" ",RC7*STDEV(R[-1]C[-2]:R[3]C[-2])
R5C14:R48C14	+(1-RC7)*STDEV(R[-2]C[-2]:R[2]C[-2]))

Figure 12-5 Calculated Cell Formulas from the Weekly Price Index Worksheet

the cell formulas for the calculated cells on the subsetted Weekly Price Index Worksheet. On the full worksheet, the same formulas are used over greater cell ranges to accommodate the additional data from the time period from August 14, 1987 until the present.

Because all of the monthly price model inputs must coincide in time with the sentiment model inputs, the price inputs are calculated as an interpolation of two 5-week centered averages and standard deviations. The use of 5-week centered averages and standard deviations provides the models the most timely price data and does not introduce unnecessary delay in the monthly model updates due to the approximately 2.5-week delay in the availability of the CFTC supplied data. The values shown on Fig. 12-4 under the heading End of Month Date Adjustment represent the difference between the last Friday in a month and the last trading day in a month expressed as the percent of a trading week (5 days). This value is used in the interpolation process.

Each market model has one output. That output is a forecast of the model's monthly centered mean price input for the subsequent month. As shown in Fig. 12-6, the Price Index Forecast Worksheet, a model's output can be compared with a calculated current monthly centered mean futures price index. This worksheet allows this comparison to be made weekly. The results can be used to plan the opening and closing of speculative positions or for assessing how well the model did at forecasting. The price index values and end-of-month date adjustment are copied from the Weekly Price Index Worksheet. The forecast monthly averages come from the output of each respective market model. The formulas for the calculated cells on this worksheet are shown in Fig. 12-7.

The transfer function for each market model has evolved from a relatively simple neural network. The properties of this network are de-

	1	2	3	4	5	6	7	8	9	10	11
1											
2											
3											
4					End of Month						
5		S&P 500 Price Index	T-Bond Price Index	Gold Price Index	Date Adjustment					Current Monthly Averages	
6	Date								SPX	T-Bond	Gold
7	2nd or 3rd Friday of the Month	130.67	108.93	74.48		130.67	108.93	74.48			
8	3rd or 4th Friday of the Month	131.20	107.73	73.60		131.20	107.73	73.60			
9	Last Friday of the Month	124.65	105.17	75.83	0.60	124.65	105.17	75.83	127.70	106.23	74.96
10	1st Friday of the Next Month	127.07	105.65	75.21		127.07	105.65	75.21			
11	2nd Friday of the Next Month					127.07	105.65	75.21			
12	3rd Friday of the Next Month					127.07	105.65	75.21			
13											
14											
15										Forecast Monthly Averages	
16									SPX	T-Bond	Gold
17									135.67	109.81	68.52
18											
19											
20										Error	
21									SPX	T-Bond	Gold
22									6.24%	3.37%	-8.58%

Figure 12-6 Price Index Forecast Worksheet.

Cell Range	Formula
R8C6: R8C8	$=RC[-4]$
R9C6: R13C8	$= IF(RC[-4] = "\quad", R[-1]C, RC[-4])$
R10C9: R10C11	$= SUM(R[-2]C[-3]:$
	$R[2]C[-3]) + R10C5*(R[3]C[-3] - R[-2]C[-3]))/5$
R23C9: R23C11	$= (R[-5]C - R[-12]C)/R[-12]C$

Figure 12-7   Calculated Cell Formulas from the Price Index Forecast Worksheet.

scribed by its topology, nodal activation functions, input/output representations, and learning rule. Although many variations of these four properties were tried during the development of the network, the current version of the network is not very sophisticated. A great deal of useful experience can be gained by trying some of the "tricks" recommended in the references. However, my general experience is that any performance improvement due to these tricks is often problem specific or that the tricks provide such marginal improvements that a network must be of significant size to justify their incorporation.

The current network's topology is a three-layer structure with feedforward data flow. There are input, hidden, and output layers. The network is fully interconnected between adjacent layers with no input-to-output node connections. The network has 20 continuous-valued inputs, a hidden layer consisting of 41 nodes, and one output node. The selection of 41 nodes in the hidden layer is due to a classical mathematical result of Kolmogorov [102]. This result allows that for any continuous mapping function there exists a three-layer neural network of n inputs, m output units, and $2n + 1$ hidden units that implements the function exactly. In reality this may be an upward limit for a network to solve the market modeling problem, but the motivation for experimenting with three-layer networks with fewer nodes did not really exist because the three-layer networks were already small. Early in the effort, four-layer networks with continuous-valued inputs and multiple discrete-valued outputs were tried. This approach was eventually discarded because of the difficulty of maintaining relatively small networks with meaningful output representations in which some sense of both the direction and magnitude of the forecasts was desired. Because these networks are implemented on digital computers in which noise and resolution are not issues, a continuous-valued output simplifies the network topology and provides more information content [113].

The hidden and output nodes of the current network use a symmetric logistic activation function with a range of $(-1, 1)$. The literature [101] suggests that the use of symmetric activation functions tends to decrease learning times and improves a network's ability to generalize. Even though I also used asymmetric logistic activation functions early in this effort, I can't verify or dispute the conclusions in the literature.

The basic argument was convincing enough when I was using discrete-valued outputs, although with continuous-valued outputs it seems less convincing. Because the required computational burden of calculating the symmetric activation functions for the forward-propagation and their derivatives for the back-propagation of error does not seem significant, symmetric activation functions continue to be used in the current networks. Other activation functions such as the arctangent and the hyperbolic tangent were tried. They worked but did not seem to offer any distinct advantages over the symmetric logistic activation function.

The network processes 20 continuous-valued inputs per presentation. Each presentation represents a 4-month input window of five input values per month. An epoch consists of all the windows in the training set, currently 36, and the trial window from which the forecast is made. The windows are presented in time order, but there is no significance to this other than that the most recent window is the trial window and the last presentation in an epoch. All inputs are scaled to fall within a $(-1, 1)$ range. The mean price input and price deviation input channels are scaled separately whereas the net commitment channels are scaled together. The net commitment channels are scaled together simply to maintain the zero sum relationship of these channels at the input to the network. The output is scaled to achieve a range of $(-0.5, 0.5)$. This tends to keep the network operating within a more linear part of the range of its nodal activation functions. The literature [103] suggests that in networks with continuous-valued outputs, lower training error levels can be achieved by staying in the linear part of the range of the activation functions. Doing that also allows for forecasts outside of the known mean price input range.

The current network's training algorithm uses a simplified version of the standard back-propagation of Rumelhart, Hinton, and Williams [2]. Standard back-propagation uses the approach of updating the network's interconnection weights after every data window presentation. Although updating weights after every epoch results in a learning rule that more closely approximates a gradient descent algorithm and allows for the incorporation of sophisticated speed-up refinements, this was a level of algorithmic complexity and an additional storage requirement, for holding the accumulated errors over the epoch, that did not seem justified by the size of the networks envisioned [105].

Not only does the current network use the simplification of updating the weights after every window presentation, it also doesn't incorporate a momentum term in the learning algorithm to smooth the error gradient. Earlier versions of the network used momentum, but the current version absorbs the training set in a reasonable time without momentum. There is some evidence [104] that the use of momentum has a less significant effect on improving the performance of a learning algorithm that updates weights after each input window presentation than it does on one that updates the weights after every epoch. Furthermore, for some networks the best results occur with the use of no momentum at all [105]. It seems that part of the improvement due to the incorporation of momentum is compensation for a rather poor selection of a network's learning rate.

In the current network, the learning rate eta is set to 1 at the beginning of the learning process and remains fixed unless the error gradient goes positive. If the error gradient goes positive, the network is reinitialized and rerun with an eta value of one half the previous value. The selection of eta is determined by the network itself through a process of trial and error. The process ends up with a value for eta that is high enough for reasonable learning times but not so high that the gradient goes positive or the variance among the residual output error terms is excessive. For the model runs shown in this chapter, eta was in the range 0.5–0.03125. As the training set grows, larger eta terms are tolerated.

The initialization of the learning process consists of zeroing the input to hidden layer weights while randomly initializing the hidden to output layer weights over a range of $(-0.5, 0.5)$. Smaller ranges for initialization were tried, but they did not seem to produce any meaningful improvement in the performance of the network. The learning process continues until the maximum mean-squared error for any training window presentation is less than a predetermined amount. For the model runs shown in this chapter, that amount was 0.030625 for the T-bond model, 0.0225 for the S&P 500 model, and 0.015625 for the gold model.

The variations of network properties tried represent a useful learning experience. Gaining that experience was, after all, one of the goals of this effort. However, I caution you to keep in mind how easy it is to forget that your main goal is the application of neural network technology and not the improvement of that technology. It becomes too easy a trap to work on the inadequacies of the technology when a model fails rather than to accept the inappropriateness of your model. Clearly, one of the problems with neural network applications, and one that contributes to the trap, is the richness of possibilities and the lack of specific guidelines for using the technology. Nevertheless, this technology is well worth learning and is a good choice for the market modeling effort.

Why Neural Networks

Neural networks were chosen as the basis for developing the transfer functions of the market models because they seem ideal for the problem and they're the "in thing." There's no denying it, the application of neural network technology is in vogue. The recent apparent growth in this area is phenomenal. Even though neural network technology is getting more than its share of hype, as you study the technology and try to apply it, you start to realize its potential. This technology can solve some interesting real problems in pattern recognition. Nets learn to recognize input/output patterns in the training data presented to them. They then recall those patterns and associate them with new inputs. They can do this when the input data is fuzzy, apparently contradictory, or even faulty. This is an exciting, capable technology; and when you consider some of the unique characteristics that make it a particularly good candidate for VLSI implementations, it gets even more interesting. So it makes good sense to learn it, and the best way to learn something is to apply it to a real problem—a problem that will keep your interest peaked even when at first you don't know what you're doing. Trying to develop a tool to help make money in speculative investments seemed like such a problem.

The basic issue in developing transfer functions for the futures market models was that they had to have the ability to recognize time-based patterns of human behavior from market price and market sentiment input data and associate those patterns of behavior with future price movements. This is a difficult task because the input data are often fuzzy, inaccurate, and untimely. The mappings of inputs to outputs are often subtle and counterintuitive. The rules for the mapping are often more qualitative than quantitative in nature. In other words, these rules are not easily or precisely described. Neither are they static; as the markets evolve, the rules must adapt. Finally, the mapping rules of the transfer functions must be extracted empirically from a historical database. There doesn't seem to be much useful theory to be built into the mapping rules a priori. When I considered the problem of modeling human behavior, the nature of the data and the available anecdotal theory for interpreting the data, neural networks seemed a good way and perhaps the only way to build the adaptive transfer functions I needed for the market modeling effort.

Why Excel?

You may be thinking that the models and the use of neural networks to develop them may be interesting and even of some value, but why use Excel to implement the neural networks? There are a number of "good" reasons. One of the reasons I used Excel is that I'm a Macintosh bigot. Overall, I believe, when you consider all the factors that go into doing a wide range of tasks on a personal workstation, the Macintosh system is clearly superior at this time to anything else. You may disagree. I don't care. The subject is not open for discussion. That's why I have a Mac at home and at work.

The Mac is, however, an application engine. Writing programs in procedural languages on the Mac, whether compiled or interpreted, seems unsatisfying and difficult. Spreadsheet application packages have been one of the few significant software developments coming out of the personal computer environment. Excel is one of the best, and it opens up the Mac to a number of numeric business and scientific problem domains that have been characteristically solved on computers with procedural languages. Unfortunately, though Excel is used extensively for business problems, it is often considered a joke when applied to scientific problems.

Far from a joke, I found the Excel/Macintosh combination to suit my needs in implementing neural networks. Beyond the fact that this combination was available and I was familiar with it, there is useful knowledge and experience to be gained by pushing a powerful, generally applicable tool such as this to its limits. Developing more facility with Excel, particularly macros, was one of my secondary goals in this effort. Excel provided a convenience and power of expression that was extremely valuable. It allowed me an extraordinary amount of flexibility in trying different network topologies, node characteristics, and training rules. It enabled me to create, maintain, and easily interface to the training set database. The usefulness of worksheets and charts for pre- and postprocessing of the network's input and output shouldn't be underestimated. In other words, the efficiency of developing networks in Excel outweighed the inefficiency of running networks in Excel.

However, to be completely fair, I must admit that my networks are relatively small and that it became clear to me early in the effort that if I wanted to run feedforward back-propagation neural nets with an adequate level of efficiency, I would have to make extensive use of Excel's macro capability. It was necessary to use macros to control the flow of cell execution on the neural net "spreadsheets" (in quotes because my neural net "spreadsheets" are actually macros that are structured to look like spreadsheets). I should emphasize that it is possible to implement a feedforward back-propagation neural network with an Excel worksheet, but it requires a particularly inefficient use of Excel's iterative capability.

Figure 12-8 shows the complete Excel neural network macro that was used to implement the three market models described in this chapter. The figure is shown with S&P 500 market input data entered into cells R5C6:R44C10, but otherwise the macro is identical for the S&P 500, T-bond, and gold market models. The input data came from the CFTC

Neural Network Based Futures Market Model

Row	Flag	Operation	Date	Price Inputs: Monthly Centered Mean	Deviation	Net Commitments Inputs: Large Speculator	Large Hedger	Small Trader	LMS Pattern Errors	Forecast	Eaverage	Estdev	Edelta	Epoch	Current Eta
2	Initialize														
3	FALSE	Init Eta								136.55	0.0027	0.0045	-	175	0.5
4	TRUE		Oct-86	103.07	1.75	-4.34%	6.88%	-2.54%							
5	TRUE	Init Input to Hidden Layer Weights	Nov-86	105.30	1.23	-1.53%	4.81%	-3.28%							
6	TRUE	Init Hidden to Output Layer Weights	Dec-86	106.97	3.15	-1.36%	0.24%	1.12%							
7	TRUE		Jan-87	116.45	2.93	-4.91%	7.72%	-2.81%							
8	FALSE	Init Average Error	Feb-87	121.42	1.64	-2.77%	4.55%	-1.79%	0.0086						
9	FALSE	Init LMS Pattern Errors	Mar-87	125.10	2.21	-4.21%	4.59%	-0.38%	0.0000						
10	FALSE	Init Epoch Count	Apr-87	121.58	2.14	-2.78%	0.88%	1.90%	0.0042						
11	TRUE	Init Mscale	May-87	122.52	3.21	-4.17%	2.74%	1.43%	0.0003						
12	TRUE	Init Mbias	Jun-87	129.41	1.17	-0.37%	1.05%	-0.68%	0.0013						
13	TRUE	Init Dscale	Jul-87	134.70	4.23	-3.14%	10.21%	-7.06%	0.0006						
14	TRUE	Init Dbias	Aug-87	136.94	3.79	-1.22%	-1.65%	2.87%	0.0007						
15	TRUE	Init Pscale	Sep-87	131.78	6.07	0.43%	-2.34%	1.90%	0.0003						
16	TRUE	Init Pbias	Oct-87	105.73	6.87	0.62%	0.63%	-1.25%	0.0017						
17	TRUE		Nov-87	97.91	3.49	-3.22%	2.36%	0.86%	0.0001						
18		Restart	Dec-87	101.87	2.23	-2.47%	4.49%	-2.01%	0.0002						
19	FALSE	Test Errors	Jan-88	104.29	1.92	-1.90%	2.38%	-0.48%	0.0004						
20	TRUE		Feb-88	108.71	1.30	-1.19%	1.43%	-0.24%	0.0006						
21	#N/A	Update Presentation Index	Mar-88	108.15	2.91	-4.71%	6.70%	-1.98%	0.0026						
22	TRUE	Perform Forward Propagation	Apr-88	106.30	0.79	-2.29%	4.22%	-1.94%	0.0223						
23	#N/A	Update Error Values	May-88	106.86	3.57	-2.41%	2.50%	-0.09%	0.0000						
24	TRUE	Perform Back Propagation	Jun-88	111.34	0.56	1.06%	0.30%	0.52%	0.0000						
25			Jul-88	109.56	2.27	-0.82%	-0.09%	-0.97%	0.0087						
26	TRUE	Output Prediction	Aug-88	107.52	1.44	-0.30%	1.65%	-1.35%	0.0102						
27	TRUE	Output Eaverage	Sep-88	111.19	1.61	-1.96%	3.38%	-1.41%	0.0016						
28	TRUE	Output Estdev	Oct-88	111.90	2.69	-1.49%	4.98%	-3.49%	0.0013						
29	TRUE	Output Edelta	Nov-88	109.52	2.11	-1.72%	3.26%	-1.54%	0.0001						
30	TRUE	Output Epoch Count	Dec-88	112.82	1.25	-1.35%	1.35%	0.00%	0.0026						
31	TRUE	Output Warning	Jan-89	117.83	1.99	0.46%	-1.35%	0.89%	0.0007						
32	TRUE	Save State	Feb-89	117.48	1.57	-3.71%	6.88%	-3.17%	0.0037						
33	TRUE	Remove Warning	Mar-89	118.15	1.92	-4.02%	7.91%	-3.90%	0.0000						
34			Apr-89	123.32	1.89	-2.32%	3.45%	-1.13%	0.0018						
35	TRUE	Gradient Test	May-89	129.06	1.47	-1.90%	1.66%	0.25%	0.0011						
36	TRUE		Jun-89	129.20	2.33	-4.79%	7.10%	-2.30%	0.0088	129.52	0.0037	0.0050		368	0.5
37	TRUE		Jul-89	135.10	2.03	-0.46%	-0.48%	0.94%	0.0080	136.90	0.0037	0.0049		457	0.5
38	TRUE	Reduce Eta	Aug-89	138.10	1.51	-3.61%	2.15%	1.47%	0.0013	135.31	0.0035	0.0048		335	0.5
39	TRUE		Sep-89	135.93	5.24	-4.53%	4.70%	-0.17%	0.0011	132.65	0.0034	0.0048		289	0.5
40	TRUE		Oct-89	132.36	2.85	-6.92%	11.38%	-4.46%	0.0000	135.06	0.0033	0.0048		304	0.5
41	TRUE		Nov-89	134.83	1.73	-6.43%	7.92%	-1.49%	0.0000	144.19	0.0032	0.0048		303	0.5
42	TRUE		Dec-89	135.12	2.62	-3.44%	2.91%	0.53%	0.0000	135.67	0.0032	0.0047		251	0.5
43	TRUE		Jan-90	127.90	2.49	-5.78%	7.75%	-1.97%	0.0000	136.55	0.0027	0.0045		175	0.5

Row	Output Vector	
47	Output Vector	
48	Input	0.714534
49	Input	0.837282
50	Input	0.851932
51	Input	0.492453
52	Input	-0.27572
53	Input	-0.63051
54	Input	-0.34826
55	Input	-0.39017
56	Input	-0.98435
57	Input	-0.93074
58	Input	-0.60705
59	Input	-0.86045

Figure 12-8 S&P 500 futures market model macro. (*Figure continues.*)

273

Input to Hidden Layer
Weight Matrix

	1	2	3	4	5	6	7	8	9	10	11	12	13	14	15	16	17
60	Input	1															
61	Input	0.624568															
62	Input	0.081325															
63	Input	0.606499															
64	Input	-0.71743															
65	Input	-0.39562															
66	Input	-0.17607															
67	Input	-0.44784															
68	Threshold	1		To\From	Input	Input	Input	Input	Input	Input	Input	Input	Input	Input	Input	Input	Input
69		0.008614		Hidden	-0.08049	-0.09874	0.374049	-0.3366	0.033995	0.144557	0.09095	0.107064	-0.07916	0.067707	-0.20217	-0.05885	-0.1184
70		0.074295		Hidden	0.131312	0.199557	-0.54956	0.583179	-0.09316	-0.26141	-0.13296	-0.14174	0.119678	-0.11791	0.326141	0.089673	0.217683
71		-0.03326		Hidden	-0.11243	-0.15542	0.492441	-0.48558	0.065585	0.214873	0.119412	0.131291	-0.10525	0.098759	-0.27875	-0.07923	-0.17749
72		-0.02207		Hidden	-0.10504	-0.14227	0.470045	-0.45351	0.057731	0.199387	0.114028	0.127059	-0.10009	0.092232	-0.2637	-0.07519	-0.16443
73		-0.01817		Hidden	0.028761	0.032564	-0.14848	0.122616	-0.00786	-0.05155	-0.03643	-0.047	0.031528	-0.02339	0.077232	0.023245	0.041443
74		-0.07991		Hidden	-0.13368	-0.20527	0.555245	-0.59477	0.096773	0.266651	0.134265	0.142821	-0.12128	0.120129	-0.33135	-0.09063	-0.22239
75		0.110337		Hidden	0.146961	0.235062	-0.58019	0.651958	-0.11531	-0.29008	-0.07614	-0.14823	0.128951	-0.13114	0.355593	0.093818	0.245027
76		-0.01812		Hidden	0.08517	0.072216	-0.31239	0.272295	-0.02396	-0.11578	-0.09246	0.066114	0.066114	-0.05406	0.166286	0.04893	0.094346
77		0.959929		Hidden	0.840001	0.759972	-0.70365	1.602694	0.466936	0.906925	-0.30658	-0.1474	0.082784	-1.08799	-0.05266	-0.29931	0.234572
78		-0.00478		Hidden	0.084851	0.105359	-0.39102	0.355492	-0.03733	-0.1532	-0.09502	-0.11084	0.055856	-0.07172	0.139103	0.061636	0.125643
79		-0.02147		Hidden	0.053694	0.06241	-0.26371	0.225246	-0.01787	-0.09527	-0.06441	-0.07993	-0.01232	0.128806	-0.04418	0.041253	0.072299
80		-0.08692		Hidden	-0.13664	-0.21232	0.561821	-0.60278	0.10122	0.272814	0.135759	0.144114	-0.03247	0.128806	-0.33753	-0.09167	-0.22806
81		0.021435		Hidden	-0.05392	-0.06269	0.264678	-0.22615	0.019978	0.095658	0.064639	0.080183	0.094097	0.04437	-0.13963	-0.0414	-0.07762
82		0.01853		Hidden	-0.02967	-0.03361	0.152925	-0.1264	0.008157	0.053151	0.037518	0.048342	-0.03247	0.024139	-0.07957	0.0394	-0.0474
83		0.011033		Hidden	0.098655	0.128363	-0.4432	0.41798	-0.04973	-0.1824	-0.10757	-0.12179	0.094097	0.024139	0.245502	0.070463	0.150148
84		-0.1647		Hidden	-0.17685	-0.28097	0.608962	-0.73179	0.140285	0.30722	-0.10786	-0.12203	0.094361	0.148945	-0.38164	-0.09023	-0.27204
85		0.011478		Hidden	0.09898	0.128948	-0.4444	0.419507	-0.05005	-0.1693	-0.10217	0.159732	0.094361	-0.0852	0.230966	0.066616	0.150757
86		0.003418		Hidden	0.092644	0.117919	-0.42076	0.390196	-0.04396	-0.08921	-0.19509	-0.1172	0.089191	-0.07906	0.291719	-0.02037	0.13915
87		0.476191		Hidden	0.413585	0.401091	-0.69642	0.91726	-0.05594	0.121447	0.079205	-0.29229	0.108055	-0.29354	-0.17356	-0.05096	0.275267
88		0.016674		Hidden	-0.06827	-0.08139	0.325162	-0.28513	0.025804	0.056264	0.039618	0.095601	0.06881	0.057772	0.008412	-0.02528	-0.09908
89		0.019187		Hidden	-0.03144	-0.03566	0.161535	-0.13378	0.008753	0.215841	0.119733	0.050932	-0.03429	0.025595	-0.08412	-0.02528	-0.04527
90		-0.03399		Hidden	-0.11282	-0.15626	0.493779	-0.48758	0.066094	0.056264	0.039618	0.131539	-0.10557	0.099162	0.082637	-0.07948	-0.17831
91		-0.01998		Hidden	0.03086	0.034994	-0.15873	0.131374	-0.00856	-0.05525	-0.03893	-0.05009	0.033698	-0.02512	-0.02074	0.024846	0.044446
92		-0.15098		Hidden	0.16833	-0.27054	0.602918	-0.71429	0.135318	0.306141	0.144512	0.156311	-0.13678	0.144461	-0.37725	-0.0923	-0.2669
93		-0.01477		Hidden	0.02166	0.02442	-0.11309	0.092775	-0.00566	-0.28595	-0.02778	-0.03612	0.024028	-0.12897	0.058671	0.017714	0.03127
94		0.017646		Hidden	-0.06625	-0.07866	0.31665	-0.38428	0.024593	0.117741	0.077207	0.093563	-0.06705	0.054997	-0.16882	-0.04964	-0.09598
95		-0.00191		Hidden	-0.09134	-0.11574	0.415822	-0.65926	0.042281	0.117207	0.100985	0.116161	-0.08812	0.077808	-0.22783	-0.06578	-0.13683
96		-0.20986		Hidden	-0.20891	-0.30905	0.625972	-0.77781	0.149119	0.295569	0.15027	0.174165	-0.14283	0.16465	-0.38625	-0.07874	-0.28181
97		0.019295		Hidden	-0.06219	-0.07329	0.299995	-0.26004	0.022278	0.110397	0.073151	0.089351	-0.0635	0.05147	-0.15928	-0.04697	-0.08986
98		0.019777		Hidden	-0.06078	-0.07144	0.294036	-0.25422	0.021502	0.107851	0.071717	0.087836	-0.06224	0.050245	-0.15594	-0.04602	-0.08775
99		-0.00246		Hidden	0.003268	0.003665	-0.01734	0.014099	-0.0008	-0.00592	-0.00427	-0.00561	0.003688	-0.00265	0.008966	0.002719	0.004735
100		0.016228		Hidden	-0.06914	-0.08256	0.326688	-0.28871	0.026333	0.123036	0.080053	0.096458	-0.06955	0.057531	-0.17559	-0.05152	-0.1004
101		0.104025		Hidden	0.144082	0.229064	-0.57572	0.640853	-0.11165	-0.28595	-0.13883	-0.14713	0.127493	-0.12897	0.351114	0.093446	0.240754
102		0.012506		Hidden	-0.01774	-0.01996	0.093097	-0.07615	0.004537	0.031989	0.02288	0.029854	-0.01979	0.014398	-0.04825	-0.01459	-0.02564
103		-0.11461		Hidden	-0.14897	-0.23906	0.353048	-0.65926	0.117724	0.292637	0.140401	0.148989	-0.1299	0.132585	-0.35846	-0.09398	-0.24779
104		0.021296		Hidden	-0.03937	-0.04497	0.199239	-0.1666	0.011841	0.070165	0.048794	0.062023	-0.04226	0.032153	-0.10416	-0.09398	-0.05662
105		0.016783		Hidden	0.102661	0.135751	-0.45788	0.437056	-0.05393	-0.19149	-0.1111	-0.1247	0.097354	-0.08884	0.255328	0.073028	0.157787
106		-0.02138		Hidden	0.054266	0.063129	-0.2662	0.227586	-0.01815	-0.09628	-0.06501	-0.08059	0.05638	-0.04467	0.140473	0.041643	0.078137
107		0.016442		Hidden	-0.06873	-0.08201	0.327017	-0.28701	0.026081	0.122281	0.079651	0.096052	-0.0692	0.057171	-0.17463	-0.05126	-0.09977
108		-0.01579		Hidden	0.0236	0.026634	-0.12286	0.10096	-0.00624	-0.04243	-0.03017	-0.03915	0.026101	-0.01917	0.063783	0.019242	0.034052
109		0.026586		Hidden	0.108724	0.147669	-0.47957	0.466843	-0.06092	-0.20582	-0.11632	-0.12888	0.102267	-0.09496	0.270421	0.076897	0.169843
110		0.461557		Output	TRUE	TRUE	TRUE	TRUE	TRUE	TRUE	TRUE	TRUE	TRUE	TRUE	TRUE	TRUE	TRUE
111																	
112		TRUE															
113					0.892368	0.714534	0.837282	0.851932	0.483129	-0.27572	-0.63051	-0.34826	-0.72479	-0.98435	-0.93074	-0.60705	0.275184
114					TRUE												0.275184

Figure 12-8 (Continued)

274

Hidden to Output Layer Weight Vector

	18	19	20	21	22	23	24	25	27	28	30
									FromTo	Output	Error Vector
67/68	Input	Input	Input	Input	Input	Input	Input	Threshold	Threshold		
69	0.070039	-0.01271	-0.06194	0.108178	-0.22713	0.125493	0.031399	0.127372	Hidden	0.10103	0.001801
70	-0.09575	0.024951	0.101497	-0.18986	0.361146	-0.20361	-0.04369	-0.21015	Hidden	-0.08544	-0.00015
71	0.087182	-0.01748	-0.08428	0.159198	-0.30949	0.173688	0.039967	0.176046	Hidden	0.141072	0.000251
72	0.083963	-0.01605	-0.07936	0.148437	-0.29228	0.163665	0.038463	0.165409	Hidden	-0.11815	-0.00021
73	-0.03094	0.006332	0.025143	-0.03732	0.089981	-0.04792	-0.01274	-0.0508	Hidden	-0.11102	-0.0002
74	0.096649	-0.02631	-0.10394	0.193194	-0.36726	0.20718	0.044093	0.214425	Hidden	0.034061	6.13E-05
75	-0.10053	0.035536	0.11828	-0.20821	0.397434	-0.22536	-0.04633	-0.23621	Hidden	-0.14396	-0.00026
76	-0.06045	0.01126	0.051869	-0.08614	0.188827	-0.10323	-0.02648	-0.1059	Hidden	0.158856	0.000284
77	1.347393	0.752587	0.74949	0.0593	-0.09375	-0.53427	-0.28453	-0.23604	Hidden	0.071005	0.000127
78	-0.07256	0.01314	0.064792	-0.11471	0.237999	-0.13186	-0.03271	-0.13354	Hidden	0.636863	1.51E-05
79	-0.05233	0.010039	0.044015	-0.07036	0.159306	-0.08634	-0.02247	-0.08948	Hidden	0.089593	0.00016
80	0.097689	-0.02815	-0.10707	0.197106	-0.37465	0.211527	0.044592	0.219654	Hidden	0.059985	0.000107
81	0.052494	-0.01006	-0.04417	0.070659	-0.15989	0.086674	0.022551	0.089805	Hidden	-0.0602	-0.00026
82	0.031818	-0.0065	-0.02588	0.038508	-0.09266	0.04937	0.01312	0.052298	Hidden	-0.03507	-0.00011
83	-0.08013	0.014798	0.074062	-0.1363	0.272948	-0.15236	-0.03658	-0.15381	Hidden	0.103225	-6.3E-05
84	0.1027	-0.06158	-0.14963	0.2232	-0.43927	0.255597	0.052232	0.267357	Hidden	-0.18099	0.000184
85	-0.0803	0.014846	0.074288	-0.13683	0.273786	-0.15285	-0.03667	-0.15431	Hidden	0.103558	-0.00032
86	-0.0769	0.013999	0.069955	-0.12672	0.25758	-0.14334	-0.03495	-0.1448	Hidden	0.09717	0.000184
87	0.001735	0.313117	0.340941	-0.18319	0.491943	-0.4047	-0.12043	-0.26518	Hidden	0.216006	0.000173
88	0.062497	-0.01156	-0.05393	0.090503	-0.19665	0.107744	0.027515	0.110261	Hidden	-0.07393	0.000317
89	0.033508	-0.00682	-0.02731	0.04082	-0.09785	0.052192	0.013854	0.055205	Hidden	-0.03702	-0.00013
90	0.087376	-0.01758	-0.08459	0.159861	-0.31056	0.174308	0.040055	0.176716	Hidden	-0.1186	-6.7E-05
91	-0.03296	0.006714	0.026848	-0.04007	0.096158	-0.05127	-0.01361	-0.05426	Hidden	0.036382	-0.00021
92	0.102826	-0.05375	-0.14103	0.220749	-0.43022	0.24806	0.050395	0.260671	Hidden	-0.17611	6.55E-05
93	-0.02381	0.004943	0.019219	-0.02808	0.068616	-0.0364	-0.00971	-0.03879	Hidden	0.026013	-0.00032
94	0.061169	-0.01136	-0.05259	0.087652	-0.19155	0.104798	0.026842	0.107418	Hidden	-0.07202	4.69E-05
95	0.076189	-0.01384	-0.06908	0.124673	-0.25427	0.141403	0.034584	0.142885	Hidden	-0.09588	-0.00013
96	0.098685	-0.09256	-0.17981	0.226065	-0.46191	0.280231	0.059972	0.282957	Hidden	-0.1931	-0.00017
97	0.058432	-0.01096	-0.04987	0.081998	-0.18127	0.098877	0.025467	0.101693	Hidden	-0.06818	-0.00035
98	0.05745	-0.01082	-0.04891	0.080037	-0.17765	0.0968	0.024978	0.099678	Hidden	-0.06683	-0.00012
99	-0.00371	0.000784	0.002963	-0.00423	0.010542	-0.00556	-0.00149	-0.00597	Hidden	0.004006	7.23E-06
100	0.063056	-0.01164	-0.0545	0.091726	-0.19882	0.108999	0.0278	0.111471	Hidden	-0.07475	-0.00013
101	-0.09986	0.033343	0.115133	-0.20551	0.39157	-0.22172	-0.04584	-0.23189	Hidden	0.155881	0.000278
102	0.019699	-0.00412	-0.01585	0.022987	-0.05652	0.029926	0.008001	0.031968	Hidden	-0.02144	-3.9E-05
103	0.100938	-0.03711	-0.12047	0.209924	-0.40129	0.227806	0.046681	0.23906	Hidden	-0.16083	-0.00029
104	0.040728	-0.00812	-0.03353	0.051236	-0.12052	0.064636	0.017056	0.067889	Hidden	-0.04551	-8.2E-05
105	-0.08222	0.015543	0.076894	-0.14284	0.283366	-0.15846	-0.03762	-0.16002	Hidden	0.107397	0.000191
106	-0.05276	0.010105	0.044417	-0.07113	0.160807	-0.0872	-0.02268	-0.09032	Hidden	0.060544	0.000108
107	0.062791	-0.0116	-0.05423	0.091145	-0.19779	0.108404	0.027665	0.110897	Hidden	-0.07436	-0.00013
108	-0.0258	0.005337	0.020861	-0.0306	0.074523	-0.03957	-0.01055	-0.04211	Hidden	0.028241	5.09E-05
109	-0.08533	0.016602	0.081383	-0.15294	0.299458	-0.16785	-0.03911	-0.16981	Hidden	0.113968	0.000203
110	TRUE	TRUE	TRUE	TRUE	TRUE	TRUE	TRUE	TRUE		TRUE	TRUE
113	1	0.824568	0.081325	-0.25218	-0.71743	-0.39562	-0.17607	1			

Figure 12-8 *(Continued)*

275

	1	2
1	Neural Network Based Futures Market Model	
2	Initialize	
3	=SET.NAME("Eta",1)	Init Eta
4	=SET.VALUE(R5C17,Eta)	
5	=SET.VALUE(R69C5:R109C25,0)	Init Input to Hidden Layer Weights
6	=FOR("Index",1,ROWS(R68C28:R109C28))	Init Hidden to Output Layer Weights
7	=SET.VALUE(INDEX(R68C28:R109C28,Index),RAND()-0.5)	
8	=NEXT()	
9	=SET.NAME("Eaverage",4)	Init Average Error
10	=SET.VALUE(Errors,4)	Init LMS Pattern Errors
11	=SET.VALUE(R5C16,0)	Init Epoch Count
12	=SET.NAME("Mscale",(MAX(Means)-MIN(Means))/2)	Init Mscale
13	=SET.NAME("Mbias",(MAX(Means)+MIN(Means))/2)	Init Mbias
14	=SET.NAME("Dscale",(MAX(Deviations)-MIN(Deviations))/2)	Init Dscale
15	=SET.NAME("Dbias",(MAX(Deviations)+MIN(Deviations))/2)	Init Dbias
16	=SET.NAME("Pscale",(MAX(Positions)-MIN(Positions))/2)	Init Pscale
17	=SET.NAME("Pbias",(MAX(Positions)+MIN(Positions))/2)	Init Pbias
18	=GOTO(R20C1)	
19	Restart	
20	=WHILE(MAX(Errors)>0.0225)	Test Errors
21	=ECHO(FALSE)	
22	=FOR("Index",1,ROWS(Errors)+1)	Update Presentation Index
23	=R48C2()	Perform Forward Propagation
24	=IF(Index=ROWS(Errors)+1,GOTO(R[3]C))	
25	=SET.VALUE(INDEX(Errors,Index),((INDEX(Means,Index+4)-Mbias)/Mscale/2-R110C2)^2)	Update Error Values
26	=R113C5()	Perform Back Propagation
27	=NEXT()	
28	=SET.VALUE(R5C12,(R110C2+0.5)*(MAX(Means)-MIN(Means))+MIN(Means))	Output Prediction
29	=SET.VALUE(R5C13,AVERAGE(Errors))	Output Eaverage
30	=SET.VALUE(R5C14,STDEV(Errors))	Output Estdev
31	=IF(AVERAGE(Errors)<Eaverage,SET.VALUE(R5C15,"-"),SET.VALUE(R5C15,"+"))	Output Edelta
32	=SET.VALUE(R5C16,R5C16+1)	Output Epoch Count
33	=MESSAGE(TRUE,"The state of the network is currently being saved.")	Output Warning
34	=SAVE()	Save State
35	=MESSAGE(FALSE)	Remove Warning
36	=ECHO(TRUE)	
37	=IF(R5C15="+",BREAK(),SET.NAME("Eaverage",DEREF(R5C13)))	Gradient Test
38	=NEXT()	
39	=IF(R5C15="-",GOTO(R42C1))	
40	=SET.NAME("Eta",Eta/2)	Reduce Eta
41	=GOTO(R4C1)	
42	=RETURN()	
43		
44		

Figure 12-9 S&P 500 futures market model macro formulas. (*Figure continues.*)

Data Worksheet and the Weekly Price Index Worksheet. Figure 12-9 shows the contents of the macro's cells in the ranges R1C1:R44C2 and R45C1:R114C30. In this figure, columns 7–23 are omitted for brevity because their contents are identical to those of columns 6 and 24. (The contents of the range R113C5:R113C25 and cell R110C2 are array formulas that don't show in the figure.) The macro can be executed by defining the ranges for the names Means, Deviations, Positions, and Errors using the Excel Define Name command. These ranges are R5C6:R44C6, R5C7:R44C7, R5C8:R44C10, and R8C11:R43C11, respectively, for the training set shown in Fig. 12-8. The name Emax must also be defined. Emax is used in cell R20C1 as the test limit that determines when network training is complete and macro execution should cease. Once these names are defined, the macro can be started at R3C1. The macro updates its display and automatically saves itself after every epoch. The displayed values of particular interest are in cells R5C12:R5C17. The macro can be interrupted as long as it is not in the process of saving itself. The interrupted macro should not be saved or restarted. To restart the macro, it must be reloaded and restarted at R20C1.

	1	2	3	4	5
45					
46					
47		Output Vector			
48	Input	=(INDEX(Means,Index)-Mbias)/Mscale			
49	Input	=(INDEX(Means,Index+1)-Mbias)/Mscale			
50	Input	=(INDEX(Means,Index+2)-Mbias)/Mscale			
51	Input	=(INDEX(Means,Index+3)-Mbias)/Mscale			
52	Input	=(INDEX(Deviations,Index)-Dbias)/Dscale			
53	Input	=(INDEX(Deviations,Index+1)-Dbias)/Dscale			
54	Input	=(INDEX(Deviations,Index+2)-Dbias)/Dscale			
55	Input	=(INDEX(Deviations,Index+3)-Dbias)/Dscale			
56	Input	=(INDEX(Positions,Index,1)-Pbias)/Pscale			
57	Input	=(INDEX(Positions,Index+1,1)-Pbias)/Pscale			
58	Input	=(INDEX(Positions,Index+2,1)-Pbias)/Pscale			
59	Input	=(INDEX(Positions,Index+3,1)-Pbias)/Pscale			
60	Input	=(INDEX(Positions,Index,2)-Pbias)/Pscale			
61	Input	=(INDEX(Positions,Index+1,2)-Pbias)/Pscale			
62	Input	=(INDEX(Positions,Index+2,2)-Pbias)/Pscale			
63	Input	=(INDEX(Positions,Index+3,2)-Pbias)/Pscale			
64	Input	=(INDEX(Positions,Index,3)-Pbias)/Pscale			
65	Input	=(INDEX(Positions,Index+1,3)-Pbias)/Pscale			
66	Input	=(INDEX(Positions,Index+2,3)-Pbias)/Pscale			
67	Input	=(INDEX(Positions,Index+3,3)-Pbias)/Pscale			
68	Threshold	1		To\From	Input
69	Hidden	=2/(1+EXP(-MMULT(RC5:RC25,R48C:R68C)))-1		Hidden	=RC30*R113C+RC
70	Hidden	=2/(1+EXP(-MMULT(RC5:RC25,R48C:R68C)))-1		Hidden	=RC30*R113C+RC
71	Hidden	=2/(1+EXP(-MMULT(RC5:RC25,R48C:R68C)))-1		Hidden	=RC30*R113C+RC
72	Hidden	=2/(1+EXP(-MMULT(RC5:RC25,R48C:R68C)))-1		Hidden	=RC30*R113C+RC
73	Hidden	=2/(1+EXP(-MMULT(RC5:RC25,R48C:R68C)))-1		Hidden	=RC30*R113C+RC
74	Hidden	=2/(1+EXP(-MMULT(RC5:RC25,R48C:R68C)))-1		Hidden	=RC30*R113C+RC
75	Hidden	=2/(1+EXP(-MMULT(RC5:RC25,R48C:R68C)))-1		Hidden	=RC30*R113C+RC
76	Hidden	=2/(1+EXP(-MMULT(RC5:RC25,R48C:R68C)))-1		Hidden	=RC30*R113C+RC
77	Hidden	=2/(1+EXP(-MMULT(RC5:RC25,R48C:R68C)))-1		Hidden	=RC30*R113C+RC
78	Hidden	=2/(1+EXP(-MMULT(RC5:RC25,R48C:R68C)))-1		Hidden	=RC30*R113C+RC
79	Hidden	=2/(1+EXP(-MMULT(RC5:RC25,R48C:R68C)))-1		Hidden	=RC30*R113C+RC
80	Hidden	=2/(1+EXP(-MMULT(RC5:RC25,R48C:R68C)))-1		Hidden	=RC30*R113C+RC
81	Hidden	=2/(1+EXP(-MMULT(RC5:RC25,R48C:R68C)))-1		Hidden	=RC30*R113C+RC
82	Hidden	=2/(1+EXP(-MMULT(RC5:RC25,R48C:R68C)))-1		Hidden	=RC30*R113C+RC
83	Hidden	=2/(1+EXP(-MMULT(RC5:RC25,R48C:R68C)))-1		Hidden	=RC30*R113C+RC
84	Hidden	=2/(1+EXP(-MMULT(RC5:RC25,R48C:R68C)))-1		Hidden	=RC30*R113C+RC
85	Hidden	=2/(1+EXP(-MMULT(RC5:RC25,R48C:R68C)))-1		Hidden	=RC30*R113C+RC
86	Hidden	=2/(1+EXP(-MMULT(RC5:RC25,R48C:R68C)))-1		Hidden	=RC30*R113C+RC
87	Hidden	=2/(1+EXP(-MMULT(RC5:RC25,R48C:R68C)))-1		Hidden	=RC30*R113C+RC
88	Hidden	=2/(1+EXP(-MMULT(RC5:RC25,R48C:R68C)))-1		Hidden	=RC30*R113C+RC
89	Hidden	=2/(1+EXP(-MMULT(RC5:RC25,R48C:R68C)))-1		Hidden	=RC30*R113C+RC
90	Hidden	=2/(1+EXP(-MMULT(RC5:RC25,R48C:R68C)))-1		Hidden	=RC30*R113C+RC
91	Hidden	=2/(1+EXP(-MMULT(RC5:RC25,R48C:R68C)))-1		Hidden	=RC30*R113C+RC
92	Hidden	=2/(1+EXP(-MMULT(RC5:RC25,R48C:R68C)))-1		Hidden	=RC30*R113C+RC
93	Hidden	=2/(1+EXP(-MMULT(RC5:RC25,R48C:R68C)))-1		Hidden	=RC30*R113C+RC
94	Hidden	=2/(1+EXP(-MMULT(RC5:RC25,R48C:R68C)))-1		Hidden	=RC30*R113C+RC
95	Hidden	=2/(1+EXP(-MMULT(RC5:RC25,R48C:R68C)))-1		Hidden	=RC30*R113C+RC
96	Hidden	=2/(1+EXP(-MMULT(RC5:RC25,R48C:R68C)))-1		Hidden	=RC30*R113C+RC
97	Hidden	=2/(1+EXP(-MMULT(RC5:RC25,R48C:R68C)))-1		Hidden	=RC30*R113C+RC
98	Hidden	=2/(1+EXP(-MMULT(RC5:RC25,R48C:R68C)))-1		Hidden	=RC30*R113C+RC
99	Hidden	=2/(1+EXP(-MMULT(RC5:RC25,R48C:R68C)))-1		Hidden	=RC30*R113C+RC
100	Hidden	=2/(1+EXP(-MMULT(RC5:RC25,R48C:R68C)))-1		Hidden	=RC30*R113C+RC
101	Hidden	=2/(1+EXP(-MMULT(RC5:RC25,R48C:R68C)))-1		Hidden	=RC30*R113C+RC
102	Hidden	=2/(1+EXP(-MMULT(RC5:RC25,R48C:R68C)))-1		Hidden	=RC30*R113C+RC
103	Hidden	=2/(1+EXP(-MMULT(RC5:RC25,R48C:R68C)))-1		Hidden	=RC30*R113C+RC
104	Hidden	=2/(1+EXP(-MMULT(RC5:RC25,R48C:R68C)))-1		Hidden	=RC30*R113C+RC
105	Hidden	=2/(1+EXP(-MMULT(RC5:RC25,R48C:R68C)))-1		Hidden	=RC30*R113C+RC
106	Hidden	=2/(1+EXP(-MMULT(RC5:RC25,R48C:R68C)))-1		Hidden	=RC30*R113C+RC
107	Hidden	=2/(1+EXP(-MMULT(RC5:RC25,R48C:R68C)))-1		Hidden	=RC30*R113C+RC
108	Hidden	=2/(1+EXP(-MMULT(RC5:RC25,R48C:R68C)))-1		Hidden	=RC30*R113C+RC
109	Hidden	=2/(1+EXP(-MMULT(RC5:RC25,R48C:R68C)))-1		Hidden	=RC30*R113C+RC
110	Output	=2/(1+EXP(-SUM(R68C28:R109C28*R68C:R109C)))-1			=GOTO(R[-41]C[1])
111		=RETURN()			
112					
113					=TRANSPOSE(R48C2:R68C2)
114					=GOTO(R68C30)

Figure 12-9 (Continued)

Current Status, Future Plans and Money Made

As I sit on the aft deck of my yacht in the south of France pondering the success of these models, I can honestly say they aren't too bad. Well, I'm not in the south of France, and I don't have a yacht; but would you believe, the models do a fair job of forecasting futures market price

	6	24	25	26
45				
46				
47				
48				
49				
50				
51				
52				
53				
54				
55				
56				
57				
58				
59				
60				
61				
62				
63				
64				
65				
66				
67				
68	Input	Input	Threshold	
69	=RC30*R113C+RC	=RC30*R113C+RC	=RC30*R113C+RC	
70	=RC30*R113C+RC	=RC30*R113C+RC	=RC30*R113C+RC	
71	=RC30*R113C+RC	=RC30*R113C+RC	=RC30*R113C+RC	
72	=RC30*R113C+RC	=RC30*R113C+RC	=RC30*R113C+RC	
73	=RC30*R113C+RC	=RC30*R113C+RC	=RC30*R113C+RC	
74	=RC30*R113C+RC	=RC30*R113C+RC	=RC30*R113C+RC	
75	=RC30*R113C+RC	=RC30*R113C+RC	=RC30*R113C+RC	
76	=RC30*R113C+RC	=RC30*R113C+RC	=RC30*R113C+RC	
77	=RC30*R113C+RC	=RC30*R113C+RC	=RC30*R113C+RC	
78	=RC30*R113C+RC	=RC30*R113C+RC	=RC30*R113C+RC	
79	=RC30*R113C+RC	=RC30*R113C+RC	=RC30*R113C+RC	
80	=RC30*R113C+RC	=RC30*R113C+RC	=RC30*R113C+RC	
81	=RC30*R113C+RC	=RC30*R113C+RC	=RC30*R113C+RC	
82	=RC30*R113C+RC	=RC30*R113C+RC	=RC30*R113C+RC	
83	=RC30*R113C+RC	=RC30*R113C+RC	=RC30*R113C+RC	
84	=RC30*R113C+RC	=RC30*R113C+RC	=RC30*R113C+RC	
85	=RC30*R113C+RC	=RC30*R113C+RC	=RC30*R113C+RC	
86	=RC30*R113C+RC	=RC30*R113C+RC	=RC30*R113C+RC	
87	=RC30*R113C+RC	=RC30*R113C+RC	=RC30*R113C+RC	
88	=RC30*R113C+RC	=RC30*R113C+RC	=RC30*R113C+RC	
89	=RC30*R113C+RC	=RC30*R113C+RC	=RC30*R113C+RC	
90	=RC30*R113C+RC	=RC30*R113C+RC	=RC30*R113C+RC	
91	=RC30*R113C+RC	=RC30*R113C+RC	=RC30*R113C+RC	
92	=RC30*R113C+RC	=RC30*R113C+RC	=RC30*R113C+RC	
93	=RC30*R113C+RC	=RC30*R113C+RC	=RC30*R113C+RC	
94	=RC30*R113C+RC	=RC30*R113C+RC	=RC30*R113C+RC	
95	=RC30*R113C+RC	=RC30*R113C+RC	=RC30*R113C+RC	
96	=RC30*R113C+RC	=RC30*R113C+RC	=RC30*R113C+RC	
97	=RC30*R113C+RC	=RC30*R113C+RC	=RC30*R113C+RC	
98	=RC30*R113C+RC	=RC30*R113C+RC	=RC30*R113C+RC	
99	=RC30*R113C+RC	=RC30*R113C+RC	=RC30*R113C+RC	
100	=RC30*R113C+RC	=RC30*R113C+RC	=RC30*R113C+RC	
101	=RC30*R113C+RC	=RC30*R113C+RC	=RC30*R113C+RC	
102	=RC30*R113C+RC	=RC30*R113C+RC	=RC30*R113C+RC	
103	=RC30*R113C+RC	=RC30*R113C+RC	=RC30*R113C+RC	
104	=RC30*R113C+RC	=RC30*R113C+RC	=RC30*R113C+RC	
105	=RC30*R113C+RC	=RC30*R113C+RC	=RC30*R113C+RC	
106	=RC30*R113C+RC	=RC30*R113C+RC	=RC30*R113C+RC	
107	=RC30*R113C+RC	=RC30*R113C+RC	=RC30*R113C+RC	
108	=RC30*R113C+RC	=RC30*R113C+RC	=RC30*R113C+RC	
109	=RC30*R113C+RC	=RC30*R113C+RC	=RC30*R113C+RC	
110	=GOTO(R[-41]C[1])	=GOTO(R[-41]C[1])	=GOTO(R68C28)	
111				
112				
113	=TRANSPOSE(R48C2:R68C2)	=TRANSPOSE(R48C2:R68C2)	=TRANSPOSE(R48C2:R68C2)	
114				

Figure 12-9   (*Continued*)

moves. Could they be better? Absolutely. Are they on the right track? I think so.

Several criteria can be used in judging whether these models are on the right track. First, do they tend to identify and lock in on developing trends in prices? This is probably the easiest task for the model to ac-

	27	28	29	30
45				
46				
47				
48				
49				
50				
51				
52				
53				
54				
55				
56				
57				
58				
59				
60				
61				
62				
63				
64				
65		Hidden to Output Layer		
66		Weight Vector		
67	From\To	Output		Error Vector
68	Threshold	=R68C30*RC2+RC		=Eta*((INDEX(Means,Index+4)-Mbias)/Mscale/2-R110C2)*(1-R110C2^2)
69	Hidden	=R68C30*RC2+RC		=RC28*R68C*(1-RC2^2)
70	Hidden	=R68C30*RC2+RC		=RC28*R68C*(1-RC2^2)
71	Hidden	=R68C30*RC2+RC		=RC28*R68C*(1-RC2^2)
72	Hidden	=R68C30*RC2+RC		=RC28*R68C*(1-RC2^2)
73	Hidden	=R68C30*RC2+RC		=RC28*R68C*(1-RC2^2)
74	Hidden	=R68C30*RC2+RC		=RC28*R68C*(1-RC2^2)
75	Hidden	=R68C30*RC2+RC		=RC28*R68C*(1-RC2^2)
76	Hidden	=R68C30*RC2+RC		=RC28*R68C*(1-RC2^2)
77	Hidden	=R68C30*RC2+RC		=RC28*R68C*(1-RC2^2)
78	Hidden	=R68C30*RC2+RC		=RC28*R68C*(1-RC2^2)
79	Hidden	=R68C30*RC2+RC		=RC28*R68C*(1-RC2^2)
80	Hidden	=R68C30*RC2+RC		=RC28*R68C*(1-RC2^2)
81	Hidden	=R68C30*RC2+RC		=RC28*R68C*(1-RC2^2)
82	Hidden	=R68C30*RC2+RC		=RC28*R68C*(1-RC2^2)
83	Hidden	=R68C30*RC2+RC		=RC28*R68C*(1-RC2^2)
84	Hidden	=R68C30*RC2+RC		=RC28*R68C*(1-RC2^2)
85	Hidden	=R68C30*RC2+RC		=RC28*R68C*(1-RC2^2)
86	Hidden	=R68C30*RC2+RC		=RC28*R68C*(1-RC2^2)
87	Hidden	=R68C30*RC2+RC		=RC28*R68C*(1-RC2^2)
88	Hidden	=R68C30*RC2+RC		=RC28*R68C*(1-RC2^2)
89	Hidden	=R68C30*RC2+RC		=RC28*R68C*(1-RC2^2)
90	Hidden	=R68C30*RC2+RC		=RC28*R68C*(1-RC2^2)
91	Hidden	=R68C30*RC2+RC		=RC28*R68C*(1-RC2^2)
92	Hidden	=R68C30*RC2+RC		=RC28*R68C*(1-RC2^2)
93	Hidden	=R68C30*RC2+RC		=RC28*R68C*(1-RC2^2)
94	Hidden	=R68C30*RC2+RC		=RC28*R68C*(1-RC2^2)
95	Hidden	=R68C30*RC2+RC		=RC28*R68C*(1-RC2^2)
96	Hidden	=R68C30*RC2+RC		=RC28*R68C*(1-RC2^2)
97	Hidden	=R68C30*RC2+RC		=RC28*R68C*(1-RC2^2)
98	Hidden	=R68C30*RC2+RC		=RC28*R68C*(1-RC2^2)
99	Hidden	=R68C30*RC2+RC		=RC28*R68C*(1-RC2^2)
100	Hidden	=R68C30*RC2+RC		=RC28*R68C*(1-RC2^2)
101	Hidden	=R68C30*RC2+RC		=RC28*R68C*(1-RC2^2)
102	Hidden	=R68C30*RC2+RC		=RC28*R68C*(1-RC2^2)
103	Hidden	=R68C30*RC2+RC		=RC28*R68C*(1-RC2^2)
104	Hidden	=R68C30*RC2+RC		=RC28*R68C*(1-RC2^2)
105	Hidden	=R68C30*RC2+RC		=RC28*R68C*(1-RC2^2)
106	Hidden	=R68C30*RC2+RC		=RC28*R68C*(1-RC2^2)
107	Hidden	=R68C30*RC2+RC		=RC28*R68C*(1-RC2^2)
108	Hidden	=R68C30*RC2+RC		=RC28*R68C*(1-RC2^2)
109	Hidden	=R68C30*RC2+RC		=RC28*R68C*(1-RC2^2)
110		=RETURN()		=GOTO(R69C5)
111				
112				
113				
114				

Figure 12-9   (Continued)

complish. Second, can they forecast price reversals after a trend has been in effect for some time? This is a difficult task. It means the models must determine that excesses in market sentiment inputs are occurring. They then must forecast the strength of the reversal. Finally, do they make wildly wrong forecasts? In other words, do the models encourage

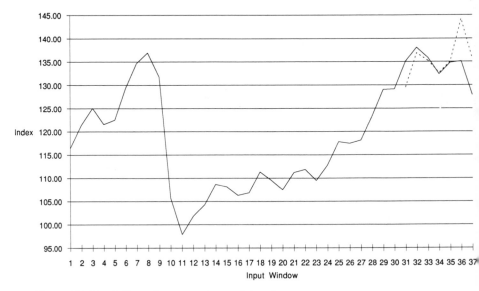

Figure 12-10   S&P 500 futures market model performance.

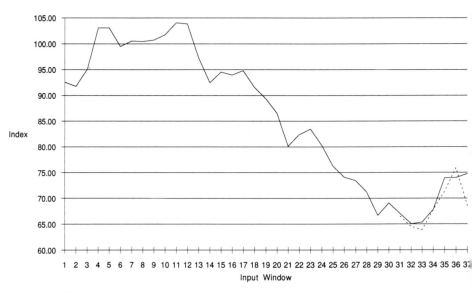

Figure 12-11   Comex gold futures market model performance.

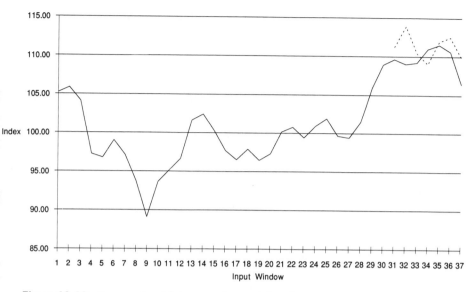

Figure 12-12 Treasury bond futures market model performance.

us to do foolish things? After all, we can do that without their help. Figures 12-10, 12-11, and 12-12 show the performance of the models for the last 7 months. In these figures the solid lines represent the actual values for the mean price index, and the dotted lines are the forecasted values plotted with one-month delay. Based on the criteria for judging the performance of these models, the gold market model appears to be the best, followed by the S&P 500 market model, with the T-Bond market model performing very poorly.

Ideally, the performance of these models should be evaluated over a longer period of time than 7 months, but my current training set only covers a period of 3 years. Going back any further than 7 months is simply working with too limited a training set. I believe that the training set should cover a period of 4–5 years or perhaps the length of time of a complete business cycle. This is necessary so that the network has an opportunity to see patterns of trader behavior during bullish, bearish, and trendless market periods.

Another problem that the models must cope with is the timeliness of the CFTC supplied data. Due to the time needed by the CFTC to compile, publish, and mail the *Commitments of Traders in Futures Report*, the data needed to calculate the sentiment model inputs are delayed approximately 2.5 weeks. Perhaps providing the model additional input on changes in total open interest, which is readily available, could help. Providing the models with trends in total open interest before the end of the month and during the period of delay could give it a better way of gauging the strength of price moves, or whether the traders' net commitments may have changed during the period of delay.

The literature suggests [93, 95] that many commodities are strongly affected by certain influences of a cyclic nature. This may manifest itself as a seasonal (yearly) or commodity-specific cycle-driven positioning of traders that may exaggerate or reduce the shorter term patterns of behavior that the model sees due to the 4-month input window. It might be useful to filter out these cyclic effects if they exist in the input data. I did not detect any seasonal influence in the data for the three markets modeled; however, that is not to say it does or does not exist. It only says that my training set covers too short a time to determine whether real cyclic influences exist in these markets.

Nothing is sacrosanct about the 4-month input window. Four months seemed like a good compromise. I ran a few similar models with 6-month input windows and observed similar forecasting patterns. There may be a benefit in lengthening the input window so that the networks receive more data at each presentation. The additional data might help them develop and analyze more rate-of-change information, for example. Of course, larger input windows require larger networks, which run slower, take up more memory, and require a larger training set to learn the greater number of weight relationships.

It might also be of benefit to filter out certain windows of input data. For example, the windows corresponding to the stock market "meltdown" of October 1987 seem to be very difficult for the S&P 500 model's network to absorb. Although this hasn't been demonstrated, I believe that removing those windows from the training set would improve the overall performance of the S&P 500 model. Observing the worsening predictions of that model as those data windows were absorbed leads me to this belief. This type of input filtering could become the basis of a useful data preprocessing rule though the resulting model might expose a trader to higher levels of risk.

As I write this case study, I have made only a few commodity option spread trades based on these models and their predecessors. To date, my financial success has been mixed. That in itself is perhaps no small feat in markets that are very hard on small traders. Keep in mind also that models such as these can only provide some insight and guidance. As stated in the introduction, no matter how good our (small traders) market forecasting skills may be or how timely our information may be, our fear and greed accentuated by our modest financial wherewithal tend to cause us to do foolish things at precisely the wrong time. This is the hardest thing to overcome. It takes work and experience. A good set of models may improve our odds and help us stay in the game long enough to gain that experience. If you decide to read some of the references, you will see that there is really nothing basically new here, it is simply the different way I put it all together. I hope this case study encourages you to build on what I've tried or use it as a point of departure. Good luck.

CHAPTER 13

Case Study IV: Optical Character Recognition

Gary Entsminger

From .PCX to .TXT Via a Neural Network

Amy's desk, piled high with typewritten pages, was a research assistant's nightmare. A gothic soap opera. For years her boss and a legion of bosses had accumulated enough reports, abstracts, and just plain gossip to fill up the Greek Theatre. Now they wanted all those pages WordStar compatible.

Her mission (would she take it?) was to retype the pages, line by line, character by character, until her fingers and mind numbed with futility. Going crazy, really.

She looked at me. Glancing up, I pretended I was handsome, dark, and perhaps mysterious, as if I were Fred MacMurray in *Double Indemnity* or Jack Nicholson in *Chinatown*—two of my favorite movies. Amy loves movies.

"Can't you do something?" she asked.

I cleared my throat in my hand, considered the possibilities, remembering the plots of *Double Indem* and several other B movies. A diabolic solution like murder, of course, was out of the question. I really liked her boss. Anyway, it's messy and immoral. Fred found that out. I took the Jack Nicholson approach.

This chapter appeared in slightly different form in *Micro Cornucopia*, #51, January–February 1990.

Neural Network PC Tools

"Well, Ms. Seidl," I said, "I don't know what I can do; you're in an unusual situation."

"Not really," she interrupted, "a lot of people are in my position."

I noticed her legs, long and crossed and turned a little toward me, but not far enough to be suggestive. I glanced past her, out toward the grassy hill that led up and then broke into a forested valley.

Sighing, I didn't know what to do, I said, "Okay, I'll poke around a little and get back to you."

She may have mistaken my tone. I don't know.

"Thanks," she managed a semi-smile, semi-sweet and semi-ambivalent.

"Save the thanks," I muttered underneath my breath, "until I deserve it."

Her problem was simple enough in theory, but I must admit I felt a little uneasy. She had a bunch of typed paper; she wanted it to appear magically in WordStar. A case of optical character recognition, or OCR as we say in the business. She was right: A lot of people are in her position.

Why OCR Is Such a Bear

OCR, in short, is the task of converting letters from a printed page into letters that a computer can recognize. I investigated and got my hands on a few tools—a scanner, a graphics editor, and a neural network— enough, I hoped, to handle the job.

1. *A scanner*, which I could use to get an image of a page into a computer. An "image," I say, because scanners inherently scan pixels not characters. A graphic image of a character (a matrix of pixels) may look like a character to you and me, but to a computer it's garbage. Images can be beautiful, of course; but moving, entering, and deleting characters, pixel by pixel, isn't a giant step for computer science. A computer must recognize the characters lurking in these matrices of pixels (bit maps), a difficult task for several reasons:

   - A scanned image may not be aligned perfectly, and even one skewed row of bits can create an unrecognizable pattern.
   - Text can be variously sized, so the computer must recognize not only the shapes of the characters but also the shapes at different sizes (8 pt, 10 pt, 12 pt, etc.).
   - Text can be monospaced (all letters allocated the same amount of space regardless of letter shape) or proportionately spaced (space allocated according to letter width).
   - Line spacing can vary.

- Text can be in many different fonts, and each font will have distinct patterns for many of the characters.
- Letters can be squeezed together to form a composite character (a ligature) and printed as a single symbol.
- Two adjacent characters can be kerned (overlapped without touching each other).
- And so on.

2. A *graphics editor*, which I could use to manipulate pixels (to realign them, for example).
3. A *neural network*, which I could use to evaluate and correct input patterns.

Neural networks effectively filter input to produce output. More specifically, a net looks for patterns in a set of examples (called a training set, the input) and learns from these examples to produce new patterns (the output). Then using what it has learned (these input/output pattern-associations), it classifies a new set of examples (called a test set).

The net uses patterns of bits instead of individual bits to process information. Because a network recognizes patterns, not bits, no particular bit is crucial for the network to recognize a pattern successfully. The network can accept minor variations in bit alignment (Fig. 13-1) and still produce the right pattern.

You input a pattern into a neural network; it compares the pattern with the patterns it knows (the patterns it learned from its training set); and it outputs a "best guess" pattern. (Note: The network's best guess might even be no pattern. We tell the network (using a threshold value) how much variation (or error) we'll accept, and if no output exceeds the threshold, the network could produce a space, for example.)

Scanning typewritten pages is, at best, an imperfect operation. We can expect the scanned patterns (our input) to be incomplete or contain errors such as bit misalignment. A neural network can correct these kinds of problems and produce reliable output by making good guesses.

We train the network by showing it a set of input patterns and their corresponding output patterns. For example, we show the network an 8-by-8 bit picture of a character and the corresponding ASCII character. We say, in effect, that when you see this input pattern (a bit picture), output an ASCII character.

This part is tricky and requires a shuffling of examples. Eventually, after we toggle a switch or two and add or delete a few examples, the network "learns" to "guess" well enough for our problem. A pattern is good enough when it reaches the threshold value we set.

I shopped around for a neural network. I was in a hurry and it beat programming a net from scratch (though Russ Eberhart and Roy Dob-

```
(Input 1)
........
...XX...
..XXX...
...XX...
...XX...
...XX...
...XX...                              (Output 1)
.XXXXXX.    >>>>>>>>>>>>              ........
                                     ...XX...
                                     ..XXX...
                                     ...XX...
                                     ...XX...
                                     ...XX...
 (Input 2)                           ...XX...
........    >>>>>>>>>>>>              .XXXXXX.
....X...
...XX...
...XX...
....X...
...XX...
....X...
...XX...
```

Figure 13-1 Both inputs produce output 1.

bins show us how to do just that in this book). I found four contenders: NeuroShell (from Ward Systems), NeuralWorks (from Neuroware), NNT (Shareware), BrainMaker (from California Scientific).

Each works well alone but has even more interesting potential for use within other systems. I found that developers have taken distinctive approaches to implementing neural networks. Everything from the user interface to operational theory varies.

I won't discuss NNT, the Shareware net, because it's detailed elsewhere in this book, but I recommend it for low-level explorer/researcher types. The code for NNT goes far toward illuminating the confusion surrounding neural networks. And because it's written in C, many programmers can embed it quickly in their programs.

NeuroShell is probably the easiest of these four networks to use, in part because it has a friendly user interface and acts a lot like an expert system. It extends expert systems in one crucial way, by solving rule-based problems that lack precise rules. Problem classification, diagnosis, forecasting, and, in general, advisory services that rely on fuzzy data can be easily implemented with NeuroShell. In sum, NeuroShell is a strong text-based neural network, but it doesn't readily allow matrix-type pattern input and analysis. You could probably solve OCR-type problems with NeuroShell, but it would require an extra step or two.

NeuralWorks, the most complex neural network system I tested, allows the most experimentation with various algorithms and network models:

- back-propagation
- counter-propagation
- bidirectional associate memory
- adaptive resonant theory
- hamming
- recirculation
- probabilistic
- Boltzmann machine
- functional-link
- Hopfield
- perceptron
- Adaline and Madaline

If you want to explore neural network technology in general, need this kind of model flexibility, are willing to sift through 700 or so pages of documentation, and can afford it (NeuralWorks Professional II costs a whopping $1495), check out this package.

I conclude that neural networks are at that inchoate stage where they share some fundamental qualities (such as the use of training sets, thresholds, and normalization), but they diverge widely in the details.

I chose BrainMaker for the OCR project because

- it is relatively inexpensive;
- it has a neat batch mode that I can call from my programs;
- it is fast enough (at least with small sets); and
- it allows two-dimensional picture input (which makes it easy for me to see and edit 8-by-8 bit characters).

I had three tools. It was a start, the nucleus of a project, but much was missing. As usual, the tools didn't fit together well enough to solve Amy's problem. My computing skills had gotten my foot in the door, but I still wasn't sure I'd solve anything. I proceeded.

Step 1.

I scanned in an image (you can simulate this step in any of the Turbo languages using the Borland Graphics Interface, or BGI):

1. Initialize graphics.
2. Open a viewport.

3. Use OutTextXY to create some graphics text.
4. Save the text to a file.

Step 2.

I loaded the image into a graphics editor (PaintShowPlus) and examined it bit by bit. Right away I discovered that text sizes, fonts, styles, and horizontal and vertical alignments vary. Too much variation is a problem. I decided to teach the neural net to handle size, font, and style matters. We teach networks by showing them a training set.

Realignment I did by bit (in PaintShowPlus). I didn't teach my network much, so it wasn't all that smart. A one-column pixel shift introduced more variation than it could handle. So I corrected a lot of bits. Ugh! In the future, I'll either train the network more extensively or automate column and row shifts.

Step 3.

PaintShowPlus writes three kinds of output files: .TIF, .IMG, and .PCX. These file formats represent various approaches to storing image files, that is, bit-mapped representations of pages. In a world of shifting standards, they're as close as we can currently get to a standard for images (i.e., patterns of bits or pixels).

BrainMaker, the neural net, wants its input as a text pattern (a matrix of Xs and periods representing a character).

Problem: Bridge the abyss between these two.

I had a copy of the PCX Toolkit, which displays, loads, saves, and in various other ways manipulates .PCX images, so I decided to work toward it.

I created a .PCX file with PaintShowPlus. I planned to translate images from the screen instead of from a file, so any file format will do (if you can display it). Eventually I had to create a two-dimensional "text" picture for BrainMaker (Fig. 13-2).

The programming problem at this juncture was

1. To prepare input for BrainMaker (in this case, to translate a bit-by-bit image of a .PCX file, or screen) to a text picture; and
2. To evaluate and translate the output from BrainMaker to a WordStar (or other text editor) readable format.

Objects

I decided to glue everything together in a couple of Turbo Pascal objects: one to translate a graphics screen into a text picture for Brain-

```
.XXXXX..
XX...XX.
XX...XX.
XX...XX.
XX...XX.
XX...XX.
.XXXXX..

........
...XX...
..XXX...
...XX...
...XX...
...XX...
...XX...
.XXXXXX.

........
.XXXXX..
XX...XX.
.....XX.
...XXX..
.XXX....
XX...XX.
XXXXXXX.
```

Figure 13-2   Examples of BrainMaker Input

```
.909 0 .001 1 .018 2 .009 3 .001 4 .033 5 .021 6 .050 7 .097 8 .081 9
.000 0 .988 1 .009 2 .049 3 .034 4 .091 5 .018 6 .067 7 .012 8 .001 9
.017 0 .034 1 .929 2 .033 3 .002 4 .038 5 .000 6 .050 7 .068 8 .034 9
.009 0 .017 1 .053 2 .918 3 .000 4 .053 5 .003 6 .020 7 .100 8 .087 9
.003 0 .085 1 .005 2 .017 3 .911 4 .021 5 .016 6 .027 7 .030 8 .000 9
.081 0 .014 1 .008 2 .072 3 .000 4 .900 5 .006 6 .042 7 .070 8 .031 9
.095 0 .025 1 .000 2 .049 3 .001 4 .003 5 .936 6 .020 7 .100 8 .001 9
.066 0 .046 1 .030 2 .008 3 .000 4 .006 5 .000 6 .972 7 .041 8 .004 9
.020 0 .000 1 .032 2 .078 3 .001 4 .001 5 .071 6 .007 7 .902 8 .018 9
.088 0 .000 1 .006 2 .050 3 .000 4 .000 5 .005 6 .064 7 .094 8 .910 9
```

Figure 13-3   BrainMaker Output; 3 Digits Weight and 1 Digit Output

Maker and one to translate BrainMaker's output (symbols plus numerical values; see Fig. 13-3) into pure text (i.e., characters).

In sum, the case seemed to hinge on five parts:

1. A scanner (or simulated) part
2. A .PCX (or screen display) part
3. A screen to neural network translator

4. A neural network part
5. A neural network to pure text part

I created parts 3 and 5 with Turbo Pascal and ran parts 2 and 4 out of a Turbo Pascal shell. The Turbo Pascal program (see Appendix C) does the following:

1. Initializes graphics
2. Opens a viewport
3. Translates the screen (looking at 8 bit × 8 bit images) into a text picture
4. Writes an output file for BrainMaker
5. Calls BrainMaker (via a batch file executed by the built-in procedure exec)
6. Translates BrainMaker's output to characters

In brief, note the following:

- To use the Turbo Pascal exec procedure, you need to reduce the large heap size in order to have enough memory to run the neural network from a batch file. I used 64K for this one. Experiment.
- Viewports and the many constants in my OCR shell are screen specific. An 80-by-25 character screen needs to have an array of 2000 characters (Num_of_characters).

The PCX files are screen-specific. I've set the constant in my code (Appendix C) for a CGA, 600-by-200 screen. OCR_shell then sets the adapter type, Viewport size, and displays the correct .PCX for your screen.

Notes and Conclusions

As I told Amy later, my initial results were revealing and incomplete. I initially trained the network to recognize numbers by using a set of number "facts" that came with BrainMaker. Then I tested a screen of numbers I created with the BGI. I wrote text (using OutTextXY and a default 8-by-8 bit font). Results: terrible; BrainMaker couldn't recognize more than two or three.

Problem: The default BGI font and the BrainMaker font both use seven rows and lines of pixels to represent a number. But the .BGI's font is shifted 1 row and 1 column down and right of BrainMaker's. So I retrained the network, using the .BGI default font. Results: great. As long as the bits aren't skewed, my first little attempt will recognize a one-size, one-font character set.

Problem: scanning text with a hand scanner. If you're working from a limited budget (as I am), you might opt for one of the nifty little hand scanners from Logitech or DFI. These are affordable ($200 or so, if you shop around) and useful for scanning images into desktop publishing software. You can also use them to scan in text, but expect to juggle a bit if your text is wider than 4 inches (the width of most hand scanners). You can scan larger images in multiple passes. Then, use a paint program (such as PaintShow Plus, which comes with the Logitech hand scanner, or PC Paintbrush Plus, which comes with the DFI scanner) to edit the image.

If you can, try to scan documents in "natural" chunks: columns or paragraphs, for example. If you're scanning paragraphs, you first rotate the document 90 degrees, and then scan. After you've scanned the page, you rotate the scanned image with your paint program. Usually, this operation goes more or less smoothly, but you'll probably have to touch up (i.e. edit) the image a little. If you're scanning a few documents for personal use, this rotation-edit process is probably good enough. If you're planning to start an OCR scanning business, you'll probably want to opt for a full page scanner.

To create a full-blown optical character recognizer, you'll need to focus on training the neural network to recognize different fonts, styles, and sizes. Labor intensive, of course, but doable. Perhaps a better alternative would focus on patterns smaller than characters. For example, you might recognize the shapes—loops, bars, and stems. Then from the sizes, locations, and numbers of these shapes, you could reconstruct character patterns.

"Amy," I said, "I figured it out and it works, but I'll have to get back to you because there's no more room in this article."

Acknowledgments

Thanks to Dave Schultz at California Scientific Software and Chris Howard at Genus Programming for timely conversations while I was working on this project.

For more information, consult the following:

Turbo Pascal Professional 5.5 $250
Borland International
4585 Scotts Valley Dr.
Scotts Valley, CA 95066
(800) 345-2888

BrainMaker $199
California Scientific Software
160 E. Montecito #E
Sierra Madre, CA 91024
(818) 355-1094

PCX Toolkit $195
Genus
11315 Meadow Lake
Houston, TX 77077
(800) 227-0918

PaintShowPlus plus scanner $339
Logitech
(800) 231-7717
(800) 552-8885 (in CA)

NeuroShell $195
Ward Systems Group, Inc.
245 West Patrick Street
Frederick, MD 21701
(301) 662-7950

NeuralWorks $1495
Neuralware
Penn Center West—Bldg. IV
Suite 227
Pittsburgh, PA 15276

CHAPTER 14

Case Study V: Making Music

Russell C. Eberhart
Roy W. Dobbins

Introduction

Neural network tools are being used in the field of music for a variety of applications. In one special issue of *Computer Music* devoted to neural networks, applications reviewed included using NNTs to investigate pitch perception, tonal analysis, quantizing musical time, exploring complex musical patterns, and optimizing fingering for string instruments [56]. Each of these subjects is appropriate for investigation using neural network tools, but most of them appeal primarily to music theorists.

This chapter deals with a subject that we feel has a broader appeal: the composition of music using NNTs. We'll look at how music is presented to an NNT for training and composition. Then we'll review network configurations that can be used for music composition. We'll look at ways you can implement code on your personal computer for music composition. One variation that uses the Batchnet back-propagation network described in Chapter 2 is explored in some depth, including the source code listings for pattern and run files. We'll also briefly explore the use of the industry standard Musical Instrument Digital Interface (MIDI) to play the music once it's composed. (Well, at least MIDI is sort of a standard. Like RS-232, it's a brave attempt at one. More about that later.)

One of the authors (RCE) has a checkered musical background, including three (grudging) years of piano lessons, and about 10 years' experience playing trumpet in marching and dance bands, not to men-

tion soprano bugle in a drum and bugle corps and smatterings of guitar
and harmonica in recent years. To gain the needed MIDI knowledge and
experience, we relied on several technical sources, most notable (no
pun intended) of which is Terry Turpin, from whom a MIDI-compatible
Yamaha CX5M music computer (with an SFG-05 FM sound synthesizer) was borrowed to complete the work in this chapter. It should be
noted that the above-mentioned author has become hooked on MIDI
and has purchased a Casio PMP-500 MIDI keyboard with synthesizer
to continue the work (play) described.

You can probably tell that the motivation for this case study is somewhat different from others in this volume. The other case studies can
be considered at least potentially work related, with the exception of
the analysis of the commodities futures market, which is concerned
with making money. The motivation for this case study is *fun*. It is fun
to play with different network configurations and training and with different types of music. And it is *fun* to actually *listen* to the output of
the neural network.

The composition of music using rule-based systems such as those
that are found in the "traditional" artificial intelligence field has been
around for a long time. Some basic problems exist with rule-based systems, however. First, it is almost impossible to articulate all of the rules
that go into any particular type of music. Second, much of the per-
ceived beauty of music stems from the elements of surprise and variety,
elements which, by definition, break rules. So it seems that a sort of
catch-22 situation exists: You only win if you can think of all the rules,
but you lose if you compose only to rules.

The use of NNTs allows us to compose music by presenting the network with examples of the kind of music we want to produce. It isn't
necessary to derive and state any explicit musical rules. We do have to
figure out how to represent the music as patterns for the NNTs, though.

Representing Music for Neural Network Tools

At the most basic level, music can be thought of and dealt with as a
series of notes. The notes are comprised of melody notes and harmony
notes. In this chapter, we deal only with the melody line, restricting
ourselves to monophonic melodies (single pitch at any one time). Although the techniques described here are applicable to polyphonic music (several notes at a time), that application is beyond the scope of this
chapter.

Once we've restricted ourselves to monophonic music, there are two
basic attributes of each note that we need to take into account. The first

is the pitch or frequency of the note. The second is duration or how long the note lasts. The absence of a note (silence) is called a *rest* and is generally considered to be a possible value of pitch because a rest has a duration just like a note.

Exactly how notes are represented has been the subject of extensive discussion. Only recently have neural networks been applied to composing music, but previous reviews of music representation for the purposes of analysis and for music composition with rule-based systems are generally relevant.

There are two basic issues in music representation for NNT implementations. First is the question of whether to represent notes (pitches and durations) as discrete values or as transition values. The second is whether to use output neurodes to represent notes or to represent time slices. We'll look at each of these issues, but for a more detailed discussion, see Todd [58].

The issue of representation is, of course, tied up with network architecture. It's hard to talk about one without considering the other. In fact, it's almost a chicken and egg situation. To get started, though, let's assume that we have something that at least vaguely resembles a back-propagation network so that we can look at the two issues of representing music. We'll further assume that we train each of the network output neurodes to be on or off, which means that we won't attempt to represent multiple values—say, an entire scale of notes—with one neurode's output.

Now, let's consider whether to represent notes as discrete values or as transitions. In the first case, each neurode represents a single note, in other words, the actual value of a note. In the second case, each neurode represents one particular magnitude, in musical half-steps, of the transition from one note to the next. To help understand the difference, consider the note sequence D, E, F. In the first case, output neurodes for the notes D, E, and F would become active sequentially. In the second case, the output sequence would be D, $+2$, $+1$. (F is a half-step above E, which is two half-steps above D.)

The transition version has advantages such as the fact that a large range of notes can be covered with relatively few output neurodes. There is one major flaw, however, which derives from the fact that neural networks don't always behave perfectly. If a "mistaken" note is produced, all of the melody that follows is shifted, or transposed. It doesn't take very many transpositions to turn a pleasant melody into the contents of a dog's dish! In agreement with Todd [58], then, we'll adopt the "one note—one neurode" rule.

The second issue, whether to use output neurodes to represent notes or time slices, is a bit more difficult to resolve. If output neurodes are used to represent note durations, a separate group of "duration" neurodes is needed. The complete representation of a note thus requires activation of both a note-value neurode and a note-duration neurode. On the other hand, if each iteration of the net represents one time slice, then the duration of notes with repetitions of the same output neurode can be indicated by the state of a "note-begin" neurode, which activates only when a note begins in a given time slice.

For example, say that a given output neurode (middle C, for instance) turns on for four successive time slices and that the time slice, which corresponds to the smallest time increment represented by the network, is equivalent to a sixteenth note. If the note-begin neurode is only active for the first time slice, the actual note represented is a quarter note (four sixteenth-notes tied together). If note begin is active for the first and third slices, then two eighth notes are represented, and so on.

The time slice approach has advantages, including simplicity. It requires only one additional note-begin neurode to represent duration fully. This is the approach chosen by Todd [58]. There are disadvantages, however, that have led us to take the approach of using a group of note-duration neurodes. One disadvantage is having to deal with the ambiguity that arises whenever a note of a different pitch is indicated *without* the note-begin neurode becoming active. Even worse is dealing with a pitch that becomes active immediately after a rest without the note begin activated. It is uncertain what is to be done in these cases. There also are ambiguities if you try to use the note-begin approach in polyphonic music.

We therefore use one group of output neurodes for pitch, each of which represents a distinct pitch value, including a rest. We use another group of output neurodes, each of which represents a distinct value, for note duration. The number needed in each group depends on the music to which the network is trained. More on that later. Now let's take a look at network configurations that can be used to compose music.

Network Configurations

Relatively little has been done in using neural networks to compose music. Probably the most generally known work has been done by Kohonen, and it doesn't strictly use neural networks [59]. Instead, it uses a context-sensitive generative grammar that has some attributes of an associative memory. Some interesting things can be learned from his work that we'll refer to later.

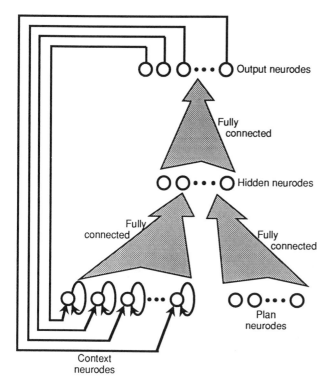

Figure 14-1 Sequential network for musical applications with feedback from output neurodes (after Jordan [60]).

One thing that should be intuitively obvious is that you need some kind of time history, or recurrence, to train a network to compose music. That is, you can't expect a network to generate a new note based entirely on the basis of the single note that immediately precedes it.

One of the first recurrent network architectures resembling back-propagation that was used for music was described by Jordan in 1986 [60]. Figure 14-1 illustrates the scheme. Note that each context neurode on the input side receives an input from the corresponding output neurode as well as feedback from its own immediately previous value. The coding of the plan neurodes represents the particular melody being learned. The coding is usually a simple binary code that uniquely identifies each melody. This general architecture has been used by several investigators, including Todd [58] to analyze melody lines and rhythms.

In Jordan's model, feedback from output neurodes to context neurodes occurs with a weight of 1.0, and the self-feedback on each context

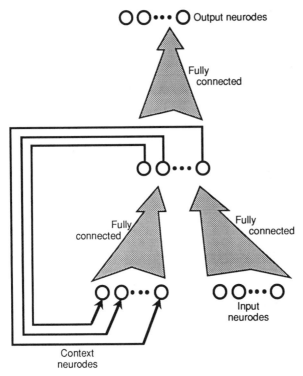

Figure 14-2 Sequential network for musical applications with feedback from hidden neurodes [after Dolson (61)].

neurode has a weight value of about 0.6–0.8 [58]. A somewhat different approach is used by Dolson; he feeds back the values of the hidden neurodes rather than the output neurodes. He contends that "feeding back the hidden-unit values may allow the network far greater flexibility in building up useful, time-varying, internal representations" [61]. This general scheme is illustrated in Fig. 14-2. If you rigidly adhere to the constraints imposed by the mathematical derivation, then the back-propagation learning algorithm would not appear to be usable in this configuration of feedback from hidden nodes. Despite this "fact," back-propagation has been applied successfully in this situation [60, 62].

In the networks for music composition that we present in the remainder of this chapter, we achieve the needed "time history," or recurrence, with a fairly standard back-propagation network with some nonstandard properties. We also suggest variations of our method. Remember that we are choosing to represent each note by two groups of neurodes: one group that represents the pitch (including a rest) and one that represents duration. The number of neurodes needed in each group depends on the melodies to which the network is trained.

Our scheme is to present a number of notes, say five, to the input neurodes and train to the next note, in this case the sixth. Then we rotate the sixth note down to the input neurodes where the fifth note was, move the fifth note to where the fourth note was, and so on until we replace the first note with the second. (The first note is now gone.) We first saw this general scheme described in an article by Duff [63], but he represented note values only as inputs, not durations.

We now train the second through the sixth note to the seventh note. We then rotate the seventh note down in a like manner and train the third through the seventh note to the eighth note. We continue doing this until we run out of notes. Figure 14-3 illustrates the network model for the case in which N notes are used to train to the $(N+1)$th note. Looks pretty simple, doesn't it? Well, it is straightforward, but we wouldn't necessarily call it simple. There are some things you need to know to make it work well.

For one thing, because the network model looks like our standard back-propagation implementation called Batchnet, the source code, which is in Appendix A, that we'd like to be able to use Batchprop. So we need some pattern files that can be used as input to Batchnet. Also, even though we've decided in general how to represent notes (two groups of neurodes, one for pitch and one for duration), we haven't said exactly how we're going to *code* the pattern file for the notes. For example, do we code the pitch that's *on* to 1 and all others to zero, or what?

Before we can tackle either of these issues, we somehow have to cap-

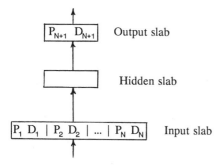

Figure 14-3   Basic three-layer back-propagation network for music composition. Note pitches and durations are represented by P and D. The number of notes in depth used for training is represented by N.

ture the data from the melodies we're going to use for training into machine-readable form. We'll use a small portion of a very simple melody as an example.

One of the constraints we're going to impose on our melodies is that they are in the key of C major. To those of you who don't know what that means, it restricts us to only seven notes per octave, and we don't have to worry about sharps and flats. We deal only with the notes C, D, E, F, G, A, and B. In general, we won't restrict ourselves to only one octave; so we have to add an octave identifier to the note value. In this book, we restrict ourselves to a two-octave range, with "middle C" defined as the beginning of the lower octave. Therefore, we represent middle C as C1 (or C middle), the C above middle C as C2, and so on. (Yes, for you nonmusicians, our octaves begin with C, not with A. What's so unusual about that? Most of you computer freaks start counting with zero, instead of one like normal folks.)

Our simple example melody fragment consists of the note pitch sequence E1 D1 C1 D1 E1 E1 E1. The durations are all eighth notes, with the exception of the last E1, which is a quarter note. This example ends with a quarter note rest. We thus have three note pitches, a rest, and two note durations to code; the initial coded list, which we call the *text file* for the melody fragment, is as follows (each note is on one line). Note that the information in parenthesis isn't part of the file; it labels the pitches, rest, and duration columns.

(C	D	E	R	E	Q)
0	0	1	0	1	0
0	1	0	0	1	0
1	0	0	0	1	0
0	1	0	0	1	0
0	0	1	0	1	0
0	0	1	0	1	0
0	0	1	0	0	1
0	0	0	1	0	1

Those of you who grew up in an English-speaking culture probably recognize the melody as the first few notes of "Mary Had a Little Lamb." This fragment obviously isn't enough to train a network (we'll discuss that subject later), but it *is* enough to show you how to build text files and pattern files, which is all we're trying to do right now.

Note that we use just enough values in each neurode group (pitch, duration) to code the information at hand. Thus, for our simple example, we needed four pitch values (remember to include a value for a rest) and two duration values. If we had coded the entire song, we obviously would have needed more neurodes. And we usually don't code just one song. So, when we're doing this for real, we have to allow for the entire pitch range and all values of durations, for all songs that are part of the training pattern set.

Starting from the left, we listed the note values in the first three spots of the line that represents the note, the presence or absence of a rest came next, and the two duration values are last, on the right end of the line. Now, how do we turn this text file into a pattern file for Batchnet?

Remember that for Batchnet we list each pattern on one line with the values for the input nodes first, followed by the target values for the output neurodes, followed by a pattern ID number. We'll list the output targets as 1s and 0s, similar to the test file, but let's think about the input representation for a moment.

If we represent the input neurode values as 1s and 0s, the weight changes propagated back to the input-to-hidden weights will be 0 for all input neurodes set to 0. This is because the back-propagation algorithm defines the change in weight for the input-to-hidden weights as proportional to the output of the input neurodes o_i,

$$\Delta w_{ji} = \eta \delta_j o_i$$

as discussed in Chapter 2 (see Eq. 2-12 and the surrounding discussion for more information). There are several ways to work around this, including the use of other activation functions [63]. The way we've chosen is to represent the input neurode values as 0.1 and 0.9 instead of 0 and 1. This allows the updating of the weights attached to input neurodes that are off. Note that we don't really have to change the on neurodes to 0.9; we just did it for symmetry in weight changes. Also note that we still represent the targets for the output neurodes as 0s and 1s.

Now that the representation issue is settled, we need to decide how many notes deep to train the network. That is, do we use the first four notes to train to the fifth, then the second through fifth notes to train to the sixth, and so on (four notes deep); or do we use the first five notes to train to the sixth, then the second through sixth to train the seventh, and so on (five notes deep); or what?

In the process of answering this question, we become aware of many more questions, most of them beyond the scope of this book. Suffice it to say that there are some analogies here with Markov sources [64], for those of you familiar with them. Those of you not familiar with them really aren't missing much.

What it boils down to is that there are trade-offs between the number of notes deep you train the network and such things as the complexity of the network (the deeper you train the more complex the network), the faithfulness of the composed music to the music used for training (the deeper you train the more faithful the sound), and the extent of variability or surprise in your music (the deeper you train, the less the element of surprise). Most of these trade-offs have two sides: For example, if you were to train 10 or 25 or 50 notes deep (assuming you could stand waiting for the network to train), you'd probably produce pretty close to the exact music with which you trained the network, which isn't what most of us are setting out to do. Of course, if you try to train too deeply, the network probably won't train at all; it probably won't have enough examples of note sequences.

The bottom line is that training three to five notes deep seems to work pretty well. Once in a while (frequently?), we'd like to go only two or three notes deep, as discussed by Kohonen [59]. For now, we settle for a fixed training depth, but we return to the depth subject later as we look at variations to this approach.

Let's return to our simple example of a few notes from "Mary Had a Little Lamb." For purposes of illustration, we assume we're training the network three notes deep, just to show you how the pattern file would evolve from the text file. The pattern file looks like this:

			(target)	
(pitch1 dur1)	(pitch2 dur2)	(pitch3 dur3)	(pitchdur)	ID
.1 .1 .9 .1 .9 .1	.1 .9 .1 .1 .9 .1	.9 .1 .1 .1 .9 .1	0 1 0 0 1 0	1
.1 .9 .1 .1 .9 .1	.9 .1 .1 .1 .9 .1	.1 .9 .1 .1 .9 .1	0 0 1 0 1 0	2
.9 .1 .1 .1 .9 .1	.9 .1 .1 .1 .9 .1	.1 .1 .9 .1 .9 .1	0 0 1 0 1 0	3
.1 .9 .1 .1 .9 .1	.1 .1 .9 .1 .9 .1	.1 .1 .9 .1 .9 .1	0 0 1 0 0 1	4
.1 .1 .9 .1 .9 .1	.1 .1 .9 .1 .9 .1	.1 .1 .9 .9 .1 .1	0 0 0 1 0 1	5

(Remember that the information in parentheses isn't part of the pattern file.) A useful training pattern file would have many more notes from several songs (probably at least 100 notes total, probably a minimum of 3 or 4 songs). Also, training could be four or five notes deep. Note again that the representation for each training note is on one line. The three input note representations are listed in order first (0.1s and 0.9s), followed by the output neurode target (0s and 1s), followed by the ID number of the pattern (1–5). This pattern file is now in a form that can be used directly by Batchnet.

We decided to pursue the training of a network with what we call "music Americana." With that goal in mind, we used as our training set three songs: "Oh, Susanna," "The Yellow Rose of Texas," and "She'll Be Comin' 'Round the Mountain." The text files for these songs are listed in Appendix D. You can create your pattern files for them to whatever depth you want and then run them with Batchnet. You should generate the pattern file for each individual song first and then combine them into one large pattern file. If you first combine the songs end to end and *then* build the pattern file, you will train the end of "Oh, Susanna" to the beginning of "The Yellow Rose of Texas," or whatever, which is probably not what you want to do.

Once the pattern file is built, you can train the network to whatever level of average sum-squared error you choose and then use the network to compose music. These three songs, when taken together to make a pattern file, require 13 pitch neurodes (including one for a rest) and 6 duration nodes, for a total of 19 input neurodes per note. The pitch neurodes represent the whole steps (key of C major) from C1 (middle C) to G2. The duration neurodes represent 16th, 8th, dotted 8th, quarter, dotted quarter, and dotted half notes. Dotted notes have 50 percent longer duration than nondotted notes.

Once the network is trained to your satisfaction, you can begin to compose music. Be careful about training your network to too small an average sum-squared error. It seems that, at least occasionally, networks trained less rigorously produce better sounding music. This may have something to do with the network "memorizing" the music to which it is trained.

You start composing music by "seeding" the network with a few notes; the number of notes in your seed is the same as the depth to which you trained the network. If, for example, you trained it four notes deep, you'll need to seed it with four notes. You then just run it in the forward-propagation mode, generating one note at a time, sliding that newly generated note down into the highest number note slot in the input pattern, sliding all of the notes in the previous input pattern down one (discarding the first), and present the new input pattern to generate the next note. You do this for as many notes as you want to compose. The seed pattern must consist of both pitches and durations for each of your seed notes.

Finally, you *play* the music you composed. This is where the real fun comes in. We describe two ways to do that later. You can edit the song text files produced by the network with any text editor, taking out parts you don't like and making revisions to parts you do like.

Figure 14-4 is an example of a melody we generated using a training pattern file built from the three song text files in Appendix D. The durations of a few of the notes were adjusted slightly so that the music

NEWSONG

Russ Eberhart & Roy Dobbins

Figure 14-4 Melody composed by neural network trained to three "music Americana" songs.

adheres to a 2/4 tempo, but pitches are unaltered except for the last three notes, which were rearranged to bring the melody to a close. A text file listing, newsong. txt, of the melody with the minor rearrangements, appears in Appendix D. Whether or not you like the tune, the "feel" or "style" of the music is reminiscent of the training songs.

The process of music composition using Batchnet consists of five main steps:

1. Encode the songs to be used for training as text files.
2. Build the training pattern file choosing how many notes deep you're going to train and how to represent notes.
3. Train a network using Batchnet, choosing the number of hidden nodes, eta, alpha, and so on, and generating an appropriate weights file before you train.
4. Compose the music one note at a time by seeding Batchnet with as many seed notes as the depth of training, using the weight file output from the training process.
5. Play the music through the computer speaker or an external synthesizer.

To help you in the five-step process, we've provided the source code for several C programs in Appendix D. To help you with the first step, the three music Americana songs we mentioned have been coded into text files, and these files appear in Appendix D. You are on your own as far as coding other songs for training. One person we know is training networks to the works of Stephen Foster.

A program called music. c in Appendix D, will help you build pattern files, the second step. As you can tell from the header to the program source code, the number of notes deep that you want to train is a command line option, as are the values you want to set the input values to for the off and on conditions (we usually use 0.1 and 0.9, respectively).

You indicate your input song text file and output song pattern file names with the redirection symbols < and >. If your text file with the coding for "Oh Susanna" is ohsus19. txt, for example, and you want to code four notes deep with input pitches and durations at the 0.1 and 0.9 levels for inactive and active neurodes, respectively, and you want your song pattern file to be called ohsu4n19. pat, your command line would be

```
music -n5 -1.1 -w.9 <ohsus19.txt >ohsu4n19.pat
```

The -n5 indicates that there are four notes in depth plus one target note for each pattern line. Note that the name of the output song pattern file reminds us that it is four notes deep and has 19 neurodes per note.

Once a pattern file is built for each song, you can concatenate them into one training pattern file. For example, if your three song pattern

files are ohsu4n19.pat, sbcr4n19.pat, and yelr4n19.pat, give
the following command:

```
copy ohsu4n19.pat+sbcr4n19.pat+yelr4n19.pat mu3s4n19.pat
```

For the third step, training the network, you need Batchnet, discussed at some length in Chapter 2, and an appropriate run file and
initial random weights file. In Appendix D, we have listed a typical run
file, named mu41901d.run, for the pattern file we built from the three
songs. You can generate a weights file using weights.c. Your command line for training the network then might be

```
batchnet -e10 -d.02 mu41901d.run
```

The command line options request batchnet to report error values each
10 iterations, and to stop training when the average sum-squared error
is less than 0.02.

The fourth step, composing the music, can be done by feeding one
input at a time, beginning with the seed notes, to Batchnet; getting the
output; making a new input pattern from it and all but one note of the
previous input; feeding that to the network; and so on. The process can
be tedious, so we have provided a program called mshell.c that does
it for you. On our machines (10-mHz AT clones), it takes about 3 sec to
produce each note when the program is run in RAM disk (a highly
recommended procedure).

In Appendix D, we have listed a typical seed pattern file, yan.pat,
which is the first four notes of Yankee Doodle, and a typical run file,
newsong.run, for use with mshell.exe. A command line for
mshell.exe could be

```
mshell -n5 -s100 -1.1 -w.9 yan.pat newsong.txt batchnet
newsong.run
```

The command line options specify that the patterns are four notes
deep (plus target note), that the program produces 100 new music
notes, that off input nodes given the value 0.1, and that on input nodes
are set to 0.9. Newsong.txt contains the new music composition.
Newsong.txt in Appendix D includes minor rearrangements of the
network output, as discussed earlier.

To play your masterpiece on your computer's speaker, all you need
is play.c. If your newly composed song text file is named
newsong.txt, for example, all you need to say on the command line is

```
play newsong.txt
```

You can include a change in tempo with the -t option on the command
line. The default tempo is 125 msec per 16th note.

It's handy to use play.exe to play your training pattern song text files, as well. It's a good way to check that the training songs have been properly coded. Note that each of the programs especially designed to help you through the five steps (music.c, mshell.c, and play.c) assume that you have a total of 19 input neurodes for each note. These consist of 13 pitches (from middle C to G2 and a rest), and six durations (sixteenth, eighth, dotted eighth, quarter, dotted quarter, and dotted half notes). There is no neurode coded as a half note because there are no half notes in the three songs used for the training pattern file.

You can change the header parts of the programs to customize them to your applications and then recompile them. Note that if you want to extend the range of pitches in play.c, you have to include the frequency values for the new notes. Similarly, additional note duration values have to be defined in terms of 16th note durations.

All of the described programs and run files are included on the Shareware diskette that is available from the editors of this book. Instructions on how to get the diskette are in Chapter 2. In addition to source code, the Shareware diskette includes executable code for the example we've just described. Everything you need to compose your own music and play it on your PC is on the diskette. You can make changes to whatever extent you wish. You may only want to change the learning or momentum factors in a run file used for training, or the seed notes in a seed text file to start the composition process. These are minor changes and can be done with any text editor or word processor that produces ASCII text files. Or you may want to do something requiring changing the source code and recompiling.

Please remember that, whether you use the source code in the appendix or on the diskette, all of the code is copyrighted. You may make changes for your own use only, and you may not sell it in any form, modified or not. You are free, under the concept of Shareware, to distribute the unmodified code with the understanding that anyone using it will pay the shareware fee.

Stochasticity, Variability, and Surprise

We've alluded several times to the issue of putting variability and surprise into the composed music. In this section, we discuss the subject and offer a few approaches to achieve some element of surprise in our music.

It should be obvious, even though we haven't explicitly said so, that the approach to music composition we described earlier is deterministic. There are an almost infinite number of ways to get from where you start, the training music text file, to your composed music in the output music text file; you can vary the depth of training, eta, alpha, and so on. But it's still a deterministic process. The purely deterministic approach has a practical disadvantage in addition to its aesthetic one. It isn't unusual for a note sequence being composed to get into a repeating loop. For example, it gets into a 10-note sequence that it repeats endlessly. When this happens, of course, the ball game is over unless you have some way to break out of it, such as by putting some randomness into the process.

We decided to try to put some randomness into the composition process. Remember that the note pitch and duration selected for each new note are those for which the output neurode has the highest activation value in each group. That value is often relatively high (over 0.9) but can be lower (0.5–0.6). One way to incorporate randomness is to select the pitch neurode with the probability of its output value. That is, if the highest pitch output value is 0.8, we could select that pitch with the probability of 80 percent. If we don't select it, we select the next highest output neurode with the probability of its activation value, and so on. We tried this. The results, at least for the few attempts we made, sounded horrible!

We thought the problem might be that the value of the winning output neurode is often only 0.8 or so, and the second highest value is often only 0.4 or so (sometimes even less). This makes the probability of not taking the winning value (and of not taking the second highest value either) rather high, and the note that was eventually selected often had a pitch and/or duration activation of only 0.2 or less. So then we implemented a variation in which we have a constant probability that the winning note is taken, and we use that same probability that the second note is taken, and so on. This probability is usually set fairly high (0.80–0.95), and the results are a little better. You can set this non-deterministic switch in our mshell program with a -d0 on the command line of mshell.exe and try it for yourself.

Even this adjustment didn't give results as pleasing as we wanted. Another approach is to train and run two or more networks. This basic idea can be implemented in at least two ways. As an example of the first, train one network four notes deep and one network five notes deep. Now run them in parallel. Take the new note from the five note deep network with some high probability, perhaps the value of the winning neurode or perhaps some constant high probability. If you don't take the new note from the five deep network, take it from the four deep one. You can extend this idea to several networks trained to various depths. We started to implement this idea, thinking that we'd train three networks, three, four, and five notes deep. However, the computational complexity associated with the network system started to bother us. It seems to us that to get a little variation in time history into our system is too computationally expensive.

An example of the second way is to use a *set* of song pattern files instead of just one pattern file. (Each is trained to the same depth, say four notes.) In our example, one pattern file could be derived from "Oh Susanna" and "The Yellow Rose of Texas," another from "She'll Be Comin' 'Round the Mountain" and "Oh, Susanna," and a third from "She'll Be Comin' 'Round the Mountain" and "The Yellow Rose of Texas." Now, take the new note from a network trained to one of the pattern files with some probability. Switching among pattern files would seem to lessen the chance of falling into repeating loops of notes.

As this book goes to press, we are exploring these and other possibilities for putting recurrence and randomness into the process. Hopefully, this will not be the last you hear from us on the subject of music composition!

Playing Your Music with MIDI

In this section, we outline one option to playing your music on the speaker of your computer. If you wonder why we'd suggest an option to your computer speaker, you've probably never played any musical melody on it. It is quintessential low fidelity! Also, when you use our play.exe program, you don't have very many options. Our program gives you some control over the tempo, but that's about it.

Enter the Musical Instrument Digital Interface, or MIDI for short. This is a communications protocol to standardize and facilitate the connection of electronic synthesizers, keyboards, instruments, and computers. With appropriate MIDI software running on your PC, you can play music on a keyboard or synthesizer with a MIDI interface. You can also record music from the external unit for later feedback. You can even edit the music and mix tracks. The possibilities are virtually endless. MIDI was introduced in 1982 and has been in a constant state of evolution since then. The major specifications, however, have remained stable, and it appears that they will continue to remain so.

The major specifications include the fact that MIDI is a serial link running at 31.25 Kbaud. Note that this is not one of the standard serial interface baud rates. To use MIDI on your personal computer, you need a special MIDI interface board unless you happen to own an Atari ST or Yamaha computer, which are the only ones with MIDI built in.

A company called Roland (known mainly for their keyboards) devised one of the earliest MIDI interfaces, the MPU-401. The MPU-401 has become the "standard" for MIDI interfaces. To say that your MIDI interface is MPU-401 compatible is analogous to saying that your computer modem is Hayes compatible. Once you have your computer with an MPU-401 compatible interface board and the appropriate software, you're ready to talk to some MIDI music equipment.

Physically, MIDI information travels between computer and synthesizer, keyboards, etc., on shielded, twisted-pair cable, terminated in male 5-pin DIN connectors. Pins 4 and 5 carry the information (4 to 4, 5 to 5), and pin 2 is connected to the shield and grounded at MIDI Out and Thru ports. There are three types of ports: In, Out, and Thru. Out ports are always connected to In ports; Thru ports pass information to other In ports. For example, in a simple setup, the MIDI Out port of your computer's MPU-401 is connected to the MIDI In port of your synthesizer; the synthesizer Out port is connected to the In port at the computer.

Communicating with the MIDI music equipment is simply a matter of reading/writing data from/to the MPU-401. To do this, you work with ports 330H and 331H on your PC. You verify that the 401 is ready by checking the status bit (bit 7) on port 331H. If it's 0, the unit is ready. You then put information out by writing to port 330H.

At the most basic level, all you need to know to play your neural network music is how to turn notes on, and turn them off. A typical message that turns on a note is: 90 3c 70 (all data in hex). The 90 hex stands for *note on* (the 9) on MIDI Channel 1 (the 0). There are 16 MIDI channels, but most synthesizers and keyboards communicate on Channel 1 as the default setting. *Note on* in Channel 2 would be 91 hex. The 3c hex is the MIDI representation for middle C. Note D above middle C is 3e hex, and so on. The 70 hex represents the strength of the keypress, or the loudness, which is medium in this case.

To turn off a note, you turn it on with a loudness of 0. So to turn off the middle C, you send 90 3c 00 (in hex). Add some software to provide timing for various note (and rest) lengths, and you're about ready.

You can do many other things with MIDI, including setting the synthesizer for the instrument sound (harpsicord, flute, etc.), but further details are beyond the scope of this book. Several good references will help you do whatever you want. One of the most useful books is the *MIDI Programmer's Handbook*, which presents details on programming for MIDI in a way that is useful for owners of almost any personal computer, whether it's a PC, a Macintosh, or whatever [66]. More specific to IBM PCs and compatibles are two books on programming in C for MIDI [67, 68].

One of the things that we were looking for, however, wasn't available in the software in any of the books mentioned: a relatively painless way to implement MIDI control with a song file format that is easy to understand, easy to write, and uses plain ASCII code. The software in the books put the song files in some inscrutable binary code that makes them impossible to edit with an ASCII text editor or word processor.

We finally came across The CMU MIDI Toolkit from the Center for Art and Technology, Carnegie Mellon University, Pittsburgh, PA 15213. For $20 we received a manual and the software on diskette (C source and executable code) to do everything we want to do (at least for now) in MIDI. Part of the Toolkit is the Adagio music language, which features song files written in easy-to-understand ASCII format. To play a song through your MIDI equipment, all you have to do is give the command: adagio filename.gio. That's what we call painless! And the Toolkit contains many other software tools for mucking about with MIDI to your heart's content. In Appendix D, in addition to the song text file, we've provided an Adagio program listing of the song composed by our network (Fig. 14-4).

Now What?

If you hadn't already guessed, there's a reason for learning about and using MIDI that we haven't stated yet. We would like to be able to generate music with our neural network tools and play it real time via MIDI. This is a somewhat ambitious goal. It may take a combination of heavy doses of Assembly language (groans!) and a 20-mHz 80386 machine (cheers!). We really do need a *reason* to get our next computer.

GLOSSARY

What is the use of a glossary? It alerts you to terms that are relevant to neural networks. In many cases, you will know these terms from domains such as engineering, mathematics, biology, and physics; but the glossary puts these terms into perspective for neural networks. You may be surprised by some of the definitions. People often use terms without having a solid understanding of their exact meaning. The glossary helps to clear the fog.

We cannot make this list exhaustive; that would probably require a tome longer than the book itself. Instead we highlight some major terms needed to get started in the field. Note that because this is a book about practical tools, the emphasis is on implementation techniques rather than neurobiology. With few exceptions, terms are defined using engineering or mathematical, not biological, terminology.

The glossary is an alphabetical list of important neural network words and phrases. Synonymous terms, more fully defined elsewhere in the glossary, are indicated in parentheses.

Activation function Algorithm for computing the activation value of a neurode as a function of its net input. The net input is usually the sum of the weighted inputs to the neurode, but may take on many other forms.

Activation rule (Activation function)

Activation state Set of activation values of all neurodes.

Activation value Output value of a neurode; may be continuous or discrete. Continuous values may further be bounded to some interval. Discrete values may be restricted to some small set of values.

Adaline Adaptive linear element devised by Widrow and Hoff for use in adaptive filters.

Architecture Specification of the slabs, number of neurodes per slab, and interconnections among the slabs in a network.

Associative memory Memory with the ability to recall an entire pattern from a partial pattern.

Axon Sending fiber of a neuron. Action potential of the neuron cell body is transmitted along the axon, from which it is received via synapses by the dendrites of other neurons.

Back–propagation A learning rule for multilayer feedforward networks, in which weights are adjusted by backward propagation of the error signal from outputs to inputs.

Batch training Procedure for training neural networks, in which the weights are adjusted after each epoch. See also Interactive training.

Bias Weight from a neurode that is always on. Acts on a neurode like an offset. All neurodes in a network, except those in the input layer, usually have a bias.

Bundle Collection of one or more links among slabs. A bundle indicates a fully connected unidirectional path between two slabs. That is, every element of one slab is connected to every element of the other slab. A bundle is a convenient shorthand notation for working with network architectures.

Cell (Neurode)

Competitive learning Unsupervised learning scheme in which neurodes compete for the right to respond to a given subset of inputs. The response of a neurode to an input pattern tends to inhibit other units. After learning, some neurodes become feature detectors. See Lateral inhibition.

Connection Pathway linking neurodes in a network, typically conducting information in one direction only. See Bundle.

Connection strength Strength of a connection between two neurodes, which determines the amount of effect that one neurode can have on the other. Connections have a positive, zero, or negative weight. Positive values are excitatory, and negative values are inhibitory.

Content addressable memory (Associative memory)

Delta rule (Widrow–Hoff rule)

Dendrite Receiving fibers of a neuron. Receive action potentials via synapses from other neurons.

Distributed representation Information representation scheme in which entities are represented by patterns of activity, distributed over many neurodes. Long-term memory is represented by the weights; short-term memory is represented in recurrent networks by activation states. Stored knowledge cannot be isolated to a single location as in the von Neumann computer. The robustness of neural networks is due to this property.

Dot product (Inner product)

Element (Neurode)

Epoch Presentation of a set of training patterns to a neural network. See Batch training and Interactive training.

Epoch training (Batch training)

Error term Measure of difference between actual state and desired state of a neurode.

Error signal (Error term)

Euclidean distance   Geometric distance between two points, given by the square root of the sum of the squares of the differences between vector components.

Euclidean normalization   Normalization of vectors to unit length (the length of a vector is the square root of the inner product of the vector with itself, or the square root of the sum of the squares of the elements.)

Fan-in   Number of neurodes connected to the input of a unit.

Fan-out   Number of neurodes to which the output of a unit is connected.

Feedback network   Network with feedback paths within the same layers or between layers.

Feedforward network   Network ordered into layers with no feedback paths. The lowest layer is the input layer, the highest is the output layer. The outputs of a given layer go only to higher layers, and its inputs come only from lower layers.

Generalization   Property of a system to abstract features from the input space that define a particular class or, the ability to perform well on patterns not seen before in the training set.

Generalized delta rule   The delta rule for semilinear activation functions in layered feedforward networks.

Gradient descent   Algorithm for minimizing some error measure by making small incremental weight adjustments proportional to the gradient of the error.

Hebbian learning rule   Fundamental law of learning, formulated by Hebb. Essentially, the connection strength between two neurodes is adjusted in proportion to the product of the activation values. Many other learning rules are founded on Hebb's original rule.

Hidden layer   A layer of neurodes with no direct connections to the outside world. All connections from the hidden layer are to other layers within the system.

Hierarchical network   Network consisting of several layers with connections between layers chosen to achieve some kind of processing in stages. Such networks can have feedforward and/or feedback connections and can combine different learning paradigms at each stage.

Hill-climbing   Algorithm for maximizing some function. See Gradient descent.

Hinton diagram   Compact graphic display of activations or weights for a layer of a network. Weights are represented by small rectangles whose sizes are proportional to the weights; negative values are shown in black, positive values in white.

Hyperplane   Surface defined in higher than three-dimensional space.

Inner product   Scalar sum of the products of components of two vectors. The activation state of a neurode is typically a function of the inner product of the weight and input vectors.

Input layer   A layer of neurodes receiving inputs from sources external to the system. These may be either sensory inputs or signals from other systems outside the one being modeled.

Input vector   Set of inputs to a network.

Interactive training   Procedure for training neural networks in which the weights are adjusted after each pattern is presented. See also Batch training.

Interconnection   (Connection)

Interconnections per second   Performance measure of a neural network. Function of number of neurode interconnections calculated per second.

Iteration   Process of setting activation states of layers and applying their activation rules according to the update procedure.

Lateral inhibition   Inhibitory action of neurodes within a layer whereby strong positive activation of one neurode results in negative influence on the activations of neighboring neurodes. Typically used in competitive learning.

Layer   A slab in a network with strict hierarchical ordering between groups of elements. See Slab.

Learning   Procedure during which the network adapts its weights by successive applications of the learning rules.

Learning rate   Parameter that regulates the relative magnitude of weight changes during learning.

Learning rule   An algorithm for adjusting the weights and connections of a network based on experience.

Least mean-square rule   (Widrow–Hoff rule)

Link   (Connection)

Local storage   Storage that is accessible only to a given neurode and not to other units.

Mexican hat   A function used in self-organizing networks to adjust the weights of neurodes in the neighborhood of a winning neurode. Weights at the center are most strongly excited, weights further away are slightly inhibited, and weights a long way out are not changed at all. The distribution of these weight changes resembles a Mexican hat.

Momentum factor   Constant used to promote stability of weight adaptation in a learning rule. To prevent excessive weight change and possible oscillation, weight changes are moderated by a term that is proportional to the previous weight change and the momentum factor.

Neighborhood   Set of neurodes topologically adjacent to a particular neurode in a network.

Network paradigm   Particular choice of a set of network attributes to achieve a particular kind of processing.

Network attributes   Distinguishing characteristics of a network, describing its architecture, activation rule, learning rule, update procedure. Attributes of a network specify its form and function.

Neural network model   Abstract specification of a network paradigm. This model is independent of any implementation. It can be simulated in software or implemented as a neurocomputer.

Neurocomputer   Hardware implementation of neural network using electronic, optical, or other components.

Node   (Neurode)

Neurode   Active unit in a neural network. Consists of a set of inputs from other neurodes and an output that can go to any number of other neurodes. Performs an activation function on its inputs to produce an activation value that is placed on the output. Can contain local storage that is used to compute the activation value. A neurode is activated by the update procedure.

Neuron   Nerve cell composed of a body, an axon, and dendrites. The fundamental unit of neural activity in biological systems. In artificial neural networks, the neuron is modeled by a processing element and connection weights.

Normalization of vectors   Adjustment of vectors so that the values of their components lie within a stipulated range, typically 0 to 1, or -1 to 1. In self-organizing networks, vectors are normalized to unit length. See Euclidean normalization.

Normalization of weights   Normalization of weight vectors so that they have unit length. Necessary in self-organizing networks in which weight vectors are compared with input vectors. See Euclidean normalization.

Output layer   Layer of neurodes sending output signals out of the system. These may be either motor signals or signals sent to other systems external to the system being modeled.

Output vector   Set of activation values of a layer.

Parallel distributed processing   Processing paradigm used in neural networks. Refers to the way in which neural networks are composed of many neurodes operating in parallel. Also indicates that computation and information storage is distributed across many neurodes.

Pattern   (Input vector)

Perceptron   Simple network developed by Rosenblatt, consisting of an input layer connected to a single neurode. The activation function of this unit is a linear threshold function applied to the inner product of the input and weight vectors.

Perceptron convergence procedure   Learning rule for a perceptron.

Presentation of a pattern   Set the state of the input layer by applying an input (pattern) vector.

Processing element   (Neurode)

Processing unit   (Neurode)

Recurrent network   Feedback network in which the current activation state is a function of the previous activation state as well as the current inputs.

Response   (Output vector)

Self-organization   Unsupervised learning neural network. Adjusts its weights to reflect the probability distribution of features that are found in the input patterns.

Sigmoid function   Nonlinear activation function whose output is a nondecreasing and differentiable function of the input with maximum and minimum saturation values.

Slab   Group of one or more neurodes sharing the same activation function and learning rule and having equivalent connection topologies. A network composed of slabs allows arbitrary connections among slabs with no implied hierarchical ordering. A slab can be used to model any network topology.

Squashing function   Function whose value is always between finite limits, even when the input is unbounded.

Sum-squared error   Measure of total error of a network for a given set of input target pairs.

Supervised learning   Learning procedure in which a network is presented with a set of input pattern target pairs. The network compares its output to the target and adapts itself according to the learning rules.

Synapse   Contact point between neurons in which the dendrites of several neurons are attached to an axon through the synaptic cleft.

Synaptic weight   (Weight)

Target   Desired output of a network corresponding to a given input pattern. See Supervised learning.

Threshold   Function whose output is one of two possible levels; the first level when the input is below a certain value (threshold), and the second level when the input is above the value.

Topology preserving map   Neural network representation that preserves topological features of the environment such that the weight vectors are distributed to resemble the distribution of the input vectors.

Training   (Learning)

Unit   (Neurode)

Unsupervised learning   Learning procedure in which a network is presented with a set of input patterns. The network adapts itself according to the statistical associations in the input patterns.

Update procedure   Timing of the application of the activation functions of elements in the network. The update procedure can be synchronous, in which case all activation values are determined simultaneously, or asynchronous, in which case units are updated at random. In hierarchical networks, there can be more elaborate update procedures in which units in some layers are not activated until other layers have been sufficiently trained.

Weight   (Connection strength)

Weight vector   Set of weights for the inputs of a neurode. The dimension (number of components) of the weight vector is given by the fan-in of the neurode but can also include an additional component for the bias.

Widrow–Hoff rule   Learning rule in which change of weight is proportional to the difference between the actual activation and the desired activation. The rule leads to minimization of mean-squared error.

REFERENCES

1. E. L. House and B. Pansky, "A Functional Approach to Neural Anatomy." McGraw-Hill, New York, 1967.
2. D. E. Rumelhart and J. L. McClelland, "Parallel Distributed Processing, Explorations in the Microstructure of Cognition, Vol. 1: Foundations." MIT Press, Cambridge, MA, 1986.
3. D. Stubbs, Neurocomputers. M. D. Computing, 5(3): 14–24 (1988).
4. J. L. McClelland and D. E. Rumelhart, "Parallel Distributed Processing, Explorations in the Microstructure of Cognition, Vol. 2: Psychological and Biological Models." MIT Press, Cambridge, MA, 1986.
5. J. L. McClelland and D. E. Rumelhart, "Explorations in Parallel Distributed Processing, A Handbook of Models, Programs, and Exercises." MIT Press, Cambridge, MA, 1986.
6. J. A. Anderson and E. Rosenfeld, Eds., "Neurocomputing: Foundations of Research." MIT Press, Cambridge, MA, 1988.
7. W. James, "Psychology (Briefer Course)." Holt, New York, 1890.
8. W. C. McCulloch and W. Pitts, A logical calculus of the ideas immanent in nervous activity. Bulletin of Mathematical Biophysics, 5:115–133 (1943).
9. R. C. Eberhart, R. W. Dobbins, and W. R. S. Webber, CaseNet: A neural network tool for EEG waveform classification. Proc. IEEE Symposium on Computer Based Medical Systems, Minneapolis, MN, 60–68 (1989).
10. J. D. Cowan and D. H. Sharp, Neural nets and artificial intelligence. Daedalus, 117(1): 85–121 (1988).
11. D. O. Hebb, "The Organization of Behavior." John Wiley, New York, 1949.
12. F. Rosenblatt, The perceptron: a probabilistic model for information storage and organization in the brain. Psychological Review, 65:386–408 (1958).
13. B. Widrow and M. E. Hoff, Adaptive switching circuits. 1960 IRE WESCON Convention Record: Part 4, Computers: Man-Machine Systems, Los Angeles, 96–104 (1960).
14. W. R. S. Webber, "JHH EMU Spike Viewer Manual." The Johns Hopkins Hospital Neurology Department, Baltimore, MD, 1988.
15. W. R. S. Webber, "JHH EMU View Spike Reference Manual." The Johns Hopkins Hospital Neurology Department, Baltimore, MD, 1988.
16. M. Minsky and S. Papert, "Perceptrons." MIT Press, Cambridge, MA, 1969.
17. S. Papert, One AI or many? Daedalus, 117(1): 1–14 (1988).
18. R. M. Stern, W. J. Ray, and C. M. Davis, "Psychophysiological Recording." Oxford University Press, New York, 1980.
19. T. Kohonen, Correlation matrix memories. IEEE Transactions on Computers, C-21(4): 353–359 (1972).
20. J. A. Anderson, A simple neural network generating on interactive memory. Mathematical Biosciences, 14:197–220 (1972).
21. S. A. Grossberg, "Neural Networks and Natural Intelligence." MIT Press, Cambridge, MA, 1988.
22. T. Kohonen, "Self-Organization and Associative Memory." Springer-Verlag, New York, 1988.
23. S. A. Grossberg, "Studies of Mind and Brain." Reidel Press, Dordrecht, Holland, 1982.
24. S. A. Grossberg, Contour enhancement, short term memory, and constancies in reverberating neural networks. Studies in Applied Mathematics, 52(3): 213–257 (1973).
25. M. Caudill, Neural networks primer: part VIII. AI Expert, 61–67 (August, 1989).

26. M. Caudill, personal communication. August 2, 1989.

27. G. A. Carpenter and S. A. Grossberg, ART2: self-organization of stable category recognition codes for analog input patterns. *Applied Optics,* **26**(23): 4919–4930 (1987).

28. K. Fukushima, Neocognitron: a self-organizing neural network model for a mechanism of pattern recognition unaffected by shift in position. *Biol. Cybernetics,* **36**:193–202 (1980).

29. K. Fukushima and S. Miyake, Neocognitron: a new algorithm for pattern recognition tolerant of deformations and shifts in position. *Pattern Recognition,* **15**:455–469 (1982).

30. K. Fukushima, S. Miyake, and T. Ito, Neocognitron: a neural network model for a mechanism of visual pattern recognition. *IEEE Transactions on Systems, Man and Cybernetics,* **SMC-13**:826–834 (1983).

31. K. Fukushima, a neural network model for selective attention in visual pattern recognition. *Biol. Cybernetics,* **55**:5–15 (1986).

32. J. J. Hopfield, Neural networks and physical systems with emergent collective computational abilities. *Proc. Natl. Acad. Sci.,* **79**:2554–2558 (1982).

33. J. J. Hopfield, Neurons with graded response have collective computational properties like those of two-state neurons. *Proc. Natl. Acad. Sci.,* **81**:3088–3092 (1984).

34. D. E. Rumelhart, G. E. Hinton, and R. J. Williams, Learning representations by back-propagating errors. *Nature* **323**(9): 533–536 (1986).

35. K. Saito and R. Nakano, Medical diagnostic expert system based on PDP model. *Proc. IEEE Intl. Conf. on Neural Networks,* San Diego, **I**:255–262 (1988).

36. C. Stanfill and B. Kahle, Parallel free-text search on the connection machine system. *CACM,* **29**(12): 1229–1239 (1986).

37. T. Kohonen, Tutorial on self-organizing feature maps. *Intl. Joint Conf. on Neural Networks,* Washington, D.C. (1989).

38. D. G. Lee, Jr., Preliminary results of applying neural networks to ship image recognition. *Proc. Int'l. Joint Conf. on Neural Networks,* Washington, D.C., **II**:576 (1989).

39. M. Caudill, Neural networks primer, part IV. *AI Expert,* 61–67 (August 1988).

40. M. Caudill, "Naturally Intelligent Systems." MIT Press, Cambridge, MA, 1989.

41. C. Mead, "Analog VLSI and Neural Systems." Addison Wesley, Reading, MA, 1989.

42. K. P. Adlassnig and W. Scheithauer, Performance evaluation of medical expert systems using ROC curves. *Computers and Biomedical Research,* **22**:297–313 (1989).

43. M. L. Meistrell and K. A. Spackman, Evaluation of neural network performance by receiver operating characteristic analysis: examples from the biotechnology domain. *Proc. 13th Ann. Symp. on Computer Applications in Medical Care,* Washington, D.C. 295–301 (1989).

44. J. A. Swets, Measuring the accuracy of diagnostic systems. *Science,* **240**:1285–1293 (1988).

45. R. M. Centor and G. E. Keightley, Receiver operating characteristics (ROC) curve area analysis using the ROC analyzer. *Proc. 13th Ann. Symp. on Computer Applications in Medical Care,* Washington, D.C. 222–226 (1989).

46. D. M. Green and J. A. Swets, "Signal Detection Theory and Psychophysics." John Wiley and Sons, New York, NY, 1966.

47. J. A. Swets, Ed., "Signal Detection and Recognition by Human Observers." John Wiley and Sons, New York, NY, 1964.

48. J. A. Hanley and B. J. McNeil, The meaning and use of the area under a receiver operating characteristic (ROC) curve. *Radiology,* **143**:29–36 (1982).

49. J. A. Hanley and B. J. McNeil, A method of comparing the areas under receiving operating characteristic curves derived from the same cases. *Radiology,* **148**:839–843 (1983).

50. D. K. McClish, Comparing the areas under more than two independent ROC curves. *Med. Decis. Making*, **7**:149–155 (1987).
51. J. T. Roscoe, "Fundamental Research Statistics for the Behavioral Sciences." Holt, Rinehart and Winston, Inc., New York, NY, 1969.
52. W. F. Allman, "Inside the Neural Network Revolution." Bantam Books, New York, NY, 1989.
53. F. J. Pineda, Dynamics and architecture for neural computation. *Jour. of Complexity*, **4**:216–245 (1988).
54. B. Gaines, An overview of knowledge acquisition and transfer. *Intl. Journ. of Man-Machine Studies*, **26**:453–472 (1987).
55. G. Bradshaw, R. Fozzard, and L. Ceci, A connectionist expert system that really works. *Proc. Neural Information Processing Systems Conference*, Denver, CO, 248–255 (1988).
56. D. G. Loy, Preface to the special issue on parallel distributed processing and neural networks. *Computer Music Journal*, **13**(3): 24–27 (1989).
57. D. C. Park, M. El-Sharkawi, R. J. Marks II, L. E. Atlas, and M. Damborg, Electric load forecasting using an artificial neural network. *Proc. PES Winter Meeting*, in press.
58. P. Todd, A sequential network design for musical applications. *Proceedings of the 1988 Connectionist Models Summer School*, Morgan Kaufmann Publishers, San Mateo, CA 76–84 (1989).
59. T. Kohonen, A self-learning musical grammar, or associative memory of the second kind. *Proc. Int'l. Joint Conf. on Neural Networks*, Washington, D.C., **I**:1–5 (1989).
60. M. I. Jordan, Serial order: a parallel distributed processing approach. Technical Report 8604, Institute for Cognitive Science, University of California, San Diego (1986).
61. M. Dolson, Machine tongues XII: neural networks. *Computer Music Journal*, **13**(3): 28–40 (1989).
62. J. L. Elman, Finding structure in time. Technical Report 8801, Center for Research in Language, University of California, San Diego (1988).
63. M. O. Duff, Backpropagation and Bach's 5th Cello Suite (Sarabande). *Proc. Int'l. Joint Conf. on Neural Networks*, Washington, D.C. (1989).
64. I. Xenakis, "Formalized Music." Indiana University Press, Indianapolis, IN, 1971.
65. R. B. Allen, Using verbs and remembering the order of events. *Proc. Int'l. Joint Conf. on Neural Networks*, Washington, D.C., **I**:210–213 (1990).
66. S. De Furia and J. Scacciaferro, "MIDI Programmer's Handbook." M & T Books, Redwood City, CA, 1989.
67. J. Conger, "MIDI Sequencing in C." M & T Books, Redwood City, CA, 1989.
68. J. Conger, "C Programming for MIDI." M & T Books, Redwood City, CA, 1988.
69. R. B. Dannenberg, The CMU MIDI toolkit manual. Center for Art and Technology, Carnegie Mellon University, Pittsburgh, PA (1988).
70. L. Sterling and E. Shapiro, "The Art of Prolog." MIT Press, Cambridge, MA, 1986.
71. R. Hawley (Ed), "Artificial Intelligence Programming Environments." Ellis Horwood, 1987.
72. P. T. Ward and S. J. Mellor, "Structured Development for Real-Time Systems." Yourdon Press, New York, NY, 1985.
73. S. Shlaer and S. J. Mellor, "Object-oriented Systems Analysis." Yourdon Press, New York, NY, 1988.
74. W. Bright, Secrets of compiler optimization. *Microcornucopia*, 26–33, Jan–Feb 1989.
75. B. W. Kernighan and D. M. Ritchie, "The C Programming Language." Prentice-Hall, Englewood Cliffs, NJ, 1978.
76. R. Eckmiller and C.vd Malsburg, "Neural computers." Springer-Verlag, New York, 1988.

77. G. Korn, A new environment for interactive neural network experiments. *Neural Networks*, **2**, 229–237 (1989).

78. C. Lynne, et al., A general purpose simulation environment for developing connectionist models. *Simulation*, **51**(1) July 1988, 5–19.

79. A. S. Fisher, "CASE: Using Software development Tools." John Wiley and Sons, New York, NY, 1988.

80. Ashton-Tate: Programming with dBASE III Plus.

81. Nantucket Corporation: Clipper, Summer 1987.

82. Borland International: Turbo-Prolog and Turbo-C user guides.

83. cadSys Software Tools: cadSYS User's Guide, 1989.

84. Microsoft Corporation: Microsoft C and MS-DOS.

85. T. DeMarco, "Structured Analysis and System Specification." Yourdon Press, New York, NY, 1978.

86. D. J. Hatley and I. A. Phirbhai, "Strategies for Real Time System Specification." Dorset House, 1987.

87. A. M. Davis, The design of a family of application oriented requirements languages. *IEEE Computer*, 21–28 (May 1982).

88. U. Leibrandt and P. Schnupp, An evaluation of prolog as a prototyping system. In R. Budde et al. (Eds.), "Approaches to Prototyping." Springer-Verlag, New York, 1984.

89. R. Venken and M. Bruynooghe, Prolog as a language for prototyping of information systems. In R. Budde et al. (Eds.), "Approaches to Prototyping." Springer-Verlag, New York, 1984.

90. G. Tate and T. W. Docker, A rapid prototyping system based on data flow principles. *ACM SIGSOFT SEN-10*, **2**, 28–34 (April 1985).

91. A. McGettrick and Gehani (Eds.), "Software Specification Techniques." Addison-Wesley, Reading, MA.

92. G. L. Heileman, H. K. Brown, and M. Georgiopolous, Simulation of artificial neural network models using an object-oriented software paradigm. *International Joint Conference on Neural Networks*, Washington D.C., 1990.

93. R. J. Teweles and F. J. Jones. "The Futures Game," 2d ed. McGraw-Hill, Inc., New York, NY, 1987.

94. R. E. Hadady, "Contrary Opinion—How to Use It For Profit in Trading Commodity Futures." Hadady Publications, Inc., Pasadena, CA, 1983.

95. P. J. Kaufman, "The New Commodity Trading Systems and Methods." John Wiley & Sons, Inc., New York, NY, 1987.

96. R. E. Hadady, I. L. Finberg, and D. Rahfeldt, "Winning With the Insiders." Weiss Research, Inc., West Palm Beach, FL, 1987.

97. R. E. Band, "Contrary Investing." Viking Penguin, Inc., New York, NY, 1986.

98. L. G. McMillan, "Options as a Strategic Investment." Simon & Schuster, Inc., New York, NY, 1986.

99. T. J. Sejnowski and C. R. Rosenberg, NETtalk: a parallel network that learns to read aloud, Technical report JHU/EECS-86/01. The Johns Hopkins University, Electrical Engineering and Computer Science, 1986.

100. D. Cobb, J. Mynhier, and S. Cobb, "EXCEL in Business." Microsoft Corp., Redmond, WA, 1985.

101. S. Ahmad and G. Tesuro, Scaling and generalization in neural networks: a case study. *In* "Proceedings of the 1988 Connectionist Models Summer School," D. S. Touretzky, G. E. Hinton, and T. J. Sejnowski (Eds.). Morgan Kaufman, San Mateo, CA, 1989.

102. R. Hecht-Nielsen, Theory of the backpropagation neural network. *In* "Proceedings of the 1989 International Joint Conference on Neural Networks." IEEE Service Center, Piscataway, NJ, 1989.

103. P. J. B. Hancock, Data representation in neural nets: an empirical study. *In* Proceedings of the 1988 Connectionist Models Summer School," D. S Touretzky, G. E. Hinton, and T. J. Sejnowski (Eds.). Morgan Kaufman, San Mateo, CA, 1989.

104. S. Becker and Y. le Cun, Improving the Convergence of Back-Propagation Learning with Second Order Methods. *In* "Proceedings of the 1988 Connectionist Models Summer School," D. S. Touretzky, G. E. Hinton, and T. J. Sejnowski (Eds.). Morgan Kaufman, San Mateo, CA, 1989.

105. S. E. Fahlman, Faster learning variations on back-propagation: an empirical study. *In* "Proceedings of the 1988 Connectionist Models Summer School," D. S. Touretzky, G. E. Hinton, and T. J. Sejnowski (Eds.). Morgan Kaufman, San Mateo, CA, 1989.

106. R. P. Gorman and T. J. Sejnowski, Analysis of hidden units in a layered network trained to classify sonar targets. *Neural Networks*, 1:75−89 (1988).

107. R. P. Gorman and T. J. Sejnowski, Learned classification of sonar targets using a massively parallel network. *IEEE Trans. on Acoustics, Speech and Signal Processing*, 36:1135−1140 (1988).

108. J. B. Boone, V. G. Sigillito, and G. S. Shaber, Signal detection capabilities of neural networks: radiology applications. *Medical Physics*, in press.

109. A. Lapedes and R. Farber, Nonlinear signal processing using neural networks: prediction and system modeling, LA-UR-87-2662. Los Alamos National Laboratory, Los Alamos, NM, 1987.

110. R. D. Lippmann, An introduction to computing with neural nets. *IEEE ASSP*, 4:22 (1987).

111. A. D. M. Walker, R. A. Greenwald, and K. B. Baker, Determination of the fluctuation level of ionospheric irregularities from radar backscatter measurements. *Radio Sci.*, 22:689−705 (1987).

112. R. A. Greenwald, K. B. Baker, R. A. Hutchins, and C. Hanuise, An HF phased array radar for studying small-scale structure in the high latitude ionosphere. *Radio Sci.*, 20:63−79 (1985).

113. K. B. Baker, R. A. Greenwald, J. P. Villain, and S. P. Wing, Spectral characteristics of high frequency backscatter from high latitude ionospheric irregularities: A statistical survey, Tech. Report to Rome Air Development Center, RADC-TR-87-284 (1987).

114. M. Pelczarski, System review: Microsoft softcard. *Byte*, 6(11): 152−162 (1981).

115. Inmos Limited, "The Transputer Reference Manual." Prentice Hall, London, 1988.

116. Phil Atkin, Performance Maximisation, Technical Note 17. Inmos-SGS Thomson, Bristol, UK, March 1987.

117. Inmos Ltd., Some issues in scientific language application porting and farming using transputers. *In* "The Transputer Development and Systems Databook," Inmos Ltd., 1989.

118. D. A. Pomerleau, G. L. Gusciora, D. S. Touretzky, and H. T. Kung, Neural network simulation at warp speed: How we got 17 million connections per second. *Proc. IEEE Intl. Conf. on Neural Networks*, San Diego, II:143−150 (1988).

119. M. W. H. Chang and F. Fallside, Implementation of neural networks for speech recognition on a transputer array, Technical Report CUED/F-INFENG/TR8. Cambridge University, Cambridge, UK, March 1988.

120. T. Beynon, A parallel implementation of the back-propagation algorithm on a network of transputers, Research Initiative in Pattern Recognition, Royal Signals and Radar Establishment, Malvern, UK. Poster paper, IEEE International Conference on Neural Networks, 1988.

121. E. Di Zitti, D. D. Caviglia, G. M. Bisio, and G. Parodi, Neural networks on a transputer array. *Proc. Int'l. Conf. on Acoustics, Speech, and Signal Processing*, 2513−2516 (1989).

122. F. Abbruzzese, A transputer implementation of a McCulloch and Pitts network. In "Parallel Processing and Applications," E. Chiricozzi and A. D'Amico (Eds.). North-Holland, New York, NY 1988, pp. 135–140.

123. J. A. Board, Jr., and J. S. J. Lu, Performance of parallel neural network simulations. In "Proceedings of the Second Conference of the North American Transputer Users Group," J. A. Board, Jr. (Ed.)., North American Transputer Users Group, Durham, NC, 1989, pp. 185–200.

124. D. G. Lee, Jr., Preliminary results of applying neural networks to ship image recognition. Proc. Intl. Joint Conf. on Neural Networks, Washington, D.C., II:576 (1989).

125. D. E. Rumelhart, G. E. Hinton, and R. J. Williams, Learning internal representations by error propagation. In "Parallel Distributed Processing, Volume 1: Foundations," Rumelhart and McClelland (Eds.). MIT Press, Cambridge, MA, 1986, pp. 318–362.

126. H. C. Leung and V. W. Zue, "Applications of error back-propagation to phonetic classification. In "Proceedings of the Neural Information Processing Systems—Natural and Synthetic Conference," D. S. Touretzky (Ed.). Morgan-Kaufman, San Mateo, CA, 1989.

127. Donald A. Waterman, "A Guide to Expert Systems." Addison-Wesley, Reading, MA, 1986.

128. Frederick Hayes-Roth, Donald A. Waterman, and Douglas B. Lenat, Eds., "Building Expert Systems." Addison-Wesley, Reading, MA, 1983.

129. Peter Jackson, "Introduction to Expert Systems." Addison-Wesley, Reading, MA, 1986.

130. Bruce G. Buchanan and Edward H. Shortliffe, "Rule-Based Expert Systems: The MYCIN Experiments of the Stanford Heuristic Programming Project." Addison-Wesley, Reading, MA, 1984.

131. William B. Gevarter, Expert systems: Limited but powerful. In "Applications of AI," Stephen J. Andriole (Ed.). Petrocelli Books, Princeton, NJ, 1985, pp. 125–139.

132. Constantin Virgil Negoita, "Expert Systems and Fuzzy Systems." Benjamin Cummings, Menlo Park, CA, 1985.

133. Abraham Kandel, "Fuzzy Mathematical Techniques with Applications." Addison-Wesley, Reading, MA, 1986.

134. M. A. Styblinski and B. D. Meyer, Fuzzy cognitive maps, signal flow graphs, and qualitative circuit analysis. Proc. IEEE Intl. Conf. on Neural Networks, II:549–556 (1988).

135. Maureen Caudill and Charles Butler, "Naturally Intelligent Systems." MIT Press, Cambridge, MA, 1990.

136. Richard Fozzard, Gary Bradshaw, and Louis Ceci, A connectionist expert system that actually works. In "Advances in Neural Information Processing Systems 1," David Touretzky, (Ed.). Morgan-Kaufman, San Mateo, CA, 1989, pp. 248–255.

137. D. G. Bounds, P. J. Lloyd, B. Mathew, and G. Waddell, A multilayer perceptron network for the diagnosis of low back pain. Proc. IEEE Intl. Conf. on Neural Networks, II:481–490 (1988).

138. E. Collins, S. Ghosh, and C. L. Scofield, An application of multiple neural network learning system to emulation of mortgage underwriter judgements. Proc. IEEE Intl. Conf. on Neural Networks, II:459–466 (1988).

139. Rodney M. Goodman, John W. Miller, and Padhraic Smyth, An information theoretic approach to rule-based connectionist expert systems. In "Advances in Neural Information Processing Systems 1," David Touretzky (Ed.). Morgan Kaufman, San Mateo, CA, 1989, pp. 256–263.

140. R. Paul Gorman and Terrence J. Sejnowski, Analysis of hidden units in a layered network trained to classify sonar targets. Neural Networks, 1(1): 75–89 (1988).

141. S. Dutta and S. Shekhar, Bond rating: A non-conservative application of neural networks. *Proc. IEEE Intl. Conf. on Neural Networks*, **II**:443–450 (1988).
142. W. E. Dietz, E. L. Kiech, and M. Ali, Jet and rocket engine fault diagnosis in real time. *Journal of Neural Network Computing*, **1**(1), 5–18 (1989).
143. Maureen Caudill, Ed., "Proceedings of the International Joint Conference on Neural Networks, 1990, Washington DC" L. Erlbaum Publishers, 1990. Many papers in the section on Expert Systems and Other Real World Applications, **II**:463–723.
144. T. Samad, Towards connectionist rule-based systems. In *Proc. IEEE Intl. Conf. on Neural Networks*, **II**:525–532 (1988).
145. T. J. Sejnowski and C. R. Rosenberg, A parallel network that learns to pronounce English text. *Complex Systems*, **1**:145–168 (1987).
146. S. R. Lehky and T. J. Sejnowski, Network model of shape-from-shading: neural function arises from both receptive and projective fields. *Nature*, **333**(6172): 452–454 (1988).
147. S. C. Johnson, Hierarchical clustering schemes. *Psychometrika*, **32**:241–253 (1967).
148. P. B. Andreassen, Market Psychology—economic variables not the only factors in stock price shifts. The Sun Newspaper, November 1, 1987, Baltimore, MD.

APPENDIX A

```
1        /* batchnet.c
2
3            Generic back-propagation neural network
4
5            Copyright (c)  1988, 1989  R.W.Dobbins and R.C.Eberhart
6            All Rights Reserved
7
8            *** SHAREWARE ***
9            You may distribute unmodified copies of the diskette or software.
10           If you find the software of value, please send $20 or any amount,
11           to :-
12                       R. W. Dobbins
13                       5833 Humblebee Road
14                       Columbia, MD, 21045
15                       Tel. (301) 740-5325
16
17           Your support is greatly appreciated.
18           $Revision:   1.2  $              $Date:    02 Jan 1990 14:29:04  $
19       */
20
21       #include <stdio.h>
22       #include <stdlib.h>
23       #include <math.h>
24       #include <conio.h>
25       #include <ctype.h>
26       #include <string.h>
27
28       #define    ESC          27
29       #define    ERRORLEVEL   0.02
30       #define    ITEMS        8
31
32       /* typedefs and prototypes for dynamic storage of arrays */
33       typedef float *PFLOAT;
34       typedef PFLOAT VECTOR;
35       typedef PFLOAT *MATRIX;
36
37       void   VectorAllocate(VECTOR *vector, int nCols);
38       void   AllocateCols(PFLOAT matrix[], int nRows, int nCols);
39       void   MatrixAllocate(MATRIX *pmatrix, int nRows, int nCols);
40       void   MatrixFree(MATRIX matrix,  int nRows);
41
42       /* define storage for net layers */
43       /* Arrays for inputs, outputs, deltas, weights & targets */
44       MATRIX   out0;          /* input layer  */
45       MATRIX   out1;          /* hidden layer */
46       MATRIX   delta1;        /* delta at hidden layer  */
47       MATRIX   delw1;         /* change in weights input:hidden */
48       MATRIX   w1;            /* weights input:hidden */
49       MATRIX   out2;          /* output layer */
50       MATRIX   delta2;        /* delta at output layer  */
51       MATRIX   delw2;         /* change in weights hidden:output */
52       MATRIX   w2;            /* weights hidden:output */
53       MATRIX   target;        /* target output */
54       VECTOR   PatternID;     /* identifier for each stored pattern */
55
56       void  main(int argc, char *argv[])
57       {
58           float eta   = 0.15,         /* default learning rate           */
```

```
59                 alpha = 0.075;        /* default momentum factor           */
60        int    nReportErrors = 100;    /* error reporting frequency         */
61        float  ErrorLevel = ERRORLEVEL; /* satisfactory error level         */
62        char   MonitorError = 0;       /* true when monitor error display   */
63        float  error;                  /* latest sum squared error value    */
64        register int   h;              /* index hidden layer                */
65        register int   i;              /* index input layer                 */
66        register int   j;              /* index output layer                */
67        int    p,                      /* index pattern number              */
68               q,                      /* index iteration number            */
69               r,                      /* index run number                  */
70               nPatterns,              /* number of patterns desired        */
71               nInputNodes,            /* number of input nodes             */
72               nHiddenNodes,           /* number of hidden nodes            */
73               nOutputNodes,           /* number of output nodes            */
74               nIterations,            /* number of iterations desired      */
75               nRuns;                  /* number of runs (or input lines)   */
76        FILE   *fpRun,                 /* run file                          */
77               *fpPattern,             /* source pattern input file         */
78               *fpWeights,             /* initial weight file               */
79               *fpWeightsOut,          /* final weight output file          */
80               *fpResults,             /* results output file               */
81               *fpError;               /* error output file                 */
82        char   szResults[66];          /* various filenames (pathnames)     */
83        char   szError[66];
84        char   szPattern[66];
85        char   szWeights[66];
86        char   szWeightsOut[66];
87        char   *progname = *argv; /* name of executable DOS 3.x only  */
88
89        /* read optional - arguments */
90        for (; argc > 1; argc--)
91        {
92            char *arg = *++argv;
93
94            if (*arg != '-')
95                break;
96
97            switch (*++arg)
98            {
99                case 'e': sscanf(++arg, "%d", &nReportErrors);  break;
100               case 'd': sscanf(++arg, "%f", &ErrorLevel);     break;
101               default:  break;
102           }
103       }
104
105       if (argc < 2)
106       {
107           fprintf(stderr, "Usage:  %s {-en -df} runfilename\n",  progname);
108           fprintf(stderr, "  -en  =>  report error every n iterations\n");
109           fprintf(stderr, "  -df  =>  done if mean squared error < f\n");
110           exit(1);
111       }
112
113       /* Open run file for reading */
114       if ((fpRun = fopen(*argv, "r"))  ==   NULL)
115       {
116           fprintf(stderr, "%s: can't open file %s\n", progname, *argv);
117           exit(1);
118       }
119
120       /* Read first line: no. of runs (lines to read from run file) */
121       fscanf(fpRun,  "%d", &nRuns);
122
```

```
123        /*------------ beginning of work loop ------------------------*/
124        for (r = 0;    r < nRuns;    r++)
125        {
126            /* read and parse the run specification line; */
127            fscanf(fpRun,
128                "%s %s %s %s %s %d %d %d %d %d %f %f",
129                szResults,            /* output results file */
130                szError,              /* error output file */
131                szPattern,            /* pattern input file */
132                szWeights,            /* initial weights file */
133                szWeightsOut,         /* final weights output file */
134                &nPatterns,           /* number of patterns to learn */
135                &nIterations,         /* number of iterations through the data */
136                &nInputNodes,         /* number of input nodes */
137                &nHiddenNodes,        /* number of hidden nodes */
138                &nOutputNodes,        /* number of output nodes */
139                &eta,                 /* learning rate */
140                &alpha);              /* momentum factor */
141
142            /*----------allocate dynamic storage for all data ---------------*/
143            MatrixAllocate(&out0,      nPatterns,    nInputNodes);
144            MatrixAllocate(&out1,      nPatterns,    nHiddenNodes);
145            MatrixAllocate(&out2,      nPatterns,    nOutputNodes);
146            MatrixAllocate(&delta2,    nPatterns,    nOutputNodes);
147            MatrixAllocate(&delw2,     nOutputNodes, nHiddenNodes + 1);
148            MatrixAllocate(&w2,        nOutputNodes, nHiddenNodes + 1);
149            MatrixAllocate(&delta1,    nPatterns,    nHiddenNodes);
150            MatrixAllocate(&delw1,     nHiddenNodes, nInputNodes + 1);
151            MatrixAllocate(&w1,        nHiddenNodes, nInputNodes + 1);
152            MatrixAllocate(&target,    nPatterns,    nOutputNodes);
153            VectorAllocate(&PatternID, nPatterns);
154
155            /*--------- Read the initial weight matrices: ------------------*/
156            if ((fpWeights = fopen(szWeights,"r"))  == NULL)
157            {
158                fprintf(stderr, "%s: can't open file %s\n", progname, szWeights);
159                exit(1);
160            }
161
162            /* read input:hidden weights */
163            for (h = 0;  h < nHiddenNodes;  h++)
164                for (i = 0;  i <= nInputNodes;  i++)
165                {
166                    fscanf(fpWeights,  "%f",        &w1[h][i]);
167                    delw1[h][i] = 0.0;
168                }
169
170            /* read hidden:out weights */
171            for (j = 0;  j < nOutputNodes;  j++)
172                for (h = 0;  h <= nHiddenNodes;  h++)
173                {
174                    fscanf(fpWeights,  "%f",        &w2[j][h]);
175                    delw2[j][h] = 0.0;
176                }
177
178            fclose(fpWeights);
179
180            /*------------ Read in all patterns to be learned:---------------*/
181            if ((fpPattern = fopen(szPattern, "r"))  == NULL)
182            {
183                fprintf(stderr, "%s: can't open file %s\n", progname, szPattern);
184                exit(1);
185            }
186
```

```
187          for (p = 0;  p < nPatterns;  p++)
188          {
189             for (i = 0;   i < nInputNodes;   i++)
190                if (fscanf(fpPattern,  "%f",   &out0[p][i])  != 1)
191                   goto  ALLPATTERNSREAD;
192
193
194             /* read in target outputs for input patterns read */
195             for (j = 0;  j < nOutputNodes;  j++)
196                fscanf(fpPattern,  "%f",   &target[p][j]);
197
198             /* read in identifier for each pattern */
199             fscanf(fpPattern,  "%f ",   &PatternID[p]);
200          }
201
202          ALLPATTERNSREAD:
203          fclose(fpPattern);
204
205          if (p < nPatterns)
206          {
207             fprintf(stderr, "%s:  %d out of %d patterns read\n",
208                     progname,  p,  nPatterns);
209             nPatterns = p;
210          }
211
212          /* open error output file */
213          if ((fpError = fopen(szError, "w"))  ==  NULL)
214          {
215             fprintf(stderr,  "%s: can't open file %s\n",  progname, szError);
216             exit(1);
217          }
218
219          fprintf(stderr, nIterations > 1  ?  "Training...\n" : "Testing\n");
220
221          /*-------------- begin iteration loop -----------------------*/
222          for (q = 0;  q < nIterations;  q++)
223          {
224             for (p = 0;  p < nPatterns;  p++)
225             {
226                /*-------------- hidden layer -------------------------*/
227                /* Sum input to hidden layer over all
228                   input-weight combinations */
229                for (h = 0;  h < nHiddenNodes;  h++)
230                {
231                   float sum = w1[h][nInputNodes];  /* begin with bias  */
232
233                   for (i = 0;  i < nInputNodes;  i++)
234                      sum   +=   w1[h][i]  *  out0[p][i];
235
236                   /* Compute output (use sigmoid) */
237                   out1[p][h]  =  1.0  /  (1.0 +  exp(-sum));
238                }
239
240                /*-------------- output layer -------------------------*/
241                for (j = 0;  j < nOutputNodes;  j++)
242                {
243                   float  sum = w2[j][nHiddenNodes];
244
245                   for (h = 0;  h < nHiddenNodes;  h++)
246                      sum  +=  w2[j][h]  *  out1[p][h];
247
248                   out2[p][j]  =  1.0  /  (1.0 +  exp(-sum));
249                }
250
```

```
251                     /*------------- delta output --------------------------*/
252                     /* Compute deltas for each output unit for a given pattern */
253                     for (j = 0;  j < nOutputNodes;  j++)
254                         delta2[p][j]  =  (target[p][j] - out2[p][j])  *
255                                          out2[p][j]  *  (1.0 - out2[p][j]);
256
257
258                     /*------------- delta hidden --------------------------*/
259                     for (h = 0;  h < nHiddenNodes;  h++)
260                     {
261                         float  sum = 0.0;
262
263                         for (j = 0;  j < nOutputNodes;  j++)
264                             sum  +=  delta2[p][j] * w2[j][h];
265
266                         delta1[p][h]  =  sum  *  out1[p][h]  *  (1.0 - out1[p][h]);
267                     }
268                 }
269
270                 /*-------- adapt weights hidden:output --------------------*/
271                 for (j = 0;  j < nOutputNodes;  j++)
272                 {
273                     float  dw;                        /* delta weight */
274                     float  sum = 0.0;
275
276                     /* grand sum of deltas for each output node for one epoch */
277                     for (p = 0;  p < nPatterns;  p++)
278                         sum  +=  delta2[p][j];
279
280                     /* Calculate new bias weight for each output unit */
281                     dw  =  eta * sum  +  alpha * delw2[j][nHiddenNodes];
282                     w2[j][nHiddenNodes]  +=  dw;
283                     delw2[j][nHiddenNodes] =  dw;          /* delta for bias */
284
285                     /* Calculate new weights */
286                     for (h = 0;  h < nHiddenNodes;  h++)
287                     {
288                         float  sum = 0.0;
289
290                         for (p = 0;  p < nPatterns;  p++)
291                             sum  +=  delta2[p][j] * out1[p][h];
292
293                         dw            =  eta * sum  +  alpha * delw2[j][h];
294                         w2[j][h]      +=  dw;
295                         delw2[j][h]   =  dw;
296                     }
297                 }
298
299                 /*------------- adapt weights input:hidden ----------------*/
300                 for (h = 0;  h < nHiddenNodes;  h++)
301                 {
302                     float  dw;                        /* delta weight */
303                     float  sum = 0.0;
304
305                     for (p = 0;  p < nPatterns;  p++)
306                         sum  +=  delta1[p][h];
307
308                     /* Calculate new bias weight for each hidden unit */
309                     dw  =  eta * sum  +  alpha * delw1[h][nInputNodes];
310                     w1[h][nInputNodes]  +=  dw;
311                     delw1[h][nInputNodes] =  dw;
312
313                     /* Calculate new weights */
314                     for (i = 0;  i < nInputNodes;  i++)
```

```
315                     {
316                         float   sum = 0.0;
317
318                         for (p = 0;  p < nPatterns;  p++)
319                             sum  +=  delta1[p][h] * out0[p][i];
320
321                         dw          =   eta * sum  +  alpha * delw1[h][i];
322                         w1[h][i]    +=  dw;
323                         delw1[h][i] =   dw;
324                     }
325                 }
326
327                 /* -------- monitor keyboard requests --------------------*/
328                 if (kbhit())
329                 {
330                     int   c = getch();
331
332                     if ((c = toupper(c))  == 'E')
333                         MonitorError++;
334                     else if (c == ESC)
335                         break;                      /* Terminate gracefully on quit key */
336                 }
337
338                 /*-------------- Sum Squared Error --------------------*/
339                 if (MonitorError || (q % nReportErrors  ==  0))
340                 {
341                     for (p = 0, error = 0.0;  p < nPatterns;  p++)
342                     {
343                         for (j = 0;  j < nOutputNodes;  j++)
344                         {
345                             float  temp  =  target[p][j] - out2[p][j];
346
347                             error += temp * temp;
348                         }
349                     }
350
351                     /* Average error per node over all patterns */
352                     error  /=  (nPatterns * nOutputNodes);
353
354                     /* Print iteration number and  error value */
355                     fprintf(stderr,"Iteration %5d/%-5d  Error %f\r",
356                             q, nIterations, error);              /* to console */
357                     MonitorError = 0;
358
359                     if (q % nReportErrors  ==  0)
360                         fprintf(fpError, "%d  %f\n",  q,  error);  /* to file */
361
362                     /* Terminate when error satisfactory */
363                     if (error < ErrorLevel)
364                         break;
365                 }
366             }
367             /* ---------- end of iteration loop --------------------------*/
368
369             for (p = 0, error = 0.0;  p < nPatterns;  p++)
370             {
371                 for (j = 0;  j < nOutputNodes;  j++)
372                 {
373                     float  temp  =  target[p][j] - out2[p][j];
374
375                     error += temp * temp;
376                 }
377             }
378
```

```
379                /* Average error over all patterns */
380                error /= (nPatterns * nOutputNodes);
381
382                /* Print final iteration number and error value */
383                fprintf(stderr, "Iteration %5d/%-5d  Error %f\n", q, nIterations,
                            error); /* to console */
384                fprintf(fpError, "\n%d  %f\n",  q,  error);            /* to file */
385                fclose(fpError);
386
387                /*---------- print final weights ----------------------------*/
388                if ((fpWeightsOut = fopen(szWeightsOut,"w"))  ==  NULL)
389                {
390                    fprintf(stderr, "%s: can't write file %s\n", progname,
                                szWeightsOut);
391                    exit(1);
392                }
393
394                for (h = 0;  h < nHiddenNodes;  h++)
395                    for (i = 0;  i <= nInputNodes;  i++)
396                        fprintf(fpWeightsOut,  "%g%c", w1[h][i], i%ITEMS==ITEMS-1 ?
                                '\n':' ');
397
398                for (j = 0;  j < nOutputNodes;  j++)
399                    for (h = 0;  h <= nHiddenNodes;  h++)
400                        fprintf(fpWeightsOut,  "%g%c", w2[j][h], j%ITEMS==ITEMS-1 ?
                                '\n':' ');
401
402                fclose(fpWeightsOut);
403
404                /*------------- Print final activation values------------------- */
405                if ((fpResults = fopen(szResults,"w"))  ==  NULL)
406                {
407                    fprintf(stderr, "%s: can't write file %s\n", progname, szResults);
408                    fpResults = stderr;
409                }
410
411                /* Print final output vector */
412                for (p = 0;  p < nPatterns;  p++)
413                {
414                    fprintf(fpResults, "%d   ",  p);
415
416                    for (j = 0;  j < nOutputNodes;  j++)
417                        fprintf(fpResults, " %f",  out2[p][j]);
418
419                    fprintf(fpResults, "  %-6.0f\n", PatternID[p]);
420                }
421
422                fclose(fpResults); '
423
424                /*----------- free dynamic storage for data --------------------*/
425                MatrixFree(out0,        nPatterns);
426                MatrixFree(out1,        nPatterns);
427                MatrixFree(delta1,      nPatterns);
428                MatrixFree(delw1,       nHiddenNodes);
429                MatrixFree(w1,          nHiddenNodes);
430                MatrixFree(out2,        nPatterns);
431                MatrixFree(delta2,      nPatterns);
432                MatrixFree(delw2,       nOutputNodes);
433                MatrixFree(w2,          nOutputNodes);
434                MatrixFree(target,      nPatterns);
435                free(PatternID);
436            }
437
438            fclose(fpRun);                           /* close run file */
```

```
439      }
440
441
442      /*----------- Array storage allocation routines --------------------*/
443      /* Allocate space for vector of float cells for
444         one dimensional dynamic vector[cols]
445      */
446      void VectorAllocate(VECTOR *vector, int nCols)
447      {
448          if ((*vector = (VECTOR) calloc(nCols, sizeof(float))) == NULL)
449          {
450              fprintf(stderr, "Sorry! Not enough memory for nodes\n");
451              exit(1);
452          }
453      }
454
455
456      /* Allocate space for columns (float cells) for
457         dynamic two dimensional matrix[rows][cols]
458      */
459      void AllocateCols(PFLOAT matrix[], int nRows, int nCols)
460      {
461          int i;
462
463          for (i = 0; i < nRows; i++)
464              VectorAllocate(&matrix[i], nCols);
465      }
466
467      /* Allocate space for a two dimensional dynamic matrix [rows] [cols]
468      */
469
470      void MatrixAllocate(MATRIX *pmatrix, int nRows, int nCols)
471      {
472          if ((*pmatrix = (MATRIX) calloc(nRows, sizeof(PFLOAT))) == NULL)
473          {
474              fprintf(stderr, "Sorry! Not enough memory for nodes\n");
475              exit(1);
476          }
477
478          AllocateCols(*pmatrix, nRows, nCols);
479      }
480
481      /* free space for two dimensional dynamic array */
482      void MatrixFree(MATRIX matrix, int nRows)
483      {
484          int i;
485          for (i = 0; i < nRows; i++)
486              free(matrix[i]);
487          free(matrix);
488      }
489
490
491      /* weights.c
492
493         For use with a Neural Network with learnable biases, such as batchnet
494
495         Program invocation on MS-DOS:
496
497         weights seed in hidden out [abs_max_wt]
498
499         Specifying abs_max_wt is optional, default value is 0.3.
500         Output is to stdout; can be redirected to weights.dat
501
502         This program generates random weights to be used in a neural network
```

```
503          which has the number of nodes as specified above.
504      */
505
506      #include <stdio.h>
507      #include <stdlib.h>
508      #define     MAXWEIGHT    ((float)0.3)    /* maximum weight */
509      #define     SCALEWEIGHT  ((float)32767)  /* normalising scale factor */
510      #define     ITEMS        8               /* items printed per line */
511
512      void main(int argc,  char *argv[])
513      {
514          float     scale = SCALEWEIGHT;     /* normalize weights in range +- 1 */
515          float     wmax;                    /* wmax is abs val of max weight */
516          int       i,
517                    j,
518                    nInputNodes,
519                    nHiddenNodes,
520                    nOutputNodes;
521
522          if (argc < 5)                      /* specifying abs_max_wt is optional */
523          {
524              printf("Usage:  weights  seed in hidden out [abs_max_wt]\n");
525              exit(1);
526          }
527
528          srand((unsigned)atoi(argv[1]));    /* parameter is random seed */
529          nInputNodes   = atoi(argv[2]);     /* number of input nodes  */
530          nHiddenNodes  = atoi(argv[3]);     /* number of hidden nodes */
531          nOutputNodes  = atoi(argv[4]);     /* number of output nodes */
532
533          /* set range of initial weights */
534          if ((wmax = atof(argv[5]))  ==  0)
535              wmax = MAXWEIGHT;              /* default value, if not specified */
536
537
538          /* set weights to random number between -wmax and wmax  */
539
540          /* generate initial layer 1 weights, including a learnable bias
541             for each hidden unit */
542          for (i = 0;   i < nHiddenNodes;   i++)
543          {
544              for (j = 0;    j < nInputNodes + 1;   j++)
545              {
546                  float frand =  rand();
547                  float w1    =  wmax * (1.0 - 2 * frand/scale);
548                  printf("%9.6f%c",
549                         w1,
550                         (j%ITEMS == ITEMS-1 || j == nInputNodes) ? '\n' : ' ');
551              }
552          }
553
554          /* generate layer 2 weights with bias, as above */
555          for (i = 0;   i < nOutputNodes;   i++)
556          {
557              for (j = 0;    j < nHiddenNodes + 1;   j++)
558              {
559                  float frand =  rand();
560                  float w2    =  wmax * (1.0 - 2 * frand/scale);
561                  printf("%9.6f%c",
562                         w2,
563                         (j%ITEMS == ITEMS-1 || j == nHiddenNodes) ? '\n' : ' ');
564              }
565          }
566      }
```

```
567
568     ****************************************************************
569     rem   Demonstration of batchnet
570     rem   -e10  saves error value every 10 iterations
571     batchnet -e10 demo.run
572
573     ****************************************************************
574     2
575     train.out train.err train.pat weights.wts train.wts 100 1000 9 4 2 0.15
                                                                            0.075
576     test.out test.err test.pat  train.wts  test.wts  166   1 9 4 2 0.15 0.075
577
578     Format of this run file:
579         number of runs,    followed by:
580         run specification lines
581         ...
582     Format of each run specification line:
583     fOut   fErr   fPat   fWts   fWtso   nPats   nIter   nInp   nHid   nOut   eta   alpha
584
585     Description of parameters:
586         fOut      output nodes file          fErr    error output file
587         fPat      input pattern file         fWts    weight file input
588         fWtso     weight file output         nPats   number of patterns to
read
589         nIter     number of iterations       nInp    number of input nodes
590         nHid      number hidden nodes        nOut    number of output nodes.
591         eta       learning rate              alpha   momentum factor
592
593
594     ****************************************************************
595     0.363636 0.191667 0.7 0.75 0.666667 0.531225 0.0898333 0.0504219 0.684434
596     1 0 1234567
597     0.327273 0.1875 0.733333 0.75 0.8 0.531038 0.0819442 0.0504219 0.801057
598     1 0 1234567
599     0.363636 0.2375 0.683333 0.683333 0.666667 0.531225 0.100878 0.0504219
                                                                        0.801057
600     1 0 1234567
601     0.3 0.25 0.716667 0.683333 0.666667 0.532375 0.119778 0.0488441 0.801057
602     1 0 1234567
603     0.454545 0.341667 0.666667 0.733333 0.633333 0.531417 0.0803663 0.0315223
                                                                        0.801057
604     1 0 1234567
605     0.327273 0.254167 0.733333 0.783333 0.633333 0.532183 0.0977224 0.0488441
                                                                        0.715305
606     1 0 1234567
607     0.881818 0.891667 0.716667 0.883333 0.666667 0.534675 0.0441106 0.0756328
                                                                        0.715305
608     1 0 1234567
609     1 0.829167 0.85 0.766667 0.766667 0.534867 0.0441106 0.0709337 0.715305
610     1 0 1234567
611     0.390909 0.279167 0.683333 0.7 0.633333 0.531038 0.0961446 0.0362557
                                                                        0.783906
612     1 0 1234567
613     0.509091 0.2875 0.616667 0.683333 0.733333 0.531992 0.083522 0.0331001
                                                                        0.783906
614     1 0 1234567
615     0.4 0.2625 0.65 0.75 0.633333 0.532758 0.0977224 0.0362557 0.783906
616     1 0 1234567
617     0.290909 0.1125 0.7 0.75 0.7 0.5318 0.092989 0.0425328 0.783906
618     1 0 1234567
619     0.413636 0.295833 0.716667 0.733333 0.633333 0.532183 0.0850998 0.0425328
                                                                        0.783906
620     1 0 1234567
621     0.359091 0.2125 0.65 0.766667 0.633333 0.530846 0.105612 0.0409549 0.783906
```

```
22    1 0 1234567
23    0.386364 0.241667 0.7 0.733333 0.666667 0.530271 0.0819442 0.0519997
                                                                    0.681004
24    1 0 1234567
25    0.331818 0.158333 0.716667 0.766667 0.666667 0.530463 0.0898333 0.0362557
                                                                    0.681004
26    1 0 1234567
27    0.413636 0.295833 0.65 0.733333 0.7 0.531417 0.0977224 0.0504219 0.612403
28    1 0 1234567
29    0.336364 0.133333 0.666667 0.75 0.766667 0.532375 0.0882555 0.0315223
                                                                    0.612403
30    1 0 1234567
31    0.404545 0.275 0.7 0.733333 0.7 0.531225 0.0693558 0.025211 0.581533
32    1 0 1234567
33    0.386364 0.241667 0.65 0.7 0.666667 0.530846 0.0945668 0.025211 0.406599
34    1 0 1234567
35    0.363636 0.333333 0.666667 0.733333 0.633333 0.528546 0.0914111 0.0441106
                                                                    0.530082
36    1 0 1234567
37    0.395455 0.145833 0.75 0.683333 0.733333 0.530846 0.0866776 0 0.530082
38    1 0 1234567
39    0.459091 0.1125 0.733333 0.733333 0.7 0.531608 0.0662002 0.0409549 0.97942
40    1 0 1234567
41    0.236364 0.075 0.716667 0.75 0.733333 0.530846 0.0961446 0.025211 0.97942
42    1 0 1234567
43    0.381818 0.2375 0.65 0.75 0.633333 0.531038 0.0914111 0.0456884 0.873088
44    1 0 1234567
45    0.322727 0.0125 0.733333 0.816667 0.7 0.531417 0.0914111 0.0441106 0.790766
46    1 0 1234567
47    0.259091 0.120833 0.666667 0.8 0.7 0.528354 0.104034 0.0393771 0.790766
48    1 0 1234567
49    0.445455 0.1625 0.716667 0.716667 0.7 0.532183 0.0709337 0.025211 0.917679
50    1 0 1234567
51    0.295455 0 0.716667 0.783333 0.8 0.531417 0.0819442 0.0362557 1
52    1 0 1234567
53    0.236364 0.0458333 0.733333 0.75 0.766667 0.530079 0.0882555 0.0220553 1
54    1 0 1234567
55    0.272727 0.0583333 0.683333 0.75 0.7 0.529312 0.083522 0.0393771 0.814777
56    1 0 1234567
57    0.313636 0.1375 0.733333 0.75 0.666667 0.5318 0.110345 0.0378336 0.818207
58    1 0 1234567
59    0.386364 0.225 0.683333 0.766667 0.666667 0.527587 0.083522 0.0472662
                                                                    0.632983
60    1 0 1234567
61    0.422727 0.166667 0.65 0.75 0.7 0.530463 0.0787885 0.0362557 0.598683
62    1 0 1234567
63    0.372727 0.258333 0.716667 0.683333 0.7 0.5318 0.0914111 0.0331001 0.684434
64    1 0 1234567
65    0.390909 0.245833 0.683333 0.733333 0.733333 0.531992 0.0850998 0.0409549
                                                                    0.684434
566   1 0 1234567
567   0.490909 0.320833 0.616667 0.733333 0.633333 0.530463 0.0772107 0.0472662
0.632983
568   1 0 1234567
569   0.368182 0.175 0.666667 0.783333 0.8 0.531608 0.083522 0.0362557 0.598683
570   1 0 1234567
571   0.390909 0.316667 0.716667 0.7 0.633333 0.530846 0.0993003 0.025211
0.506071
572   1 0 1234567
573   0.427273 0.195833 0.666667 0.733333 0.766667 0.531417 0.0819442 0.0519997
0.574672
574   1 0 1234567
575   0.35 0.208333 0.683333 0.783333 0.733333 0.531992 0.0819442 0.0362557
0.643274
```

```
676     1 0 1234567
677     0.340909 0.141667 0.766667 0.75 0.666667 0.5318 0.105612 0.0173218 0.85250
678     1 0 1234567
679     0.309091 0.145833 0.65 0.766667 0.633333 0.529504 0.108767 0.0409549
0.852507
680     1 0 1234567
681     0.331818 0.166667 0.766667 0.766667 0.666667 0.532758 0.092989 0.0141662
0.866228
682     1 0 1234567
683     0.327273 0.1875 0.7 0.75 0.666667 0.527779 0.0961446 0.0220553 0.763326
684     1 0 1234567
685     0.427273 0.2 0.683333 0.783333 0.733333 0.531038 0.0803663 0.0456884
0.540372
686     1 0 1234567
687     0.313636 0.15 0.716667 0.75 0.6 0.529504 0.0898333 0.0204775 0.588393
688     1 0 1234567
689     0.436364 0.2375 0.683333 0.833333 0.733333 0.532183 0.0662002 0.0456884
0.506071
690     1 0 1234567
691     0.290909 0.0375 0.666667 0.75 0.666667 0.532567 0.129245 0.0331001 0.93825
692     1 0 1234567
693     0.309091 0.170833 0.716667 0.75 0.7 0.529887 0.0725115 0.0441106 0.938259
694     1 0 1234567
695     0.581818 0.783333 0.566667 0.866667 0.633333 0.533525 0.0472662 0.0646224
0.615833
696     0 1 1234567
697     0.3 0.420833 0.866667 0.916667 0.566667 0.532183 0.0646224 0.0346779
0.615833
698     0 1 1234567
699     0.590909 0.7625 0.6 0.85 0.566667 0.533908 0.0504219 0.0646224 0.615833
700     0 1 1234567
701     0.322727 0.525 0.85 0.583333 0.566667 0.532567 0.0646224 0.0535776 0.61583
702     0 1 1234567
703     0.163636 0.525 0.85 0.55 0.766667 0.5318 0.0567332 0.058311 0.739315
704     0 1 1234567
705     0.804545 0.5625 0.933333 0.583333 0.566667 0.533908 0.0393771 0.0803663
0.739315
706     0 1 1234567
707     0.186364 0.504167 0.866667 0.65 0.633333 0.530654 0.058311 0.0614667
0.739315
708     0 1 1234567
709     0.181818 0.5 0.866667 0.616667 0.566667 0.532375 0.0709337 0.0598889
0.739315
710     0 1 1234567
711     0.272727 0.4875 0.866667 0.616667 0.6 0.531038 0.067778 0.0519997 0.763326
712     0 1 1234567
713     0.2 0.308333 0.9 0.866667 0.6 0.532183 0.0646224 0.0220553 0.763326
714     0 1 1234567
715     0.290909 0.516667 0.85 0.616667 0.566667 0.531608 0.0630445 0.0535776
0.639844
716     0 1 1234567
717     0.259091 0.483333 0.833333 0.65 0.566667 0.531417 0.0725115 0.0567332
0.639844
718     0 1 1234567
719     0.159091 0.383333 0.866667 0.833333 0.666667 0.531225 0.0646224 0.0551554
0.866228
720     0 1 1234567
721     0.118182 0.475 0.85 0.65 0.666667 0.530846 0.0772107 0.0598889 0.866228
722     0 1 1234567
723     0.554545 0.358333 0.583333 0.866667 0.6 0.532375 0.0725115 0.0472662
0.506071
724     0 1 1234567
725     0.763636 0.595833 0.866667 0.616667 0.633333 0.53525 0.0472662 0.0756328
0.506071
```

```
726      0 1 1234567
727      0.586364 0.708333 0.566667 0.816667 0.6 0.533525 0.0315223 0.0598889
0.506071
728      0 1 1234567
729      0.381818 0.483333 0.816667 0.683333 0.7 0.530271 0.0598889 0.0614667
0.506071
730      0 1 1234567
731      0.113636 0.504167 0.833333 0.6 0.6 0.531225 0.067778 0.0425328 0.694725
732      0 1 1234567
733      0.313636 0.504167 0.9 0.583333 0.566667 0.531225 0.0646224 0.0425328
0.509501
734      0 1 1234567
735      0.313636 0.516667 0.8 0.583333 0.6 0.533525 0.0614667 0.0409549 0.509501
736      0 1 1234567
737      0.595455 0.679167 0.6 0.766667 0.6 0.533717 0.0425328 0.0551554 0.509501
738      0 1 1234567
739      0.413636 0.520833 0.766667 0.566667 0.666667 0.531608 0.0551554 0.0346779
0.509501
740      0 1 1234567
741      0.336364 0.516667 0.8 0.55 0.566667 0.531417 0.0598889 0.0519997 0.578102
742      0 1 1234567
743      0.590909 0.691667 0.616667 0.833333 0.6 0.533908 0.0488441 0.0598889
0.578102
744      0 1 1234567
745      0.4 0.529167 0.833333 0.583333 0.566667 0.532375 0.0598889 0.0567332
0.578102
746      0 1 1234567
747      0.795455 0.541667 0.966667 0.566667 0.566667 0.534867 0.0504219 0.0709337
0.468341
748      0 1 1234567
749      0.577273 0.666667 0.583333 0.816667 0.566667 0.5341 0.0519997 0.0567332
0.468341
750      0 1 1234567
751      0.427273 0.529167 0.816667 0.55 0.566667 0.532758 0.0567332 0.0504219
0.468341
752      0 1 1234567
753      0.268182 0.541667 0.883333 0.566667 0.633333 0.530271 0.0472662 0.0409549
0.574672
754      0 1 1234567
755      0.145455 0.520833 0.866667 0.566667 0.566667 0.531417 0.058311 0.0393771
0.907388
756      0 1 1234567
757      0.213636 0.504167 0.916667 0.65 0.566667 0.531038 0.067778 0.0662002
0.907388
758      0 1 1234567
759      0.136364 0.520833 0.95 0.583333 0.566667 0.532567 0.067778 0.0425328
0.855937
760      0 1 1234567
761      0.668182 0.783333 0.65 0.766667 0.633333 0.536012 0.0441106 0.0567332
0.855937
762      0 1 1234567
763      0.3 0.529167 0.766667 0.566667 0.566667 0.5318 0.0567332 0.0519997 0.855937
764      0 1 1234567
765      0.277273 0.529167 0.766667 0.55 0.666667 0.528546 0.058311 0.0646224
0.910818
766      0 1 1234567
767      0.0545455 0.504167 0.983333 0.616667 0.6 0.532375 0.0662002 0.0772107
0.910818
768      0 1 1234567
769      0.236364 0.479167 0.783333 0.616667 0.6 0.5318 0.0740893 0.0188996 0.910818
770      0 1 1234567
771      0.590909 0.745833 0.583333 0.85 0.733333 0.533717 0.0488441 0.0567332
0.468341
772      0 1 1234567
```

```
773     0.340909 0.529167 0.85 0.566667 0.566667 0.532375 0.0567332 0.0456884
0.468341
774     0 1 1234567
775     0.722727 0.558333 0.8 0.6 0.6 0.53525 0.0456884 0.0614667 0.468341
776     0 1 1234567
777     0.1 0.483333 1 0.633333 0.566667 0.532183 0.0772107 0.0551554 0.96913
778     0 1 1234567
779     0 0.504167 0.883333 0.65 0.566667 0.531417 0.0709337 0.058311 0.96913
780     0 1 1234567
781     0.186364 0.529167 0.833333 0.55 0.566667 0.531417 0.058311 0.0535776
0.807917
782     0 1 1234567
783     0.527273 0.3875 0.616667 0.766667 0.6 0.531992 0.0756328 0.0409549 0.48549
784     0 1 1234567
785     0.731818 0.554167 0.766667 0.583333 0.566667 0.535629 0.0409549 0.0567332
0.485491
786     0 1 1234567
787     0.486364 0.341667 0.7 0.766667 0.633333 0.530654 0.0725115 0.0409549
0.684434
788     0 1 1234567
789     0.781818 0.745833 0.766667 0.866667 0.566667 0.53525 0.0409549 0.0709337
0.684434
790     0 1 1234567
791     0.340909 0.4375 0.866667 0.733333 0.633333 0.531417 0.0709337 0.0630445
0.684434
792     0 1 1234567
793     0.15 0.516667 0.833333 0.583333 0.566667 0.531225 0.058311 0.0456884
0.684434
794     0 1 1234567
```

APPENDIX B

```
 1      ************** Source and run files for Self-organizing network
 2      rem demo.bat
 3      kohonen -e1 -t1000 -T5 -n.5 -a.2  demo.run
 4      rem This batch command runs a simple demo of the Kohonen net.
 5      rem The command options are as follows:
 6      rem -e1      display network every iteration
 7      rem -t1000   time steps during which neighborhood decreases linearly
 8      rem -T5      factor by which above time interval is lengthened
 9      rem -n.5     size of initial neighborhood as fraction of whole layer
10      rem -a.2     factor by which learning rate is decreased
11
12      ****************************************************************
13
14      demo.run    sample run file
15      1
16      kohonen.out my.dat RANDOM kohonen.wts 100 200 2 64 .3
17
18      format of run file:
19      line 1:  number of runs
20      line 2:  description of run 1
21      ...
22      line n:  description of run n
23
24      format of run description line:
25         fres fpat fwtsin fwtsout npats nepochs nin nout eta
26      where:
27      fres     results out filename
28               final output activations
29      fpats    patterns in filename
30               training or test set. If name is RANDOM then patterns are
31               generated automatically with a random distribution:
32               RANDOM/S    square probability distribution
33               RANDOM/C    cross
34               RANDOM/T    triangle
35      fwtsin   weights in filename
36               Initial values of weights. If name is RANDOM then weights
37               are generated automatically.
38
39      fwtsout  weights out filename
40               final weight values.
41
42      npats    number of patterns
43               Maximum number of patterns to read from pattern in file.
44
45      nepochs  number of epochs
46               Maximum number of epochs (complete presentations of pattern
47               set).
48
49      nin      number of input nodes
50
51      nout     number of output nodes
52               A rectangular output array is assumed.
53
54      eta      learning factor
55
56      ****************************************************************
57
58      my.dat    sample data file
59      .2   .2   0
60      .2   .2   1
```

```
61        .2   .2   2
62        .8   .2   3
63        .2   .2   4
64        .2   .2   5
65        .1   .9   6
66        .2   .2   7
67        .2   .2   8
68        .2   .8   9
69        .8   .2   10
70        .8   .2   11
71        .2   .2   12
72        .2   .8   13                      ∋
73        .8   .2   14
74        .2   .2   15
75
76        ****************************************************************
77
78        /* kohonen.c
79
80            Kohonen self-organizing neural network
81
82            version 1.0     RWD  28 Jan 1990
83
84            Copyright (c)  1990  R.W.Dobbins and R.C.Eberhart
85            All Rights Reserved
86
87            *** SHAREWARE ***
88            You may distribute unmodified copies of the diskette or software.
89            If you find the software of value, please send $20 or any amount,
90            to :-
91
92                      R. W. Dobbins
93                      5833 Humblebee Road
94                      Columbia, MD, 21045
95                      Tel. (301) 740-5325
96
97            Your support is greatly appreciated.
98            $Revision:    1.0   $                 $Date:     10 Apr 1990 10:41:42  $
99        */
100
101       #include <stdio.h>
102       #include <stdlib.h>
103       #include <math.h>
104       #include <conio.h>
105       #include <ctype.h>
106       #include <string.h>
107       #include <graphics.h>
108       #include <time.h>
109       #include "vector.h"
110       #include "graphnet.h"
111       #include "kohonen.h"
112
113       void help(void);
114       void readweights(char *szWeights);
115       void readpatterns(char *szPattern);
116       void writeweights(char *szWeights);
117       void writeactivations(char *szResults);
118       int  findwinner(int p);
119       void normalizeweights(int  j);
120
121       /* define storage for net layers and weights */
122       MATRIX    out0;              /* input layer   */
123       MATRIX    out2;              /* output layer */
124       MATRIX    Weights;           /* weights input:output */
125       VECTOR    PatternID;         /* identifier for each stored pattern */
126
127       int    nInputNodes;          /* number of input nodes              */
```

```
128      int    nOutputNodes;       /* number of output nodes           */
129      int    nPatterns;          /* number of patterns desired       */
130      int    nIterations;        /* number of iterations desired     */
131      int    p;                  /* index pattern number             */
132      int    Side;               /* size of one side of output rectangle */
133      long   Tk;                 /* elapsed time in time steps */
134      float  eta;                /* actual learning rate */
135      int    DensityFunction;    /* probability density function of patterns */
136      int    q;                  /* epoch (iteration) number         */
137      int    t;                  /* time step in current segment  */
138
139      void  main(int argc, char *argv[])
140      {
141          float eta0    = 0.3;         /* default initial learning rate    */
142          float etaShrink0 = .2;       /* learning rate decrease factor     */
143          register int   i;            /* index input layer                 */
144          register int   j;            /* index output layer                */
145          int    r;                    /* run number                       */
146          int    n;                    /* requested number of nodes         */
147          int    nRuns;                /* number of runs */
148          int    T1 = 1000;            /* time interval during which eta decreases */
149          int    T1f = 5;              /* time interval increase factor    */
150          int    T2 = 10;              /* display updating interval         */
151          char   MonitorNet = 0;       /* true when network monitor request */
152          int    Neighborhood0;        /* initial neighborhood              */
153          float  NeighborSize = .5;    /* size as fraction of net           */
154          int    Neighborhood;         /* current neighborhood              */
155          FILE   *fpRun;               /* run file                          */
156          char   szResults[66];        /* various file pathnames            */
157          char   szPattern[66];
158          char   szWeights[66];
159          char   szWeightsOut[66];
160          char   *progname = *argv;    /* name of executable (DOS 3.x only) */
161          int    WinnerHorizontal;     /* location of winner in output rectangle */
162          int    WinnerVertical;
163          int    left;                 /* neighborhood boundary of winner */
164          int    right;
165          int    top;
166          int    bottom;
167          int    h;                    /* horiz/vert location of current node */
168          int    v;
169
170          /* read optional - arguments */
171          for (; argc > 1; argc--)
172          {
173              char *arg = *++argv;
174
175              if (*arg != '-')
176                  break;
177
178              switch (*++arg)
179              {
180                  case 'e':  sscanf(++arg,  "%d",  &T2);  break;
181                  case 't':  sscanf(++arg,  "%d",  &T1);  break;
182                  case 'T':  sscanf(++arg,  "%d",  &T1f);  break;
183                  case 'n':  sscanf(++arg,  "%f",  &NeighborSize); break;
184                  case 'a':  sscanf(++arg,  "%f",  &etaShrink0); break;
185                  default:   break;
186              }
187          }
188
189          if (argc < 2)
190              help();
191
192          /* Open run file for reading */
193          if ((fpRun = fopen(*argv, "r"))  ==  NULL)
194          {
```

```
195              fprintf(stderr, "%s: can't open file %s\n", progname, *argv);
196              exit(1);
197          }
198
199          /* Read first item: number of runs */
200          fscanf(fpRun,  "%d",  &nRuns);
201
202      /*-------------------- beginning of work loop ------------------------*/
203          for (r = 0;   r < nRuns;   r++)
204          {
205              /* read and parse the run specification line; */
206              fscanf(fpRun,
207                  "%s %s %s %s %d %d %d %d %f %f",
208                  szResults,             /* output results file */
209                  szPattern,             /* pattern input file */
210                  szWeights,             /* initial weights file */
211                  szWeightsOut,          /* final weights output file */
212                  &nPatterns,            /* number of patterns to learn */
213                  &nIterations,          /* number of iterations through the data */
214                  &nInputNodes,          /* number of input nodes  */
215                  &nOutputNodes,         /* number of output nodes */
216                  &eta0);                /* learning rate */
217
218              /* must be rectangular output layer topology */
219              Side = sqrt((double)nOutputNodes);
220              n    = Side * Side;
221              if (n != nOutputNodes)
222              {
223                  fprintf(stderr,
224                      "Rectangular output layer of %n by %n used\n",  n,  n);
225                  nOutputNodes = n;
226              }
227
228              /*----------allocate dynamic storage for all data --------------*/
229              MatrixAllocate(&out0,      nPatterns,    nInputNodes);
230              MatrixAllocate(&out2,      nPatterns,    nOutputNodes);
231              MatrixAllocate(&Weights,   nOutputNodes, nInputNodes);
232              VectorAllocate(&PatternID, nPatterns);
233
234              /*--------- Read the initial weight matrices: ------------------*/
235              readweights(szWeights);
236
237              /*----------- Read in all patterns to be learned:---------------*/
238              readpatterns(szPattern);
239
240              fprintf(stderr, nIterations > 1 ? "Training...\n" : "Testing\n");
241
242          /*-------------------- begin iteration loop ----------------------*/
243              /* set initial values for iterations */
244              eta           = eta0;        /* learning rate */
245              Neighborhood0 = Side * NeighborSize;
246              Tk            = 0;              /* number of time steps elapsed */
247              t             = 0;
248              /* basic unit of operation is time step t;
249                    this inner loop presents T1 time steps;
250                    for each time step:
251                      - one pattern is presented;
252                      - a winner selected;
253                      - weights of neighborhood adapted
254              */
255
256              /* each iteration q is one epoch (complete pattern set) */
257              for (q = 0;  q < nIterations  && eta > 0;  q++)
258              {
259                  for (p = 0;  p < nPatterns;  p++)
260                  {
261                      int   Winner;        /* index in output layer of winning unit */
```

```
262
263                    /*------------------ compute output layer activation --------*/
264                    for (j = 0;  j < nOutputNodes;  j++)
265                    {
266                        float  sum = 0;
267
268                        for (i = 0;  i < nInputNodes;  i++)
269                            sum  +=  Weights[j][i]  *  out0[p][i];
270
271                        out2[p][j]  =  sum;
272                    }
273                    /* !NB! want only the winner to output a value;
274                       all other nodes should be quiescent.
275                       This can be done by a post processing layer
276                    */
277
278                    /*------------------ find winning unit -------------------*/
279                    Winner = findwinner(p);
280
281                    /*------------------ adapt weights input:output -----------*/
282
283                    /* Define the neighborhood:
284                       Only the weights to those units in the neighborhood of the
285                       winner are adjusted.
286                    */
287
288                    /* horizontal and vertical coordinates of winner in
289                       two dimensional output space */
290                    WinnerHorizontal    =  Winner % Side;
291                    WinnerVertical      =  Winner / Side;
292
293                    /* Neighborhood width is a linear shrinking function of
294                       the discrete time step, t: */
295                    Neighborhood = Neighborhood0 * (1 - t / T1) + 1;
296                    /* constrain neighborhood to limits of array */
297                    left   =  max(0, WinnerHorizontal - Neighborhood);
298                    right  =  min(Side - 1, WinnerHorizontal + Neighborhood);
299                    top    =  max(0, WinnerVertical - Neighborhood);
300                    bottom =  min(Side - 1, WinnerVertical + Neighborhood);
301
302                    /* learning coefficient is a linear shrinking function of
303                       the discrete time step, t */
304                    eta  =  eta0 * (1 - t / T1);
305
306                    /* update weights in the neighborhood of the winner */
307                    for (h = left;  h <= right;  h++)
308                        for (v = top;  v <= bottom;  v++)
309                        {
310                            j   = Side * v + h;
311
312                            /* each component of the weight vector changes by some
313                               fraction, eta of its difference from the input vector */
314                            for (i = 0;  i < nInputNodes;  i++)
315                                Weights[j][i]  +=  eta * (out0[p][i] - Weights[j][i]);
316                        }
317
318                    /* ------------- monitor keyboard requests -------------*/
319                    {
320                        int   c = kbreq();
321
322                        if (c)
323                        {
324                            if (c == 'E')
325                                MonitorNet++;        /* request network display */
326                            else if (c == ESC)
327                                goto DONE;           /* Terminate gracefully (save)*/
328                            else if (c == ABORT)
```

```
329                      goto QUIT;              /* terminate ungracefully */
330                  }
331              }
332
333              Tk++;                           /* count time steps */
334              if (++t >= T1)
335              {
336                  /* completed a linear time segment, T1 */
337                  t        = 0;               /* begin new segment */
338                  eta0     *=  etaShrink0;    /* reduce learning factor */
339                  Neighborhood0  = 0;
340                  T1       *=  T1f;           /* adjust length of next segment */
341              }
342          }
343          /* display network state */
344          if (MonitorNet || (q % T2  ==  0))
345          {
346              displaynet();
347              MonitorNet = 0;
348          }
349      }
350      /* -------------- end of iteration loop --------------------------*/
351      DONE:
352      displaynet();       /* display final state */
353      /* browse loop while user examines network state */
354      for (;;)
355      {
356          int    c = kbreq();
357
358          if (c == ESC || c == ABORT)
359              break;
360      }
361      ResetScreen();
362
363      /* print final weights */
364      writeweights(szWeightsOut);
365
366      /* Print final activation values */
367      writeactivations(szResults);
368
369      /* free dynamic storage for data */
370      MatrixFree(out0,     nPatterns);
371      MatrixFree(out2,     nPatterns);
372      MatrixFree(Weights,  nOutputNodes);
373      free(PatternID);
374  }
375  QUIT:
376  ResetScreen();
377 }
378
379 void help()
380 {
381     fprintf(stderr, "Usage:  kohonen {-etTna} runfilename\n");
382     fprintf(stderr, "  -en   => display state every n iterations (100)\n");
383     fprintf(stderr, "  -tn   => initial learning time interval steps
                (1000)\n");
384     fprintf(stderr, "  -Tn   => learning time interval increase factor
                (5)\n");
385     fprintf(stderr, "  -nf   => initial neighborhood size fraction of
                net\n");
386     fprintf(stderr, "  -af   => learning rate decreasing factor (.2)\n");
387     exit(1);
388 }
389
390 /*------------------ find winning unit --------------------*/
391 /* Compute Euclidean distance between weight vector and
392     input vector, for each output unit.
```

```
93          o  Winner is unit whose weight vector has minimum Euclidean
94                        distance to the input pattern vector.
95          o  Euclidean distance of vectors Weights and out0 is
96                        square root(sum(square(Weights - out0))
97          o  Here we are only interested in finding the minimum, so
98                        we don't need the square root.
99     */
00     int  findwinner(int p)
01     {
02        int    Winner;
03        int    i;
04        int    j;
05
06        float MinimumDistance = 0;          /* used to find winner */
07
08        for (j = 0;  j < nOutputNodes;  j++)
09        {
10           float EuclideanDistance = 0;
11
12           for (i = 0;  i < nInputNodes;  i++)
13           {
14              float d  = out0[p][i] - Weights[j][i];
15              EuclideanDistance += d * d;
16           }
17
18           if (j == 0  ||  EuclideanDistance <= MinimumDistance)
19           {
20              MinimumDistance  = EuclideanDistance;
21              Winner  = j;
22           }
23        }
24        return  Winner;
25     }
26
27     void readweights(char *szWeights)
28     {
29        int    i;
30        int    j;
31
32        if (strcmp(szWeights, "RANDOM") == 0)
33        {
34           /* randomize weights */
35           randomize();
36           for (j = 0;  j < nOutputNodes;  j++)
37           {
38              for (i = 0;  i < nInputNodes;  i++)
39              {
40                 float  r  = (float)rand() / RAND_MAX;   /* 0.0 .. 1.0 */
41
42                 Weights[j][i]  = r;
43              }
44              normalizeweights(j);
45           }
46        }
47        else
48        {
49           FILE  *fpWeights;            /* initial weight file           */
50           if ((fpWeights = fopen(szWeights,"r"))  ==  NULL)
51           {
52              fprintf(stderr,  "can't open file %s\n", szWeights);
53              exit(1);
54           }
55
56           /* read input:output layer connection weights */
57           for (j = 0;  j < nOutputNodes;  j++)
58           {
59              for (i = 0;  i < nInputNodes;  i++)
```

```
460                     {
461                         fscanf(fpWeights,   "%f",        &Weights[j][i]);
462                     }
463                     normalizeweights(j);
464                 }
465                 fclose(fpWeights);
466         }
467     }
468
469
470     /* normalize weight vector */
471     void normalizeweights(int   j)
472     {
473         int    i;
474         float  d =  0;
475
476         /* sum squares of vector components */
477         for (i = 0;  i < nInputNodes;  i++)
478         {
479             float r =  Weights[j][i];
480             d  +=  r * r;
481         }
482
483         /* Euclidean norm is sqrt (sum of the squares) */
484         d = sqrt((double) d);          /* length of vector */
485         /* dividing each component by the length gives a vector
486            of unit length */
487         for (i = 0;  i < nInputNodes;  i++)
488             Weights[j][i]  /=  d;
489     }
490
491     void readpatterns(char *szPattern)
492     {
493         int    i;
494         int    j;
495         if (strncmp(szPattern, "RANDOM/", 7) == 0)
496         {
497             char c = szPattern[7];
498
499             /* generate random input distribution */
500             c = toupper(c);
501             if (strchr("TCS", c) == NULL)
502             {
503                 fprintf(stderr,  "can't understand RANDOM/%c %s\n",
504                         c, szPattern);
505                 exit(1);
506             }
507             DensityFunction = c;
508             for (p = 0; p < nPatterns;  p++)
509             {
510                 float n0, n1, norm;
511                 for (;;)
512                 {
513                     int  Inside = FALSE;
514                     /* generate a random set of samples */
515                     n0  = (float)rand() / RAND_MAX;  /* 0.0 .. 1.0 */
516                     n1  = (float)rand() / RAND_MAX;  /* 0.0 .. 1.0 */
517                     switch(c)
518                     {
519                     case 'S':
520                         /* square distribution ==> accept all */
521                         Inside = TRUE;
522                         break;
523                     case 'T':
524                         /* triangular distribution */
525                         if (n1 >= 2 * fabs((double)n0 - 0.5))
526                             Inside = TRUE;
```

```
 7                         break;
 8                     case 'C':
 9                         /* cross shape distribution */
 0                         if (fabs((double)n0 - 0.5) <= .25  ||
 1                             fabs((double)n1 - 0.5) <= .25)
 2                             Inside = TRUE;
 3                         break;
 4                     }
 5                     if (Inside)
 6                         break;
 7                 }
 8                 out0[p][0]  =  n0;
 9                 out0[p][1]  =  n1;
 0                 PatternID[p] = p;
 1             }
 2         }
 3         else
 4         {
 5             FILE  *fpPattern;              /* source pattern input file        */
 6             if ((fpPattern = fopen(szPattern, "r")) == NULL)
 7             {
 8                 fprintf(stderr, "can't open file %s\n", szPattern);
 9                 exit(1);
50             }
51
52             for (p = 0;  p < nPatterns;  p++)
53             {
54                 float   d  =  0;
55                 for (i = 0;  i < nInputNodes;   i++)
56                 {
57                     float  r;
58                     if (fscanf(fpPattern, "%f",   &r)  != 1)
59                         goto  ALLPATTERNSREAD;
60                     out0[p][i]  =  r;
61                     d  += r * r;    /* sum of squares of components */
62                 }
63
64                 /* normalize pattern vector to unit length */
65                 d = sqrt((double) d);       /* Euclidean norm */
66                 for (i = 0;  i < nInputNodes;  i++)
67                     out0[p][i]  /=  d;
68
69                 /* read in identifier for each pattern */
70                 fscanf(fpPattern,  "%f ",   &PatternID[p]);
71             }
72
73             ALLPATTERNSREAD:
74             fclose(fpPattern);
75
76             if (p < nPatterns)
77             {
78                 fprintf(stderr, "%d out of %d patterns read\n",
79                         p,  nPatterns);
80                 nPatterns = p;
81             }
82         }
83     }
84
85     void writeweights(char *szWeightsOut)
86     {
87         int   i;
88         int   j;
89         FILE  *fpWeightsOut;              /* final weight output file         */
90         if ((fpWeightsOut = fopen(szWeightsOut,"w")) == NULL)
91         {
92             fprintf(stderr,  "can't write file %s\n", szWeightsOut);
93             exit(1);
```

```
594                }
595
596                for (j = 0;  j < nOutputNodes;  j++)
597                   for (i = 0;  i < nInputNodes;  i++)
598                      fprintf(fpWeightsOut,  "%g%c", Weights[j][i], j%ITEMS==ITEMS-1
                            '\n':' ');
599
600                fclose(fpWeightsOut);
601          }
602
603          void writeactivations(char *szResults)
604          {
605              int   i;
606              int   j;
607              FILE  *fpResults;              /* results output file              */
608              if ((fpResults = fopen(szResults,"w"))  ==  NULL)
609              {
610                  fprintf(stderr,  "can't write file %s\n",  szResults);
611                  fpResults = stderr;
612              }
613
614              /* Print final output vector */
615              for (p = 0;  p < nPatterns;  p++)
616              {
617                  for (j = 0;  j < nOutputNodes;  j++)
618                      fprintf(fpResults, "%g ",  out2[p][j]);
619
620                  fprintf(fpResults, " %-6.0f\n", PatternID[p]);
621              }
622
623              fclose(fpResults);
624          }
625
626          *****************************************************************
627
628          /* netshow.c
629
630              display network activation state of
631              Kohonen self-organizing neural network
632
633              Copyright (c)  1990   R.W.Dobbins and R.C.Eberhart
634              All Rights Reserved
635
636              $Revision:   1.0  $              $Date:   10 Apr 1990 10:41:48  $
637          */
638
639          #include <stdio.h>
640          #include <stdlib.h>
641          #include <math.h>
642          #include <conio.h>
643          #include <ctype.h>
644          #include <string.h>
645          #include <graphics.h>
646          #include "graphnet.h"
647          #include "vector.h"
648          #include "kohonen.h"
649
650          /* possible display modes */
651          #define SELECTPATTERN   1        /* display selected pattern only */
652          #define WINNER          2        /* accumulate only winning nodes */
653          #define TABULATE        4        /* tabulate data */
654
655          static int GraphicsMode = 0;  /* true when graphics mode set */
656          static int colornegative = LIGHTRED;
657          static int colorpositive = WHITE;
658          static int patternnegative = CLOSE_DOT_FILL;
659          static int patternpositive = SOLID_FILL;
```

```
660    static int Zoom = 1;
661    static int displaypattern = 0;      /* pattern number to display */
662    static int displaymode     = SELECTPATTERN | TABULATE;
663
664    void DisplayActivation(void);
665    void DisplayPattern(void);
666    void DisplayWeights(void);
667    void displaylayer(VECTOR vect, int hSide, int vSide);
668    void setwindows(void);
669
670    VIEW    screen;
671    VIEW    view  = {0,0,0,0,1};
672    VIEW    viewin = {0,0,0,0,1};
673    VIEW    viewwt = {0,0,0,0,1};
674    VIEW    title = {0,0,0,0,1};
675    int     DX;
676    int     DY;
677    int     xt;
678    int     yt;
679    float   Vmax;                       /* maximum positive value     */
680    float   Vmin;                       /* minimum negative value     */
681    float   Vscale;                     /* display scale factor       */
682    int     fieldwidth = 7;             /* characters per text field */
683    char    dump[81];
684    char    *lines[]  = {dump, dump, dump};
685
686    /* display network state (two dimensional Hinton type display) */
687    void displaynet()
688    {
689        if (!GraphicsMode)
690        {
691            InitScreen();        /* enter graphics mode screen */
692            GraphicsMode++;
693            setwindows();
694        }
695        DisplayActivation();     /* display network activation state */
696        DisplayPattern();        /* display network input pattern */
697        DisplayWeights();        /* display weight vectors */
698    }
699
700
701    void displaytitle(int argc, char *argv[])
702    {
703        int   y = 0;
704
705        openviewport(&title);
706        outtextxy(20, y, "Kohonen self organizing network");
707        while (argc-- > 0)
708        {
709            y += yt;        /* advance to next line */
710            moveto(0, y);
711            outtext(*argv++);
712        }
713    }
714
715    /* setup display windows */
716    void setwindows()
717    {
718        if (view.bottom == 0)
719        {
720            /* define viewports for title and activation state */
721            getviewsettings(&screen);
722            /* x,y increments for a numeric activation display */
723            xt           = textwidth("0") * fieldwidth + 1;
724            yt           = textheight("0") + 1;
725            title.right  = getmaxx();
726            title.bottom = 3 * yt;    /* 3 lines in title */
```

```
727              /* network view */
728              view.left    = 0;
729              view.top     = title.bottom + 2;
730              view.right   = getmaxx() / 2;
731              view.bottom  = getmaxy() / 2;
732              /* input view */
733              viewin.left    = view.right + 2;
734              viewin.top     = title.bottom + 2;
735              viewin.right   = getmaxx();
736              viewin.bottom  = getmaxy() / 2;
737              /* weights view */
738              viewwt.left    = 0;
739              viewwt.top     = view.bottom + 2;
740              viewwt.right   = getmaxx();
741              viewwt.bottom  = getmaxy();
742              /* x,y increments for Hinton activation display */
743              DX             = (view.right - view.left + 1)   /   Side;
744              DY             = (view.bottom - view.top + 1)   /   Side;
745          }
746      }
747
748      /* monitor keyboard requests */
749      int kbreq()
750      {
751          if (kbhit())
752          {
753              int    c = getch();
754
755              c = toupper(c);
756              if (!GraphicsMode)
757                  return c;                /* suppress keyboard until in graphics mode */
758
759              if (c == 'T')
760              {
761                  /* toggle tabulate mode */
762                  displaymode ^= TABULATE;
763                  displaynet();   /* request display */
764              }
765              if (c == 'P'  ||  c == '+'  ||  c == '-')
766              {
767                  displaymode |= SELECTPATTERN;
768                  if (c == 'P')
769                  {
770                      /* set pattern */
771                      lines[0] = "Enter pattern # to view:   ";
772                      displaytitle(1, lines);
773                      GraphicsGetString(dump, 10);
774                      sscanf(dump, "%u", &displaypattern);
775                  }
776                  else if (c == '+')
777                      displaypattern++;
778                  else if (c == '-')
779                      displaypattern--;
780                  if (displaypattern >= nPatterns)
781                      displaypattern = 0;
782                  else if (displaypattern < 0)
783                      displaypattern = nPatterns - 1;
784                  displaynet();   /* request display */
785              }
786              else if (c == 'M')
787              {
788                  /* set mode */
789                  lines[0] = "Enter display mode: P-Pattern  A-All   ";
790                  displaytitle(1, lines);
791                  c = GraphicsGetChar();
792                  c = tolower(c);
793                  if (c == 'p')
```

```
794                     {
795                         /* display single pattern */
796                         displaymode |= SELECTPATTERN;
797                         lines[0] = "Display nodes: A-All  W-Winner ";
798                         displaytitle(1, lines);
799                         c = GraphicsGetChar();
800                         c = tolower(c);
801                         if (c == 'w')
802                             displaymode |= WINNER;
803                         else
804                             displaymode &= ~WINNER;
805                     }
806                     else if (c == 'a')
807                     {
808                         /* display all patterns */
809                         displaymode &= ~SELECTPATTERN;
810                         lines[0] = "Display patterns: A-Averages W-Winners ";
811                         displaytitle(1, lines);
812                         c = GraphicsGetChar();
813                         c = tolower(c);
814                         if (c == 'w')
815                             displaymode |= WINNER;
816                         else
817                             displaymode &= ~WINNER;
818                     }
819                     displaynet();    /* request display */
820                 }
821             return c;             /* keypress request */
822         }
823         else
824             return  0;           /* no keypress */
825     }
826
827     void DisplayActivation()
828     {
829         int     h;
830         int     v;
831         int     X;
832         int     Y;
833         char    dump1[81];
834         static VECTOR  activation;            /* local storage for layer */
835         static int HaveVector = 0;
836
837         lines[0] = "^Q-Quit   Esc-End   E-Display   T-Tabulate   P/+/--Pattern
                M-Mode";
838         lines[1] = dump;
839         lines[2] = "Activations                              Patterns";
840         sprintf(dump1, "pattern %d", displaypattern);
841         sprintf(dump,
842             "State: %s  Epoch %-4d  %s  %s",
843             q == nIterations ? "done" : "training",
844             q,
845             displaymode & SELECTPATTERN ? dump1 : "  ",
846             displaymode & WINNER ? "Winner" : "All");
847         displaytitle(2, lines);
848         openviewport(&view);
849
850         /* capture storage for the display pattern */
851         if (!HaveVector)
852         {
853             int  p;
854
855             VectorAllocate(&activation, nOutputNodes);
856             HaveVector++;
857         }
858         if (displaymode & SELECTPATTERN)
859         {
```

```
860              /* look at selected pattern only
861                 save pattern in display buffer
862                 note: this could be done without copying:
863                 simply set activation = out2; but we may want
864                 to manipulate this pattern before displaying it
865              */
866              /* set scale factors for patterns */
867              Vmax  =  1.0;
868              Vmin  =  0.0;
869              if (displaymode & WINNER)
870              {
871                  int   Winner = 0;
872                  /* clear display vector */
873                  for (h = 0;  h < nOutputNodes;  h++)
874                      activation[h] = 0;
875                  for (h = 1;  h < nOutputNodes;  h++)
876                      if (out2[displaypattern][h] > out2[displaypattern][Winner])
877                          Winner = h;
878                  activation[Winner] = Vmax;
879              }
880              else
881                  for (h = 0;  h < nOutputNodes;  h++)
882                  {
883                      float a = out2[displaypattern][h];
884                      activation[h] = a;
885                      if (a > Vmax)
886                          Vmax = a;
887                  }
888          }
889          else
890          {
891              /* look at all patterns */
892              /* clear display vector */
893              for (h = 0;  h < nOutputNodes;  h++)
894                  activation[h] = 0;
895
896              if (displaymode & WINNER)
897              {
898                  /* accumulate winners for each pattern */
899                  /* set scale factors for patterns */
900                  Vmax  =  1.0;
901                  Vmin  =  0.0;
902                  for (p = 0; p < nPatterns;  p++)
903                  {
904                      int   Winner = 0;
905
906                      for (h = 1;  h < nOutputNodes;  h++)
907                          if (out2[p][h] > out2[p][Winner])
908                              Winner  =  h;
909
910                      /* count number of times this node wins */
911                      activation[Winner] += 1;
912                      /* scale if not displaying tabulated data */
913                      if (!(displaymode & TABULATE)  &&  activation[Winner] > Vmax)
914                          Vmax  =  activation[Winner];
915                  }
916              }
917              else
918              {
919                  /* sum all nodes across all patterns */
920                  /* set scale factors for patterns */
921                  Vmax  =  1.0;
922                  Vmin  =  0.0;
923                  for (p = 0; p < nPatterns;  p++)
924                  {
925                      for (h = 0;  h < nOutputNodes;  h++)
926                      {
```

```
927                    activation[h] += out2[p][h];
928                    if (!(displaymode & TABULATE)  &&  activation[h] > Vmax)
929                        Vmax = activation[h];
930                }
931            }
932        }
933    }
934    Vscale = Vmax - Vmin;
935    displaylayer(activation, Side, Side);
936    setviewport(screen.left, screen.top, screen.right,
937                    screen.bottom, 1);
938 }
939
940
941 void DisplayPattern()
942 {
943    openviewport(&viewin);
944    Vscale = 1;
945    displaylayer(out0[displaypattern], nInputNodes, 1);
946    setviewport(screen.left, screen.top, screen.right,
947                    screen.bottom, 1);
948 }
949
950
951 void DisplayWeights()
952 {
953    int     h;
954    int     v;
955    int     Y;
956
957    if (nInputNodes > 2)      /* suppress display if higher than 2 dimension*/
958        return;
959
960    openviewport(&viewwt);
961    Y    = Top;              /* initial position in window */
962    Vscale = 1;
963
964    for (h = 0;   h < Side;   h++)
965    {
966        Top  = Y;       /* start at top of viewport */
967
968        for (v = 0;   v < Side;   v++)
969        {
970            /* display weight vector for this node */
971            displaylayer(Weights[Side * v + h], nInputNodes, 1);
972            Top  += DY;    /* advance viewport to next position */
973        }
974        Left += DX * nInputNodes + 2;   /* next column in viewport */
975    }
976    setviewport(screen.left, screen.top, screen.right, screen.bottom, 1);
977 }
978
979
980 /* display a vector as a rectangular array */
981 void displaylayer(VECTOR vect, int hSide, int vSide)
982 {
983    int  h, v;
984    int  X, Y;
985
986    X  = Left;
987
988    for (h = 0;   h < hSide;   h++)
989    {
990        Y  = Top;
991
992        for (v = 0;   v < vSide;   v++)
993        {
```

```
994               if (displaymode & TABULATE)
995               {
996                   /* display value as text string */
997                   char   dump[21];
998
999                   sprintf(dump, "%4.2f", vect[hSide * v  + h]);
1000                  outtextxy(X, Y, dump);
1001              }
1002              else
1003              {
1004                  /* display value as filled rectangle */
1005                  float    f = vect[hSide * v  + h];   /* actual value */
1006                  float    fn = f - Vmin;               /* relative to minimum*/
1007                  float    dx;
1008                  float    dy;
1009
1010                  /* scale value to range 0 .. 1 */
1011                  dx  = dy  = sqrt((double)fn / Vscale);
1012
1013                  if (dx  >  0)
1014                  {
1015                      int    fillcolor  =  f < 0  ?  colornegative :
                                colorpositive;
1016                      int    fillpattern = f < 0  ?  patternnegative :
                                patternpositive;
1017                      int    fx;
1018                      int    fy;
1019                      int    rx;
1020                      int    ry;
1021
1022                      dx  *= DX - 1;     /* scale values to available screen space
                                                */
1023                      dy  *= DY - 1;     /* rectangle size + 1 pixel margin */
1024                      rx  = X  + dx;
1025                      ry  = Y  + dy;
1026                      setcolor(fillcolor);
1027                      rectangle(X, Y, rx, ry);
1028                      fx  = X + 1;
1029                      fy  = Y + 1;
1030                      fx  = min(fx, rx);
1031                      fy  = min(fy, ry);
1032                      setfillstyle(fillpattern,  fillcolor);
1033                      floodfill(fx,  fy,  getcolor());
1034                  }
1035              }
1036              Y  +=  DY;
1037          }
1038          X  +=  DX;
1039      }
1040  }
1041
1042  *****************************************************************
1043
1044  /* graphnet.c
1045
1046     graphics support for network display
1047
1048     version 1.0    RWD 28 Jan 1990
1049
1050     Copyright (c)  1990  R.W.Dobbins and R.C.Eberhart
1051     All Rights Reserved
1052
1053     $Revision:   1.0  $              $Date:   10 Apr 1990 10:41:52  $
1054  */
1055
1056  #include <stdio.h>
1057  #include <stdlib.h>
```

```
1058    #include <graphics.h>
1059    #include <ctype.h>
1060    #include "graphnet.h"
1061
1062    void InitScreen()
1063    {
1064        /* Initialise graphics screen */
1065        for (;;)
1066        {
1067            int     graphdriver;
1068            int     graphmode;
1069            static char     drivers[66] = "\\tc";
1070            int     len;
1071            int     result;
1072
1073            graphdriver = DETECT;
1074            initgraph(&graphdriver, &graphmode, drivers);
1075            if ((result = graphresult()) == 0)
1076                break;
1077            printf("Trouble loading BGI driver!  Error code %d\n",  result);
1078            if (result != -3)
1079                exit(1);
1080            printf("Can't find driver file. Enter driver directory pathname: ");
1081            fgets(drivers, 65, stdin);
1082            if ((len = strlen(drivers) - 1)   <=   0)
1083                exit(1);
1084            if (drivers[len]  ==   '\n')
1085                drivers[len]  =   '\0';
1086        }
1087    }
1088
1089    void ResetScreen()
1090    {
1091        closegraph();
1092    }
1093
1094    int Left;
1095    int Top;
1096    int Right;
1097    int Bottom;
1098
1099    void openviewport(VIEW *v)
1100    {
1101        setviewport(v->left, v->top, v->right,
1102                        v->bottom, 1);
1103        clearviewport();
1104        /* Define some handy parameters for the active viewport */
1105        Left   = 0;
1106        Top    = 0;
1107        Right  = v->right - v->left;
1108        Bottom = v->bottom - v->top;
1109        rectangle(Left, Top, Right, Bottom);
1110    }
1111
1112
1113    int   GraphicsGetString(char *s, int maxchars)
1114    {
1115        int     i;
1116        char    c;
1117        char    cDump[2];
1118        char    done = 0;
1119
1120        cDump[1] = '\0';
1121
1122        for (i = 0; i <= maxchars  && !done;)
1123        {
1124            c = GraphicsGetChar();
```

```
1125            if ( !isprint(c))
1126            {
1127                /* Any non-printable key */
1128                switch(c)
1129                {
1130                    case 8:
1131                        /* Backspace */
1132                        if (i)
1133                        {
1134                            /* Not at beginning yet */
1135                            moveto(getx() - textwidth("_"), gety());
1136                            s--;
1137                            i--;
1138                        }
1139                        break;
1140                    case '\n':
1141                    case '\r':
1142                        /* Finish */
1143                        done++;
1144                        break;
1145                    default:
1146                        break;
1147                }
1148            }
1149            else
1150            {
1151                *s++ = c;
1152                *cDump = c;
1153                outtext(cDump);
1154                i++;
1155            }
1156        }
1157        *s = '\0';
1158
1159        return i;
1160    }
1161
1162
1163    int    GraphicsGetChar()
1164    {
1165        int         i;                      /* blink counter */
1166        int         X;
1167        int         Y;
1168        char        cursoron;               /* TRUE when cursor displayed */
1169        static void *cursorblt;             /* address of bit image */
1170        static char HasBlt = 0;       /* TRUE when cursor bit image captured */
1171        int         CursorBlinkRate = 1000;
1172
1173        cursoron = ~0;                      /* Initially, cursor displayed */
1174        X       = getx();                   /* Current position */
1175        Y       = gety();
1176
1177        if (!HasBlt)
1178        {
1179            int         XRight   = X + textwidth("X");
1180            int         YBottom = Y + textheight("X");
1181            unsigned    size;                   /* Size of cursor image */
1182
1183            /* Generate a cursor bit image */
1184            outtext("_");           /* Put initial cursor symbol */
1185            size = imagesize(X, Y, XRight, YBottom);
1186            if ((cursorblt = (void *)malloc(size)) == NULL)
1187            {
1188                GraphAbort("Not enough memory");
1189            }
1190            getimage(X, Y, XRight, YBottom, cursorblt);
1191            moveto(X, Y);
```

```
92              HasBlt = 1;
93          }
94          putimage(X, Y, cursorblt, COPY_PUT);
95
96          for (;;)
97          {
98              for (i = 0; i < CursorBlinkRate; i++)
99              {
00                  if (kbhit())
01                  {
02                      /* Key has been pressed: erase cursor before returning */
03                      if (cursoron)
04                      {
05                          putimage(X, Y, cursorblt, XOR_PUT);
06                      }
07                      return   getch();
08                  }
09              }
10
11              /* Blink cursor */
12              putimage(X, Y, cursorblt, XOR_PUT);
13              cursoron = ~cursoron;
14          }
15      }
16
17
18      int     FoldColor(int  color)
19      {
20          int    MaxColor = getmaxcolor();
21
22          return   min(MaxColor, color);
23      }
24
25
26      int     GraphAbort(char *Message)
27      {
28          outtext(Message);
29          getch();
30          closegraph();
31          exit(1);
32      }
33
34      ****************************************************************
35
36      /* kohonen.h
37      */
38
39      #define     TRUE        1
40      #define     FALSE       0
41      #define     ESC         27
42      #define     ABORT       17      /* ^Q */
43      #define     ITEMS       8
44
45      extern MATRIX   out0;               /* input layer  */
46      extern MATRIX   out2;               /* output layer */
47      extern MATRIX   Weights;            /* weights input:output */
48      extern VECTOR   PatternID;          /* identifier for each stored pattern */
49      extern int      nInputNodes;        /* number of input nodes         */
50      extern int      nOutputNodes;       /* number of output nodes        */
51      extern int      nPatterns;          /* number of patterns desired    */
52      extern int      nIterations;        /* number of iterations desired  */
53      extern int      p;                  /* index pattern number          */
54      extern int      Side;               /* size of one side of output rectangle */
55      extern long     Tk;                 /* elapsed time in time steps */
56      extern float    eta;                /* actual learning rate */
57      extern int      DensityFunction;    /* probability density of patterns
                                            */
```

```
1258    extern int      q;              /* epoch count */
1259    extern int      t;              /* time step in current segment */
1260
1261    ****************************************************************
1262
1263    /* vector.h
1264
1265        typedefs and prototypes for dynamic storage of arrays
1266
1267    */
1268
1269    typedef float *PFLOAT;
1270    typedef PFLOAT VECTOR;
1271    typedef PFLOAT *MATRIX;
1272
1273    void   VectorAllocate(VECTOR *vector, int nCols);
1274    void   AllocateCols(PFLOAT matrix[], int nRows, int nCols);
1275    void   MatrixAllocate(MATRIX *pmatrix, int nRows, int nCols);
1276    void   MatrixFree(MATRIX matrix,  int nRows);
1277
1278    ****************************************************************
1279
1280    /* graphnet.h
1281    */
1282    extern int Left;
1283    extern int Top;
1284    extern int Right;
1285    extern int Bottom;
1286    typedef struct viewporttype VIEW;
1287
1288    void InitScreen(void);
1289    void ResetScreen(void);
1290    void openviewport(VIEW *v);
1291
1292    ****************************************************************
1293
```

APPENDIX C

```
1       Program OCR_Shell
2       uses
3         Crt,Dos,Graph,pcx_tp;{pcx_tp from Genus Toolkit}
4
5       var
6         F, F2 : text;
7
8       const
9         { BGI fonts }
10        Fonts : array[0..4] of string[13] =
11        ('DefaultFont', 'TriplexFont', 'SmallFont',
12         'SansSerifFont', 'GothicFont');
13        { BGI text directions }
14        TextDirect : array[0..1] of string[8] =
15        ('HorizDir', 'VertDir');
16        Num_of_patterns = 10;
17        Num_of_characters = 2000; { for 80x25 viewport }
18        Input_file_from_neural_net =
19                        'C:\TP\EXE\BrainRTS.Out';
20        Output_file_for_neural_net =
21                        'C:\TP\EXE\BrainRTS.In';
22        OCR_Output_file = 'C:\TP\EXE\OCR.Out';
23        PCX_file = 'C:\TP\EXE\a.PCX';
24        Line_length = 79; Threshold = 0.60;
25        PCX_type = pcxCGA_6;
26
27      type
28        Weights = array[1..Num_of_characters]
29                    of string[4];
30        Patterns = array[1..Num_of_characters]
31                    of string[1];
32      { objects }
33
34      NNIptr = ^neural_net_interpreter;
35      neural_net_interpreter = object
36        Array_index: integer; First_char, S: string;
37        Weight: Weights; Output_pattern: Patterns;
38        constructor Init; destructor Done; virtual;
39        procedure Get_weights;
40        procedure Output_characters;
41      end;
42
43      Screenptr = ^screen;
44      screen = object
45        GraphDriver: integer; { Graphics device driver }
46        GraphMode: integer;          { Graphics mode value }
47        MaxX, MaxY: word;  { Maximum screen resolution }
48        ErrorCode: integer;   { Reports graphics errors }
49        MaxColor: word;     { Max color value available }
50        pcxReturn: integer; PixelStatus: integer;
51        ViewInfo: ViewPortType; constructor init;
52        destructor done; virtual; procedure Initialize;
53      end;
```

```pascal
54
55      var
56        OldExitProc : Pointer;        {Saves exit proc addr}
57
58      {$F+}
59      procedure MyExitProc;
60      begin
61        ExitProc := OldExitProc;{Restore exit proc addr}
62        CloseGraph;        { Shut down the graphics system }
63      end; { MyExitProc }
64      {$F-}
65
66      procedure screen.Initialize;
67      { Initialize graphics and report errors}
68      var
69        InGraphicsMode: boolean; { Flags graphics init}
70        PathToDriver  : string;  {path to *.BGI & *.CHR}
71
72      begin
73        { When using Crt & graphics, turn off Crt's
74          memory-mapped writes }
75        DirectVideo := False;
76        OldExitProc := ExitProc; { Save prev exit proc }
77        ExitProc := @MyExitProc; { Insert our exit proc}
78        PathToDriver := '';
79        repeat
80          GraphDriver := Detect;{detect graphic adapter}
81          InitGraph(GraphDriver,GraphMode,PathToDriver);
82          ErrorCode := GraphResult;{Preserve err return}
83          if ErrorCode <<>> grOK then       { Error? }
84          begin
85            Writeln('Graphics error: ',
86                       GraphErrorMsg(ErrorCode));
87            if ErrorCode = grFileNotFound then begin
88              Writeln('Enter full path to BGI driver');
89              Writeln('or type <<Ctrl-Break>> to quit.');
90              Readln(PathToDriver); Writeln;
91            end
92            else Halt(1);{ Some other error: terminate }
93          end;
94        until ErrorCode = grOK;
95      end; { Initialize }
96
97      { object constructors & destructors }
98
99      constructor screen.init;
100     begin end;
101
102     destructor screen.done;
103     begin end;
104
105     constructor neural_net_interpreter.init;
106     begin end;
107
108     destructor neural_net_interpreter.done;
109     begin end;
110
111     { object methods }
112
113     procedure neural_net_interpreter.Get_weights;
114     var
115        This_weight  : string[4];
116        This_pattern : string[1];
117        Count        : integer; Char_Ptr: integer;
```

```
118
119      begin
120        FOR Count := 1 TO Num_of_characters DO
121          begin      { Initialize arrays }
122            Weight[Count]          := ' ';
123            Output_pattern[Count] := ' ';
124          end;
125        Assign(F,Input_file_from_neural_net);
126        Reset(F); Array_index := 1;
127        WHILE Array_index <<= Num_of_characters DO begin
128          Readln(F,S); First_char := Copy(S,1,1);
129            IF First_char = ' ' THEN begin
130                Char_Ptr  := 2;
131                FOR Count := 1 TO Num_of_patterns DO
132                   begin
133                     This_weight:=Copy(S,Char_Ptr,4);
134                     Weight[Array_index]:=This_weight;
135                     Char_Ptr := Char_Ptr + 5;
136                     This_pattern:=Copy(S,Char_Ptr,1);
137                     Output_pattern[Array_index] :=
138                       This_pattern;
139                     Char_Ptr := Char_Ptr + 2;
140                     Inc(Array_index);
141                   end;
142                end;
143          end;
144        Close(F);
145      end;
146
147      procedure neural_net_interpreter.output_characters;
148      var
149        Output_char   : string;
150        Pattern_count, Char_count, ReturnCode : integer;
151        Wt, New_weight : real;
152
153      begin
154        Assign(F2,OCR_Output_file); Rewrite(F2);
155        Array_index := 1; Char_count   := 1;
156        WHILE Array_index <<= Num_of_characters DO
157        begin
158         Pattern_count := 1;
159         Wt := 0; Output_char := ' ';
160         WHILE Pattern_count <<= Num_of_patterns DO
161          begin
162            Val(Weight[Array_index],New_weight,
163               ReturnCode);
164            IF New_weight >> Wt THEN begin
165               Wt := New_weight;
166               Output_char :=
167                 Output_pattern[Array_index];
168              end;
169            Inc(Pattern_count); Inc(Array_index);
170           end;
171         IF Wt >>= Threshold THEN Write(F2,Output_char)
172         ELSE
173           Write(F2,' ');
174         IF Char_count >> Line_length THEN
175         begin
176           Writeln(F2); Char_count := 0;
177         end;
178         Inc(Char_count);
179        end;
180        Close(F2);
181      end;
```

```
182
183
184      procedure pcx_to_neural_net;
185      {get PCX; display; convert to txt for BrainMaker.}
186      var
187        SPort              : Screenptr;
188        X, Y               : integer;
189        XPt, YPt, RowPt : integer;   S: string;
190
191      begin
192        New(SPort,init);
193        WITH SPort^ DO begin
194          Initialize;
195          Maxx := GetMaxx; Maxy := GetMaxy;
196          SetViewPort(0,0,Maxx,Maxy,ClipOn);
197          SetTextStyle(DefaultFont, HorizDir, 1);
198          pcxReturn := pcxSetDisplay(PCX_type);
199          pcxReturn := pcxFileDisplay(PCX_file,0,0,0);
200          IF (pcxReturn = pcxSuccess) THEN begin
201            Assign(F,Output_file_for_neural_net);
202            Rewrite(F);
203            GetViewSettings(ViewInfo); { coordinates of
204                                                Viewport }
205            XPt   := 0; YPt   := 0; RowPt := 0;
206            WHILE RowPt <<= ViewInfo.y2 DO begin
207              WHILE XPt <<= ViewInfo.x2 DO begin
208                FOR Y := YPt to (YPt + 7) DO begin
209                  FOR X := XPt to (XPt + 7) DO begin
210                      PixelStatus := GetPixel(X,Y);
211                      IF PixelStatus = 0 THEN
212                        write(F,'.'){BrainMaker wants}
213                      ELSE        { either a . or an X }
214                        write(F,'X');
215                    end;
216                  writeln(F);
217                end;
218              YPt := RowPt; XPt := XPt + 8;
219            end;
220            XPt := 0; RowPt := RowPt + 8; YPt := RowPt;
221          end;
222        end;
223        Close(F);
224      end;
225      Dispose(SPort,done);
226    end;  { pcx_to_neural_net}
227
228    var
229      NNI : NNIptr;
230
231    begin { main program body }
232      pcx_to_neural_net;{Prep PCX file for BrainMaker}
233      New(NNI, init);
234      WITH NNI^ DO begin
235        SwapVectors;
236        exec('C:\COMMAND.COM','/C C:\BATCH\net'); {BM}
237        SwapVectors;
238        IF DosError <<>> 0 THEN
239          Writeln('Dos error # ',DosError)
240        ELSE
241          Get_weights; {Translate BrainMaker's output}
242          Output_characters;    {write a file of ASCII}
243          Dispose(NNI, done);            { Clean up }
244      end;
245    end. { main }
```

```
246
247
248      /* OCR addendum */
249
250      /* The main listing (OCR.PAS) sets a default graphics mode for
251      the CGA adapter in the "type" section --
252
253        PCX_type = pcxCGA_6;
254
255      To run this code with other adapters, you need to tell the .PCX
256      toolbox what kind of adapter you're using. To do this, replace
257      this constant with one of the following, and have the
258      appropriate .BGI file in the current directory --
259
260      PCX_type = pcxEGA_E (640x200x16)
261      PCX_type = pcxVGA_12 (640x480x16)
262      etc....
263
264      For more information on specific types, check the PCX
265      Programmer's Toolkit manual.
266
267      The screen.Initialize procedure then uses --
268
269        GraphDriver := Detect;{detect graphic adapter}
270        InitGraph(GraphDriver,GraphMode,PathToDriver);
271
272      to automatically detect and link in the correct graphics
273      adapter.  */
```

APPENDIX D

```
1
2                         OHSUS19.TXT
3
4      1 0 0 0 0 0 0 0 0 0 0   0   1 0 0 0 0 0
5      0 1 0 0 0 0 0 0 0 0 0   0   1 0 0 0 0 0
6      0 0 1 0 0 0 0 0 0 0 0   0   0 1 0 0 0 0
7      0 0 0 0 1 0 0 0 0 0 0   0   0 1 0 0 0 0
8      0 0 0 0 1 0 0 0 0 0 0   0   0 0 1 0 0 0
9      0 0 0 0 0 1 0 0 0 0 0   0   1 0 0 0 0 0
10     0 0 0 0 1 0 0 0 0 0 0   0   0 1 0 0 0 0
11     0 0 1 0 0 0 0 0 0 0 0   0   0 1 0 0 0 0
12     1 0 0 0 0 0 0 0 0 0 0   0   0 0 1 0 0 0
13     0 1 0 0 0 0 0 0 0 0 0   0   1 0 0 0 0 0
14     0 0 1 0 0 0 0 0 0 0 0   0   0 1 0 0 0 0
15     0 0 1 0 0 0 0 0 0 0 0   0   0 1 0 0 0 0
16     0 1 0 0 0 0 0 0 0 0 0   0   0 1 0 0 0 0
17     1 0 0 0 0 0 0 0 0 0 0   0   0 1 0 0 0 0
18     0 1 0 0 0 0 0 0 0 0 0   0   0 0 0 1 0 0
19     0 0 0 0 0 0 0 0 0 0 0   1   0 1 0 0 0 0
20     1 0 0 0 0 0 0 0 0 0 0   0   1 0 0 0 0 0
21     0 1 0 0 0 0 0 0 0 0 0   0   1 0 0 0 0 0
22     0 0 1 0 0 0 0 0 0 0 0   0   0 1 0 0 0 0
23     0 0 0 0 1 0 0 0 0 0 0   0   0 1 0 0 0 0
24     0 0 0 0 1 0 0 0 0 0 0   0   0 0 1 0 0 0
25     0 0 0 0 0 1 0 0 0 0 0   0   1 0 0 0 0 0
26     0 0 0 0 1 0 0 0 0 0 0   0   0 1 0 0 0 0
27     0 0 1 0 0 0 0 0 0 0 0   0   0 1 0 0 0 0
28     1 0 0 0 0 0 0 0 0 0 0   0   0 0 1 0 0 0
29     0 1 0 0 0 0 0 0 0 0 0   0   1 0 0 0 0 0
30     0 0 1 0 0 0 0 0 0 0 0   0   0 1 0 0 0 0
31     0 0 1 0 0 0 0 0 0 0 0   0   0 1 0 0 0 0
32     0 1 0 0 0 0 0 0 0 0 0   0   0 1 0 0 0 0
33     0 1 0 0 0 0 0 0 0 0 0   0   0 1 0 0 0 0
34     1 0 0 0 0 0 0 0 0 0 0   0   0 0 0 0 1 0
35     0 0 0 0 0 0 0 0 0 0 0   1   0 0 1 0 0 0
36     0 0 0 1 0 0 0 0 0 0 0   0   0 0 0 1 0 0
37     0 0 0 1 0 0 0 0 0 0 0   0   0 0 0 1 0 0
38     0 0 0 0 0 1 0 0 0 0 0   0   0 1 0 0 0 0
39     0 0 0 0 0 1 0 0 0 0 0   0   0 0 0 1 0 0
40     0 0 0 0 0 1 0 0 0 0 0   0   0 1 0 0 0 0
41     0 0 0 0 1 0 0 0 0 0 0   0   0 0 1 0 0 0
42     0 0 0 0 1 0 0 0 0 0 0   0   1 0 0 0 0 0
43     0 0 1 0 0 0 0 0 0 0 0   0   0 1 0 0 0 0
44     1 0 0 0 0 0 0 0 0 0 0   0   0 1 0 0 0 0
45     0 1 0 0 0 0 0 0 0 0 0   0   0 0 0 1 0 0
46     0 0 0 0 0 0 0 0 0 0 0   1   0 1 0 0 0 0
47     1 0 0 0 0 0 0 0 0 0 0   0   1 0 0 0 0 0
48     0 1 0 0 0 0 0 0 0 0 0   0   1 0 0 0 0 0
49     0 0 1 0 0 0 0 0 0 0 0   0   0 1 0 0 0 0
50     0 0 0 0 1 0 0 0 0 0 0   0   0 1 0 0 0 0
51     0 0 0 0 1 0 0 0 0 0 0   0   0 1 0 0 0 0
52     0 0 0 0 0 1 0 0 0 0 0   0   0 1 0 0 0 0
53     0 0 0 0 1 0 0 0 0 0 0   0   0 1 0 0 0 0
54     0 0 1 0 0 0 0 0 0 0 0   0   0 1 0 0 0 0
55     1 0 0 0 0 0 0 0 0 0 0   0   0 0 1 0 0 0
56     0 1 0 0 0 0 0 0 0 0 0   0   1 0 0 0 0 0
57     0 0 1 0 0 0 0 0 0 0 0   0   0 1 0 0 0 0
```

```
58    0 0 1 0 0 0 0 0 0 0 0 0   0   0 1 0 0 0 0
59    0 1 0 0 0 0 0 0 0 0 0 0   0   0 1 0 0 0 0
60    0 1 0 0 0 0 0 0 0 0 0 0   0   0 1 0 0 0 0
61    1 0 0 0 0 0 0 0 0 0 0 0   0   0 0 0 1 0 0
62    0 0 0 0 0 0 0 0 0 0 0 0   1   0 0 0 1 0 0
63
64
65                      SBCRM19.TXT
66
67    0 0 0 0 1 0 0 0 0 0 0 0   0   0 1 0 0 0 0
68    0 0 0 0 0 1 0 0 0 0 0 0   0   0 1 0 0 0 0
69    0 0 0 0 0 0 0 1 0 0 0 0   0   0 1 0 0 0 0
70    0 0 0 0 0 0 0 1 0 0 0 0   0   0 1 0 0 0 0
71    0 0 0 0 0 0 0 1 0 0 0 0   0   0 1 0 0 0 0
72    0 0 0 0 0 0 0 1 0 0 0 0   0   0 1 0 0 0 0
73    0 0 0 0 0 1 0 0 0 0 0 0   0   0 1 0 0 0 0
74    0 0 0 0 1 0 0 0 0 0 0 0   0   0 1 0 0 0 0
75    0 0 1 0 0 0 0 0 0 0 0 0   0   0 1 0 0 0 0
76    0 0 0 0 1 0 0 0 0 0 0 0   0   0 1 0 0 0 0
77    0 0 0 0 0 0 0 1 0 0 0 0   0   0 0 0 0 0 1
78    0 0 0 0 0 0 0 1 0 0 0 0   0   0 1 0 0 0 0
79    0 0 0 0 0 0 0 0 1 0 0 0   0   0 1 0 0 0 0
80    0 0 0 0 0 0 0 0 0 1 0 0   0   0 1 0 0 0 0
81    0 0 0 0 0 0 0 0 0 1 0 0   0   0 1 0 0 0 0
82    0 0 0 0 0 0 0 0 0 1 0 0   0   0 1 0 0 0 0
83    0 0 0 0 0 0 0 0 0 1 0 0   0   0 1 0 0 0 0
84    0 0 0 0 0 0 0 0 0 0 0 1   0   0 1 0 0 0 0
85    0 0 0 0 0 0 0 0 0 1 0 0   0   0 1 0 0 0 0
86    0 0 0 0 0 0 0 0 1 0 0 0   0   0 1 0 0 0 0
87    0 0 0 0 0 0 0 1 0 0 0 0   0   0 1 0 0 0 0
88    0 0 0 0 0 0 0 1 0 0 0 0   0   0 0 0 0 0 1
89    0 0 0 0 0 0 0 0 0 0 0 1   0   0 1 0 0 0 0
90    0 0 0 0 0 0 0 0 0 0 1 0   0   0 1 0 0 0 0
91    0 0 0 0 0 0 0 0 0 1 0 0   0   0 1 0 0 0 0
92    0 0 0 0 0 0 0 0 0 1 0 0   0   0 1 0 0 0 0
93    0 0 0 0 0 0 0 0 0 1 0 0   0   0 1 0 0 0 0
94    0 0 0 0 0 0 0 0 0 1 0 0   0   0 1 0 0 0 0
95    0 0 0 0 0 0 0 0 1 0 0 0   0   0 1 0 0 0 0
96    0 0 0 0 0 0 0 1 0 0 0 0   0   0 1 0 0 0 0
97    0 0 0 0 0 0 0 1 0 0 0 0   0   0 1 0 0 0 0
98    0 0 0 0 0 0 0 1 0 0 0 0   0   0 1 0 0 0 0
99    0 0 0 0 0 1 0 0 0 0 0 0   0   0 1 0 0 0 0
100   0 0 0 0 0 1 0 0 0 0 0 0   0   0 1 0 0 0 0
101   0 0 0 0 0 1 0 0 0 0 0 0   0   0 1 0 0 0 0
102   0 0 0 0 0 1 0 0 0 0 0 0   0   0 1 0 0 0 0
103   0 0 0 0 0 0 0 0 1 0 0 0   0   0 1 0 0 0 0
104   0 0 0 0 0 0 0 1 0 0 0 0   0   0 1 0 0 0 0
105   0 0 0 0 0 0 1 0 0 0 0 0   0   0 1 0 0 0 0
106   0 0 0 0 0 1 0 0 0 0 0 0   0   0 1 0 0 0 0
107   0 0 0 0 1 0 0 0 0 0 0 0   0   0 1 0 0 0 0
108   0 0 0 0 1 0 0 0 0 0 0 0   0   0 1 0 0 0 0
109   0 0 0 0 0 0 0 1 0 0 0 0   0   0 0 1 0 0 0
110   0 0 0 0 0 0 0 0 1 0 0 0   0   1 0 0 0 0 0
111   0 0 0 0 0 0 0 0 0 1 0 0   0   0 1 0 0 0 0
112   0 0 0 0 0 0 0 0 1 0 0 0   0   0 1 0 0 0 0
113   0 0 0 0 0 1 0 0 0 0 0 0   0   0 1 0 0 0 0
114   0 0 0 0 0 0 1 0 0 0 0 0   0   0 1 0 0 0 0
115   0 0 0 0 0 0 0 1 0 0 0 0   0   0 0 0 0 0 1
116   0 0 0 0 0 0 0 0 0 0 0 0   1   0 0 0 1 0 0
117
118
119                      YELRO19.TXT
120
121   0 0 0 0 1 0 0 0 0 0 0 0   0   1 0 0 0 0 0
```

```
122    0 0 0 1 0 0 0 0 0 0 0 0    0    1 0 0 0 0 0
123    0 0 1 0 0 0 0 0 0 0 0 0    0    0 1 0 0 0 0
124    0 0 0 0 1 0 0 0 0 0 0 0    0    0 1 0 0 0 0
125    0 0 0 0 1 0 0 0 0 0 0 0    0    0 1 0 0 0 0
126    0 0 0 0 1 0 0 0 0 0 0 0    0    0 1 0 0 0 0
127    0 0 0 0 0 1 0 0 0 0 0 0    0    0 1 0 0 0 0
128    0 0 0 0 1 0 0 0 0 0 0 0    0    0 0 0 1 0 0
129    0 0 0 1 0 0 0 0 0 0 0 0    0    0 1 0 0 0 0
130    0 0 1 0 0 0 0 0 0 0 0 0    0    0 1 0 0 0 0
131    0 0 0 0 1 0 0 0 0 0 0 0    0    0 1 0 0 0 0
132    0 0 0 0 0 0 0 1 0 0 0 0    0    0 0 1 0 0 0
133    0 0 0 0 0 0 0 0 1 0 0 0    0    1 0 0 0 0 0
134    0 0 0 0 0 0 0 0 0 1 0 0    0    0 0 0 0 1 0
135    0 0 0 0 0 0 0 0 0 0 0 0    1    0 1 0 0 0 0
136    0 0 0 0 0 0 0 0 0 1 0 0    0    0 1 0 0 0 0
137    0 0 0 0 0 0 0 0 0 1 0 0    0    0 1 0 0 0 0
138    0 0 0 1 0 0 0 0 0 0 0 0    0    0 1 0 0 0 0
139    0 0 0 1 0 0 0 0 0 0 0 0    0    0 1 0 0 0 0
140    0 0 0 0 0 0 0 0 0 1 0 0    0    0 1 0 0 0 0
141    0 0 0 0 0 0 0 0 0 1 0 0    0    0 1 0 0 0 0
142    0 0 0 0 0 0 0 0 1 0 0 0    0    0 0 0 1 0 0
143    0 0 0 0 0 0 0 1 0 0 0 0    0    0 1 0 0 0 0
144    0 0 0 0 0 0 1 0 0 0 0 0    0    0 1 0 0 0 0
145    0 0 0 0 0 0 0 1 0 0 0 0    0    0 1 0 0 0 0
146    0 0 0 0 0 0 0 0 1 0 0 0    0    0 0 1 0 0 0
147    0 0 0 0 0 0 0 0 0 1 0 0    0    1 0 0 0 0 0
148    0 0 0 0 0 0 0 0 1 0 0 0    0    0 0 0 0 1 0
149    0 0 0 0 0 0 0 0 0 0 0 0    1    0 1 0 0 0 0
150    0 0 0 0 1 0 0 0 0 0 0 0    0    1 0 0 0 0 0
151    0 0 0 1 0 0 0 0 0 0 0 0    0    1 0 0 0 0 0
152    0 0 1 0 0 0 0 0 0 0 0 0    0    0 1 0 0 0 0
153    0 0 0 0 1 0 0 0 0 0 0 0    0    0 1 0 0 0 0
154    0 0 0 0 1 0 0 0 0 0 0 0    0    0 1 0 0 0 0
155    0 0 0 1 0 0 0 0 0 0 0 0    0    0 1 0 0 0 0
156    0 0 0 0 0 1 0 0 0 0 0 0    0    0 1 0 0 0 0
157    0 0 0 0 1 0 0 0 0 0 0 0    0    0 1 0 0 0 0
158    0 0 0 0 1 0 0 0 0 0 0 0    0    0 0 1 0 0 0
159    0 0 0 1 0 0 0 0 0 0 0 0    0    1 0 0 0 0 0
160    0 0 1 0 0 0 0 0 0 0 0 0    0    0 1 0 0 0 0
161    0 0 0 0 1 0 0 0 0 0 0 0    0    0 1 0 0 0 0
162    0 0 0 0 0 0 0 1 0 0 0 0    0    0 0 1 0 0 0
163    0 0 0 0 0 0 0 0 1 0 0 0    0    1 0 0 0 0 0
164    0 0 0 0 0 0 0 0 0 1 0 0    0    0 0 0 0 1 0
165    0 0 0 0 0 0 0 0 0 0 0 0    1    0 1 0 0 0 0
166    0 0 0 0 1 0 0 0 0 0 0 0    0    1 0 0 0 0 0
167    0 0 0 0 1 0 0 0 0 0 0 0    0    1 0 0 0 0 0
168    0 0 0 0 1 0 0 0 0 0 0 0    0    0 1 0 0 0 0
169    0 0 0 0 0 0 0 0 0 0 1 0    0    0 1 0 0 0 0
170    0 0 0 0 0 0 0 0 0 0 1 0    0    0 1 0 0 0 0
171    0 0 0 0 0 0 0 0 0 0 1 0    0    0 1 0 0 0 0
172    0 0 0 0 0 0 0 0 0 0 1 0    0    0 1 0 0 0 0
173    0 0 0 0 0 0 0 0 1 0 0 0    0    0 1 0 0 0 0
174    0 0 0 0 0 0 0 0 1 0 0 0    0    0 0 1 0 0 0
175    0 0 0 0 0 0 0 1 0 0 0 0    0    1 0 0 0 0 0
176    0 0 0 0 0 0 1 0 0 0 0 0    0    0 1 0 0 0 0
177    0 0 0 0 1 0 0 0 0 0 0 0    0    0 1 0 0 0 0
178    0 0 0 0 0 0 0 0 0 1 0 0    0    0 0 1 0 0 0
179    0 0 0 0 0 0 0 1 0 0 0 0    0    1 0 0 0 0 0
180    0 0 0 0 0 0 0 1 0 0 0 0    0    0 0 0 0 1 0
181    0 0 0 0 0 0 0 0 0 0 0 0    1    0 1 0 0 0 0
182
183
184
185
```

```
186
187
188                         MU41901D.RUN
189
190     1
191     tr41901d.out tr41901d.err mu4n1901.pat w761119.wts tr41901d.wts 158 1500 7
            11 19 0.15 0.075
192
193
194     Format of this run file:
195         number of runs,    followed by:
196         run specification lines
197         ...
198     Format of each run specification line:
199     fOut  fErr  fPat  fWts  fWtso  nPats  nIter  nInp  nHid  nOut  eta  alpha
200
201     Description of parameters:
202         fOut    output nodes file         fErr    error output file
203         fPat    input pattern file        fWts    weight file input
204         fWtso   weight file output        nPats   number of patterns to read
205         nIter   number of iterations      nInp    number of input nodes
206         nHid    number hidden nodes       nOut    number of output nodes.
207         eta     learning rate             alpha   momentum factor
208
209
210
211
212
213
214
215
216
217
218
219                         NEWSONG.RUN
220
221     1
222     netm.out netm.err  net.in  tr41901d.wts  junk.wts  1  1  76  11  19  0.001
            0.0001
223
224
225
226                     YAN.PAT
227
228     0 0 0 0 0 0 0 1 0 0 0 0  0  1 0 0 0 0 0
229     0 0 0 0 0 0 0 1 0 0 0 0  0  1 0 0 0 0 0
230     0 0 0 0 0 0 0 1 0 0 0 0  0  0 1 0 0 0 0
231     0 0 0 0 0 0 0 0 1 0 0 0  0  0 1 0 0 0 0
232
233
234
235
```

NEWSONG.TXT

```
236
237    0 0 0 0 0 0 0 1 0 0 0 0 0 1 0 0 0 0 0
238    0 0 0 0 0 0 0 0 1 0 0 0 0 1 0 0 0 0 0
239    0 0 0 0 0 0 0 0 0 1 0 0 0 0 1 0 0 0 0
240    0 0 0 0 0 0 0 0 0 1 0 0 0 0 1 0 0 0 0
241    0 0 0 0 0 0 0 0 0 1 0 0 0 0 1 0 0 0 0
242    0 0 0 0 0 0 0 0 0 1 0 0 0 0 1 0 0 0 0
243    0 0 0 0 0 0 0 0 1 0 0 0 0 0 1 0 0 0 0
244    0 0 0 0 0 0 0 1 0 0 0 0 0 0 1 0 0 0 0
245    0 0 0 0 0 0 0 1 0 0 0 0 0 0 1 0 0 0 0
246    0 0 0 0 0 0 0 1 0 0 0 0 0 0 1 0 0 0 0
247    0 0 0 0 0 1 0 0 0 0 0 0 0 0 1 0 0 0 0
248    0 0 0 0 1 0 0 0 0 0 0 0 0 0 1 0 0 0 0
249    0 0 1 0 0 0 0 0 0 0 0 0 0 0 1 0 0 0 0
250    0 0 0 1 0 0 0 0 0 0 0 0 0 0 1 0 0 0 0
251    0 0 0 1 0 0 0 0 0 0 0 0 0 0 0 0 1 0 0
252    0 0 0 0 0 0 0 0 0 0 0 0 1 0 1 0 0 0 0
253    0 1 0 0 0 0 0 0 0 0 0 0 0 1 0 0 0 0 0
254    0 1 0 0 0 0 0 0 0 0 0 0 0 1 0 0 0 0 0
255    0 0 1 0 0 0 0 0 0 0 0 0 0 0 1 0 0 0 0
256    0 0 0 1 0 0 0 0 0 0 0 0 0 0 1 0 0 0 0
257    0 0 0 0 1 0 0 0 0 0 0 0 0 0 1 0 0 0 0
258    0 0 0 0 1 0 0 0 0 0 0 0 0 0 1 0 0 0 0
259    0 0 0 0 0 1 0 0 0 0 0 0 0 0 1 0 0 0 0
260    0 0 0 0 1 0 0 0 0 0 0 0 0 0 1 0 0 0 0
261    0 0 0 0 1 0 0 0 0 0 0 0 0 0 0 0 1 0 0
262    0 0 0 1 0 0 0 0 0 0 0 0 0 0 0 1 0 0 0
263    0 0 0 0 0 0 0 1 0 0 0 0 0 1 0 0 0 0 0
264    0 0 0 1 0 0 0 0 0 0 0 0 0 0 1 0 0 0 0
265    0 0 1 0 0 0 0 0 0 0 0 0 0 0 1 0 0 0 0
266    1 0 0 0 0 0 0 0 0 0 0 0 0 0 1 0 0 0 0
267    0 1 0 0 0 0 0 0 0 0 0 0 0 1 0 0 0 0 0
268    0 0 0 1 0 0 0 0 0 0 0 0 0 0 1 0 0 0 0
269    0 0 1 0 0 0 0 0 0 0 0 0 0 0 1 0 0 0 0
270    0 1 0 0 0 0 0 0 0 0 0 0 0 0 1 0 0 0 0
271    1 0 0 0 0 0 0 0 0 0 0 0 0 1 0 0 0 0 0
272    0 0 0 1 0 0 0 0 0 0 0 0 0 0 1 0 0 0 0
273    0 0 1 0 0 0 0 0 0 0 0 0 0 0 1 0 0 0 0
274    1 0 0 0 0 0 0 0 0 0 0 0 0 0 1 0 0 0 0
275    0 1 0 0 0 0 0 0 0 0 0 0 1 0 0 0 0 0 0
276    0 0 0 1 0 0 0 0 0 0 0 0 0 0 1 0 0 0 0
277    0 0 1 0 0 0 0 0 0 0 0 0 0 0 1 0 0 0 0
278    0 1 0 0 0 0 0 0 0 0 0 0 0 0 1 0 0 0 0
279    0 0 0 1 0 0 0 0 0 0 0 0 0 1 0 0 0 0 0
280    0 0 1 0 0 0 0 0 0 0 0 0 0 0 1 0 0 0 0
281    1 0 0 0 0 0 0 0 0 0 0 0 0 0 0 0 1 0 0
282    0 0 0 0 0 0 0 0 0 0 0 0 1 0 0 0 1 0 0
283
284
285
286
287                         NEWSONG.GIO
288
289    * america1.gio  composed by neural network 2/25/90 [Russ Eberhart]
290    * net trained with Oh Susanna, Yellow Rose of Texas, and She'll Be
291    *    Comin' 'Round the Mountain
292    r q z26 v1
293    c5 s 1f; d5; e5 i; e5; e5; e5; d5; c5; c5; c5; a4; g4; e4; g4; g4 q; r i;
294    d4 s; d4; e4 i; g4; g4; g4; a4; g4; g4 q; f4 i.; d5 s; f4 i; e4; c4 i.;
295    d4 s; g4 i; e4; d4 i.; c4 s; f4 i; e4; c4 i.; d4 s; g4 i; e4; d4 i.; f4 s;
296    e4 i; c4 q; r
297
298
```

```
299                        MUSIC19.C
300
301     /* music19.c
302        Generates a set of patterns for music generator neural network.
303        Input is a text file of notes, where each note consists of a pitch
304        plus a duration.  Note value and duration are represented as a
305        string of 0's and one 1's, separated by spaces, for example:
306                    note value            duration in 16ths
307           c d e f g a b c d e f g  R    1 2 3 4 6 12
308           0 0 0 0 0 0 0 1 0 0 0 0  0    0 1 0 0 0 0
309           ^middle C                     ^rest
310
311        command line parameters:
312           -nN                   N is the number of notes in context (each
313                                 pattern line consists of N - 1 notes plus 1
314                                 target note).
315     */
316     #include <stdio.h>
317     #include <stdlib.h>
318
319     #define MAXNOTES      6       /* maximum notes in a context */
320     #define NOTES         6       /* default notes in context */
321     #define MAXSCALE      13      /* maximum pitch scale including rest */
322     #define NOTESCALE     13      /* actual pitch scale */
323     #define MAXDURATION   6       /* maximum number of note durations */
324     #define NOTEDURATION  6       /* actual number of note durations */
325     #define LOSER         0       /* loser value for all inactive neurodes */
326     #define WINNER        1       /* winner value for active neurodes */
327                                   /* only one active pitch, one duration */
328
329     void   main(int argc,  char *argv[])
330     {
331        int *note[MAXNOTES];    /* notes already seen plus the next note */
332        int notesize = NOTESCALE + NOTEDURATION;
333        int notes   = NOTES;        /* number of notes in context */
334        int i, j, k;
335        int need;
336        int *ptemp;
337        float loser  = LOSER;       /* loser value for nodes */
338        float winner = WINNER;      /* winner value for nodes */
339
340        /* process command line options */
341        while (--argc)
342        {
343           char *arg;
344
345           arg = *++argv;                          /* next argument */
346           if (*arg++ == '-')                        /* options */
347              switch (*arg++)
348              {
349                 case 'n':
350                     /* expecting number of notes */
351                     sscanf(arg, "%d", &notes);
352                     break;
353                 case 'l':
354                     /* expecting number */
355                     sscanf(arg, "%f", &loser);
356                     break;
357                 case 'w':
358                     /* expecting number */
359                     sscanf(arg, "%f", &winner);
360                     break;
361                 case '?':
362                     fprintf(stderr,
```

```
                              "Usage:\nmusic -nN -1L -wW <notes >patterns\n");

                 fprintf(stderr, "N number of notes including target\n");
                 fprintf(stderr, "L loser node value (0)\nW winner node value
      (1)\n");
                     exit(1);
                 default:
                     break;
             }
         }

         /* allocate buffers for notes */
         for (i = 0;  i < notes;  i++)
             if ((note[i] = (int *)malloc(notesize * sizeof(int))) == NULL)
             {
                 printf("not enough memory\n");
                 exit(1);
             }

         for (k = 0, need = 0;  ;  k++)
         {
             for (i = need;  i < notes;  i++)
               for (j = 0;  j < notesize;  j++)
                 if (scanf("%d", &note[i][j])  !=  1) /* read another note */
                   goto DONE;

             /* have a set of notes; write pattern: */
             for (i = 0;  i < notes;  i++)
             {
                 for (j = 0;  j < notesize;  j++)
                 {
                     int   n = note[i][j];

                     /* map input pattern to floating point output:
                        all nodes are "losers" except for one "winner".
                        In case of the target, use the original (binary) values
                     */
                     printf("%g ", i == notes - 1 ?  n  :  (n ? winner : loser));
                 }
                 printf(" ");
             }

             printf(" %d\n", k);     /* append a pattern ID (sequence number) */

             /* shift notes:
                drop first one leave last slot open for next note */
             need = notes - 1;                /* request another note */
             ptemp   = note[0];
             /* this simply swaps pointers to the storage area */
             for (i = 0;  i < need;  i++)
                 note[i] = note[i + 1];
             note[i] = ptemp;
         }
     DONE:;
     }


                              MSHELL19.C


     /* mshell19.c
        Generate (compose) a set of patterns for music generator neural network.
        Input is a string of notes, where each note consists of a pitch
        plus a duration. Note pitch and duration are each represented as a
        string of 0's and one 1's, separated by spaces, for example:
```

```
426          note pitch                      duration in 16ths
427          c d e f g a b c d e f g   R   1 2 3 4 6 12
428          0 0 0 0 0 0 0 0 1 0 0 0   0   0 1 0 0 0 0
429          ^middle C                     ^rest
430
431      R.W. Dobbins
432    */
433    #include <stdio.h>
434    #include <stdlib.h>
435
436    #define MAXNOTES     6      /* maximum notes in a context */
437    #define NOTES        6      /* default notes */
438    #define MAXSCALE     13     /* maximum no. of note pitches including rest */
439    #define NOTESCALE    13     /* actual no. of note pitches */
440    #define MAXDURATION  6      /* maximum no. of note durations */
441    #define NOTEDURATION 6      /* actual no. of note durations */
442    #define LOSER        0      /* loser value for neurodes */
443    #define WINNER       1      /* winner value for neurodes */
444    #define NOTESIZE     (NOTESCALE + NOTEDURATION)
445    #define THRESHOLD    90      /* random number probability threshold */
446    #define NONDETERMINISTIC
447
448    int  notesize       = NOTESIZE;
449
450    int  deterministic  = 1;  /* default choice of winning notes is determ. */
451
452    void   main(int argc,  char *argv[])
453    {
454       int    *note[MAXNOTES];      /* notes already seen plus the next note */
455       float  *notegen;             /* note generated by net */
456       int    notes         = NOTES;/* number of notes in context */
457       int    SequenceLen   = 0;    /* generated sequence length */
458       unsigned  seed       = 1;    /* random number seed value */
459       float  loser  = LOSER;       /* loser value for nodes */
460       float  winner = WINNER;      /* winner value for nodes */
461       int    i, j, k;
462       int    need;
463       int    *ptemp;
464       FILE   *fnet;
465       FILE   *fRun;                /* run file */
466       FILE   *fin;                 /* input - seed sequence */
467       FILE   *fout;                /* output - generated composition */
468       char   seedname[66];         /* input filename */
469       char   outname[66];          /* output filename */
470       char   netshell[66];         /* neural network command */
471       char   netrun[66];           /* neural network run filename */
472       char   netin[66];            /* neural network input/output */
473       char   netout[66];
474       char   netcommand[66];       /* constructed net command line */
475
476       /* process command line options */
477       for ( ; argc > 1;  --argc)
478       {
479          char *arg = *++argv;                      /* next argument */
480
481          if (*arg != '-')                          /* options */
482             break;
483
484          switch (*++arg)
485          {
486             case 'n':
487                /* expecting number of notes */
488                sscanf(++arg, "%d", &notes);
489                break;
```

```
490                    case 's':
491                       /* expecting sequence length */
492                       sscanf(++arg, "%d", &SequenceLen);
493                       break;
494                    case 'l':
495                       /* expecting number */
496                       sscanf(++arg, "%f", &loser);
497                       break;
498                    case 'w':
499                       /* expecting number */
500                       sscanf(++arg, "%f", &winner);
501                       break;
502                    case 'd':
503                       /* expecting a digit */
504                       sscanf(++arg, "%d", &deterministic);
505                       break;
506                    case 'r':
507                       /* expecting number */
508                       sscanf(++arg, "%d", &seed);
509                       break;
510                    case '?':
511                       help();
512                       exit(1);
513                    default:
514                       break;
515                }
516        }
517
518        if (argc < 5)
519        {
520            help();
521            exit(1);
522        }
523
524        /* expecting input and output filenames */
525        sscanf(*argv++, "%s", seedname);
526        sscanf(*argv++, "%s", outname);
527        /* expecting neural net command name string */
528        sscanf(*argv++, "%s", netshell);
529
530        /* open files */
531        if ((fin = fopen(seedname, "r"))   ==   NULL)
532        {
533            fprintf(stderr, "Can't open file %s\n", seedname);
534            exit(1);
535        }
536        if ((fout = fopen(outname, "w"))   ==   NULL)
537        {
538            fprintf(stderr, "Can't open file %s\n", outname);
539            exit(1);
540        }
541
542        /* Open run file for reading */
543        sscanf(*argv, "%s", netrun);
544
545        if ((fRun = fopen(netrun, "r"))   ==   NULL)
546        {
547            fprintf(stderr, "Can't open file %s\n", netrun);
548            exit(1);
549        }
550
551        strcpy(netcommand, netshell);
552        strcat(netcommand, " ");
553        strcat(netcommand, netrun);
```

```
554
555          fscanf(fRun, "%d", &i);
556          /* read and parse (part of) the run specification line; */
557          fscanf(fRun,
558                 "%s %*s %s",
559                 netout,              /* output results file */
560                 netin);              /* pattern input file */
561          fclose(fRun);
562
563          /* allocate buffers for notes */
564          for (i = 0;  i < notes;  i++)
565              if ((note[i] = (int *)malloc(notesize * sizeof(int))) == NULL)
566              {
567                  fprintf(stderr, "not enough memory\n");
568                  exit(1);
569              }
570
571          if ((notegen = (float *)malloc(notesize * sizeof(float))) == NULL)
572          {
573              fprintf(stderr, "not enough memory\n");
574              exit(1);
575          }
576
577          need = notes - 1;    /* length of note seed sequence */
578
579          /* read initial seed sequence */
580          for (i = 0;   i < need;   i++)
581          {
582              for (j = 0;   j < notesize;   j++)
583              {
584                  if (fscanf(fin, "%d", &note[i][j])  != 1)
585                  {
586                      fprintf(stderr, "unexpected end of net seed sequence\n");
587                      exit(1);
588                  }
589                  fprintf(fout, "%d ", note[i][j]);
590              }
591
592              fprintf(fout, "\n");
593          }
594
595          /* don't care initial target note: */
596          for (j = 0;  j < notesize; j++)
597              note[i][j] = 0;
598
599          srand(seed);
600
601          /* generate a sequence of notes, starting from seed */
602          for (k = 0;  k < SequenceLen;   k++)
603          {
604              /* present partial sequence to net */
605              if ((fnet = fopen(netin, "w")) == NULL)
606              {
607                  fprintf(stderr, "can't write net file\n");
608                  exit(1);
609              }
610
611              for (i = 0;  i < notes;  i++)
612              {
613                  for (j = 0;  j < notesize;  j++)
614                  {
615                      int   n = note[i][j];
616                      float f = i == notes - 1 ? n :  (n ? winner : loser);
617
```

```
618                     /* map input pattern to floating point output:
619                         all nodes are "losers" except for one "winner".
620                         In case of the target, use the original (binary) values
621                     */
622                     fprintf(fnet, "%g ", f);
623                 }
624                 fprintf(fnet, " ");
625             }
626
627             fprintf(fnet, " %d\n", k);   /* append pattern ID (sequence number) */
628
629             fclose(fnet);
630
631             /* ***************** RUN THE NEURAL NETWORK PROCESS **********/
632             system(netcommand);
633
634             /* get net outputs */
635             if ((fnet = fopen(netout, "r")) == NULL)
636             {
637                 fprintf(stderr, "can't open net file\n");
638                 exit(1);
639             }
640
641             fscanf(fnet, "%d", &j);      /* skip the sequence number */
642
643             for (j = 0;   j < notesize;   j++)
644                 if (fscanf(fnet, "%f", &notegen[j])    != 1)
645                 {
646                     fprintf(stderr, "unexpected end of net file\n");
647                     exit(1);
648                 }
649
650             fclose(fnet);
651
652             /* select note duration and value */
653             selectnote(notegen, note[need], NOTESCALE);
654           selectnote(&notegen[NOTESCALE], &note[need][NOTESCALE], NOTEDURATION);
655
656             /* have a set of notes; write generated pattern: */
657             for (j = 0;  j < notesize; j++)
658                 fprintf(fout, "%d ", note[need][j]);
659
660             fprintf(fout, "\n");
661
662             /* shift notes:
663                 drop first one; leave last slot open for next note */
664             ptemp    = note[0];
665             for (i = 0;  i < need;  i++)
666                 note[i] = note[i + 1];
667             note[i] = ptemp;
668         }
669     }
670
671
672     /* select winning note from candidates */
673     int selectnote(float candidate[], int note[], int  n)
674     {
675         int    j;
676         int    winner;
677
678         /* clear the whole note result area */
679         for (j = 0;  j < n;  j++)
680             note[j]   = 0;
681
```

```
682          /* pick winning value */
683          for (;;)
684          {
685              int    i;
686              float  work[NOTESIZE];
687
688              /* copy candidates to work area */
689              for (j = 0;  j < n;  j++)
690                  work[j]  =  candidate[j];
691
692              /* nondeterministic loop: give every candidate a chance;
693                 priority ordered from highest to lowest */
694              for (i = 0;  i < n;  i++)
695              {
696                  /* pick winner so far */
697                  for (winner = 0, j = 1;  j < n;   j++)
698                      if (work[j] > work[winner])
699                          winner  =  j;
700
701                  /* make deterministic or nondeterministic choice: */
702                  if (deterministic  ||  random(100) < THRESHOLD)
703                  {
704                      note[winner]  =  1;
705                      return;
706                  }
707                  /* when nondeterministic choice fails,
708                     erase the winner; try another one */
709                  work[winner]  =  0;
710              }
711          }
712      }
713
714
715      int help()
716      {
717          fprintf(stderr,
                 "Usage:\nmshell -rR -dD -nN -sS -lL -wW seed comp net run\n");
718
719          fprintf(stderr, "   R     random seed value (1)\n");
720          fprintf(stderr, "   D     deterministic choice (1)\n");
721          fprintf(stderr, "   N     number of notes in context\n");
722          fprintf(stderr, "   S     sequence length\n");
723          fprintf(stderr, "   L     loser node value (0)\n");
724          fprintf(stderr, "   W     winner node value (1)\n");
725          fprintf(stderr, "   seed  note seed sequence filename (N - 1 notes)\n");
726          fprintf(stderr, "   comp  composed note filename\n");
727          fprintf(stderr, "   net   neural net command name\n");
728          fprintf(stderr, "   run   net run filename\n");
729      }
730
731
732                                  PLAY19.C
733
734      /* play19.c
735         Plays music from music composition text file
736         Composition is a string of notes, where each note consists of a pitch
737         plus a duration.  Note pitch and duration are represented as a
738         string of 0's and one 1's, separated by spaces, for example:
739             note value                    duration in 16ths
740             c d e f g a b c d e f g  R    1 2 3 4 6 12
741             0 0 0 0 0 0 0 1 0 0 0 0  0    0 1 0 0 0 0
742             ^middle C                     ^rest
743         R.W. Dobbins
744      */
```

```
745     #include <stdio.h>
746     #include <stdlib.h>
747     /* #include <dos.h> */
748
749     void delay(unsigned milliseconds);
750     void sound(unsigned frequency);
751
752     #define MAXNOTES     100
753     #define NOTESCALE     13       /* actual no. of note pitch values incl rest */
754     #define NOTEDURATION 6        /* actual no. of note duration values */
755     #define PAUSE         5        /* internote pause in milliseconds */
756
757     struct
758     {
759         int frequency;
760         int duration;
761     } note[MAXNOTES];           /* the composition file */
762     int    notes;                 /* actual number of notes in composition */
763     char   compositionfile[66];
764
765     /* note frequency mappings in cycles/sec */
766     int   mapfreq[NOTESCALE] =
767     {
768         262, 294, 330, 349, 392, 440, 494, 523, 587, 659, 698, 784, 0
769     };
770
771     /* note duration mapping in 1/16 notes:
772        1/16  1/8 3/16 1/4 3/8 3/4 */
773     int   mapdur[NOTEDURATION]  =
774     {
775         1, 2, 3, 4, 6, 12
776     };
777
778     /* duration of a sixteenth note in milliseconds, at normal tempo: */
779     float sixteenth = 125;
780
781     /* read abbreviated notation for composition */
782     int readcomposition()
783     {
784         FILE  *fRun;
785
786         if ((fRun = fopen(compositionfile, "r"))   ==    NULL)
787         {
788             fprintf(stderr, "Can't open file %s\n", compositionfile);
789             return  0;
790         }
791
792         for (notes = 0;  notes < MAXNOTES;  notes++)
793         {
794             int   j;
795
796             /* read note frequency */
797             for (j = 0;   j < NOTESCALE;   j++)
798             {
799                 int  f;
800
801                 if (fscanf(fRun, "%d",  &f)   !=   1)
802                     goto ENDCOMPOSITION;
803                 if (f)
804                     note[notes].frequency  =  mapfreq[j];
805             }
806
807             /* read note duration */
808             for (j = 0;   j < NOTEDURATION;   j++)
```

```
809              {
810                  int  d;
811
812                  if (fscanf(fRun, "%d",  &d)   !=   1)
813                      goto ENDCOMPOSITION;
814                  if (d)
815                      note[notes].duration  =  mapdur[j];
816              }
817          }
818
819          ENDCOMPOSITION:
820          fclose(fRun);
821          return  notes;
822      }
823
824
825      int playcomposition()
826      {
827          int  i;
828
829          for (i = 0;  i < notes;  i++)
830          {
831              int  f  =  note[i].frequency;
832
833              if (f)
834                  sound(f);
835              else
836                  nosound();
837              delay(note[i].duration * sixteenth);
838              nosound();
839              delay(PAUSE);
840              if (kbhit())
841              {
842                  getch();
843                  break;
844              }
845          }
846
847          nosound();
848          return  i;
849      }
850
851      void  main(int argc,  char *argv[])
852      {
853          /* process command line options */
854          for ( ; argc > 1;  --argc)
855          {
856              char *arg = *++argv;                      /* next argument */
857              if (*arg != '-')                          /* options */
858                  break;
859
860              switch (*++arg)
861              {
862                  case 't':
863                      /* set tempo */
864                      {
865                          int  tempo;       /* tempo in beats/min */
866                          sscanf(++arg, "%d", &tempo);
867                          sixteenth = 60.0 * 1000 / 4 / tempo;
868                          break;
869                      }
870                  default:
871                      break;
872              }
```

```
873          }
874
875          if (argc < 2)
876          {
877              printf("Enter name of composition file: ");
878              if (scanf("%s", compositionfile) != 1)
879                  exit(1);
880          }
881          else
882              /* composition file name from command line */
883              sscanf(*argv, "%s", compositionfile);
884
885          for(;;)
886          {
887              int   c;
888
889              if (readcomposition())
890                  for (;;)
891                  {
892                      playcomposition();
893                      printf("Repeat?\n");
894                      c = getch();
895                      if (toupper(c) != 'Y')
896                          break;
897                  }
898
899              printf("Play another composition? ");
900              c = getch();
901              if (toupper(c) != 'Y')
902                  break;
903
904              printf("Enter name of composition file: ");
905              if (scanf("%s", compositionfile) != 1)
906                  break;;
907          }
908      }
```

Additional Resources

Russell C. Eberhart
Roy W. Dobbins

Introduction

It seems that whenever you get involved in a new technical area such as neural networks, one of the first things you do is seek out resources related to the area that are interesting and pertinent to your particular applications. Hopefully, this book has proven to be helpful in that respect. Throughout this book, we have given resources for your explorations with neural network tools (NNTs). Each chapter has included references that can give you information you need to implement NNTs in your own applications. Most of the references are to books or technical articles published in magazines and journals.

The purpose of this appendix is to supplement these references. These added resources are grouped into five main categories: organizations/societies, conferences/symposia, journals/magazines/newsletters, computer bulletin boards, and computer data bases. This division is somewhat arbitrary. Organizations sponsor conferences and also publish journals and magazines, so it's sometimes difficult to talk about only one category at a time.

Each of us learns (or prefers to learn) in different ways. Some people like hearing information presented in a classroom environment; others prefer to read and study. We hope that you can find useful avenues to enhance your learning about NNTs in the listing of resources that follows.

Two caveats: First, although the information in this book was accurate to the best of the authors' knowledge at the time it was written, some of it will probably have changed by the time you read it. Second, the information is not meant to be complete. It is strongly biased by what the authors have found to be interesting and practical in their quests to learn about and apply neural network tools.

Organizations and Societies

Currently two major U.S.-based organizations are heavily involved in neural network research, development, and applications. One is the Institute of Electrical and Electronics Engineers (IEEE) Neural Network Council (NNC). The other is the International Neural Network Society (INNS). Both are multinational organizations with several thousand members actively involved in neural networks; but their technical focuses differ slightly. The IEEE has over 300,000 members worldwide. In the technical arena, the IEEE is made up of societies, councils, and committees. Societies and councils represent the bulk of the technical activities, including, for example, the Communications Society and the Engineering in Medicine and Biology Society (EMBS).

When a new technical area receives sufficient interest, a committee is formed, with representatives of interested societies serving as members. If interest and activity is sufficiently high for a period of time, the committee can become a council, the step prior to becoming a full-fledged society. The advantage to becoming an IEEE council is that a council can publish transactions.

The NNC, which has two delegates from each of ten member societies, has, as this book is written, become a council. The first *IEEE Transactions on Neural Networks* appeared in March 1990. (Remember we said that it's hard to talk about only one category at a time.)

In addition to publishing the Transactions, the IEEE NNC cosponsors, with the INNS, the two International Joint Conferences on Neural Networks each year. If you are an IEEE member, you can contact your local section or people in one of the NNC member societies, such as EMBS, to get more information on IEEE neural network activities. You can also write to the IEEE Neural Network Council, % the IEEE Technical Activities Board, IEEE Service Center, 445 Hoes Lane, P.O. Box 1331, Piscataway, NJ 08855-1331.

IEEE membership fees vary according to whether you're a student or a full-time engineer and what options you choose to go with your basic membership. For example, you generally pay $10–16 per year to subscribe to the transactions of a society. The basic membership fee, however, is currently about $70 per year. If your field is electrical or computer engineering and you are interested in neural networks, you should probably seriously consider joining the IEEE.

The INNS is focused entirely on the theory, applications, and hardware of neural networks. In general, the INNS stresses biologically based work more than the IEEE and practical applications somewhat less. It isn't that the INNS isn't interested in applications. They are. It's just that there seems to be, in general, a broader spectrum of neural network related interests represented by the INNS membership. It's interesting to note that, at least as of early 1990, approximately 20 percent of the INNS members are also members of the IEEE.

If your interests are focused *primarily* on neural networks, you should probably consider joining the INNS. As of 1990, regular INNS membership is $55 per year and students can join for $40, annually. Membership includes a subscription to *Neural Networks*, the offical INNS journal, which is described in more detail later.

As noted earlier, the INNS cosponsors the two IJCNNs with the IEEE each year. For more information on INNS membership, write to the INNS Membership Office, P.O. Box 441166, Ft. Washington, MD 20744 USA.

If you are in Europe, you might want to look into the recently formed Joint European Neural Network Initiative (JENNI). This organization was born at the 1989 IJCNN in Washington, D.C., and represents an attempt to provide a focus for neural network activity in Europe. JENNI is planning conferences and symposia for the 1990s. For more information on JENNI, you can write to Prof. Rolf Eckmiller, Biophysics Dept., University of Duesseldorf, Universitatstrasse 1, D-400 Duesseldorf 1, Federal Republic of Germany.

The Japanese, not to be outdone by the Americans or the Europeans, have founded The Japan Neural Network Society. The first chairman of the organization, founded in July 1989, is Dr. Kunihiko Fukushima, the chief researcher at Nihon Hoso Kyokai (NHK) Broadcasting Technology Laboratory. As is the case with the INNS in the United States, the society's membership is multidisciplinary, including psychologists, biologists, engineers, and so on. It was predicted that the society would have about 500 members by the end of 1990.

In addition to the national societies, a number of local neural network organizations have sprung up around the United States. Sometimes these are billed as neural network societies and sometimes as neural network special interest groups of larger clubs and users groups. If you are a member of a PC user's group or a Mac user's group, for example, you might want to check whether a neural network SIG exists there.

Conference and Symposia

The numerous conferences and symposia on neural networks span the range from the purely theoretical to specific application areas. The two largest conferences dedicated entirely to neural nets are the International Joint Conferences on Neural Networks (IJCNNs). They are sponsored jointly by the Institute of Electrical and Electronics Engineers (IEEE) Neural Networks Council (NNC) and the International Neural Network Society (INNS). The joining of the two organizations for the purpose of sponsoring IJCNNs occurred in 1989, and the association hopefully will help keep neural network development activity unified and coordinated.

The societies alternate in terms of which one is the lead society. Starting in 1991, one conference per year is being planned in the United States and one outside the United States. One year, the INNS will take the lead for the conference in the United States, with the IEEE NNC being the lead society for the other conference. The next year, the IEEE NNC will serve as lead society for the U.S. conference, with the INNS playing the role outside the United States. Attendance at these meetings ran about 2,000 or so in 1989–1990.

For information about these conferences, you can contact the place that provides membership information about the lead society for the conference, discussed previously, or you can read the journals and magazines that feature neural network articles. These publications usually have calendars of upcoming conferences and workshops.

A smaller conference of very high quality is the Neural Information Processing System (NIPS) meeting, held annually in Denver in late November or early December. To give you an idea of the selectivity of this conference, in 1989 over 500 papers were submitted, but fewer than 100 were accepted for oral or poster presentation. Attendance at NIPS has generally been about 500. For more information on the NIPS meeting, write to the NIPS Local Committee, University of Colorado, Engineering Center, Campus Box 425, Boulder, CO 80309-0425.

Numerous conferences have sessions or tracks (a track is a group of sessions) pertaining to neural networks. Most of the major AI conferences now (sometimes grudgingly) give airtime to neural nets. Some of the very best papers, however, can be found at smaller conferences that are focused on some particular applications area. An example is the IEEE EMBS Annual Conference; another is the annual IEEE Symposium on Computer Based Medical Systems. Both of these meetings have tracks devoted to neural networks or to neural networks and expert systems combined. Announcements of the locations and dates of the meetings can be found in the IEEE *EMBS Magazine*. The CBMS meeting is announced in the IEEE *Computer* magazine.

Journals, Magazines, and Newsletters

We review the magazines in an order similar to what we used for organizations. We first talk about publications of the major societies, then other journals and magazines. Finally, we take a quick look at a few newsletters. The costs quoted were in effect when the book was being written and were verified at that time, but there is no guarantee that they will remain unchanged for any period of time. By the way, the difference between a magazine and a journal is that material submitted for publication in a journal is reviewed by other experts in the field, a process called *peer review*, prior to publication. With a magazine, there is no guarantee that anyone else in the field has ever seen the material, so *caveat emptor* applies.

The newest major journal on the scene is the *IEEE Transactions on Neural Networks*, which began publication in early 1990. Herbert Rauch of Lockheed was named the first editor. The scope of the transactions states that:

> The IEEE Transactions on Neural Networks will publish high quality technical papers in the science and technology of neural networks which disclose significant technical achivements, exploratory developments and applications of neural networks from theory to software to hardware. Emphasis will be given to artificial neural networks.

To publish short papers reporting new research results quickly, the Transactions also contains a Letters section. The Transactions costs $10 per year for IEEE members who belong to societies that participate in the IEEE Neural Networks Committee and $15 per year for IEEE members in other societies. IEEE members can subscribe via the annual membership renewal form. Or you can contact the IEEE Service Center, 445 Hoes Lane, P.O. Box 1331, Piscataway, NJ 08855-1331, USA. Telephone (201) 981-1393.

The INNS likewise publishes a journal, called, appropriately enough, *Neural Networks*. Quoting from the Aims and Scope published in each issue:

> Neural Networks is a quarterly, international journal which publishes original research and review articles concerned with the modeling of brain and behavioral processes and the application of these models to computer and related technologies. Models aimed at the explanation and prediction of bio-

logical data and models aimed at solution of technological problems are both solicited, as are mathematical and computational analyses of both types of models.

The major sections of Neural Networks are original contributions, book reviews, and current events. A subscription to Neural Networks is included with your membership fee when you join the INNS. You can also contact Pergamon Press Inc., Fairview Park, Elmsford, NY 10523 USA, publisher of the journal. At last count, there are three coeditors-in-chief (from three countries) and 67 members of the editorial board.

Of these two journals, the *IEEE Transactions on Neural Networks* tends to be more engineering and applications oriented and Neural Networks more biologically and mathematically inclined.

At about the same time as Dr. Terry Sejnowski moved to the Salk Institute and the University of California at San Diego, he took the helm as editor-in-chief of a new neural network journal, *Neural Computation.* Although he is the lone editor-in-chief, Dr. Sejnowski is assisted by a 16-member advisory board and 40 action editors. Volume 1, Number 1 of Neural Computation was published in the spring of 1989. The journal is published quarterly by MIT Press Journals. Yearly subscriptions cost $45.00 for individuals, $90 for institutions, and $35.00 for students. Although this is a hefty tariff, the first few issues of this journal have been impressive. It's hard to imagine keeping up with the field without looking at Neural Computation, so you will at least want to find a copy you can review. Subscription information can be obtained from MIT Press Journals, 55 Hayward Street, Cambridge, MA 02142 USA. Their telephone number is (617) 253-2889. *Neural Computation* considers three types of manuscripts for publication. "Letters," designed for quick reporting of research and development results, are no longer than 2,000 words. "Views" are invited minireviews of important research, up to 4,000 words. Finally, "Reviews" are comprehensive overviews summarizing significant advances in a broad area and can be up to 10,000 words.

The Lawrence Erlbaum Associates' offering in the journal field is called *Neural Network Review.* Its mission is "to help professionals in the realm of neural networks identify the significant discoveries and issues in the field." Their advertising states that "leading researchers and applications specialists provide critical reviews and analyses of neural network literature, as well as general information on current and forthcoming products and conferences." The journal is published quarterly, with a yearly subscription costing $36.00 for an individual and $72.00 for an institution. Orders from outside the United States or Canada cost $15.00 more. You can address enquiries to Lawrence Erlbaum

Associates, Inc., Journal Subscription Department, 365 Broadway, Hillsdale, NJ 07642 USA. The editor's name is Craig A. Will.

Another journal, *Network: Computation in Neural Systems*, published by the Institute of Physics and Blackwell Scientific Publications, came on the scene in 1990. It appears four times a year. The yearly subscription rate is $180.00, so it would seem that most subscribers would be libraries and commercial organizations. It bills itself as "the first genuinely interdisciplinary journal in neural networks." Its aim is to "provide a forum for integrating theoretical and experimental findings across relevant interdisciplinary boundaries." North American subscriptions are being handled by the American Institute of Physics, Marketing Services, 335 East 45th Street, New York, NY 10017 USA. From outside North America, contact the Journals Marketing Department, IOP Publishing Ltd., Techno House, Redcliffe Way, Bristol BS1 6NX, England.

Currently, no commercial magazines are devoted entirely to neural networks though almost every computer-related magazine, it seems, has had a special issue on neural networks and runs articles sporadically. At least two magazines, however, have featured neural networks on a regular basis: *Micro Cornucopia* and *AI Expert*.

Micro Cornucopia was a hacker's magazine in the very best sense of the word. It always seemed to have something useful and interesting. The articles were always clear and understandable, not obscure and out in the ozone like some other magazines aimed at programmers and computer systems hackers. It should therefore be no surprise that the authors approached *Micro Cornucopia* in the early stages of writing this book with the idea of publishing portions of some of the chapters. When asked for a written confirmation that he would publish the series of articles, editor Dave Thompson sent a letter, the total text of which was "It's a 'go' on the articles. Looking forward to it." He didn't go for excess words in his magazine either! Unfortunately, he also didn't go for continuing to publish it. He sold the magazine to Miller Freeman Publications, publishers of *AI Expert*, just before this book went to press. We understand that the magazine has been discontinued and the staff disbanded.

AI Expert bills itself as "The Magazine of Artificial Intelligence in Practice." It is concerned primarily with the expert systems side of the AI house. Neural network oriented articles appear every so often, and their frequncy has been increasing recently. *AI Expert's* main claim to fame in the neural network area is a very good series of articles by Maureen Caudill that have contained reviews of major neural net architectures and learning algorithms. She has provided a thorough introduction to a number of network architectures, and we recommend referring to her article series for those networks, such as Grossberg's ART 1 and ART 2, which we haven't covered in detail. *AI Expert* is published monthly, and the subscription rate quoted on their title page is $37 per year though most of the issues seem to advertise "special" reduced subscription rates. *AI Expert* is published by Miller Freeman Publications, 500 Howard Street, San Francisco, CA 94105. Their phone number is (405) 397-1881. *AI Expert* has a bulletin board that will be covered in the next section.

In addition to journals and magazines, a number of newsletters featuring neural networks have sprung up in the past few years. Newsletters often seem to appear whenever there is a rapidly changing high-tech area with the prospect for substantial government funding.

The newsletter *Neurocomputers* is essentially the product of one person's expertise and effort. Dr. Derek Stubbs is a familiar sight at many of the neural network conferences and symposia. He can often be seen, complete with backpack, in intense discussion with a neural network researcher or developer. *Neurocomputers* contains information on meetings (both past and future), new products, and new books. Dr. Stubbs also provides a hotline over which he dispenses advice and information on neural networks. *Neurocomputers* is published monthly and costs $32 per year. As newsletters go, this is a reasonable price, and Stubbs has been active in the neural network field long enough to bring valuable experience to his efforts. For information, or to subscribe, write to *Neurocomputers*, Gallifrey Publishing, P.O. Box 155, Vicksburg, MI 49097 USA, or call (616) 649-3772.

The other two newsletters we'll look at are published by larger organizations than that of Dr. Stubbs. The first is *Neural Network News*, published monthly by AI Week, Inc., the company that publishes *AI Week*. The publishers promise you "comprehensive news and insights of U.S. and international developments in neural network technology." A one-year subscription to *Neural Network News* costs $249. The publisher's address is AI Week, Inc., 2555 Cumberland Parkway, Suite 299, Atlanta, GA 30339-9708 USA. To order by phone, you can call (404) 434-2187.

The second is *Synapse Connection*, published by GRAEME Publishing Corporation. *Synapse Connection* is billed as "one stop shopping for the executive." They claim to "regularly cover the news from the commercial arena and describe the technical discoveries in understandable terminology." A one-year subscription to *Synapse Connection* costs $295. The publisher's address is GRAEME Publishing Corporation, 10 Northen Boulevard, Amherst, NH 03031 USA. Their telephone number is (603) 886-8221.

Of the two newsletters, *Neural Network News* seems a bit more technically oriented whereas the company that publishes *Synapse Connection* bills itself as a market research company. Both are relatively expensive and probably don't get many subscriptions from the home-based neurohacker. The typical subscriber probably works either for a company that specializes in neural network related activity, and thus needs timely notice of developments in the field, or for a medium to large sized company within which the newsletter gets passed from office to office. This type of newsletter is particularly important if you are involved in marketing neural network products. It is less so if you are a researcher, in which case your primary publication sources probably include technical journals and magazines.

Computer Bulletin Boards

As potential NNT resources go, computer bulletin boards must generally be considered the most transient, or least certain to exist over a long time. For that reason, the neural network bulletin board services we describe are limited to those we believe are the most likely to survive for at least a few years. They may change significantly between the time this book is published and you read it.

In addition, *Neuron Digest* isn't really a bulletin board at all but an on-line computer-based neural network digest made available on several major computer networks. *Neuron Digest* is disseminated weekly and is available directly on Internet and Bitnet, two of the largest computer networks in the world. It is also available as part of a "news group" on Usenet, another major network.

It contains up-to-the-minute (well, up-to-the-week, anyway) information submitted by anyone who is a subscriber. The authors access *Neuron Digest* via Bitnet, which is a worldwide computer network that contains over a thousand nodes, primarily at educational institutions. You never know what you'll find in *Neuron Digest*. There are questions from neophyte neural network enthusiasts, information on conferences, debates on hot topics by world-class experts, and announcements of breakthroughs in everything from theory to applications. (Some of the breakthroughs are mainly in the mind of the announcer, but the contents of the digest are edited to some degree by the digest moderator.)

When you subscribe, which costs nothing as long as you have a valid user ID on Bitnet or Internet, your local host computer system automatically gets your copy of *Neuron Digest* each week. You can then examine and/or download your copy whenever you sign on to the computer system. To subscribe, you simply send an e-mail message to the editor requesting that your subscription be started. On Bitnet, send the message to neuron-request@hplabs.hp.com. The moderator of *Neuron Digest*, at the time this volume was written, was Peter Marvit.

The magazine *AI Expert* maintains a computer bulletin board (BBS) network. It mainly contains information on expert systems but does have a fair amount of information on neural networks. For example, much of the source code associated with Maureen Caudill's series of articles (e.g., [25]) is available on the *AI Expert* BBS. To download files, you must have communications software capable of ASCII capture or XMODEM file transfers. Using the BBS is free. The first time you sign on, you'll be asked for your name and some more information. There are several numbers you can call, depending on where you are in the United States. The number of the Public Domain Software Exchange in Sunnyvale, California, is (408) 735-7190. The number that has been used by the authors is (617) 621-0574 in Boston, Massachusetts. If you want a number more convenient to your location or you have trouble with one of the two listed here, contact *AI Expert* at the address or telephone number given previously in the section on magazines.

Computer Databases

As resources go, this variety is a relative newcomer. Databases that are accessed on-line or are available on magnetic media for sale were until recently quite expensive and available primarily to highly specialized users or to large organizational subscribers. This has changed as several time-sharing services have made large databases available. Also, as the power of personal computers has increased and their price has decreased, multimegabyte databases can now be used by many individuals at work and at home.

The database *NeuralBase 5000* is a software package that is available for an IBM XT or workalike or for better IBM versions such as the PC/AT. The price of NeuralBase 5000 is $595, and it is available from Anza Research, 19866 Baywood Drive, Cupertino, CA 95014. Their phone number is (408) 996-2022. Although the price may not sound inexpensive to the neural network home-based hobbyist, it is clearly well worth the price to those who do full-time research and development in this fast-changing field. The software is called NeuralBase 5000 because there are, as of early 1990, approximately 5000 bibliographic references in the database, over two-thirds with abstracts. You can search NeuralBase 5000 by author, date, author and date, and keyword.

There are eight major keyword categories, with a total of 162 keywords. The database takes up about 5 Mbytes of a hard disk and comes on 17 diskettes, so it isn't appropriate for everyone. It can, however, save you several times its purchase price when compared with the cost of a consultant or technical person given the task to compile the neural network information you require.

The *PaperChase* database is an on-line system, a service of Boston's Beth Israel Hospital. To access PaperChase you need the same equipment that you need to access a computer bulletin board: a PC or terminal, a phone line, and a modem. PaperChase provides access to the continually updated MEDLINE database of over 5 million references to the biomedical literature, including references to articles published in 4000 international journals from 1966 to the present. Because of its biomedical focus, PaperChase will help you the most if you're involved in the biological, biomedical, or psychological areas related to neural networks.

Access from most locations in the United States and Canada is through the CompuServe telephone lines though the service is independent of CompuServe (you never really get into CompuServe when you call PaperChase, you just use the CompuServe lines). From many locations in Europe, as well as from other places such as Australia, Hong Kong, and Mexico, you can access PaperChase through Computer Sciences Corporation, with which PaperChase has a special arrangement. There are also PaperChase network addresses for international access via Tymnet, Telenet, ITT, and RCA Globcom. A typical 10-min PaperChase search on-line costs about $6.00. Their address is Paper-Chase, Longwood Galleria, 350 Longwood Avenue, Boston, MA 02115, USA. Their telephone number is (617) 732-4800.

Summary

In a field that's changing as fast as neural networks, it is sometimes hard to know where to obtain pertinent information; but after you get involved, sometimes it seems as though you have a tiger by the tail, given the explosion of effort in the field. Hopefully, the information in this appendix will help you. The contributors, listed near the front of this book, should be considered another resource. We echo Bernard Widrow's opinion, stated in the Foreword: All you need to get to work in neural networks is a personal computer and this book. Enjoy!

APPENDIX F

file: dmac.c   01/30/90

```
1    /***********************************************************
2    *   dmac   High speed dense matrix multiply for NN         *
3    *          DGL    11/9/88                                  *
4    *          v1.1   11/13/88 add code for 1st and last part of loop *
5    *          v1.2   11/14/88 just a little more tinkering    *
6    *                                                          *
7    *                                                          *
8    ***********************************************************/
9    static char dmacver[] = "dmac.c DGL 11/11/88 v1.2";
10
11   #pragma macro DMULT(k)
12   #pragma asm
13           FPLDNLSN
14           FPLDNLMULSN    ; multiply
15           LDNLP    +1    ; input address is on stack, point to next one
16           DUP
17           LDL      ?ws+4 ; get weight
18           LDNLP    +(k+1)
19           FPADD          ; and sum
20   #pragma endasm
21   #pragma endmacro
22
23
24   void dmac(icnt, ocnt, input, wp, op)
25   /*
26    * icnt : size of input vector
27    * ocnt : size of output vector
28    * input: pointer to 1st value in input vector
29    * wp   : pointer to 1st value in weight matrix using the following
30    *        organization:
31    *        WP11, WP12, Wp13, ... WP1icnt, WP21, WP22, ... WP2icnt, ...
32    *        WPocnt1, WPocnt2, WPocnt3, ... WPocnticnt
33    * op   : pointer to 1st value in output vector
34    */
35   int icnt, ocnt;
36   float *input, *op, *wp;
37   {
38   int i, j, iloop, offset;
39   float *inp;
40
41   iloop = icnt >> 4;
42   for(j=0;j<ocnt;j++)
43           {
44           inp = input;
45   #pragma asm
46           FPLDZEROSN
47   #pragma endasm
48           for(i=0;i<iloop;i++)
49                   {
50   #pragma asm
51                   LDL      ?ws-1  ; get input
52                   DUP
53                   FPLDNLSN
54                   LDL      ?ws+4  ; get weight
```

```
55                    FPLDNLMULSN     ; multiply
56                    LDNLP    +1     ; input address is on stack, point to next one
57                    DUP
58                    LDL      ?ws+4
59                    LDNLP    +1
60                    FPADD           ; and sum
61     #pragma endasm
62                    DMULT(1)
63                    DMULT(2)
64                    DMULT(3)
65                    DMULT(4)
66                    DMULT(5)
67                    DMULT(6)
68                    DMULT(7)
69                    DMULT(8)
70                    DMULT(9)
71                    DMULT(10)
72                    DMULT(11)
73                    DMULT(12)
74                    DMULT(13)
75                    DMULT(14)
76     #pragma asm
77                    FPLDNLSN
78                    FPLDNLMULSN     ; multiply
79                    LDNLP    +1
80                    STL      ?ws-1  ; store new increment for next loop
81                    LDL      ?ws+4
82                    ADC      +64    ; adjust weight pointer for next loop
83                    STL      ?ws+4
84                    FPADD           ; and sum
85     #pragma endasm
86                    }
87     #pragma asm
88           LDL      ?ws+5
89           FPSTNLSN
90     #pragma endasm
91           for(i=iloop<<4;i<icnt;i++)   /* Finish up with Slow approach */
92                 {
93                 *op += *wp * *inp;
94                 wp++;
95                 inp++;
96                 }
97           op++;
98           }
99     }

       file: dtmac.c  01/30/90

100    /****************************************************************
101     *  dtmac  High speed dense TRANSPOSED matrix multiply for NN *
102     *      DGL    11/16/88  Conversion of dmac for Transpose      *
103     *                                                             *
104     *                                                             *
105     *                                                             *
106     *                                                             *
107     ****************************************************************/
108    static char dtmacver[] = "dtmac.c DGL 11/16/88 v1.0";
109
110    #pragma macro DMULT(k)
111    #pragma asm
112           FPLDNLSN
113           FPLDNLMULSN      ; multiply
114           LDL      ?ws+2   ; get offset
115           LDL      ?ws-2   ; get present weight address
```

```
116                 WSUB             ; calculate new address
117                 DUP
118                 STL      ?ws-2   ; save
119                 LDL      ?ws-1   ; get input
120                 FPADD            ; and sum
121                 LDNLP    +1      ; point to next one
122                 DUP
123                 STL      ?ws-1   ; save
124     #pragma endasm
125     #pragma endmacro
126
127
128     void dtmac(icnt, ocnt, input, weights, op)
129     /*
130      * icnt : size of input vector
131      * ocnt : size of output vector
132      * input: pointer to 1st value in input vector
133      * wp   : pointer to 1st value in weight matrix using the following
134      *        organization:
135      *        WP11, WP12, Wp13, ... WP1icnt, WP21, WP22, ... WP2icnt, ...
136      *        WPocnt1, WPocnt2, WPocnt3, ... WPocnticnt
137      * op   : pointer to 1st value in output vector
138      */
139     int icnt, ocnt;
140     float *input, *op, *weights;
141     {
142     int i, j, iloop;
143     float *wp, *inp;
144
145     iloop = icnt >> 4;
146     for(j=0;j<ocnt;j++)
147             {
148             inp = input;
149             wp = weights + j;
150     #pragma asm
151             FPLDZEROSN
152     #pragma endasm
153             for(i=0;i<iloop;i++)
154                     {
155     #pragma asm
156                     LDL      ?ws-1   ; get input
157                     LDL      ?ws-2   ; get weight
158                     FPLDNLSN
159                     FPLDNLMULSN      ; multiply
160                     LDL      ?ws+2   ; get offset
161                     LDL      ?ws-2   ; get present weight address
162                     WSUB             ; calculate new address
163                     DUP
164                     STL      ?ws-2   ; save
165                     LDL      ?ws-1   ; get input
166                     FPADD            ; and sum
167                     LDNLP    +1      ; point to next one
168                     DUP
169                     STL      ?ws-1   ; save
170     #pragma endasm
171                     DMULT(1)
172                     DMULT(2)
173                     DMULT(3)
174                     DMULT(4)
175                     DMULT(5)
176                     DMULT(6)
177                     DMULT(7)
178                     DMULT(8)
179                     DMULT(9)
```

```
180                     DMULT(10)
181                     DMULT(11)
182                     DMULT(12)
183                     DMULT(13)
184                     DMULT(14)
185     #pragma asm
186             FPLDNLSN
187             FPLDNLMULSN        ; multiply
188             LDL      ?ws+2     ; get offset
189             LDL      ?ws-2     ; get present weight address
190             WSUB               ; calculate new address
191             STL      ?ws-2     ; save
192             LDL      ?ws-1     ; get input
193             LDNLP    +1        ; point to next one
194             STL      ?ws-1     ; save
195             FPADD              ; and sum
196     #pragma endasm
197                     }
198     #pragma asm
199             LDL      ?ws+5
200             FPSTNLSN
201     #pragma endasm
202             for(i=iloop<<4;i<icnt;i++)   /* Finish up with Slow approach */
203                     {
204                     *op += *wp * *inp;
205                     wp += ocnt;
206                     inp++;
207                     }
208             op++;
209             }
210     }
211
```

INDEX